Inside Criminalized Governance

For over four decades, drug-trafficking gangs have monopolized violence and engaged in various forms of governance across hundreds of
informal neighborhoods known as favelas in Rio de Janeiro. Drawing
on three years of ethnographic fieldwork, over 200 interviews with
gang members and residents, 400 archival documents, and 20,000
anonymous hotline denunciations of gang members, this book provides
a comprehensive examination of the causes and consequences of these
governance arrangements. The book documents the variation in gang–
resident relationships – from responsive ones in which gangs provide a
reliable form of order and stimulate the local economy to coercive and
unresponsive relations in which gangs offer residents few benefits – and
then identifies the factors that account for this variation. The result is
an unprecedented ethnographic study that provides readers a unique,
in-depth insight into the evolution of Rio de Janeiro's drug-trafficking
gangs, from their emergence in the 1970s to the present day.

Nicholas Barnes is a lecturer in the School of International Relations at
the University of St Andrews. This book is based on more than three
years of ethnographic fieldwork in Rio de Janeiro, eighteen months of
which the author spent living in Complexo da Maré, the city's largest group of informal neighborhoods. This project has benefitted from
numerous grants, including from the National Science Foundation, the
Department of Education through the Fulbright-Hays Program, the
Social Sciences Research Council, and the Harry Frank Guggenheim
Foundation. The dissertation on which this book is based received
the Best Fieldwork Award (2017) from the American Political Science
Association and the Best Dissertation Award (2018) from the Society
for Institutional & Organizational Economics.

Cambridge Studies in Comparative Politics

General Editor

Kathleen Thelen, *Massachusetts Institute of Technology*

Associate Editors

Lisa Blaydes, *Stanford University*
Catherine Boone, *London School of Economics and Political Science*
Thad Dunning, *University of California, Berkeley*
Anna Grzymala-Busse, *Stanford University*
Torben Iversen, *Harvard University*
Stathis Kalyvas, *University of Oxford*
Melanie Manion, *Duke University*
Prerna Singh, *Brown University*
Dan Slater, *University of Michigan*
Susan Stokes, *Yale University*
Tariq Thachil, *University of Pennsylvania*
Erik Wibbels, *University of Pennsylvania*

Series Founder

Peter Lange, *Duke University*

Editor Emeritus

Margaret Levi, *Stanford University*

Other Books in the Series

Isabel M. Perera, *The Welfare Workforce: Why Mental Health Care Varies Across Affluent Democracies*
Graeme Blair, Fotini Christia, and Jeremy M. Weinstein, *Crime, Insecurity, and Community Policing: Experiments on Building Trust*
Georgia Kernell, *Inside Parties: How Party Rules Shape Membership and Responsiveness*
Volha Charnysh, *Uprooted: How post-WWII Population Transfers Remade Europe*
Catherine Boone, *Inequality and Political Cleavage in Africa: Regionalism by Design*
Soledad Artiz Prillaman, *The Patriarchal Political Order: The Making and Unraveling of the Gendered Participation Gap in India*
Charlotte Cavaillé, *Fair Enough?: Support for Redistribution in the Age of Inequality*
Noah L. Nathan, *The Scarce State: Inequality and Political Power in the Hinterland*
Scott de Marchi and Michael Laver, *The Governance Cycle in Parliamentary Democracies: A Computational Social Science Approach*
Egor Lazarev, *State-Building as Lawfare: Custom, Sharia, and State Law in Postwar Chechnya*
Lorenza B. Fontana, *Recognition Politics: Indigenous Rights and Ethnic Conflict in the Andes*

(Continued after the index)

Inside Criminalized Governance

How and Why Gangs Rule the Streets of Rio de Janeiro

NICHOLAS BARNES

University of St Andrews

CAMBRIDGE
UNIVERSITY PRESS

Shaftesbury Road, Cambridge CB2 8EA, United Kingdom

One Liberty Plaza, 20th Floor, New York, NY 10006, USA

477 Williamstown Road, Port Melbourne, VIC 3207, Australia

314–321, 3rd Floor, Plot 3, Splendor Forum, Jasola District Centre,
New Delhi – 110025, India

103 Penang Road, #05–06/07, Visioncrest Commercial, Singapore 238467

Cambridge University Press is part of Cambridge University Press & Assessment,
a department of the University of Cambridge.

We share the University's mission to contribute to society through the pursuit of
education, learning and research at the highest international levels of excellence.

www.cambridge.org
Information on this title: www.cambridge.org/9781316513040

DOI: 10.1017/9781009072410

© Nicholas Barnes 2025

When citing this work, please include a reference to the DOI 10.1017/9781009072410

First published 2025

A catalogue record for this publication is available from the British Library

*A Cataloging-in-Publication data record for this book is available from the Library
of Congress*

ISBN 978-1-316-51304-0 Hardback
ISBN 978-1-009-06994-6 Paperback

For my grandmother, Bernadine, and my parents, Chuck and Jan

E para todas as pessoas moradoras do conjunto de favelas da Maré

Contents

Figures

Tables

Acknowledgments

This book has benefitted from the support of an incredible number of people that I wish to thank here. First and foremost, I am deeply indebted to my PhD advisor, Scott Straus, whose support has been unwavering from the first time I pitched an idea about drug-trafficking gangs in Rio de Janeiro. Since then, his training and intellect have guided me and been a constant source of inspiration. He has also been a role model for the type of scholar, advocate, and teacher that I wish to be. I also want to thank the other members of my dissertation committee, Christina Ewig, Erica Simmons, Rikhil Bhavnani, and Ivan Ermakoff, whose constructive comments and feedback during the development and writing of the dissertation, upon which this book is based, greatly improved nearly every aspect of what you see before you. To all my friends and colleagues in Madison, who also made this project better in ways large and small, thank you. In particular, I am grateful to Barry Driscoll, Rachel Feldman, Jared Gars, Martina Kunovic, Lauren Lauter, Kyle Marquardt, Benjamin Power, Ryan Powers, Taylor Price, Casey Ehrlich Rollow, Rachel Schwartz, Beth Sondel, Mark Toukan, Leigh Vierstra, and Sarah Walker. This book also owes much to Damon Bourne for all the squash games, without which I wonder what would have happened to my sanity during grad school.

   This project received generous financial assistance of several research institutes and organizations over the years. The Latin American, Caribbean, and Iberian Studies Center (LACIS) at University of Wisconsin–Madison, under the guidance of Alberto Vargas, offered support from the very beginning of the project. Two summer Foreign Language Area Studies grants completed at Middlebury's Portuguese School and the University of Florida in Rio allowed me to learn Portuguese at an accelerated rate while several pre-dissertation grants from LACIS and the Political Science Department also provided funds for two exploratory research trips. The support of the National Science Foundation, the Department of Education through the Fulbright-Hays Doctoral Dissertation

Research Abroad program, and the Social Sciences Research Council (SSRC) through the International Dissertation Research Fellowship were essential to conducting the nearly three years of fieldwork that this project required. A special thanks goes to the SSRC's Drugs, Security, and Democracy in Latin America Fellowship program that also provided funding for fieldwork and organized two fascinating workshops during my fieldwork. During the write-up stage, a Harry Frank Guggenheim Fellowship and a Mellon Summer Dissertation Fellowship gave me the financial resources to focus on writing while UW–Madison's International Institute and a Franklin Research Grant from the American Philosophical Foundation provided funds for two follow-up research visits.

A postdoctoral fellowship at Brown University's Watson Institute for International and Public Affairs offered time and a supportive, tight-knit community in which to transform my dissertation into a book. A special thanks goes to Adaner Usmani and Tara Menon who provided a home away from home in Providence, where there was never an empty stomach nor shortage of enlightening conversation. Aarti Sethi and Poulomi Saha also opened their home (and kitchen) to me on numerous occasions. Their generosity and humor will not be forgotten. I want to also thank Rawan Arar for her friendship during those years.

I am forever indebted to Barry Driscoll and Taylor Price (and Ronan too!), who helped me return to my home state of Iowa to teach some of the best undergraduate students in the world at Grinnell College. Your friendship and support were much needed and appreciated during that difficult year at the beginning of a global pandemic. At the University of St Andrews, I am beyond grateful to work with such supportive and gifted colleagues, including Ryan Beasley, Adam Bower, Ana Gutierrez Garza, Jaremey McMullin, Muireann O'Dwyer, Mateja Peter, and Rahul Rao. Each of you have been willing to listen and think with me about this project. I especially want to thank Roxani Krystalli for her sharp mind, dedication to the craft of writing, and being constantly attentive to our ethical obligations.

There are a vast number of people in Rio de Janeiro whose patience, support, and friendship made my fieldwork and the years after some of the most interesting, enjoyable, and enlightening of my life. In particular, I wish to thank Juan Albarracín, Desmond Arias, Mariana Carvalho, Will Connors, Rute Duarte, Graham and Laurie Denyer Willis, François Espcnel, Simone Gomes, Jimmy Casas Klausen, Sara Koenders, Benjamin Lessing, Ned Littlefield, Palloma Menezes, Joana Monteiro, Zak Paster, Dennis Pauschinger, Silvia Ramos, Erika Robb Larkins, Taniele Rui, Stephanie Savell and Peter Klein, Jason Scott, Nadia Sussman, Alice Taylor, Antonello Veneri, Michael Wolff, and Alba Zaluar. I am also grateful to Zeca Borges, Gabriela Franco, Evandro Barbosa, and Michelle Moreira at Disque-Denúncia and Bruna Camargos, Bruna Cruz, and all the wonderful people at AfroReggae who allowed me to accompany their work and lives in the initial part of my fieldwork. I am forever indebted to Quentin Dubois and Ana-Maria Iorgulescu who offered a much-needed space for reflection and relaxation during the entirety of my fieldwork. I want to also thank Rafaela Ramalhete Ferraz and Vera Ramalhete for their generosity and kindness.

More than anywhere else in the world, Complexo da Maré remains close to my heart. I will never be able to repay the kindness and generosity that so many of Maré's residents have shown me over the years. I was welcomed into the homes and businesses in every neighborhood that makes up the Complexo. In part, my warm reception was due to "Carlos," my research assistant, to whom I owe so much I cannot begin to express it here. Your patience with me in developing this project was endless. Your guidance and teaching made me a better researcher and person. I hope this book lives up to your example. A special thanks also goes to Alberto Aleixo, Bira Carvalho, Lourenço Cesar, Luke Dowdney, Helena Edir, Ernani Euclides, Maïra Gabriel, André Galdino, Aristênio Gomes, Gilson Jorge, Geisa Lino, Luiz Gustavo de Sousa Lucas, Lidiane Malanquine, Rodrigo Maré, Eduardo Miranda, Felipe Moulin, Rodrigo Nascimento, William Nascimento, Daniela Ferreira Nunes, Renata Pedrone, Felipe Reis, Daniel Remilik, Everton Ribeiro, Mariani Rodrigues, Ruth Rosa, Shyrlei Rosendo, Kelly Santos, Maykon Sardinha, Higor Silva, Eliana Sousa, Lino Teixeira, Juliana Tibau, and Patrícia Vianna who supported me and this project in myriad ways.

I also owe much to Maré's numerous institutions and organizations that offered their support and made this book possible. The directors, staff, and volunteers of Redes da Maré, Luta pela Paz, the Centro de Estudos e Ações Solidárias da Maré (CEASM), the Observatório de Favelas, Projeto Uerê, Vida Real, the Lona Cultural Municipal Herbert Vianna, and the Museu da Maré are each engaged in the daily work of supporting, educating, and providing resources for Maré's residents to endure and thrive in difficult and, at times, intolerable circumstances. Their efforts continue to inspire me and make me hopeful that a different, better future for Maré is possible. In addition, each of Maré's Residents' Associations opened their doors to me so that I could understand their work to improve the lives of Maré's residents in practical and meaningful ways. I also want to thank each of Maré's gang organizations and their members for allowing me to accompany their lives and activities and whose tacit and even explicit approval of my project made this entire endeavor possible. I hope that this book does justice to the lived reality of these men and women.

In the final stages of writing, I relied on a huge number of colleagues and working groups to sharpen and refine the manuscript. Juan Albarracín, Desmond Arias, Ana Arjona, Laura Blume, Sarah Daly, Corrina Jentzsch, Sandra Ley, Zachariah Mampilly, Eduardo Moncada, Ana Paula Pellegrino, Rachel Schwartz, David Skarbek, Abbey Steele, Megan Stewart, Rebecca Tapscott, Lucía Tiscornia, and Samantha Vortherms all generously read chapters and gave insightful comments. Andrew Yingling and Benjamin Weber offered much-needed copy editing. Pranjal Drall provided excellent assistance with data analysis and visualization. Charlotte Van der Lijn helped with the GIS images. It was an enormous pleasure to collaborate with Bruna Ferreira Montuori for the book's maps. A special thanks goes to Juan Masullo, Desirée Poets, and Henning Tamm who went above and beyond by reading and commenting on multiple drafts and were each willing (forced?) to have many conversations to help me better understand my own thinking. This book is much improved because of your combined patience, intellect, and friendship.

Finally, I want to thank my family. Henrique Gomes, Andreza Jorge, Alice Odara, and the entire Jorge clan became my adoptive family in Maré. Your generosity and hospitality are endless. Without you, this book would be and mean so much less. I am enormously grateful to have you in my life. To my grandmother, Bernadine, at whose kitchen table I began this project, thank you for being such an inspiration and always pushing me to take every opportunity to learn. To my sisters, Megan and Erica, I am grateful for your humor and affection that have been a constant throughout my life and for my nephew, Malcolm, and nieces, Eleanor and Winifred, that have brought so much laughter and joy to our lives these past few years. To my parents, Chuck and Jan, I will never be able to express my gratitude for your love and support through all the years. And to Luna Borges, who entered my life in the final phase of this project, thank you. Every day with you is a gift.

A Note on Translation

All translations are the author's own. Because interviews and public meetings were not recorded – for security and confidentiality reasons – the author took extensive notes in a mix of English and Portuguese, then translated the notes into English. There are, inevitably, mistakes that have occurred in this process. Through triangulation of sources, the help of a research assistant and, in some cases, the interviewees themselves, I have made every effort to verify these translations. Overall, I follow a "fidelity to the reader" approach in adapting the original spoken Portuguese, which also often included pauses, partial words or phrases, and fillers, to ensure intelligibility. I am also cognizant that the process of translation is not simply one of transforming text into another language but is a political act that requires constant and continuous reevaluation of our assumptions concerning social relations, ideologies, and power.

Abbreviations, Acronyms, and Translated Words

ADA	*Amigos dos Amigos* (Friends of Friends), one of Rio's three prison-based drug-trafficking factions
Alemão	German, a term used to refer to a rival gang and its members
AM	*Associação de Moradores* (Residents' Association)
Avenida Brasil	Brazil Avenue, Rio de Janeiro's busiest highway
Atacadista	Drug wholesaler
Avião/Aviãozinho	Airplane/little airplane, a messenger for the gang
Assaltante	Robber/mugger
Baile funk	Funk party, large gang-organized parties where a particular form of funk music is played, which features deep bass, sampled melodies, and a "bum cha-cha, bum cha-cha" beat
Barraca	A cart or stall used for selling food or other informal goods
Boca de fumo	"Mouth of smoke," open-air retail drug markets
BOPE	*Batalhão de Operações Policiais Especiais* (Special Police Operations Battalion)
Braço direito	Right-hand man, a moniker used to refer to a gang's second-in-charge
Caveirão/caveirões	Big skull/s, armored vehicles that police use to invade favela territories
CCCC	*Centro Comunitário do Combate a Criminalidade* (Community Center for Combatting Crime), small police posts often located in or near favelas
Cria	Someone born and raised in the favela
CV	*Comando Vermelho* (Red Command), one of Rio's three prison-based drug-trafficking factions

CVNH   *Comando Vermelho da Nova Holanda*
                        (Comando Vermelho of New Holland), the
                        local CV-connected gang in the Nova Holanda
                        neighborhood
CVPU   *Comando Vermelho do Parque União* (Comando
                        Vermelho of Union Park), the local CV-connected
                        gang in the Parque União neighborhood
DD   *Disque-Denúncia* (Denunciation Hotline), an
                        NGO-operated service to anonymously report
                        crimes
Dono   Don or gang leader
DPO   *Destacamento de Policiamento Ostensivo*
                        (Ostensive Policing Detachment), small police
                        posts often located in or near favelas
Endolador   Packager, sometimes but not always a gang
                        member who is paid to divide, weigh, and package
                        drugs
Facção/facções   Faction/factions, a term that refers to the three prison-
                        based drug-trafficking organizations in the city of Rio
                        de Janeiro: CV, TCP (see below), and ADA
Favela   A name given to various working-class
                        neighborhoods with informal origins in Rio de
                        Janeiro and other Brazilian cities
Fogueteiro   Firecracker, a gang member, usually an adolescent,
                        tasked with shooting off firecrackers when police
                        are seen entering the community
Gerente   Manager
Gerente de boca   Sales-point manager, a gang member responsible
                        for the operation of an open-air drug market
Gerente de cocaína/   Cocaine manager, a gang member responsible
pó/branco   for the packaging and distribution of all cocaine
                        within a gang's territory
Gerente de crack   Crack manager, a gang member responsible for the
                        packaging and distribution of all crack within a
                        gang's territory
Gerente de maconha/   Marijuana manager, a gang member
preto   responsible for the packaging and distribution of
                        all marijuana within a gang's territory
Gerente de preço   Price manager, a gang member responsible for the
                        packaging and distribution of one quantity of one
                        drug (e.g., R$50 of marijuana)
Gerente dos soldados/ Soldiers or security manager, a gang
de segurança   member responsible for organizing the schedules of
                        security personnel and keeping track of armaments

Gerente geral	General manager
Gringo	A general term for foreigner, but most often used to refer to white foreigners
Guerra	War
Jogo do bicho	Animal game, an illegal lottery (commonly referred to as the numbers racket in the US) where animals represent different numbers that are drawn weekly with the winner receiving a lump sum and the organizers taking a cut
Irmãos Metralha	Beagle Boys, a gang from Nova Holanda in the 1980s led by five brothers
Lei de silêncio	Law of silence, also referred to as the *lei do morro* "law of the hillside"
Linha Amarela	Yellow Line highway
Linha Vermelha	Red Line highway
Matuto	Supplier of retail drugs
Milícia	Militia, a term used to refer to police-connected racketeering organizations that monopolize a variety of illicit and informal markets in hundreds of favelas throughout Rio de Janeiro
OCGs	*Organized and criminalized groups*
Olheiro	Lookout
Palafita	Shack on stilts, thousands of which were built in Maré from the 1940s to the 1980s, later removed by the public authority
PPC	*Posto de Policiamento Comunitário* (Community Police Post), small police posts often located in or near favelas
Real/reais	Brazilian currency, R$1 was roughly equal to $0.40 during my fieldwork
Soldado	Soldier, a gang member tasked with security duties
Sub-gerente	Sub-manager, a gang member who works directly for/under a manager
TC	*Terceiro Comando* (Third Command), one of Rio's three prison-based drug-trafficking factions until 2002
TCP	*Terceiro Comando Puro* (Pure Third Command), one of Rio's three prison-based drug-trafficking factions since 2002; also the abbreviation I use to refer to the local TCP affiliated gang in Complexo da Maré
Vacilão	Someone that is considered disloyal or cowardly
Vapor	Seller, a gang member who exchanges drugs for money at open-air drug markets

I

Introduction

> It's bad with the gangs, but worse without. An unhappy but necessary marriage.
> —Alba Zaluar, *Condomínio do Diabo* (1994, 11)

> The gangs today don't understand why they're fighting. They know they're angry
> and willing to fight but they don't know what they're actually fighting for.
> —José, a lifelong resident of Complexo da Maré

THE PUZZLE

I had been living in Nova Holanda (New Holland) for several months when
Carlos, my research assistant, introduced me to Severino, a member of the local
Comando Vermelho (Red Command, hereon CV) affiliated gang.[1] Severino
did not raise his eyes to meet mine when we shook hands. "Hello!" I said,
"It's nice to meet you. I'm a researcher from the United States. I'm interested
in …" Severino stopped me immediately with a wave of his hand. "I already
know," he said. I looked at Carlos, who shrugged. "I've seen you around,"
Severino explained. The corner where we were standing was only a minute's
walk from my apartment. In fact, Severino had seen me nearly every day for
the past few months. I, on the other hand, had never noticed Severino. He was
a full head shorter than me, skinny, with light brown skin. That day, he was
wearing an oversized red t-shirt, baggy athletic shorts, and a pair of what used
to be white Havaiana sandals. A baseball cap with a logo I did not recognize
covered his closely shaved head. Unlike most of the other gang members I saw
on the streets, Severino was not carrying a gun. Despite his rather unassuming

---

[1] CV is a prison-based drug-trafficking faction (*facção*), which connects hundreds of gangs
throughout the city and, in recent years, has spread to nearly every state in Brazil. For more on
the history and makeup of Rio's factions, see Chapter 4.

appearance, he had been in the gang for more than fifteen years over which time he had held various positions: *aviãozinho* (messenger), *olheiro* (lookout), *soldado* (soldier), and *vapor* (seller). When I met him, Severino was work-ing directly for the gang's *gerente de crack* (crack manager) as a *sub-gerente* (sub-manager).

Carlos walked over to a small convenience store on the corner, leaving the two of us alone. Severino was still looking out at the intersection, and I began to feel a bit uncomfortable just standing in front of him, so I turned to face the bustling traffic. After a few moments of awkward silence, I felt I needed to say something. "Shit, it's really hot today, isn't it?" was all I could come up with. "Very," he replied. I decided to get straight to the point, "Do you have some time to talk?" I asked. He nodded and we went over and sat down on the curb, out of earshot of any of the passersby.

I started by reciting my oral consent script.[2] I told him that my research was focused on understanding the relationship between the gang and the commu-nity, that he did not have to answer my questions, and could stop whenever he wanted. I promised not to use his name – Severino is a pseudonym – or divulge any identifiable information about him.[3] I concluded by asking if it was alright if I took notes. "Of course," he said, "there are no secrets here. Everyone knows everything." I reached for my notepad, but before I could take it out he asked, "Why do you think I hang out on this corner?" I took a closer look at the intersection.

Unlike many other favelas (informal neighborhoods), Nova Holanda's streets have a checkerboard layout because it was originally built as a tem-porary housing project in the early 1960s. The larger of the two roads that comprised the intersection was one of the busiest in Maré. A constant stream of cars, trucks, motorcycles, and pedestrians moved past the shops, bars, and restaurants that lined both sides of the street. The intersecting street was less busy and much narrower, barely wide enough for two cars to squeeze past one another. A small barbershop was located on the corner closest to us, just a few steps away. I spotted Carlos eating a Snickers bar and chatting with the owner of the small convenience store on the opposite corner. The other two corners were home to a beverage shop and a hardware store. This intersection did not have one of the gang's *bocas de fumo* (literally, mouths of smoke), open-air drug markets where the gang sold varying quantities of marijuana, cocaine, and crack. Without a boca and no heavy gang presence, it seemed like an unre-markable intersection to me.

"I don't know," I admitted.

---

[2] This was a paragraph-length description of the project, developed with the Institutional Review Board at the University of Wisconsin–Madison, to ask for the consent of the "research subject" to conduct the interview and be included within the study.
[3] Where necessary, I have not divulged or slightly changed some specific details about Severino (and my other interlocutors) and our interactions to provide a further level of anonymity.

"Look around," Severino said and motioned down the smaller street. I turned and looked where he had gestured. In the distance, I could see all the way to Avenida Brasil, Rio's busiest highway, some 500 yards away. Then he turned and looked in the other direction. I followed his gaze. Just a couple of hundred yards away, I could see a section of the fifteen-foot concrete wall that surrounded the 22nd Battalion, an imposing police station built on the edge of Nova Holanda in 2003. I could just make out the razor wire that ran along the top of the wall, but the gun turrets and the large double doors through which the enormous, militarized vehicles would pass when the police conducted their operations were just out of sight. We then turned to look down the larger street. I saw cars and pedestrians crossing the Ponte da Amizade (Bridge of Friendship) into Parque União (Union Park), a neighboring favela controlled by another CV-allied gang. A few hundred yards in the other direction, I spotted the beginning of Baixa do Sapateiro (Cobbler's Swamp) and Morro do Timbau (Timbau Hill) rising in the distance, two favelas controlled by a gang connected to CV's longtime rival, *Terceiro Comando Puro* (Third Pure Command, hereon TCP), another prison-based faction (*facção*). Severino then looked at me, our eyes meeting for the first time. "You always have to pay attention to what's going on in the community," he said. "This is a great spot to do that."

Over the next year and a half, I found Severino hanging out on this corner most days. He was often accompanied by an assortment of young men, some with pistols tucked into their shorts, others carried semiautomatic rifles. Severino would sometimes wave me over, and we would strike up a conversation about community events, politics, football, family, or any one of a variety of other topics. He would also tell me if anything important was happening regarding the gang or the police. Over time, I noticed that various residents approached him: an elderly man requested help buying medicine, a single mother carrying an infant asked for money for diapers, a young man wanted to know where he could find his former neighbor, and a middle-aged woman wanted to resolve a domestic dispute with her husband. Although he would not solve every problem, Severino often provided information, handed out small amounts of money, told residents who to talk to, and passed the most serious problems up the chain of command.

At first glance, Severino's services may seem rather banal and inconsequential, but the longer I lived in Maré, the more I came to realize that his behavior was part of a broader set of gang activities and relations which included not just financial assistance but a series of more programmatic policies intended to control space, gather information, and ingratiate the gang with the local population. Severino was just one of the Nova Holanda gang's 150 or so members, many of whom were engaged in similar activities that included monitoring the streets, enforcing a set of rules, throwing parties, offering forms of welfare, and providing access to illicit and informal economies. Together, these activities constitute what I refer to as *criminalized governance*, or the structures and practices through which gangs control territory and manage relations with local populations.

Criminalized governance is not uncommon in Rio de Janeiro. More than 1,000 favelas dot the city's sprawling urban landscape. In most of these communities, social services are limited, public infrastructure only partially provided, and schools and basic utilities fail to meet the needs of the population. Police only appear to engage in aggressive militarized operations. In the absence of a reliable state presence, drug-trafficking gangs have been the dominant political authority in hundreds of these neighborhoods for more than three decades. Their governance activities have irrevocably shaped the social dynamics within these communities, determined the physical security of residents, influenced local levels of development, and even affected the functioning of Rio's democratic institutions.

This book seeks to explain the origins, evolution, and variation in Rio de Janeiro's criminalized governance arrangements across space and time. To do so, I seek to answer a series of interrelated questions. First, what exactly are the "structures and practices" which criminalized governance entails? What are its primary dimensions and activities? Second, why do gangs govern at all? Why would organizations that seem most interested in accumulating wealth from the drug trade, spend valuable time and resources to implement reliable systems of order, adjudicate disputes, provide welfare, or distribute gifts and other benefits to residents? Finally, I seek to explain how and why these governance practices vary. Why do some gangs rely on violence and threats to dominate local populations while others refrain from such coercive behaviors? Why do some gangs provide significant benefits to local communities while others offer little or nothing? And how and why do these practices change over time and even vary within a single gang's turf?

These questions are enduring puzzles not just for scholars of Rio de Janeiro but also a growing swath of the global urban terrain. Most contemporary cities are wracked by poverty and inequality, sparse investment in public housing, uneven infrastructure, and inadequate social services. They are mostly governed by corrupt and inefficient political institutions and bureaucracies, ill-equipped to handle the massive waves of urbanization that continue to reshape human societies across the globe.[4] As a result, a vast multitude of slums (Davis 2006), shantytowns (Goldstein 2003), hyper-shantytowns (Auyero 2001), ghettos (Venkatesh 1997), and hyperghettos (Wacquant 2008) have emerged on what has been termed the "urban periphery" (Leeds 1996) or the "urban margins" (Auyero, Bourgois, and Scheper-Hughes 2015). Together, these communities are home to an estimated one billion people worldwide (UN-Habitat 2016). Gangs and their governance activities are a fact of life for many of these communities.

---

[4] According to a recent UN report (2019), 55% of the world's population already lives in urban areas, up from just 30% in 1950, and is estimated to grow to 68% by 2050.

A growing number of scholars have begun to recognize the prevalence of criminalized governance in the contemporary world. The phenomenon is particularly prominent across Latin America and the Caribbean, where hundreds of cities have witnessed the incredible proliferation of gangs and other *organized and criminalized groups* (OCGs) – drug-trafficking organizations, cartels, mafias, smuggling networks, and protection rackets among others. Today, a staggering 77 to 101 million people ($\approx$14 percent) across the region are estimated to live in areas where OCGs operate (Uribe et al. 2024). In São Paulo, Brazil, for instance, a prison gang, the *Primeiro Comando da Capital* (First Command of the Capital, or PCC), "sits at the heart of the governance of the urban conditions of life and death" (Denyer Willis 2015, 9), where they have developed an alternative system of law and justice for imprisoned populations and marginalized communities (Biondi 2014; Feltran 2010b; Lessing and Denyer Willis 2019). In Medellín, Colombia, *combos* (street gangs) have developed a dizzying array of arrangements with drug cartels, paramilitaries, and insurgent groups as they vie for control of impoverished neighborhoods across the city's periphery (Abello-Colak and Guarneros-Meza 2014; Arias 2017; Blattman et al. 2021; Lamb 2010).

In Central America, gangs are abundant. Nicaraguan *pandillas* impose their own form of order in urban areas, creating strong neighborhood-level identities and allegiances in the process (Rodgers, 2006a, 2006b, 2009, 2017). Across the Northern Triangle countries of Honduras, Guatemala, and El Salvador, *maras* dominate poor, marginalized neighborhoods in the major urban centers where they have been known to extort residents while also providing order and protection from rivals (Córdova 2022; Cruz 2010; Cruz and Rosen 2024; Van Der Borgh and Savenije 2015). Across urban Mexico, street and prison gangs compete and collaborate with drug cartels for the control of illicit markets while imposing various forms of order in local neighborhoods (Correa-Cabrera 2017; Magaloni et al. 2020; Trejo and Ley 2020; Wolff 2018).

The Caribbean has witnessed a similar expansion of gangs in recent decades. In Kingston, Jamaica, gangs linked to political parties dominate the sprawling towns surrounding the capital and are often considered de facto sovereigns while providing order and a variety of public goods to local communities (Arias 2017; Jaffe 2013, 2015). In Port-au-Prince, Haiti, gangs linked to political patrons have long dominated areas of the capital, engaging in a complex mix of predation and protection (Mobekk and Street 2006; Olivier 2021; Schuberth 2015). Nearly each and every island in the region contains examples of criminalized governance (Bobea 2013).

Governance is also an oft-noted dynamic of gangs in the United States. Across many marginalized and impoverished urban neighborhoods, gangs can provide individuals and communities some level of security amidst chaotic and volatile circumstances (Ortiz 2018; Sobel and Osoba 2009), occasionally even constituting the dominant local authority (Sánchez-Jankowski 1991, 2003; Venkatesh 1997, 2008). Prison gangs also control much of the US penitentiary system; some of these organizations have managed to extend their governance beyond the prison walls to entire illicit markets (Skarbek 2014).

The phenomenon of criminalized governance is not exclusive to the Americas. In South Africa, gangs have a long history of dominating impoverished townships on the outskirts of the major urban centers (Jensen 2008; Kynoch 1999, 2005; Lambrechts 2012; Pinnock 1984, 2016). Slum-based gangs in Nigeria and Kenya have linked themselves to political parties and elites through which they have managed to accumulate significant local authority (LeBas 2013). In India, youth gangs are known to provide order in urban slums by punishing criminals (Sen 2014), while some have even become major players in lucrative real estate markets (Weinstein 2008, 2013). In Bangladesh, gangs control access to infrastructure and services, determine property rights, and distribute employment opportunities to impoverished communities (Jackman 2019; Khan 2000). Meanwhile, in urban Pakistan and Indonesia, gangs have long competed for control of protection rackets and illicit markets while providing some public goods, developing close relationships with a variety of political parties in the process (Siddiqui 2022; Tajima 2018).

And yet, despite the prevalence of criminalized governance in the contemporary world, gangs and other OCGs have been mostly ignored as consequential political actors. The discipline of political science has long been interested in how a variety of armed actors (states, insurgents, paramilitaries, and terrorists) control territory and govern populations, but these same behaviors by gangs and other criminalized groups have been almost completely overlooked. Why?

Historically, this oversight was justified by their lack of overt political ambitions pertaining to the state and, as I often heard from audiences when presenting this project early on, the belief that gang members "are just criminals." Such a perspective is thoroughly biased in two ways. First, political science as a discipline has incorrectly assumed that modern states, unless in the midst of war, successfully monopolize legitimate violence within their territories. This hegemonic assumption stems from Weber's iconic definition: "a human community that (successfully) claims the monopoly of the legitimate use of violence within a given territory" (1965). Drawing from the early twentieth-century European experience, Weber's idealized state shares little in common with the vast majority of states in the modern world (Barkey 1994; Centeno 2002; Davis and Pereira 2003; Herbst 2015). Seldom have states outside of Europe – or even European ones, for that matter – been able to monopolize "legitimate" violence within their borders.[5] In fact, many high capacity, democratic, and

---

[5] The very inclusion of the term legitimacy is problematic because, as Wedeen expertly points out, it can easily be conflated with "acceptance, acquiescence, consent, and/or obedience" (2015, xiv). This critique is reminiscent of Tilly's famous argument: "The distinction between 'legitimate' and 'illegitimate' force ... makes no difference to the fact. If we take legitimacy to depend on conformity to an abstract principle or on the assent of the governed (or both at once), these

seemingly "peaceful" states will often contain a variety of non-state armed groups that operate and sometimes govern specific areas within their territory. While gangs and a variety of other criminalized groups may not consider themselves rivals to the state, their use of violence and governance practices have made it abundantly clear that we can no longer ignore their origins, motivations, and behaviors if we are to understand contemporary politics in a great many locations throughout the world.[6]

The other source of bias is racial and of class. Political science has long regarded the "ordinary strategies that the black [and brown] urban poor embrace ... as apolitical" (Alves 2018, 197). This book, rather, contends that "black [and brown] youths' deviant behavior (of which the figure of the gangster has become an icon) should be understood not only as counterhegemonic protest against racism and discrimination but also as a radical refusal to comply with white civil society" (p. 197).[7] Thus, joining and becoming a gang member, instead of being seen as an act of mere deviance or criminality, should be considered a *political* one. Moreover, the residents of the communities where gangs operate – favelas, ghettos, housing projects, etc. – are overwhelmingly underrepresented in higher education, much less the research community. For anyone who grew up in a neighborhood where gangs operate, the political nature of these organizations is self-evident, though often contested and disliked. The discipline has mostly overlooked the political nature of the violence that these communities have suffered and continue to endure, in part because incredibly few political scientists come from such neighborhoods. For these reasons, criminalized governance remains a significant blind spot for the discipline. By developing the conceptual and theoretical language to describe how and why gangs govern in the contemporary world, I seek to add to our understanding of the politics of the most marginalized within our societies.

THE ARGUMENT

I argue that gangs govern not because their members are motivated by governance (it is a difficult and time-consuming task) nor by a desire to remake the political order that has placed them at the bottom of society. Instead, gangs govern because they inhabit an extremely dangerous world and need the obedience and support of local communities if they are to survive. To gain the type

---

conditions may serve to justify, perhaps even to explain, the tendency to monopolize force; they do not contradict the fact" (1985, 171).

[6] In this regard, this book joins scholars that have turned to the study of non-state armed groups that exist and even thrive within consolidated and democratic states, including vigilante groups (Bateson 2021; Moncada 2017; Tapscott 2021a), militias and paramilitaries (Acemoglu, Robinson, and Santos 2013; Daly 2022; Davis and Pereira 2003; Tajima 2018), and even political parties (Albarracín 2018; Siddiqui 2022; Straus 2012; Wilkinson 2004), among others.

[7] While not every gang is black or brown, the statement can be equally applied to marginalized and impoverished populations virtually anywhere.

and degree of support they need from the local population, they must learn
to wield power effectively, to deploy the tools – the carrots and sticks, so to
speak – at their disposal. In this regard, I conceive of criminalized governance
as comprised of two primary dimensions: *coercion* and the *provision of benefits*. On the one hand, gangs have developed a variety of coercive practices in
the areas where they operate: they monitor entry and exit to their territories,
maintain a physical and sometimes militarized presence on the streets, and can
violently punish anyone that infringes on their economic activities or disobeys
their rules. A gang that merely predates and dominates a community through
coercion alone, however, is not governing. Such contexts are better thought of
as *disorder*. To govern, gangs must place some limits on their coercive behavior and will often develop a set of beneficent practices that can include mechanisms for dispute resolution, economic stimulation, as well as opportunities
for recreation, among others.

   Not all gangs that govern, however, employ the same levels of coercion
nor provide the same quality of benefits. In fact, we observe significant variation across these two dimensions. I distinguish between gangs that use low
or high amounts of coercion and are responsive or unresponsive to resident
demands for benefits. The interaction of these two dimensions produces four
ideal-typical criminalized governance regimes. A *social bandit gang* will employ
low levels of coercion while providing responsive benefits to the community.
A *benevolent dictator gang* will use high levels of coercion but simultaneously
offer responsive benefits to residents. A *tyrant gang* also employs high levels
of coercion but is unresponsive to residents' requests for benefits. Finally, a
laissez-faire gang uses little coercion while providing few if any benefits to the
community. Some gangs may maintain a particular type of governance regime
for decades while others move back and forth across these regimes quickly.
Gangs may even vary their governance practices within the areas in which they
operate. This book seeks to explain this variation.

   Building on three years of ethnographic fieldwork in Rio de Janeiro's favelas, I argue that criminalized governance is an innate strategic response to two
kinds of threat, from rival gangs and from the police, that shape what a gang
needs from residents.[8] First, a belligerent rival represents an existential threat
to any gang organization and its membership because they are capable of con-
quering and expelling a gang from its territory.[9] In this regard, gang turf wars

---

[8] Unlike many popular conceptions of gang members as inherently irrational and even psychotic,
   this theory assumes gang members to be highly strategic actors. Although I make no strict
   "rational choice" assumptions – that all gang members are ultimately self-interested and will
   make choices that benefit themselves (see Skarbek 2014, 2–4) – the overarching organizations in which individual members are embedded shape their motivations and incentives, thus
   encouraging a set of organizational practices and behaviors.
[9] Gangs in Rio de Janeiro do not just compete for territorial control with other gangs. For years,
   off-duty police and other public security personnel in Rio have formed milícias (militias), their
   own illicit organizations, which also dominate favelas and set up their own local governance

are an oft-documented phenomenon throughout much of the world. At the same time, many gangs have also found ways to avoid violence and warfare by negotiating, making peace, forging alliances, and developing arrangements to divide territory among themselves.[10] Given this variation in intergang relations, I argue that gangs can face three different levels of rival threat: *active*, *latent*, or *absent*.

An *active* threat is when a gang faces a rival that is intent on taking over their territory, which can include everything from all-out invasions, skirmishes, and drive-by shootings to targeted kidnappings and assassinations, as well as more subtle attempts to infiltrate a territory. A *latent* threat, by contrast, applies to contexts where a gang does not currently face a rival actively trying to take over their territory but due to proximity, a history of conflict, or previous territorial turnover, the possibility of violent contestation is high. Finally, an *absent* threat means a gang faces no competitors for territorial control. This is often due to a group having successfully defeated and absorbed all local rivals, their relative geographic isolation, or the result of stable alliances or arrangements with surrounding gangs. Gangs can shift back and forth across these levels rapidly while, in other cases, rival threat builds slowly or gradually diminishes. Some gangs may experience multiple rival threats at the same time. Others may have never faced a proximate rival.

I argue that the degree of rival threat determines the coercive practices gangs will use against the population within its territory. If a gang loses its turf to a rival, incumbent gang members and their families will either be killed or expelled from the territory. Therefore, when facing an active rival threat, gang members will defend their turf at all costs, diverting any available resources and manpower to prevent their enemy from invading and infiltrating their territory. They will remove any existing limits on their coercive behavior because, in the fog of war, gangs cannot put the concern for resident well-being above the need to defend their territory. In these contexts, I predict gangs will use extreme levels of coercion directed at residents as they demand higher levels of obedience and fear collaboration with their rival. They will question, threaten, and expel anyone they think does not belong, ostentatiously display themselves and their armaments as a constant reminder to residents that they dominate the territory, and will engage in brutal and public punishments of anyone suspected of betrayal. These contexts are best understood as *disorder*. For latent threats, gangs will still closely monitor their borders, maintain an extensive

regimes (Arias 2017; Cano 2008; Cano and Duarte 2012; Manso 2020; Zaluar and Conceição 2007). Milícias are now more numerous than drug-trafficking gangs in the city (Hirata, Cardoso, et al. 2021; Hirata and Couto 2022) and are often rivals to many of Rio's gangs.

[10] See Arias (2017), Aspholm (2020), Cruz and Durán-Martínez (2016), Daly and Barham (2024), Durán-Martínez (2018), The Economist (2012), Magaloni et al. (2020), Sánchez-Jankowski (1991), Skarbek (2014), and Vargas (2016) for a description of some of these various intergang relations.

physical presence, and punish disloyalty but they will refrain from the most extreme forms of coercion and not divert all their attention and resources to the defense of their turf. Finally, an absent threat translates to a gang that will take a more relaxed approach to controlling their territory. They will not monitor their borders assiduously, be less physically present on the streets, and refrain from violent punishments.

I argue that the threat of police enforcement, unlike that of a rival, constitutes only a transient threat to gangs, one that can also vary from *active* to *absent*. Even amid active and highly militarized enforcement efforts, the police almost never represent an existential threat to gangs because they seldom seek a permanent presence within these neighborhoods and do not look to take over local illicit markets like a rival would. Instead, police enforcement the world over mostly focuses on weakening gangs and combatting illicit markets by arresting their members and by confiscating weapons, drugs, or other illicit material. Although gangs may occasionally confront police directly, they generally refrain from such tactics because: (1) they know police will only be present for a short period of time and (2) this will only cause further police attention and enforcement. Therefore, gangs do not defend their territory at all costs like they do against rivals but rather seek to evade enforcement by melting into the population. Not all gangs, however, face active enforcement. Some gangs have developed durable bribery schemes or tacit agreements with the police that prevent or limit enforcement. Other gangs operate in areas where police may seldom go, either due to a lack of resources or because they have decided that enforcement is too costly or unattractive.

I argue that the degree of transient threat from police enforcement determines a gang's willingness to provide benefits to local communities. Where enforcement is active and frequent, gangs will seek greater levels of support from the community in the effort to avoid enforcement. In these contexts, gangs need residents to at least not inform on them and sometimes their direct assistance to evade the police. As a result, they are more willing to resolve disputes for residents, provide economic stimulation, and organize opportunities for recreation. Gangs that face little or no enforcement, however, need the community less and will provide little in terms of benefits.

Although gang-level incentives may seem to predominate, criminalized governance is not merely imposed from the top-down. The role of residents is crucial. This insight has already been baked into the theory as residents are presented with a series of constraints and opportunities for gaining access to scarce resources and providing for their safety within each of the security environments described earlier. How residents respond to gangs within each of these environments shapes the nature of the threats that gangs face and, in turn, the governance outcomes observed. I argue that there are two resident behaviors, in particular, that matter to governance outcomes: *denunciations* and *demands*. On the one hand, residents of gang territories have sensitive information regarding gang members' activities, whereabouts, routines, and social relations. This information is extremely useful in the hands of rivals and the police. Where a gang faces an active or latent threat from a rival, they will employ higher levels of coercion to try to prevent and deter residents from offering sensitive information to their enemy. Residents can do little to limit coercion in these circumstances because the nature of the threat is existential.

When gangs face high levels of police attention and enforcement, however, residents have more leverage over gang behavior. First, the transient nature of enforcement does not require the same coercive gang response and, second, unlike denunciation to rivals, which is extremely difficult and dangerous, residents can often provide information to the police quite easily through emergency phone numbers or hotlines created specifically for this purpose. Thus, when enforcement is active, gangs are incentivized to seek out closer, more beneficial relations with residents because they need residents to refrain from denouncing them to the police. The use of coercion in such circumstances is counterproductive because gangs have a difficult time knowing who is informing on them and, therefore, who to target. Moreover, indiscriminate forms of coercion while enforcement is active will only lead to further denunciation and even more frequent police enforcement efforts. Where enforcement is not forthcoming, however, either through bribery schemes or the lack of police presence, denunciation does not produce the same effect and gangs are not incentivized to develop such reciprocal relations with local communities.

Finally, although gangs often manage to provide benefits to communities when and where they attempt to do so, they cannot resolve disputes, provide welfare, or create opportunities for recreation if residents refuse to accept them. Thus, when and where residents "demand" (ask for and accept) gang benefits is essential to understanding these outcomes. While perhaps not as consequential as denunciations in terms of the local security environment, demands and the more collaborative relations that they engender between gangs and residents are equally important to the survival of any gang organization. In this way, criminalized governance should be understood as a two way street; residents always play a fundamental role in shaping the nature of these arrangements. Overall, I argue that criminalized governance is a joint production, the result of frequent and repeated interactions between gang members and residents within particular security environments.

CONTRIBUTIONS TO THE LITERATURE

An emerging research agenda spanning several social scientific disciplines has slowly begun to investigate the origins, causes, and consequences of governance by gangs and other OCGs. Although the literature generally refers to this phenomenon as criminal governance, I employ the term *criminalized* governance because, ultimately, the state – both representing and shaping the interests and opinions of society at large – is the arbiter of what activities, practices, individuals, and groups are considered to be "criminal." If we are to sufficiently understand how and why such groups engage in governance, the processes by which some individuals and groups are criminalized while others are considered acceptable or even legal must be acknowledged and incorporated into our frameworks.[11] Notwithstanding this conceptual correction, the theoretical framework I develop contributes to three distinct analytical traditions within this quickly expanding literature, which implicitly or explicitly equate criminalized governance to processes of state making, rebel governance, or state perversion. In the following sections, I describe how this book borrows key insights from each of these approaches and contributes to them in multiple ways. Overall, this book attempts to build more and better bridges between these parallel literatures by highlighting points of similarity while remaining cognizant of the distinctions.

Criminalized Governance as State Making

The first framework views gangs and other OCGs as would-be states and their governance activities as incipient forms of state making. In this tradition, today's nation-states are understood as the descendants of racketeers from the late Middle Ages that created governing institutions because "the provision of a peaceful order and other public goods gives the stationary bandit a far larger take than he could obtain without providing government" (Olson 1993, 568) and because providing governance can generate "quasi-voluntary compliance" with the effort to extract resources (Levi 1989). Counter-intuitively, then, it was the self-interested and avaricious bandit that settled down and began providing services and benefits to populations.

Developing governance structures and institutions (i.e. state making) was never the explicit intent of these bandits but were "inadvertent by-products of efforts to carry out more immediate tasks, especially the creation and support of armed force" (Tilly 1992, 26). Almost by necessity, the conquest of territory through warfare involved providing some services to local populations that included redistribution of lands, encouragement of production, adjudication of disputes, and, inevitably, extraction (p. 20). This process quickly became self-reinforcing. The concentration of the means of coercion within a specific territory facilitated and demanded resource extraction that, in turn, built governing institutions, which then allowed the ruler to continue to expand their territory and build more extensive governing institutions. In this way, war making, extraction, and governance slowly (over several centuries) produced elaborate bureaucracies and governmental institutions (tax collectors, courts, exchequers, and, eventually, police forces) that would extend the power of the state directly into the lives of each and every citizen, thus bringing about

---

[11] I further develop this concept in Chapter 2.

a more peaceful order.[12] Here we have the basic components of a bellicist theory of governance that revolves around the extraction of resources amid violent competition for control of territory and population.

Like the bandits of the late Middle Ages, the governance that gangs engage in is often related to similar processes of violence and competition. Due to their criminalization by the state and society, gangs exist within what can be considered anarchic security environments (Sánchez-Jankowski 1991; Skaperdas and Syropolous 1995). Gang members must constantly be willing to use or threaten violence to protect themselves and their interests against would-be rivals, of which there can be many; single gang cities are incredibly rare. Given these anarchic conditions, gangs often fight wars for territorial supremacy. The fact that gangs fight wars has yet to be truly appreciated by scholars of political violence because they generally only occur within cities and states that we have traditionally considered to be "at peace." Moreover, such wars seldom threaten the "fortified enclaves" (Caldeira 2001) of the middle classes and elites, much less the functioning of government institutions. They are mostly contained within the marginalized and impoverished neighborhoods where gangs and other criminalized groups emerge and operate. In this book, I argue that gang warfare (and its threat) incentivizes gangs to behave in ways that resemble the state makers of yore: they seek to consolidate territorial control, eliminate all internal threats and enemies, and extract resources. If state-making theories are correct, it should come as no surprise that these contexts provide the primary examples of gangs that govern.

The state formation approach to criminalized governance seems, initially, to be a fruitful path to understanding its underlying dynamics. However, unlike early state-formers, gangs exist within states that have already accumulated the concentrated means of coercion. Thus, when contemporary gang organizations engage in warfare with rivals, they are not battling for absolute territorial control which precedes the state. Instead, they are self-consciously competing for territories *within* states. Gangs are not interested in taking over or breaking away from the state. In fact, the state plays a starring role in where violence escalates and where it is contained. The state can often be the deciding factor in which gangs emerge victorious as security forces may protect some while allowing others to perish. In addition, although the presence and responsiveness of the state and its institutions may be weak or only partial for resident

---

[12] Centeno (2002) compellingly argues that this European state formation process never happened in Latin America, where the coercive arm of the state, instead of being used to compete with external rivals, was primarily employed to dominate and repress large African and Indigenous populations or the class enemies of the state. Without external wars to incentivize the construction of a cohesive state that "pacified" and incorporated the various populations within its territory (through conscription and the building of a national identity), the Latin American state never became a fully capable one. According to Centeno, this incomplete state formation process has allowed a variety of non-state armed groups to emerge and wield considerable violence and authority in the region.

populations in areas where gangs operate, citizens and communities continue to make demands of the state, either directly to the public security apparatus or through electoral and political processes. These differences make the direct application of this framework not so straightforward, as others have pointed out (Koivu 2016; Lessing 2020).

Despite this key difference, the state making approach offers key insights to the task at hand. First, the accumulation of the means of violence is an inherently political project, whether governance is the group's primary motivation or not. By overlooking gangs' lack of overt political motivations regarding the state and focusing our attention more squarely on their actual activities and behavior, we can more clearly recognize how they have managed to accumulate political authority. Second, this approach places violent competition and the strategic environments in which these actors operate at the center of the analysis. How gangs deal with threats to their organization and the role that residents play in intensifying or diminishing those threats are crucial to understanding how and why they govern.

Criminalized Governance as Rebel Governance

The second analytical framework stems from the emerging research agenda on rebel governance. Like the state-making approach, competition over territory and population plays a central role in theories of rebel governance. Rebel groups, by definition, are engaged in violent conflict with the state and, therefore, their governance activities can only occur within this broader contestation for control of territory and population. The contours of this growing literature are still evolving but the fundamental thrust is that civil war represents "competitive state-building" (Kalyvas 2006) in which rebel groups are attempting to implement their vision of an alternative political order. To do so, they create structures and institutions that not only correspond to that vision, but which help them gain the support of the local population and maximize the byproducts of territorial control (like recruitment and access to resources) in their effort to win the war. Rebel governance has been found to vary significantly even within territories held by the same overarching rebel organization. The effort of many scholars working in this area has been to explain the causes and consequences of this variation.[13]

Rebel governance shares a surprising resemblance to criminalized governance in several respects. First, like rebels, OCGs can vary from being indifferent to territory and populations to out-administering the state in others (Kalyvas 2015a, 1534). Some OCGs have even been known to "secure the

---

[13] Some of the most prominent works include Arjona (2016), Arjona, Kasfir, and Mampilly (2015), Cunningham and Loyle (2021), Huang (2017), Mampilly (2011), Mampilly and Stewart (2021), Revkin (2020, 2021), Stewart (2017, 2021), and Loyle et al. (2022), among others.

allegiance and identification of large segments of society" (Felbab-Brown 2010, 158), thus resembling more overtly political movements. In addition, some gangs have even been known to directly confront state security forces, what has been referred to as "criminal insurgency" (Killebrew 2011; Manwaring 2005; Sullivan 2010) or "cartel-state conflict" (Lessing 2017), thus, even more closely resembling civil war contexts. Finally, although generally thought to be uniformly antagonistic, gang- and rebel-state relations have been shown to vary along a similar continuum from collaboration to competition (Barnes 2017; Staniland 2012).

Despite these numerous points of overlap, there are strong arguments against a wholesale adoption of this framework. The primary difference between gangs and rebels concerns their *raison d'être*. While I disagree with the simple distinction between criminal and political motivations that much of the literature adheres to (see Barnes 2017), rebels are almost always seeking the larger goal of secession, state capture, or political reform (Kasfir 2015, 23). In this effort, they govern not only to gain the support of local populations, but to demonstrate to the international community that they are capable and responsible rulers, what Mampilly has referred to as "juridical sovereignty" (2011, 39). Gangs and other criminalized groups may maintain de facto sovereignty but have no interest in juridical sovereignty. They certainly do not seek the support of states within the international system, thus making these forms of governance potentially quite distinct. Moreover, rebel groups that have consolidated their territorial control seldom allow state institutions and agents to continue to function in these areas. This is never the case for gangs that will allow various aspects of the state (including the police) to continue to operate in their turf even as they claim exclusive control vis-à-vis their rivals (Barnes 2022b). As such, gangs and other criminalized groups generally prefer lower profile and informal governance mechanisms that can overlap or coexist with some forms of state governance. In this regard, numerous scholars have argued that comparing gangs and OCGs with rebels is misguided and produces counter-productive policies (Arias 2006a; Lessing 2017, 2020; Rodgers and Muggah 2009). These are compelling arguments for the continued distinction between rebel and criminalized governance.

While I agree that we must not equate OCGs with rebels, discarding the parallels between these forms of governance would be equally unwise. This project borrows three important insights from existing work on rebel governance. First, while many rebel groups may obtain the obedience or acquiescence of local populations through the threat of violence, they must also gain the willing or active support of at least a segment of the population if they are said to govern.[14] In this regard, conceptualizations of rebel governance

---

[14] This is a point that both scholars and practitioners of rebel governance agree on (Arjona 2016; Guevara, Stone, and Morray 2012; Kalyvas 2006; Mampilly 2011; Weinstein 2007; Wickham-Crowley 1987; Wood 2003; Zedong 2000). Scholars of gang-community relations make the

nearly always include both the use and threat of force (coercion) as well as the provision of some benefits.[15] Similarly, I argue that we cannot understand criminalized governance without focusing on *both* the coercive as well as beneficent activities. They constitute separate but complementary sides of the same governance coin.

Second, violent competition for territorial control plays a major role in shaping rebel governance. In his seminal work on the logic of violence in civil war, for instance, Kalyvas (2006) demonstrated how armed groups shift their repertoires of violence and, thereby, relations to civilian populations depending on the type and degree of territorial contestation vis-à-vis other armed groups. Other scholars have similarly shown that governance of civilians is often subordinated to the strategic considerations regarding the ongoing civil war and may even be suspended during more conflictual periods.[16] The theory of criminalized governance I develop builds on these works by tracing the logic and mechanisms through which violent territorial competition between rivals translates to the greater use of coercion against local communities.

Finally, the role of civilians in determining the nature of rebel governance arrangements is an insight which this project applies to understanding how and why gangs govern. In civil wars, some communities have refused to cooperate with rebels, resisting their attempts to govern at every turn.[17] In other cases, communities have embraced rebels, welcomed their governance initiatives, and provided them significant support in their effort to win the overarching war in return.[18] Again, these dynamics map quite easily onto contexts of criminalized governance: existing work finds a similar variation in citizen responses to gangs and other criminalized groups, from direct support

same argument (Sánchez-Jankowski 1991, 32; Skaperdas and Syropolous 1995, 76; Zaluar 1994, 11).

[15] Kalyvas has outlined six mechanisms which encourage civilian support or collaboration: shielding, mechanical ascription, credibility of rule, the provision of benefits, monitoring, and self-reinforcing by-products (2006, 124). Of these, Mampilly argues that shielding – protecting civilians from rival groups – and the provision of benefits constitute the primary dimensions of governance (2011, 54). Arjona similarly argues that rebels govern when they provide "public goods, create new institutions, or establish quasi-legal systems with their own courts and enforcement system" (2015, 22).

[16] See Arjona (2016, 202), Kasfir (2005, 291), Mampilly (2011, 81–82), and Metelits (2009, 27).

[17] Scholars have outlined a huge number of ways civilians can resist rebel governance including by not offering them information or material support, refusing to comply with their rules, bargaining with them directly, informing on them to state authorities, or even organizing militias (Arjona 2015, 2016, 2017; Hallward, Masullo, and Mouly 2017; Idler, Belén Garrido, and Mouly 2015; Jentzsch 2022; Kaplan 2013, 2017; Krause 2018; Masullo 2021a, 2021b).

[18] Civilians can support and cooperate with rebels in a huge variety of ways, including by using their courts and legal systems, partaking in education and social services that rebels provide, or joining and supporting the rebel group more directly (Arjona 2016, 2017; Kalyvas 2006, 87–110; Parkinson 2013, 2023; Petersen 2001; Rubin 2020; Wood 2003, 122–59).

to begrudging obedience to overt resistance and even mobilization.[19] How and why individuals and communities respond in these ways has yet to be fully explained but this book offers some clues by providing a micro-level analysis of how civilian responses map onto and shape criminalized governance activities.

Criminalized Governance as State Perversion

The final approach views criminalized governance as a direct result of perverse states. Until the turn of the millennium, numerous scholars had come to view the region's increasing levels of violence and crime as a consequence of neoliberal reforms: the hollowing out of social services, the shrinking of the public sector, and the limiting of access to systems of law and justice (see Leeds 1996; O'Donnell 1993). Desmond Arias was one of the first to articulate a different explanation, arguing that the proliferation of "criminal governance" (in perhaps the first use of the term) was not the product of state absence or failure but rather the result of a state that *was* present (2006b, 294). A variety of scholars quickly followed suit, documenting how criminalized groups governed through clandestine networks involving politicians, public security officials, licit businesses, and community leaders, what Auyero (2007) referred to as the "grey zone."[20] According to Arias, these illicit networks "provide important conduits through which impoverished populations, historically excluded from basic political protections and economic opportunities, are incorporated under conditions of dependency and violence into a wider political system" (2013, 282). From this perspective, criminalized governance can be seen as a perverse form of state building in highly unequal societies.[21]

Overall, the perverse state approach offers a persuasive argument for how and why gangs and other criminalized groups emerge and engage in governance. Departing from a Weberian understanding of the state, this tradition highlights the many ways that states themselves have given rise to the very groups they are purportedly combatting. By marginalizing segments of their citizenry, refusing to provide them with rights and services, engaging in a variety of corrupt and unsavory practices within these communities, and arbitrarily and cynically applying the rule of law, it is little wonder that a variety of organizations willing to engage in crime and violence have gathered authority

---

[19] See Arias (2006a), Arias and Rodrigues (2006), Arjona (2017), Ley, Mattiace, and Trejo (2019), and Moncada (2019b, 2019a, 2022).

[20] Other works in this tradition include Abello-Colak and Guarneros-Meza (2014), Arias (2017), Arias and Goldstein (2010), Auyero and Berti (2015), Caldeira (2001, 2002), D. E. Davis (2010), G. Denyer Willis (2015), Feltran (2010a, 2018), D. Goldstein (2003), D. M. Goldstein (2004), Holston (2009), and Rodgers (2006a).

[21] More recently, scholars have developed the concept of hybrid governance, which denotes how criminalized groups, the state, and other informal actors may all contribute in myriad ways to governance in any given setting (Jaffe 2013; Pimenta, Suarez, and Ferreira 2021).

outside of the state. Instead of combatting them by striving to (re)incorporate marginalized populations within the body politic, Latin American states have overwhelmingly chosen to militarize their policing practices (Flores-Macías and Zarkin 2021), pushing citizens of these areas even further toward alternative governance arrangements (Koonings and Kruijt 2004; Wolff 2015). For anyone familiar with the politics of the Latin American region, this is a compelling vision for how and why gangs and other criminalized groups govern.

One of the major flaws of this approach, however, is that it seldom offers gangs or other criminalized groups and their members much agency. Scholars within this tradition seldom focus on the strategic behavior of gangs and their members. Instead, the networks and connections to the state often override any bottom-up processes, including how residents relate to gangs in these areas. While many studies have compellingly shown that gang violence and authority are heavily influenced by top-down processes, how gangs order space, recruit members, provide welfare, develop informal systems of law and justice, and offer access to illicit markets are not structurally determined. What this book contributes is a ground-level analysis of how gangs and their members are capable of a remarkably diverse set of actions and reactions to these difficult and constrained environments.

Existing research has mostly overlooked the bottom-up aspects of criminalized governance because these activities are extremely difficult if not impossible to observe directly. By its nature, criminalized governance is nearly always informal and clandestine. Gangs and other criminalized groups seldom keep records and always try to prevent the authorities and larger society from finding out about these activities.[22] Moreover, those receiving criminalized governance services seldom want the authorities, local institutions, or even their neighbors to know about these exchanges due to the significant stigma and perhaps even the legal repercussions of such connections. As a result, we have mostly been unable to document much less theorize a whole range of governance activities which are the bread and butter of any criminalized organization. Moreover, we have failed to understand these activities from the perspective of their protagonists, the providers and subjects/beneficiaries of such governance. This book seeks to break new ground by taking you, the reader, *inside* the organizations and communities where such practices take place. In the next section, I outline the mixed-method ethnographic approach required to provide such a perspective of criminalized governance as well as the various ethical, security, and positionality considerations necessary to conduct such research.

RESEARCH DESIGN AND FIELDWORK

This book employs a comparative ethnographic research design. By ethnography, I refer not just to interviews and long-term fieldwork but the use of

---

[22] There are exceptions (see Lessing and Denyer Willis 2019).

participant observation and "immersion in the place and lives of people under study" (Wedeen 2010, 257). Many ethnographers have focused on single case studies to highlight complexity and contextual meaning while mostly ignoring case comparisons and explicitly refuting claims of generalizability. In a recent innovation, however, Simmons and Smith have argued that ethnographers can better engage with broader theoretical debates by conducting "ethnographic research that explicitly and intentionally builds an argument through the analysis of two or more cases" (2019, 341). This book takes just such an approach by comparing the governance activities of three separate drug-trafficking gangs over four decades. It traces the evolution of each of these organizations, from their emergence as fledgling street gangs to powerful drug-trafficking organizations, with an eye toward understanding how and why their governance activities have shifted over that time. Analytical leverage is gained not only through comparison across these cases but also the temporal and spatial variation within each.

I engaged in more than three years of multi-method fieldwork in Rio de Janeiro, Brazil and eighteen months of ethnography in Complexo da Maré, a sprawling complex of fifteen favelas and housing projects, in which three separate drug-trafficking gangs operate. In June 2013, I moved to Nova Holanda (see Figure 1.1), one of three contiguous neighborhoods controlled by a gang I refer to as Comando Vermelho of Nova Holanda (CVNH). Although I resided in this one gang's territory, I travelled extensively throughout Maré, spending several days a week in Maré's two other gang territories, one of which was also affiliated with the CV faction and located in an adjacent neighborhood, Parque União (thus, CVPU). The third gang, which controlled ten contiguous favelas and housing projects in the south of Maré, was connected to CV's primary rival, Terceiro Comando Puro (TCP).

In April 2014, nine months after I moved to Maré, 2,500 Brazilian Army and Marine troops invaded and occupied the entirety of Complexo da Maré. The intervention represented the culmination of Rio's *Unidades de Polícia Pacificadora* (Police Pacification Units) or UPPs, a public security program intended to recapture the state's "monopoly of violence" from drug-trafficking gangs in hundreds of favelas throughout the city. The military occupation was initially intended to be short-term – just four months – to weaken the gangs and build local capacity before the installation of four community policing units. This would never come to pass. Instead, the military occupied Maré for fifteen months, during which time I continued my fieldwork, living in Maré for another nine months, concluding initial data collection in November 2014. I returned to Maré in July and August 2015 immediately following occupation, again in 2017 and 2018 for several more months of follow-up research, and finally in 2023 for a few months.

During the original fieldwork period, I spent 24 hours a day, seven days a week in my field site. To the extent that a *gringo* (foreigner) could, I tried to live like other favela residents. I shopped at local supermarkets, ate at favela

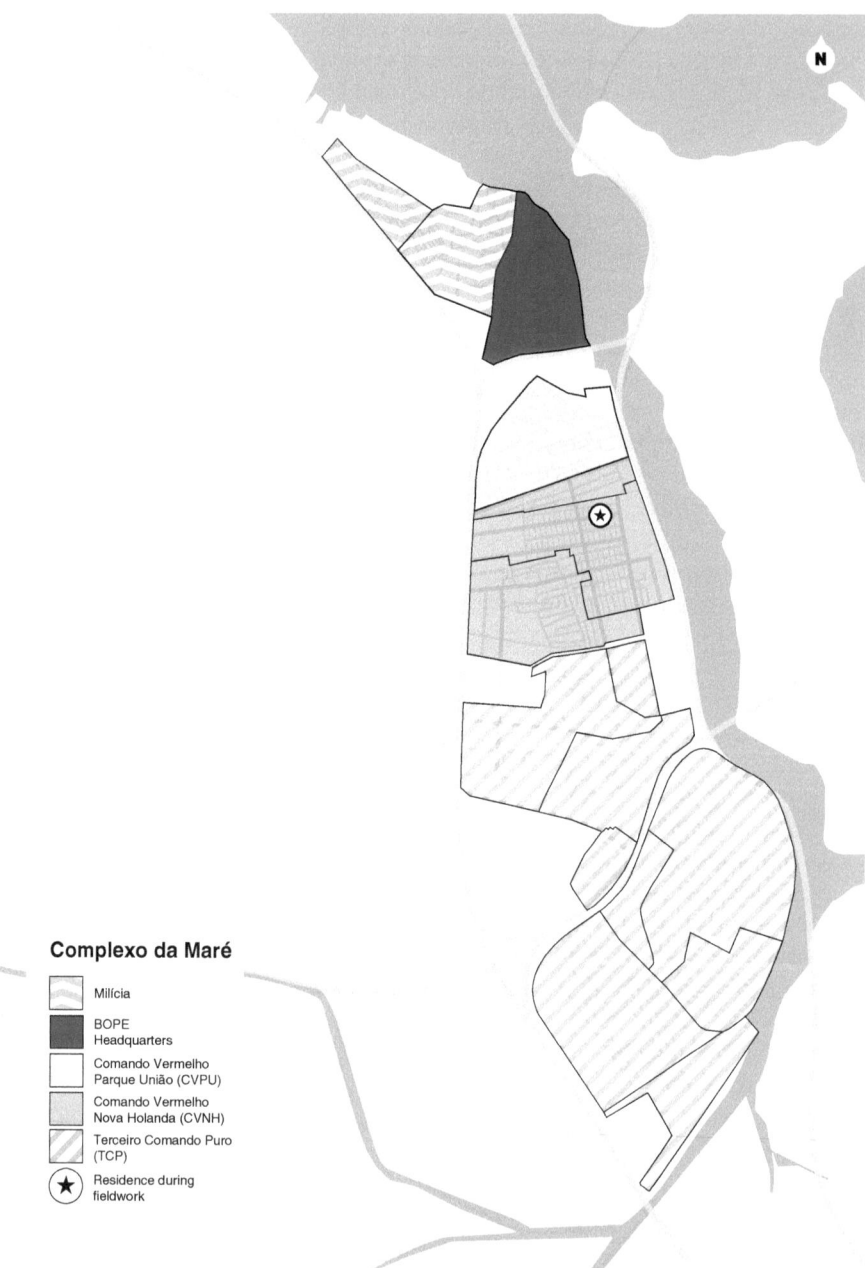

FIGURE 1.1 Map of gang territories in Complexo da Maré during fieldwork
Visualization by Bruna Montuori.

restaurants, exclusively used informal and public forms of transportation, and attended numerous music performances, sporting events, and other local cultural events. I became intimately familiar with each of Maré's fifteen neighborhoods by walking or biking through the labyrinth of streets and alleyways. Prior to military occupation, I attended dozens of gang-organized *bailes funk* (funk parties), birthday parties, and holiday celebrations while subjecting myself to gang rules. During military occupation, I attended numerous public meetings and events organized by the military and was able to observe their daily operations. Such an immersive and participatory methodology allowed me to document how each of Maré's gangs governed these communities as well as how their behavior changed over time.

Given Maré's size (roughly 1.25 square miles) and population (approximately 140,000 residents), a comprehensive accounting of criminalized governance through participant observation alone was not possible. Therefore, I also collected several other forms of data. I conducted 206 semi-structured interviews, 73 of which were with current and former gang members, 73 with community leaders, 48 with a cross-section of residents, and 12 more with scholars, researchers, and public security officials.[23] I identified most of these research subjects through a "snowball sampling" of the various social networks in which I became embedded. Interviews were conducted on the street, in public plazas, in my apartment, in my interlocutors' homes or businesses, or at local NGOs, lasting anywhere from thirty minutes to more than three hours. I did not record the interviews due to security concerns but instead took copious notes, which I immediately translated and typed up after the interviews.[24] All names are pseudonyms and I have avoided using any specific information which could be used to identify these individuals. Beyond these semi-structured interviews, I also engaged in hundreds of less formal conversations and thousands of daily encounters and interactions across all three gang territories that I wrote up in more than 400 pages of field notes. Finally, I supplement these personal observations and interviews with hundreds of newspaper articles, government reports, and archival documents, as well as micro-level data concerning gang and police behavior from *Disque-Denúncia* (Denunciation Hotline, hereon DD).[25]

Case Selection

Following two preliminary research trips in 2010 and 2011, I moved to Rio in October 2012 and quickly began searching for suitable field research sites. This sprawling city of six million has roughly 1,100 favelas

---

[23] See Table A1 for a complete list of interviews.
[24] All direct quotations included in this book were transcribed from these notes.
[25] All primary documents are cited by source and date in the footnotes with full citations in the appendix.

FIGURE 1.2 Map of fieldwork in Rio de Janeiro's favelas and housing projects
Visualization by Bruna Montuori. Basemap tiles by Esri, HERE, Garmin, FAO,
NOAA, USGS, © OpenStreetMap contributors, and the GIS User Community. Favela
and Conjunto Habitacional data provided by the Instituto Pereira Passos.

(see Figure 1.2), which vary in size from several hundred residents to more
than 70,000 (Instituto Pereira Passos 2018). Nearly all favelas have been dominated by drug-trafficking gangs or police-connected *milícias* (militias) that run
protection rackets for the past three decades. Every favela-based gang is at least
nominally connected to one of three factions located within the city's prisons:
CV, TCP, and *Amigos dos Amigos* (Friends of Friends, hereon ADA).[26] While
all the city's gangs can be considered part of these prison-based factions, they
are better understood as horizontal networks of alliance rather than singular,
hierarchical organizations (Dowdney 2003, 31). Importantly for this book,
governance practices are entirely dictated by the gang's *Dono* (leader) and its
membership on the streets of the favela, not the faction in prison.

I spent the first nine months of fieldwork taking every opportunity to visit
favelas throughout the city. In total, I visited nearly 60 separate communities
(See Figure 1.2), where I learned about the local geography, history, security
dynamics, and gang practices while also exploring the possibility of conducting

[26] For a description of the origins and connections between the factions and the gangs, see
Chapter 4.

longer-term research. During this initial phase, I also interviewed twenty rehabilitated gang and milícia leaders from favelas across the city. I connected with these former members through *AfroReggae*, an influential NGO that had developed an impressive program to assist individuals in leaving these organizations. These interviews were invaluable in helping me understand the complex histories and structures of the gangs, the breadth of their governance activities, and their evolution over time.

Through these initial visits and interviews, my understanding of Rio's gangs increased incredibly but remained superficial. Up to this point, my research had revealed the breadth and scope of criminalized governance, but even when I got access to these communities and their members, I found many of the answers to my questions were *"pra Inglês ver"* (literally, "for the English to see"), as many favela residents put it.[27] That is, they had answers to questions from outsiders that did not correspond to their lived experience because it was too difficult to explain the reality, that's what they thought I wanted to hear, or they were perhaps afraid of the legal or moral connotations of revealing the truth (Wood 2009). Alternatively, offering such canned responses could have been a way for some of my interlocutors to deny access to certain parts of their life or perhaps a subtle way of refusing to be studied or analyzed at all (Simpson 2007). Whatever the reason, I wanted a more intimate understanding that was not possible from interviews alone or from spending the occasional afternoon in favelas.[28] If I was going to understand the causes and consequences of criminalized governance, I needed to place myself inside these communities.

Over the course of the initial period of field research, one case – or set of cases, rather – began to stand out as an ideal location in which to conduct long-term fieldwork. Complexo da Maré (highlighted in Figure 1.2) is located in the Zona Norte (Northern Zone) of the city along the banks of Guanabara Bay. There are three reasons why I chose Maré as my primary field site. First, Maré is the only group of favelas in the city in which multiple OCGs control territory: two gangs connected to CV, another to TCP, as well as a police-connected milícia (see Figure 1.1). Their proximity offered a unique opportunity to compare across these organizations. In addition, the nature of competition between these groups and their shifting territorial control within Maré allowed me to focus on how gangs won and lost territory and the consequences of territorial expansion and contraction on their governance activities. Finally, because of its location at the intersection of three of the city's major traffic arteries – Avenida Brasil, Linha Vermelha, and Linha Amarela – and

---

[27] According to Lessing, this phrase "dates back to England's imposition of anti-slavery laws on the Portuguese Empire in the early nineteenth Century" (2017, xv).

[28] Hanson and Richards (2019) argue that this desire for intimacy is one of three "fixations" of gold-standard ethnographic research (danger and solitude being the other two), which can have disastrous and dangerous consequences especially for women ethnographers.

its proximity to the international airport, Maré has also been the focus of considerable public security attention over the years. In fact, Maré has the only Military Police Battalion (the 22nd) located inside its borders and the headquarters of the *Batalhão de Operações Policiais Especiais* (Special Police Operations Battalion) or BOPE was moved to the outskirts of Maré in 2011 (see Figure 1.1).[29] Together, these characteristics made Maré an ideal context in which to study criminalized governance.

I first visited Maré on a preliminary research trip in 2011 and began making regular trips soon after beginning fieldwork in 2012. For my first several visits, I met NGO workers along Avenida Brasil – the city's busiest highway that runs the length of Maré – and they brought me into the community, passing by gang *olheiros* (lookouts) that monitor all the entrances to these neighborhoods. Over time, gang members became used to my presence and, eventually, I was able to come and go without a chaperone. Then, in June 2013, one of my local contacts informed me of a studio apartment available for rent in Nova Holanda. The rooftop apartment was near a couple of local NGOs and a safe distance from the border separating Maré's rival gangs, where most inter-gang violence occurred (see Figure 1.1). Later that month, I moved to Maré and would permanently reside there until November 2014.

When I selected Maré as my field site, I did not know that the military would eventually occupy the area. On March 21st, 2014, just two months before the start of the World Cup, in a meeting with then-President Dilma Rousseff, the governor of Rio de Janeiro, Sergio Cabral, formally requested the assistance of Federal troops to occupy Maré. Three weeks later, and roughly nine months after I moved to Maré, the Brazilian military invaded all fifteen of Maré's neighborhoods and would stay there for the duration of my fieldwork.[30] Thus, the research design for this book evolved organically and, in this way, reflects how events occurring on the ground can provide opportunities for inquiry and investigation, one of the distinct advantages of long-term ethnographic field-work (Gade 2020).

Ethics and Safety

At this point, it is important to recognize that built into my desire for greater understanding and access was the considerable power and privilege that I had as a white cisgender male researcher from a prestigious university in the Global North. After all, going to the field much less spending three years there is an enormous privilege, one that the vast majority of researchers do not have (Fujii 2016, 1149). Moreover, the type of access I enjoyed in many favela communities was predicated on the existing inequalities between myself and my

[29] Military Police are responsible for ostensive policing duties while the Civil Police are tasked with investigatory duties. Both operate under the authority of each of Brazil's 27 state governors.
[30] See Chapter 8 for an analysis of this period.

interlocutors because access and its refusal are very much "a privilege of the powerful" (Krystalli 2021, 137). Especially for communities that have been, from their origins, heavily surveilled by the state and thoroughly under the microscope of social science, such inquiry can simultaneously be a form of invasion (Tuck and Yang 2014). Therefore, ethnographers and researchers of marginalized spaces must recognize the inherently extractive nature of such research and should tread with caution, sensitivity, and respect when entering these communities to study or document life there. As Lee Ann Fujii reminds us, "…to enter another's world as a researcher is a privilege not a right" (2012, 722). In the rest of this section, I first address some of the ethical and security considerations of my fieldwork before analyzing how my positionality shaped and informs the data to which I gained access.[31]

Conducting research on gangs in favelas requires significant consideration of local security dynamics, possible risks for would-be research participants, as well as issues surrounding confidentiality and anonymity.[32] In Rio's favelas, gangs have implemented their own set of rules which govern daily life: no speaking to the police, no theft in the community, no fighting between residents, and no sexual or domestic abuse, among others. Submitting myself to gang rules was an important part of the ethnographic experience but learning which behaviors were circumscribed or which topics of conversation were acceptable was a slow process. Gang rules are not written down and local customs often go unspoken. In this regard, I relied on the help of several NGO workers and residents that had grown up in Maré and who were intimately familiar with these local dynamics and whose patience and guidance were instrumental in my learning process. Several of these collaborators had worked with other researchers in the past, helping them identify suitable interview participants. Two of these collaborators would eventually complete Institutional Review Board training and become formal and paid members of my research team.[33] With one of these

---

[31] I have included these methodological considerations in the main text of the book instead of an appendix because how I collected the data is, ultimately, inseparable from and co-constitutive of "the findings" of this project (Krystalli 2021; Pachirat 2017; Wedeen 2010). Such transparency regarding the procedures and processes regarding data collection and analysis also follows recent Qualitative Transparency Deliberations (Bleich and Pekkanen 2015; Jacobs et al. 2021), in particular, Working Group IV.2 on Research in Violent or Post-Conflict Political Settings (Arjona, Mampilly, and Pearlman 2019).

[32] The Institutional Review Board at the University of Wisconsin–Madison was instrumental in developing interview protocols and a set of guidelines for minimizing many of the risks related to my project. However, as any ethnographic researcher knows, the reality of the spaces in which we conduct research often requires numerous additional considerations. In this regard, the SSRC's Drugs, Security, and Democracy Working Paper Series on Research Security (www.ssrc.org/programs/drugs-security-and-democracy-program/dsd-working-papers-on-research-security/) and the advice of numerous colleagues helped me think through many of these challenges.

[33] Their compensation was equal to what a research assistant at the University of Wisconsin–Madison received at that time. These amounts were negotiated before they began working with

research assistants, whom I refer to as Carlos (a pseudonym), we developed a set of guidelines for research activities, where and when we could engage in them, and the locations that were safe for us and the research participants.

With the support of Carlos, other research collaborators, my expanding social networks, and by merely spending a lot of time observing and listening, I learned how to stay safe. The social networks in which I became embedded not only provided me greater information and access to interlocutors but also offered increased security. Malejacq and Mukhopadhyay (2016) refer to this as building one's own "tribe" or "forming and joining different social micro-systems to collect data and, in some cases, survive" (2016, 1014). I also developed what Baird (2018, 346–47), following Bordieu (1992), refers to as "a feel for the rules of the game" and "practical sense" that helped me evade danger. I began to identify the signs of an approaching police operation or rival gang invasion by watching the traffic patterns, the movement of pedestrians, and the sights and sounds of the favela. I came to quickly recognize the far-off sounds of a police helicopter and eventually was able to differentiate between firecrackers and gunshots. Innate to most favela residents, these were indispensable skills for staying safe.

During my first several months living in Maré, I mostly refrained from conducting interviews. I first wanted to gain a better understanding of local dynamics and allow residents and gang members to become comfortable with my presence before jumping into formal interviews. I sought to take things as slowly as possible at each stage of the research process because of the inherently fraught nature of conducting research within these marginalized communities and because I had never heard of another long-term ethnographic project that focused explicitly on gangs *and* involved them as research participants. I decided to err on the side of caution. To my surprise, however, there seemed to be little suspicion and reticence about me and my project. My connections to respected NGOs and the fact that several interlocutors and collaborators vouched for me was essential. Moreover, because I was living in Maré, residents and gang members alike were assured that I was interested in more than just a superficial understanding of their lives and was not there to extract information before quickly leaving.

I found many residents were open to the possibility of being interviewed. While residents seldom speak directly about gangs in public, conversations about violence and crime are frequent. Most often, they take the form of passing comments about shootouts or police operations. In more private settings, residents are quick to share their experiences, interactions, and opinions about gangs. Such conversations are one way that residents keep informed about

the project. Research assistants documented all time and effort spent on the project, including preparation, reading, and travel. Meals were also provided when they coincided with project work. Their participation was fully voluntary and flexible, usually amounting to several hours of work per week but varied depending on availability.

local security dynamics and to deal with the stress of these environments. I had to be careful, however, not to take any stories or conversations at face value. News travels quickly through favela communities and *fofoca* (gossip) and rumors about such topics are rampant (Grillo 2013, 17–18; Menezes 2014). Therefore, I attempted to triangulate and verify accounts across several participants and with other forms of data, including newspaper articles, archival documents, and public security reports. That said, I was not only interested in ascertaining the veracity of these accounts. Gossip and the ways in which residents and gang members exaggerate, lie, prevaricate, and opine about gangs offered me important insights into what Fujii (2009) has called the "logics" or patterns of meanings, which residents and gang members use to understand violence and crime as well as daily life in Maré. Interpreting these logics was crucial if I was to understand criminalized governance.

Positionality

Despite living in Maré and eventually becoming a more integrated member of these communities is not to say that residents and gang members did not recognize my foreignness or that they were not surprised by my presence.[34] Although it was not unheard of for a gringo from the Global North to visit Maré or conduct a short-term research project there, most residents had never met one who lived there.[35] Some residents, even ones I came to know quite well, merely referred to me as "gringo." I was an oddity, to be sure. My gringo-ness, however, was a distinct advantage. First, part of the reason my research did not arouse more suspicion was because no one thought I was working for the police, a common fear for gangs and residents alike. A native Brazilian conducting research on the same subject would have faced far more suspicion in this regard.

In addition to being a gringo, my identity as a white cisgender male, a tall and bearded one at that, from a university in the Global North shaped the data I collected in ways large and small. How my race, specifically, influenced my research in Maré is difficult to pin down. First, it is important to note that racial identities and experiences of favela residents are significantly more diverse and heterogenous than is commonly thought. According to a recent census, roughly 37% of Maré's residents identify as white (*branco*), 53% as brown (*pardo*), and 9% as black (*preto*), with less than 1% as either indigenous or Asian (*amarelo*) (Redes da Maré 2019a).[36] That said, my whiteness

---

[34] For a discussion of insider/outsider status and its implications for ethics, see Holmes (2021).

[35] Although the category of gringo technically includes all foreigners irrespective of race or ethnicity, in practice, it is more commonly used to refer to white foreigners.

[36] I also found that racial identification often varies within families, a significant departure from the US, largely owing to Brazil's very different experience of colonization, slavery, and state making (Loveman 2014; Marx 1996; Nobles 2000). This is not to suggest that racism is less

surely shaped the nature of each and every interaction. Along with my gender and connection to a prestigious university in the US, it meant that I was offered immediate respect and deference in many situations and especially during interviews. I quickly gained access to people and places, not just in Maré, but in government offices, think tanks, and universities throughout the city.

My class is an equally important aspect of my identity to consider. Although Maré can be generally characterized as impoverished, it is not uniformly so. The socio-economic disparity within Maré stretches from individuals and families living in destitute poverty, without access to secure housing, water, or food, to lower middle-class families that own homes and businesses furnished with all the modern appliances and technologies. I conducted interviews across this entire spectrum. While it is impossible to change certain aspects of one's class, I sought to diminish the socio-economic difference between myself and the community in which I was living. I tried to live a lifestyle like most other favela residents. I did not eat out frequently or extravagantly spend money at local shops or bars. I did not wear expensive shoes or clothes. I traveled exclusively by walking, biking, or by taking buses or vans (informal public transportation). I attended free and inexpensive forms of entertainment along with other residents. None of my participants (or anyone else in Maré for that matter) ever asked me for money nor seemed to expect payment of any kind though I would often pay for a meal, snacks, or beverages before or after interviews if the timing and occasion called for it.[37] As far as I could tell, I was not known as someone "with money" or someone whom residents or interlocutors could garner favors and resources though it is difficult to ascertain exactly how I was spoken of and understood among residents.

My gender also had considerable and perhaps more easily identifiable consequences for my research. First, the vast majority of gang members are men, and our common gender shaped our interactions, especially how they expressed their thoughts and feelings about violence and crime as well as their familial and romantic relationships. My gender allowed me to develop a rapport with these men in public, when they hung out in groups and engaged in conversations and exchanges on the street, in a way that a woman or non-binary researcher may have not been able to. That said, I avoided performing male bravado as a means of ingratiating myself with gang members or in an effort to become "one of the guys" (Baird 2018; Theidon 2014).[38] Instead, I tried to

pervasive or insidious in Brazil. Rather, like the US, race and class overlap thoroughly and the most marginalized and impoverished populations in Brazilian society are those that identify as black and indigenous (Telles 2004).

[37] I am of two minds on compensating research participants for interviews. On one hand, paying impoverished interlocutors for a lengthy interview seems perfectly reasonable and ethically justifiable. On the other, I did not want to create perverse incentives for people to agree to interviews or unduly influence how they might answer my questions.

[38] See Grillo (2013, 17–43) for an extended discussion of these gender dynamics in relation to studying gangs in Rio and Gade (2020) in other research on violence. In another vein, Contreras

maintain a professional yet relaxed attitude when interacting with them and in interviews. I did not become close friends with gang members and decided early on not to try to interview or "hang out" with gang members while they were on duty – shifts normally run for 12 hours, beginning at 6am or 6pm – because I wanted to be respectful of their responsibilities and the nature of their jobs often meant increased security risks.[39] I also avoided prolonged interaction with gang members at parties or bars at night, where alcohol consumption and drug use were common, due to the complicated ethics of these situations. Nearly all my interviews with gang members were when they were off duty and not obviously under the influence.

As a single man, I also had significant independence and autonomy within Maré that would likely not have been afforded to a woman. Maré, like most favelas in Rio, is comprised of surprisingly tight knit communities, which can sometimes have conservative ideas concerning family structure, gender roles, and sexuality. If I was not aware of it beforehand, this disparity was driven home during meetings of an informal research group of Brazilian and US ethnographers comprised almost entirely of women researchers.[40] We met once a month for the better part of a year to discuss our fieldwork experiences. Through these meetings, conversations, and visits to the favela communities in which these women were conducting their own ethnographic research, the numerous advantages I had as a product of my positionality became abundantly clear.

For one, our security fears differed enormously. I was most afraid of gang members not recognizing me or perhaps believing I was police and threatening or using violence against me as a result. I was particularly careful around gang borders because I did not want to be mistaken for a rival gang member or off-duty police. Gang members more frequently stop and question men and mistake them for security threats than women. On the other hand, like nearly everywhere else in the world, I was little concerned with just walking down the street of a favela or in the rest of the city even at night. Many of my female colleagues were extremely worried about being sexually assaulted or robbed and,

(2013) has criticized the "cowboy ethnographer" ethos that permeates many studies of crime and violence in which a male ethnographer highlights the danger of the fieldwork and glorifies the violence he witnessed, seeking ultimately to profit from these depictions. In this regard, I have made every effort neither to glorify nor sanitize the violence and criminal behaviors I witnessed and documented. I have also chosen not to write this book in such a way that makes the book more about me, the ethnographer, than my interlocutors.

[39] The demands of being in the gang are multiple – long, tedious hours monitoring borders for police or rivals, exchanging money for drugs at open-air sales points, employing violence, or engaging in many of the other governance activities I describe in this book. For these reasons, they should most certainly be considered "workers" (Méndez 2018).

[40] During the time I lived in Rio, I found that most long-term ethnographic research in favelas was being done by women. See de Souza (2019), Denyer Willis (2018, 2023), Fahlberg (2018), Gilsing (2020), Gomes (2020), Grillo (2013), Koenders (2020), Menezes (2014), Robb Larkins (2015), Rosner (2018), Savell (2016), Souza (2020), and Suska (2015), among others.

over the course of my time living in Rio, several female friends and colleagues were victimized in these ways.[41]

Beyond security concerns, no one ever gave me a hard time or judged me for living alone, staying on the streets late, or coming and going when I pleased. Some female colleagues found that community members monitored their behavior more closely and encouraged them to have a male companion or to attend church. They were also expected to assist in childcare or help neighbors while I was never asked to do so. Some of my colleagues even became pregnant and had children over the course of fieldwork. Aside from the incredible physical and emotional energy and effort required to raise a child while conducting fieldwork, this also dramatically changed their relationship to the local community. Some reported that they were even more closely monitored but that they were also often invited to parties and people's houses, becoming even more integrated into the community. In this way, there were also research opportunities and conversations that, as a single man, I was not privy to.

Finally, the information and opinions that research participants offered me were also shaped by my gender. This was made especially clear when a female colleague and I conducted a couple of interviews jointly. These interviews offered a fascinating lens into the different behaviors and responses that research participants had to our presence. One older community leader, a man I had already interviewed individually and known to be very stoic and authoritative, became visibly emotional and openly wept when he told us about his mother. Following the interview, I marveled at his willingness to be vulnerable. My colleague told me that this did not surprise her at all as that interlocutor had cried in all her previous interviews with him as well. This example demonstrates how my gender and other intersecting identities influenced not only who I gained access to and the social networks in which I became embedded but also shaped the exchanges, assumptions, and responses during interviews. I note these dynamics here not to discount any of the information that I or other researchers gather through such methods but rather to emphasize how I tried to remain reflexive about the types of information and data to which I was given access.

ORGANIZATION OF THE BOOK

The rest of this book is organized as follows. Chapter 2 develops the concept of criminalized governance by first placing Rio de Janeiro's gangs alongside other criminalized groups and outlining the concept's scope conditions. I then differentiate between its two primary dimensions – coercion and the provision of benefits – and describe the various activities and behaviors contained

---

[41] See Hanson and Richards (2019) for a description of how these gendered and sexualized experiences of harassment during fieldwork have been systematically silenced in research findings and remain unaddressed in graduate training.

within each. I conclude the chapter by constructing a typology of criminalized governance regimes.

In Chapter 3, I use ethnographic insights to develop a generalizable theory that accounts for when and why these various criminalized governance regimes emerge. Overall, I argue it is the nature of the threats to gang organizations and their members that leads them to engage in these two dimensions of governance. I also address how resident behaviors shape the nature of these threats and, thereby, governance outcomes. I conclude the chapter by describing the dynamics that should be observed within each of the criminalized governance regimes and by addressing several additional factors left out of the theory.

Chapter 4 describes the origins of the three gangs that dominated Complexo da Maré during my fieldwork. I use dozens of oral histories and hundreds of archival documents to show how gangs emerged at very different times across Maré's neighborhoods depending on local circumstances and only after other forms of governance began to break down. I trace the evolution of three fledgling gangs as they began to compete over increasingly valuable drug selling turf and, eventually, beat out local rivals and consolidated control over distinct parts of Maré. The chapter concludes by providing a brief history of Rio's factions into which these three independent gangs integrated at the beginning of the 1990s.

Chapters 5–7 trace the evolution of these three gangs since their integration into the prison-based factions in the early 1990s until the military occupation of Maré in 2014. I show how shifting security environments – the result of competition and alliance formation between these gangs, oscillating police enforcement policies, and residents' responses to the gangs – have shaped the governance regimes of these gangs. In each chapter, I employ and triangulate data from 206 in-depth interviews, more than 400 newspaper and community-based archival documents, and hundreds of geo-located anonymous denunciations.

Chapter 8 begins by tracing the confluence of factors which led to the military intervention in Maré. I describe how the military occupied these neighborhoods and imposed a new form of order, documenting the various operations and activities the military employed to combat gangs and gain the support of Maré's residents. I analyze how and why each of the three gangs responded differently to the challenges of occupation, which offers further empirical evidence to support the theory.

Finally, in Chapter 9, I bring the reader up to date, documenting the changes and continuities in Complexo da Maré and Rio de Janeiro since end of the original fieldwork period in 2015. I then describe some of the possibilities for the future of policing and criminalized governance in Rio de Janeiro. I also address the generalizability and implications of the argument, first for other drug-trafficking gangs and milícias throughout the city, before moving onto other Brazilian cities and beyond. The epilogue concludes the book by describing a final interview I conducted with Severino, with whom I began this book.

2

Criminalized Governance: A Conceptual Framework

> ...the gang is a protean manifestation: no two gangs are just alike; some are good;
> some are bad; and each has to be considered on its own merits.
> —Frederic Thrasher, *The Gang: A Study of 1,313*
> *Gangs in Chicago* (1927, 5)

INTRODUCTION

On September 27th, 1993, a gang threw a massive street party in Nova Holanda to commemorate the public holiday for the city's two patron saints, Cosmas and Damian. The gang hired a live band, organized a fireworks show, paid for a professional clown named *Pirulito* (Lollipop) to entertain the children, and had a local bakery supply a twenty-foot cake. Residents of all ages packed the streets, drinking, eating, and dancing as they enjoyed the festivities. In the late afternoon, the gang drove a flatbed truck into the middle of the crowd as gang members tossed bags of toys, candy, and carbonated beverages into the crowd. Hundreds of partygoers swarmed the truck, shouting to the gang members, reaching out, hoping to catch some of the party favors before they ran out.

Just two days before this festive scene, the same gang engaged in a very different kind of public spectacle: the brutal and public execution of the president of the local Samba school and three of his associates. According to the gang's leader, a man nicknamed Gigante (Giant), the president was providing information to the police to try to take over drug trafficking in the area. The fact that the president was married to Gigante's sister did not save his life because, according to the gang leader, "There is no forgiveness for a snitch."[1]

---

[1] *O Globo* 9/28/1993.

These starkly contrasting events present a puzzling and frightening juxtaposition. On the one hand, Rio's gangs have sought to gain the support and consent of favela residents by providing benefits to these communities. Holiday parties such as those just described are only the most visible way that they have done so. Many gangs are known to provide a highly effective form of order within the neighborhoods where they operate by protecting private property and ensuring the personal safety of residents. They serve as an essential resource for resolving conflicts and mediating any interpersonal disputes between residents. Gangs are also known to stimulate the local economy by spending money at local businesses, facilitating transactions, and offering opportunities for residents to make ends meet through illicit and informal economies. They even provide some forms of welfare by paying for food, medicine, transportation, and even offering housing to residents in need.

On the other hand, gangs have resorted to violence and threats to maintain control of their territory and ensure resident compliance. Rio's gangs monitor the boundaries of their turf and have been known to question, threaten, and refuse entry to anyone who does not belong or those they suspect of collaborating with their rivals or the police. Within their territories, gangs can maintain a significant physical presence on the streets by ostentatiously displaying their high-powered firearms as a constant reminder to residents that they are the dominant authority in the area. Finally, gangs have been known to torture, execute, or expel anyone that has broken their rules, the most important of which is the *lei de silêncio* (law of silence), which prohibits residents from speaking with the police or rival gangs. Such acts of violence are not only intended to remove these threats but also serve as powerful reminders of what happens when gang rules are disobeyed.

I argue that these two sets of behaviors – the use of coercion and the provision of benefits – comprise the primary dimensions of *criminalized governance*, which I define as the structures and practices through which OCGs attempt to control territory and manage relations with local populations. Building on more than eighteen months of ethnography in Complexo da Maré and three years of overall fieldwork in dozens of gang-controlled neighborhoods in Rio de Janeiro, I develop this concept from the ground up. This will require significant description because "it is hard to develop [causal] explanations before we know something about the world and what needs to be explained on the basis of what characteristics" (King, Keohane, and Verba 1994, 34). Especially for a topic as clandestine as criminalized governance, perhaps the most important step in developing causal claims is "mere description" (Gerring 2012). In the rest of this chapter, I first define and then discuss the scope conditions of the concept before outlining the two dimensions of criminalized governance in turn. Using personal observations, interviews, and the extant ethnographic literature from Rio's favelas, I describe the various activities involved in each. Finally, I construct a typology of criminalized governance regimes that captures the existing variation in these practices.

GANGS AND OTHER ORGANIZED AND CRIMINALIZED GROUPS

Originally meaning "to go," "path," or "journey," the word "gang" in English has been around since the late middle ages (Merriam-Webster 2023). In the nineteenth century, the term came to refer to a diverse set of groups engaged in illegal and violent activities, from outlaws in the American West (e.g., the Wild Bunch and the James Gang), to collectives and familial networks in urban Birmingham (e.g., the Peaky Blinders), to violent ethnic-based groups in the Five Points neighborhood of New York City (e.g., the Dead Rabbits, the Plug Uglies, and the Bowery Boys).[2] Building on this popular usage, the social science concept of the gang was born in the early twentieth century when Frederic Thrasher (1927) and a team of researchers systematically documented more than a thousand delinquent youth groups that had emerged in minority neighborhoods all around Chicago.[3] Since then, an endless line of monographs, articles, and books from across the social sciences have dealt with nearly every facet of the urban gang. Once considered primarily an American phenomenon (Klein 1995), gangs are perhaps one of the most common forms of social organization in the world. They have been extensively documented throughout the Americas, Europe, Africa, and Asia.[4] And yet, despite their ubiquity and the profusion of scholarship on them, there remains considerable disagreement about what exactly constitutes a gang.

Some gangs are just a handful of adolescents engaged in antisocial and illegal behavior and could perhaps be better understood as "troublesome youth groups" (Hagedorn 2008, xxvi). Some of these groups go on to form more cohesive and durable organizations, managing to establish themselves as a relatively stable presence within a given territory and developing age cohorts as a way to reproduce themselves (Hagedorn 1988; Klein and Maxson 1996; Moore 1978; Vigil 1988). Some gangs even become "institutionalized" by consolidating their presence so thoroughly within a territory that they become the dominant political and social institution and, in doing so, may resemble a variety of other non-state armed groups (Hagedorn 2008). A few gangs go on to become "super-gangs" as they expand their organizations through prison systems, violent conquest, and strategic alliances to integrate numerous other

---

[2] For detailed histories of these nineteenth-century "gangs," see Asbury (2008), Gooderson (2010), and Horan (1997).

[3] Thrasher defined a gang as "an interstitial group, originally formed spontaneously, and then integrated through conflict. It is characterized by the following types of behavior: meeting face to face, milling, movement through space as a unit, conflict, and planning. The result of this collective behavior is the development of tradition, unreflective internal structure, esprit de corps, solidarity, morale, group awareness, and attachment to a local territory" (1927, 6).

[4] For a sample of the cross-national work on gangs, see Barnes (2022a), Decker and Pyrooz (2015b), Hagedorn (2008), Hazen and Rodgers (2014), Hazlehurst and Hazlehurst (1998), and Rodgers (1999).

gangs (Klein and Maxson 1996). There is an ocean of difference between some of these examples, yet they can all be considered gangs.[5]

Due to this incredible diversity and because gangs are in a constant state of evolution – what Thrasher (1927, 5) called "a protean manifestation" (see earlier quote) – any concept must be flexible enough to capture all of these forms. Therefore, I employ a minimal definition: Gangs are autonomous organizations that "(1) display a measure of institutional continuity independent of its membership; (2) routinely engage in violent behavior patterns that are considered illegal by the dominant authorities and mainstream society; and (3) consist of members who are principally, though not necessarily only, under the age of 25" (Hazen and Rodgers 2014, 8).

While allowing for considerable flexibility, this concept does make some necessary distinctions. First, it distinguishes gangs from more transient groups, such as hooligans and troublesome youth groups, that may engage in crime and violence, but which only exist for short periods of time. Second, it also restricts the scope to groups that engage in violence *and* are criminalized by the state and mainstream society – what Hagedorn (2008) refers to as their "resistance identities." This excludes groups that may look and act like gangs but which are not criminalized by the state (e.g., militias and vigilantes).[6] Groups that seek exclusive sovereignty over a given territory and population (e.g., rebel groups and insurgents) are also not included because they have aspirations of formal political power,[7] which gangs, except in the

---

[5] Seldom is the term "gang" or its direct translation used in many parts of the globe. In Latin America, gangs or gang-like groups have been variously referred to as *bandas, barras, chapulines, chichipatos, chimbas, clikas, combos, galeras, gallados, maltas, manchas, maras, naciones, pandillas, parches,* and *quadrilhas,* just to name a few (Imbusch, Misse, and Carrión 2011; Rodgers 1999; Rodgers and Baird 2015). The gang term is also a highly contested one. Many groups that are considered gangs refuse the label, instead referring to themselves as militias, civil defense forces, or just youth groups (Jensen 2008; LeBas 2013; Rasmussen 2014; Sen 2014).

[6] Militias and vigilante groups also emerge in urban areas and can be primarily comprised of local youth (Tapscott 2021b). The difference here lies less in their on-the-ground behavior – gangs can also fight crime and violence within areas where they operate, and vigilante groups can engage in equally illegal and violent activities – but their position vis-à-vis the state. Militias and vigilantes generally seek to bolster or strengthen the state's monopoly of violence and are better understood as "extralegal" entities rather than criminal or, more accurately, criminalized ones. According to Bateson, extralegal armed groups "go beyond the law, which implies an action that is moving in the same direction as the law, but exceeding its scope or severity" (2021, 927).

[7] While some rebel groups and insurgencies have been called "criminal gangs" by state officials in an effort to delegitimize them, these declarations are self-serving and fail to understand the origins, motivations, and behaviors of these movements (Kalyvas 2001). That said, it is often the case that gangs are incorporated into armed groups or state security services during conflict (see Arias 2017, 75–84; Daly 2016, 142–44; Doyle 2016; Hagedorn 2008, 34–35; Rodgers 2017, 649–50; Utas 2014, 179 for examples). While such transformations belie a neat distinction between gangs and more politically motivated armed groups, when absorbed into these organizations, the gang ceases to exist as an autonomous entity.

rarest of cases, lack.[8] Such restrictions are necessary because these differences fundamentally shape the objectives, organization, and governance practices of these groups.

Whether gangs are inherently "criminal" organizations is hotly debated within the criminology literature. Critical gang studies have increasingly challenged the dominant perspective of gangs as purely "predatory groups of violent criminals" (Ortiz 2023b, 6). They argue that existing positivist and pro-criminal justice gang definitions, developed by mostly middle-class and privileged scholars (Katz and Jackson-Jacobs 2004), tend to pathologize, dehistoricize, and decontextualize what they often refer to as street organizations, further encouraging the oppression and marginalization of impoverished and racialized youth (Brotherton 2015; Brotherton and Barrios 2004; Ortiz 2023a). These are valid and much-needed critiques but overlook the fact that criminalization by the state and the larger society is precisely the reason for the existence of gangs in the first place. If young men and women from impoverished and marginalized neighborhoods could rely on the state for protection, gangs would not exist at all. Thus, gangs are better understood not as inherently criminal groups but as criminalized ones. Definitional issues aside, this book shares much in common with critical gang studies, including its methodological orientation, its effort to demonstrate the highly arbitrary and biased nature of criminal justice systems and the rule of law, as well as the desire to offer a fuller accounting of gang life not reduced to merely their violent or criminal acts.

Finally, the age limit of twenty-five years restricts the gang concept from including more adult groups, which is essential if we are to avoid conceptual stretching (Collier and Mahon 1993; Sartori 1970, 1991).[9] The attribute of youth is perhaps *the* key characteristic that distinguishes gangs from other OCGs, such as cartels, mafias, syndicates, and smuggling networks, among others. While it is common for senior gang members to be older than twenty-five, they generally come of age in the gang, and most of the members continue to be youth. And yet, many gangs can still be considered OCGs so long as they attempt to "regulate and control the production and distribution of a given commodity or service unlawfully" (Varese 2010, 14).[10] Most small and newly

---

[8] Gangs seldom express overt political motivations pertaining to the state (Curry 2011; Hagedorn 2005, 321–23).

[9] The age cutoff is perhaps arbitrary because "youth" is a slippery and culturally specific term. That said, it is a reasonable estimation. The United Nations even defines "youth" as a person between the ages of 15–24 (United Nations 2023).

[10] The conventional understanding of organized crime, built from the example of the American and Sicilian mafia, understood these organizations as rigidly hierarchical, ruthlessly violent, and directed by a single person or a small group of leaders. However, as examples of organized crime have multiplied (or at least become better known and understood), the concept of organized crime has shifted to include a broader array of groups and organizational structures. See Varese (2010) for an excellent conceptual discussion of OCGs.

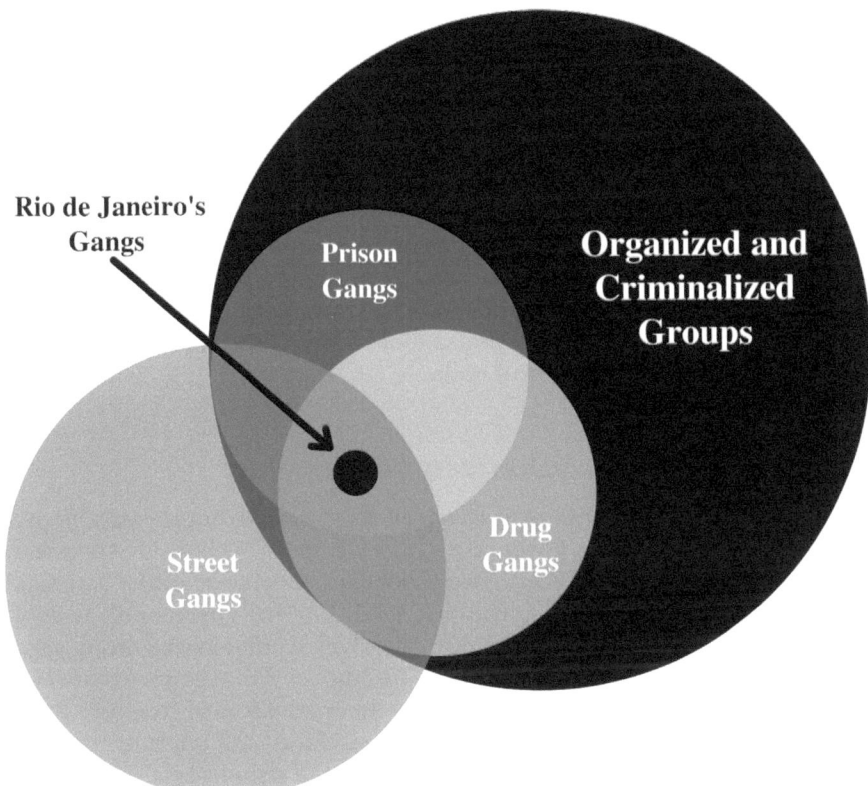

FIGURE 2.1   Gangs and other OCGs
Visualization by author.

formed gangs are incapable of such regulation but many others are able to do so.[11] In the end, the age restriction excludes other criminalized groups from being considered gangs but does not prevent gangs from being included within the larger umbrella category of OCG (see Figure 2.1).

   One final conceptual distinction concerning gangs is worth noting. Some scholars and policymakers have attempted to entirely separate the street gang phenomenon from drug and prison gangs (Decker and Pyrooz 2015a; Klein and Maxson 2006). Such efforts are misguided. First, neatly distinguishing street gangs from drug and prison gangs is proving increasingly difficult as most street gangs throughout the world maintain connections to prison gangs or are involved with the illicit drug trade, whether through production and distribution or merely retail sales. Thus, segregating prison gangs from street

---

[11] A gang can even be considered a mafia if it "produces, promotes, and sells" protection (Gambetta 1993, 1).

gangs from drug gangs is, if not empirically impossible, then highly problematic from a conceptual perspective considering how many of these organizations operate across these boundaries. Rio de Janeiro's gangs, for instance, are all involved in retail drug sales *and* are at least nominally connected to one of three prison-based factions: CV, TCP, and ADA.[12] Some scholars even argue that these overarching organizations, which they consider syndicates or cartels, should be the relevant level of analysis (Lessing 2017, 2). However, as mentioned in the introduction, Rio's factions are better understood as horizontal networks of neighborhood-level street gangs than vertically integrated and hierarchical groups (Dowdney 2003, 31).[13] Thus, Rio's gangs are the result of the intermingling of several organizational forms – street, prison, and drug gang – sharing different aspects of each.

CONCEPTUALIZING CRIMINALIZED GOVERNANCE

Criminalized governance can refer to one of three distinct but inseparable sets of activities: (1) how OCGs govern their own members; (2) how OCGs govern illicit markets; or (3) how OCGs govern populations outside of the "criminal underworld" (Lessing 2020).[14] The first level, internal governance, is comprised of the mechanisms and rules through which a criminalized group organizes itself and controls the behavior of its members.[15] From gangs to cartels to mafias, every OCG develops and maintains an organizational structure (from highly decentralized and flexible to rigidly hierarchical) and implements mechanisms for distributing resources, assigning roles and responsibilities, resolving disputes, punishing insubordination, and initiating new members.[16] Without effective internal governance, maintaining a cohesive organization is impossible and negates the possibility of an OCG extending its authority and control over illicit markets or communities.

---

[12] In common favela parlance, these organizational forms are also mixed as the gangs are variously referred to as *quadrilhas* or *gangues* (gangs), *a rapaziada* or *os meninos* (the boys), *o movimento* (the movement, referring to the retail drug trade), *o comando* (the command), *a facção* (the faction) or just *o tráfico* (the drug trade).

[13] This overarching structure is similar to other "super-gangs" such as the maras in Central America and the Bloods or Crips in the US context. Scholars continue to debate whether these groups should be considered gangs or organized crime (Albarracín and Barnes 2020; Cruz 2010; Wolf 2017).

[14] The three levels intersect in myriad ways. Elsewhere, I have argued that tension between these different levels of governance involves trade-offs (Barnes and Albarracín 2020).

[15] This form of governance is akin to corporate governance in the licit world (see Lessing 2020; Lessing and Denyer Willis 2019; Sánchez-Jankowski 1991; Skarbek 2012, 2014; Varese 2017).

[16] Some have suggested governance can exist without organizations in which case a set of diffuse norms or traditions are enforced by individuals through social sanctioning (e.g., "the convict code" and "the code of the street") (see Skarbek 2014, 18–42).

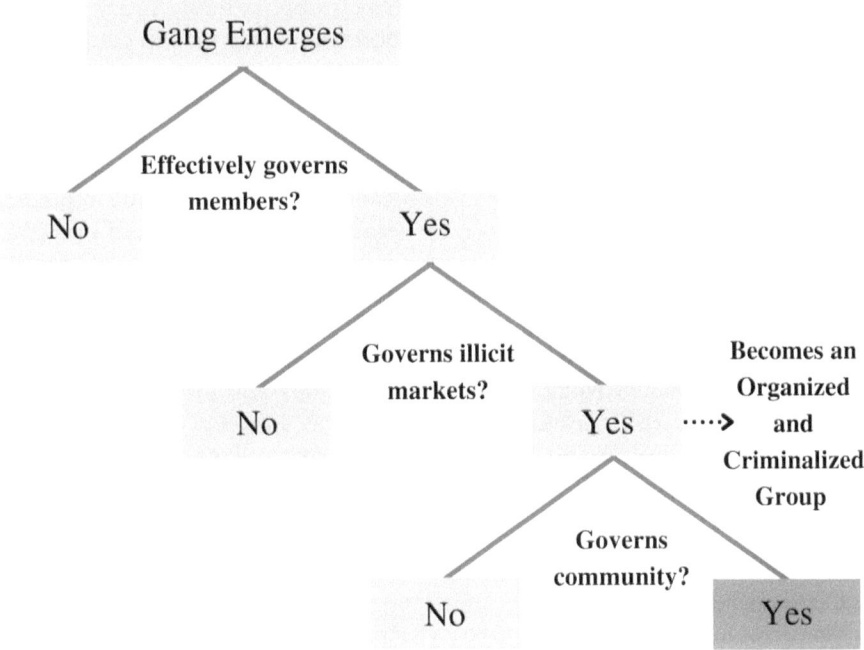

FIGURE 2.2 Levels of criminalized governance
Visualization by author.

This brings us to the second level of criminalized governance. The regulation of illicit or informal markets implies the creation of predictability (or order) in a market that is not regulated by the state.[17] Criminalized groups often seek to monopolize these markets within specific delimited areas by establishing and enforcing rules that determine who gets to produce and sell, where, at what price, as well as how disputes within the market are settled.[18] I consider the regulation or monopolization of these markets to be a precondition for OCGs to extend their governance to whole communities (see Figure 2.2). They must maintain exclusivity vis-à-vis all other OCGs because, without it, neither the gang members themselves nor residents can recognize who is the dominant authority within the area. Gangs that lack exclusivity cannot be said to constitute a governance *regime* even if they engage in some of the activities described

---

[17] A significant literature, based mostly in economics, has focused on this form of governance (see Gambetta 1993; Koivu 2016; Kostelnik and Skarbek 2013; Reuter 1983; Schelling 1971; Skaperdas 2001; Skarbek 2011, 2014). Not all illicit drug markets are governed by organizations, however. There are numerous cases where even highly lucrative and competitive drug markets are dominated by individuals or very small entrepreneurial groups (Bourgois 2002).
[18] As Thomas Schelling famously described organized crime, "In the overworld, its counterpart would not be just organized business, but monopoly" (1971, 182).

later.[19] The typology developed in this chapter applies most clearly to gangs and other criminalized groups that have successfully managed to complete the first two levels of governance.

This book is primarily concerned with the third level of criminalized governance, how and why gangs govern communities. Not every gang that has effectively managed to control the behavior of their members and regulate illicit markets can be said to govern. Some gangs may instead choose to predate on local communities, enforce no rules regarding the treatment of non-gang members, and behave with little predictability, what Arjona (2016, 26–28) refers to as *disorder*, the result of a lack of a social contract between civilians and armed groups. In Rio, Zaluar describes just such a scenario when a gang "makes an improper, preposterous, or uncontrolled use of their weapon. They humiliate, kill, and provoke residents for frivolous reasons or no reason at all, just to assert their power" (1985, 148). This situation differs markedly from even a very violent and intrusive gang, but that still maintains some rules and limitations regarding its behavior vis-à-vis residents. In Rio de Janeiro's gang-controlled favelas, this difference has been summarized in the following way:

If there are rules, even nonsensical or absurd ones, and even if it is extremely stressful to follow them, it is always possible to avoid retaliation and protect oneself by accommodating oneself to the will of the despot. It is enough to learn the tyrant's code and obey his rules. However, if there are no rules, all that remains is fear, pure fear, without end or limit: terror (Soares, Bill, and Athayde 2005, 263).

In the end, it is the predictability of gang behavior which determines whether order or disorder reigns. In other contexts, gangs may choose to intervene only minimally in community life. While it may seem that such gangs have chosen not to govern, the fact that they control their members sufficiently so that residents can make expectations about gang behavior represents a form of governance, limited though it may be. Gangs that put no limits on their behavior vis-à-vis residents – predating, threatening, abusing, and so forth – however, cannot be considered to govern even if they wield extreme power over the lives of residents. These contexts are better understood as disorder because, as Rosenau (1992, 8) argues, "without order, there can be no governance."

Before elaborating the typology of criminalized governance, two other concepts must be clarified. First, I use the term "community" to refer to *all* residents, businesses, and social and political institutions within a gang's territory or turf. The boundaries of a gang's territory can move considerably over time, shifting from one block to the next, expanding or shrinking from certain streets, corners, and alleyways but no two gangs can be said to

---

[19] In rural areas, where exclusivity is either not possible or perhaps even desirable, OCGs may share governance in a variety of ways (see Blume 2021; Blume, Sauls, and Knight 2022; Idler 2012).

govern the same territory at the same time. If more than one gang is present in an area, it is because they are incapable of establishing exclusive territorial control – and therefore are unable to regulate illicit markets (the second level of governance) – or are in the midst of a battle for outright territorial supremacy. Either way, these gangs do not maintain a governance *regime* even if they engage in some governance activities. Some gang turfs, however, can encompass large swaths of urban territory, include multiple different neighborhoods, or, in rare cases, noncontiguous areas. I refer to anyone living or working within one gang organization's territory, whether contiguous or not, as "the community."[20]

Second, I use the term "resident" to refer to any non-gang member living in a gang territory. In practice, it is often difficult to distinguish where exactly the gang ends and the community begins. Most gang members grow up in the neighborhood and are, technically speaking, residents too. I distinguish very neatly between residents and the gang here because, once a member, they must consider the gang's interests above their own, their families, and the community's or risk punishment, expulsion, or possibly even death. That said, most gangs also have what can be referred to as "hangers-on," usually male adolescents that interact frequently with gang members, do favors for them, and may eventually become part of the gang but are not yet members. A variety of other residents may also be involved in certain aspects of the retail drug trade or in various informal and illegal economies regulated by the gang while other residents are related to or intimate partners of gang members. Neither I nor the gang members I interviewed consider any of these individuals to be fully-fledged members.[21]

In other cities and countries, gangs have been known to have a membership-for-life policy but, at least in Rio, this is not the case. Many gang members have been known to end their involvement while continuing to live within the gang's territory.[22] These individuals no longer receive the benefits, nor are they subject to the responsibilities of gang membership even if they have numerous connections with the gang. They are not, strictly speaking, part of the gang. While it may be useful and necessary to blur the boundaries of the gang and the community, for the purposes of this book, I understand them to be distinct.[23] The preceding discussions constitute the primary conceptual considerations and scope conditions underlying the typology of criminalized governance presented later.

---

[20] I am mindful that all favela neighborhoods are not singular communities (Valladares 2008, 151–52) and that the various favelas and housing projects under one gang's control may not consider themselves part of the same overarching community. I disaggregate the concept of community further in the empirical portion of the book (Chapters 4–8).

[21] Gang members were quite clear on who was and was not part of the gang.

[22] See Brenneman (2011) for description of such dynamics for Central America's maras.

[23] See Cavalcanti (2007, 13) for a problematization of this distinction.

DIMENSIONS OF CRIMINALIZED GOVERNANCE

I conceptualize criminalized governance as consisting of two distinct but inseparable dimensions: coercion and the provision of benefits. Very simply, I differentiate between the carrots and sticks that gangs and other OCGs use to attempt to control their territory and manage relations with populations.[24] In the following sections, I outline the constituent activities of each dimension, describe how they can vary, then use these insights to develop a typology of criminalized governance regimes.

Coercion

The first dimension of governance revolves around coercion: the use and threat of violence to deter disobedience and encourage resident compliance with gang control.[25] By the time a gang has established its exclusive access to a territory, it has already demonstrated its capacity to wield violence. Establishing exclusivity nearly always involves violence or its threat because the gang must, first, make certain that no other gangs are operating on their turf and that they are the exclusive suppliers of the goods or services from which they earn revenue and sustain their organization. In the case of Rio de Janeiro, gangs have long sought to monopolize the retail drug trade within their respective turfs. The effect of the accumulation of violence necessary to exert exclusivity means that most of Rio's gangs also systematically regulate violence within their territory. They do so, initially, to ensure that there are no threats to their activities from the local population. While the exact means by which OCGs may exert coercion surely varies across urban and national contexts, I argue that gangs in Rio de Janeiro engage in three primary coercive activities: physical presence, punishment, and surveillance.

Physical Presence

First, gangs control space in the areas where they operate by being physically and visibly present on the streets. They will congregate and place themselves

---

[24] There remains little consensus among scholars regarding the primary components of criminalized governance in Rio. Some have focused on one aspect such as the punishment of crimes and internal security (Arias and Rodrigues 2006; Zaluar 1985), territorial domination (Silva, Fernandes, and Braga 2008), or access to benefits (Gay 1999). Others have taken a more holistic approach. Arias, for instance, includes "providing funds to individuals in need, maintaining some degree of order by preventing assault and theft, and supporting large-scale festivities for residents" (2006b, 303). Dowdney has pointed to "maintenance of social order, protection from crime, and conflict resolution" as well as "economic stimulation and investment in leisure activities" (2003, 55). Leeds has noted the provision of internal security as well as monetary and community assistance (1996, 60). Magaloni, Franco-Vivanco, and Melo (2020), meanwhile, have broadly characterized these governance relations as either abusive or cooperative.

[25] Kalyvas has similarly argued that both selective and indiscriminate forms of violence directed at civilians in civil war aim to generate collaboration via deterrence (2006, 141–42).

at strategic locations, especially points of access, where drugs (or other illicit goods) are sold or stored, and in and around the homes and businesses of their leaders. Gang members will also frequently move through their territory on foot, bicycle, motorcycle, or in cars and other vehicles. This physical presence is constitutive of their territorial control. That is, without such an observable presence, gangs would likely not be able to retain their exclusivity nor exert their priority over residents and other social and political actors.[26] Although gangs cannot maintain their physical presence throughout an entire territory at all times, the extent of their physical presence will determine the degree to which they can encourage resident compliance and deter any activities which may threaten them or bring their control and authority into question.

Rio de Janeiro's gangs are also highly militarized. The sight of young men and adolescents carrying a variety of handguns and military-grade rifles is not uncommon in these neighborhoods. Some gang members can even be seen carrying two large rifles. This would be counterproductive in any violent encounter as these weapons cannot be effectively used with one arm. That, however, is not the point. Carrying two high-powered rifles is performative and sends a clear message to residents and anyone else that this gang member and the gang, more generally, are not to be trifled with. While such displays of force do not mean that gang members are necessarily actively threatening residents, there is an implicit threat behind such a constant and ostentatious presence. Overall, the gang's visibility is intended to remind residents of who is in charge and to obey their rules.

While all of Rio's gangs will maintain some physical presence and display of force within their territories, these practices can vary considerably. During my fieldwork, I visited dozens of gang-controlled favelas in the city and the variation in the presence of gang members and how openly they displayed their weapons was significant. In some neighborhoods, gangs take a more hands-off approach to controlling space. They maintain only a limited geographical presence, are minimally visible on the streets, seldom display their firepower, and refrain from constantly riding up and down streets on their motorcycles or congregating in large groups. Other gangs will maintain a much heavier presence by placing numerous checkpoints and security positions throughout their territory, frequently riding through the streets on their motorcycles, ostentatiously displaying their firearms, and perhaps even taking on a more sinister and unapproachable aspect (e.g., mean-mugging).[27]

An essential aspect of a gang's physical presence is their treatment of residents in the course of daily events, often referred to by residents and gang

---

[26] This is reminiscent of Levi's assertion, "Enforcement is nearly always imperfect. Even with considerable coercive power and effective techniques of measurement and monitoring, a ruler cannot achieve total compliance unless there is a policeman on every corner" (1989, 49).

[27] Machado da Silva describes this as "violent sociability" (2004), Zaluar as the "warrior ethos" (2000), Sánchez-Jankowski as a "defiant individualist" character (1991, 24–26), and Katz as the feeling of "dread" in their presence (1988).

members as their *"abordagem"* (approach) or *"visão"* (vision). Because they drive on the same streets, buy food from the same supermarkets and vendors, and frequent many of the same restaurants and bars, interactions between gang members and residents are numerous. Whether gang members treat residents with respect, defer to them in certain situations, or if they consider their thoughts and feelings are the most important yet overlooked aspects of how gangs govern because they structure and organize space and social relations within the community. One resident described it in this way: "The way a gang member pays attention, how he converses, basically how he relates to the community, it all matters."[28] The gang's approach is, in part, organic, expressed through repeated interactions between gang members and residents but is also dictated from the top-down. The leadership of some gangs tightly control the behavior of their members in this regard, either encouraging them to treat residents with respect, to say *"bom dia"* (good day), *"licença"* (excuse me), and *"com respeito"* (with respect). Other gang leaders allow their members to mistreat or disrespect residents without consequence.

Punishment

Another key aspect of coercion is whether and to what degree gangs punish residents for infringing on the drug trade, not sufficiently respecting the gang's authority, or disobeying their rules. All gangs in Rio implement a law of silence to prevent residents from informing on them to police and rival gangs. Any resident known to break this rule, often referred to as a *vacilão* (traitor or coward) or *X-9* (snitch), will be dealt with harshly, usually resulting in expulsion, torture, or even execution.[29] The purpose of such punishments is not just to teach those individuals a lesson or remove them from the gang's territory but to communicate to the rest of the population that disloyalty comes at a high price.

Gangs also implement a set of rules for resident behavior. While the specific rules that exist in each favela may vary, the list of proscribed activities generally includes the following:

No theft in the community
No physical fighting between residents
No rape of women
No sexual abuse of children
No domestic abuse[30]

---

[28] Natan 8/22/2013.
[29] The term X-9 comes from the US comic series, *Secret Agent X-9*, created by Dashiell Hammett in the 1930s in which a secret agent employed by a nameless federal agency infiltrated criminal networks. These comics became popular in Brazil in the 1940s. The term, as used in favelas, applies to anyone that provides information to a gang's enemies.
[30] For a fuller description of these rules, see Dowdney (2003, 63–70).

On the one hand, there is a more benign element to these rules as they are intended to provide some degree of social order for residents. The punishments that gangs mete out for transgressing these rules, however, can vary considerably. Some gangs will publicly threaten, mutilate, torture, and execute those found breaking these rules, while other gangs use less coercive means, merely issuing a verbal warning, shaming, or perhaps expelling residents for more serious offenses. In theory, gang members must also abide by these same rules and can be held accountable for sexual assaults, theft, and abuse though some gangs will seldom punish their own members. Other gangs will not refrain from punishing and sanctioning their own members. What punishments, if any, will also depend on the type of crime and the specific residents involved.

Numerous ethnographers of Rio's favelas have described, in detail, the often violent and spectacular punishments that gangs employ against rule breakers. For example, Robb Larkins recounts when "an alleged child abuser was tied to a telephone pole in the middle of one of the busiest thoroughfares and beaten with metal chains until he was no longer recognizable" (2015, 43). Both Leeds (1996) and Goldstein (2003) similarly describe the violent nature of gang order that is largely based on the whims of the gang. Arias and Rodrigues (2006) even develop the notion of the "myth of personal security," in which gangs use violence against marginalized residents while failing to enforce the rules against their own members or more respected residents.

In another example, Penglase (2014, 108–10) describes an episode in which a gang member killed a resident's dog and murdered a drug addict who had returned to the community from which he had been expelled. Although Penglase describes this episode as an example of the arbitrariness of gang justice, it also demonstrates how a gang will limit their use of violence in important ways. For one, the gang member that killed the dog and the addict was disciplined by the gang leader by not allowing him to sell drugs for a week. Although perhaps not seen as a sufficiently severe punishment by Penglase, the gang leader prided himself on controlling the behavior of his members (p. 119). In addition, the primary issue that community members seemed to have had with the episode was the shooting of the dog and the time and location of the murder – in the afternoon on a major thoroughfare – and not the murder itself. The drug addict, known to have "caused problems" in the community, and who had already been expelled by the gang, was likely seen to have it coming by many community members.

In this regard, several scholars have suggested that even very violent punishments often comply with community notions of justice. Zaluar, for instance, argues that gang members share a moral, albeit violent, sense of order with the residents of Cidade de Deus (City of God), a set of housing projects in Rio's Zona Oeste (Western Zone) (1994, 19–26). Following numerous interviews with residents, Robb Larkins similarly realized that the residents "needed" the gang's order despite its extremely violent nature (2015, 44). Lessing also points to the benefits of such an intensive form of order by quoting a resident of one of Rio's favelas, "...the people feel there is order. A small business, for example ... outside [the favela], you would have to put security guards, cameras, but inside, no. Nobody will touch anything" (2008, 113). In this sense, even violent punishments can be a relatively well agreed upon form of justice within the community.

The important point from all these examples is how such forms of coercion are viewed by residents. While outside observers often view all gang order as equally coercive, the reality for residents of favelas is far more complex. They frequently distinguish between the violence and threats deemed necessary to maintaining social order and those that are arbitrary or gratuitous. Differentiating between these subjective understandings can be especially difficult given the oft-violent nature of gang punishments but there are important differences. In general, violence can be welcomed by many residents when used to punish those individuals engaging in theft or sexual abuse within the favela.[31] In this way, the use of coercion can sometimes be seen as a benefit. That said, some gangs can fail to provide a consistent sense of law and order or overstep these bounds by punishing residents that are either not guilty of the alleged transgression or by exceeding local norms regarding the severity of punishment.

Surveillance

Gangs also engage in the monitoring and surveillance of residents, both along the borders of their turf and throughout the territory. Gangs will often place olheiros and soldados at or near the boundaries of their territory to monitor entry and exit. They are especially watchful for any sign of rival gangs or police but can also pay close attention to the residents crossing over these borders. Gangs may fear the infiltration of their territory by outsiders intent on gathering information about their security locations and strengths. According to one gang lookout, "You have to keep an eye on things. We don't know who is by our side, don't know if it's a X-9, if it's an *alemão* (rival), we have to always keep an eye out. Eyes open and just listening" (Dowdney 2003, 140).[32] Some gangs even resort to questioning and threatening anyone who does not seem to belong. In more extreme cases, they will abuse or beat residents of a neighborhood controlled by a rival or anyone who lacks a good reason to be there. Many gangs will also construct barriers along their borders to prevent police operations or rival gang invasions. In Rio, gangs frequently place steel I-beams in holes in the middle of streets to slow down police operations. In several rare

[31] For a similar set of civilian-supported rules that armed groups may implement during civil war, see Arjona (2016, 49–50).

[32] *Alemão*, meaning "German" in Portuguese, is the term often used to refer to an enemy or rival gang in Rio's favelas. I was never able to conclusively trace the origin of its use but some residents said that it dated back to World War II when Brazil fought on the side of Allies and their "enemies" were Germans.

cases, gangs have even chosen to entirely close one or more entry points to their territory, preventing any residents from coming or going. In other cases, gangs maintain few or no security positions near their borders, allowing residents greater freedom of movement.

Gangs will also engage in monitoring and surveillance of the local population throughout their territory. Severino, with whom I began this book, is a prime example of how gang members are constantly monitoring the areas where they live and are closely attuned to what is happening in the neighborhood. Much surveillance is focused on the areas in and around where the gangs sell drugs or engage in other illicit activities but also often includes major thoroughfares, the homes of gang leaders, and areas of strategic importance. Monitoring also occurs through many of the social relations and networks that gangs maintain. Friends, family, and associates will provide the gang with information about any significant events in the neighborhood. Such relations are a normal part of life in these tight-knit communities but also have strategic importance for the gangs because they are better able to wield coercion or resolve disputes with high-quality information about the community. Overall, the monitoring and surveillance of the local population, both along the borders and throughout their territory is an essential component to the coercive capacities of the gang.

Provision of Benefits

The second dimension of criminalized governance is the provision of benefits. These activities are intended to legitimize the gang in the eyes of the local population, encourage residents to remain silent, and to gain the outright allegiance or support of some residents. Rio de Janeiro's gangs began offering some limited and sporadic benefits to favela residents early on in their development. In the 1970s and 1980s, some gangs and bandits distributed the spoils from robberies, gave small gifts, or threw parties with the resources from the fledgling drug trade.[33] By the 1990s, after consolidating their territorial control within favelas, gangs were able to provide more significant benefits to residents. I distinguish between three primary types of benefits: dispute resolution, economic stimulation, and recreation. Every gang throughout the city will engage, to varying degrees, in each of these activities. While such benefits are not distributed equally across these communities, and gangs can seldom be considered to offer truly public goods, they do offer benefits to nearly any resident willing to ask for them.[34]

---

[33] For descriptions of these early governance practices, see Arias (2006a), Gay (1999), Leeds (1996), McCann (2014), and Misse (1999).

[34] Public goods are non-excludable (anyone can use them) and non-rivalrous (if used, it does not prevent others from also using them).

Dispute Resolution

As in any other human community, interpersonal conflicts between favela residents are inevitable. Especially given the extreme population density, difficult living conditions, and the precarity and abuse from which many favela residents have and continue to suffer, interpersonal disputes can be frequent. Mechanisms for resolving such conflicts are perhaps the most important benefit that gangs provide to residents within their territories. Doing so accomplishes several goals simultaneously: they solve urgent problems for residents, they gather essential information about the local population, and, if resolved successfully, they legitimize their authority.[35] Moreover, residents of gang-controlled neighborhoods can seldom rely on the police to handle such disputes because they are either negligent or known to be corrupt and abusive. It is common for resident populations where gangs operate to have little trust in the public security apparatus. In Rio, gangs have explicitly disallowed residents from going to the police for any reason. In turn, they have implemented varyingly effective and responsive institutions to deal with interpersonal conflict. They have done so because they do not want conflicts to escalate and turn violent, which might eventually draw the attention or require the involvement of the authorities.

In most cases, residents approach the gang either directly at the local *boca de fumo* or through their friends or relatives that know someone involved.[36] The gang will offer mediation for a variety of disputes: serious disagreements or fights between neighbors, problems concerning money or debts, damage to property, or for disputes between lovers or family members. The less serious disagreements and problems will be handled by the lower-level gang members who often happen to be working at the bocas, either *vapores* or *soldados*. However, more serious conflicts require the involvement of the gang *gerentes* (managers) and, in certain cases, the Dono himself, especially if the punishment involves expulsion or the death penalty. In Rio, it is rare for dispute resolution to take on a formal process (such as a tribunal) but there are many occasions in which each party will present their side of the story before the gang makes a final decision.[37] The gang will ensure both parties abide by the

---

[35] According to Arjona, dispute resolution is the most basic and necessary institution that any ruler may provide to a local population (2016, 69–74).

[36] Numerous scholars have written about this aspect of criminalized governance. Goldstein, for example, outlines how residents seek out local gangs to help them resolve private matters including domestic abuse, sexual abuse, theft or robbery, gun control, and adultery (2003, 190–97). Dowdney also points to gangs providing these essential services when residents avail themselves of their assistance, quoting one favela resident: "They only get involved if [someone] steals from us, they get involved to defend the residents" (2003, 59).

[37] Some gangs, such as the PCC in São Paulo, have implemented highly formalized and effective judicial institutions (so-called *debates* or tribunals), first designed to deal with internal discipline, but which have been known to be used by residents of areas where they operate (Biondi 2009; Denyer Willis 2015; Feltran 2010a, 2018; Lessing and Denyer Willis 2019).

judgment with the threat of force, if necessary. In this way, like punishments, dispute resolution can overlap both dimensions of governance.

Some gangs will provide higher-quality conflict resolution mechanisms by trying to resolve disputes in an impartial or mutually agreeable way that is responsive to community notions of justice and without the use or threat of violence. They will also be more responsive to community demands for these services by dealing with whatever issues residents bring to their attention, thus involving themselves deeply in the personal lives of the residents. Some gangs have offered these services for nearly every type of disagreement including disputes between lovers or family members and instances of domestic abuse. Other gangs take a less responsive approach, refusing to deal with residents' personal issues, only addressing the most prominent forms of conflict, and not caring if residents feel the dispute was resolved in an agreeable way.[38] Some gangs even delegate the authority to deal with these issues to other social actors, including churches, non-governmental organizations (NGOs), or the *Associação de Moradores* (Residents' Association, hereon AM) within these territories.

Economic Stimulation

Drug trafficking and a range of other economic enterprises have provided some gangs with significant resources with which they have stimulated local economies and offered various forms of welfare. Most of the financial benefits of the local drug trade, however, remain within the families and social networks of the gangs. Salaries for the lowest-level gang members are often little more than minimum wage but this amount grows steadily as the member ascends the hierarchy. The gang's highest-ranking members can earn ten times the minimum wage with the Dono making even more (Silva 2006; Willadino, Nascimento, and Silva 2018). The families, girlfriends, relatives, and even friends of gang members may rely heavily on these earnings to feed and clothe their families. In this way, not a small number of residents will rely on the organization (Gay 2005). In addition, the families of imprisoned gang members will often receive stipends for the duration of a member's imprisonment.

Beyond the gang's social networks, much of the revenue generated from the drug trade stays within these neighborhoods though some gang leaders have been known to purchase real estate or engage in business ventures outside their territory. Gang members will purchase clothing, food, alcohol, and many other goods and services from local shops and vendors. The businesses that cater especially to gang members can benefit significantly though there are downsides, including being targeted by the police or reductions in other clientele. While the economic benefits of the drug trade are not felt evenly across these neighborhoods and should not be considered a public good that the gang

---

[38] According to Lessing, the *Família do Norte* (Family of the North), a prison gang from the Amazon region of Brazil, has refused to provide such services to populations that they govern (2020, 861).

provides, such stimulation remains an essential way that the gang maintains the support of many residents within the community.

In addition to revenues from the drug trade, many gangs have diversified their economic portfolio by providing access to television and internet services, developing informal transportation services, managing and speculating on real estate, and distributing and selling cigarettes, beverages, and pirated videos, among others. The revenues brought in from these other illicit activities pale in comparison to retail drugs but offer many residents not formally part of the gang additional ways to make money or to receive services that are cheaper and sometimes better than if they went through the formal market.[39] Gangs also control access to space within favelas and are often the arbiters of whether and where residents can construct new homes or place their shacks and stands on the side of roads to sell all manner of goods. Gangs also authorize dozens if not hundreds of families to sell food and beverages at their weekly parties (see later).

Finally, gangs have also been known to engage more directly in welfare. Some gangs have paid for water maintenance, home construction and repair, the asphalting of streets, and the construction of soup kitchens and daycare centers. These sorts of investments in infrastructure are not common though some gangs have become famous for such expenditures. On a more regular basis, gangs will provide monthly food baskets, refrigerators, gas cylinders, medicine, and other necessary items for residents in need, as well as transportation to hospitals for the sick.[40] Although relatively small amounts, such generosity can facilitate a lot of goodwill among residents. Other gangs, however, provide little in terms of welfare or economic stimulation to the local community. Some leaders prefer to hoard their profits by building luxurious homes and purchasing expensive consumer goods for themselves and their families.

Recreation

Gangs also play an important role within the community in providing certain forms of recreation. First, many gangs throw weekly baile funk parties which are attended by hundreds if not thousands of local youths.[41] The gangs will set up tents, stages, and sound equipment, hire popular DJs, and organize vendors to sell food and drinks. The significant drug sales at these parties are surely one of their motivating factors but there are also several ways in which gangs simultaneously use these parties to legitimize their presence and gather support within the community.

First, free forms of entertainment are hard to come by in favela communities. Favela youth can often be harassed and unwelcome in other areas of

---

[39] For instance, the CVNH gang's cable and internet services were allegedly faster, more reliable, and cheaper than the formal providers (Breno 4/4/2017).
[40] See also Arias (2006a), Dowdney (2003), and Leeds (1996) for a description of these activities.
[41] For a history of the emergence and expansion of these parties, see Vianna (1988, 1997).

the city – the city center, beaches, and touristy neighborhoods – where free entertainment is more common. Baile funk parties are one of the few places where favela youth are free to enjoy and express themselves. In this way, these parties can be seen as an important public good, especially by many of the youth from these neighborhoods. In addition, the lyrics of many funk songs venerate the local gang, its leader, and their larger faction affiliation.[42] For this reason, much funk music is referred to as either *apologia* (apologist), for the way the lyrics praise and idolize drug trafficking and the gang lifestyle, or *proibidão* (prohibited), because the state has outlawed such forms of music from being played in much of the city. Through this music, some gangs and their leaders become local if not citywide heroes, further supplementing their legitimacy in these communities.

In addition to bailes, gangs can organize large parties for Mother's, Father's, and Children's Day, as well as other holidays for which they provide free food and drink and distribute toys and other party favors to attendees. In some cases, gangs distribute larger items through raffles that include electronics (laptops, phones, and televisions), appliances (washing machines, refrigerators, and stoves), as well as bicycles. Free, family-friendly events are also in short supply in favela communities and any event at which the entire family can eat, drink, and enjoy music is a significant benefit and bolsters the reputation of the local gang in the eyes of many residents. Finally, some gang members have been known to organize weekly barbecues to which they will invite entire streets or areas of the neighborhood. They also throw lavish parties for their birthdays or in conjunction with other religious holidays for which they hire music, offer free food and drink, and block off streets or plazas. These parties and events can be an important source of free entertainment for some residents especially those that struggle to make ends meet.

Finally, gangs have occasionally been known to support local football teams and have, in certain rare cases, funded the construction of football fields. All these benefits can be broadly conceived under the category of recreation and, along with dispute resolution and economic stimulation, are the primary benefits that gangs provide to a community.

A TYPOLOGY OF CRIMINALIZED GOVERNANCE REGIMES

In the previous section, I separated criminalized governance into two dimensions, coercion and the provision of benefits, then outlined the behaviors associated with each. As I emphasized throughout, gangs can engage in varying amounts and degrees of each governance activity. For coercion, gangs can implement an extensive or limited geographical presence, use varying degrees

---

[42] For research on how gangs have used baile funks as platforms to glorify their activities, see Sneed (2007, 2008).

TABLE 2.1 *A typology of criminalized governance regimes*

Provision of benefits	Coercion	
	High	*Low*
Responsive	Benevolent dictator The gang uses high levels of coercion while providing responsive benefits to the community.	Social bandit The gang engages in low levels of coercion while providing responsive benefits to the community.
Unresponsive	Tyrant The gang uses high levels of coercion while being unresponsive to demands for benefits from the community.	Laissez-Faire The gang engages in low levels of coercion while being unresponsive to demands for benefits from the community.

of violence to punish disobedience, and engage in highly vigilant or more relaxed surveillance of residents. For the provision of benefits, gangs can provide more or less responsive mechanisms of conflict resolution, offer significant or relatively little welfare and economic assistance, and many or few forms of recreation. While each of these activities can vary independent of one another, I aggregate the variation into high and low levels of coercion and responsive or unresponsive provision of benefits. The interaction of these two dimensions produces four ideal-typical governance regimes (Table 2.1). While some gangs may be found between these ideal types, all gangs that govern can be located within these quadrants.

Benevolent dictator gangs do not refrain from using high levels of violence and threats directed toward residents while also developing a variety of responsive behaviors and practices intended to gain the loyalty of local populations. They will maintain a heavy physical presence, are more likely to resort to violent punishments for disobedience, and intensively surveil the community. At the same time, a benevolent dictator gang will provide responsive benefits by resolving interpersonal disputes, distributing significant welfare and stimulating the local economy, and offering various forms of recreation.

Tyrant gangs are less willing to provide any benefits to a local population but will not refrain from using high amounts of coercion. This governance regime is likely the worst for communities as the gang is little interested in the welfare of residents and is mostly concentrated on maintaining their position of dominance through the threat of force. They will punish with violence, maintain a heavy and ostentatious physical presence, and closely monitor resident behavior.

Social bandit gangs represent the most benevolent governance regime by providing responsive dispute resolution, significant welfare, and numerous opportunities for recreation while largely avoiding the use of threats and violence against residents. The name refers to a largely rural preindustrial phenomenon, in which outlaws and bandits were at the forefront of the resistance of the oppressed classes (Hobsbawm 1959, 2000). In Rio, the term, *bandido social* (social bandit) is still commonly used to refer to gang members which have the interests of the community at heart.

Finally, *laissez-faire* gangs represent a governance style that subscribes to a *live and let live* philosophy. The gang provides little in terms of benefits to the local population but also maintains a limited physical presence, refrains from violent punishment, and takes a lax attitude toward surveillance. Although a limited form of governance in relation to the community, laissez-faire gangs can and do engage in the same criminal and illicit activities as other gangs.

EXISTING EXPLANATIONS OF CRIMINALIZED GOVERNANCE IN RIO DE JANEIRO

The expansive anthropological and sociological literature on gangs in Rio de Janeiro offers numerous descriptive accounts of the use of coercion and the provision of benefits by gang organizations throughout the city. Although these dynamics are seldom conceptualized as governance and have yet to be systematically theorized, these works offer several plausible explanations for why these activities may vary.

Overall, there have been few attempts to understand why some gangs are more coercive than others. A couple of scholars, however, have described less coercive governing regimes and have attempted to account for them, at least anecdotally. Zaluar (2000) points to several communities in which gangs engage in less violence and threats against residents while allowing them greater freedoms. She argues that this is because police spend little time in these communities and the gangs have little fear of enforcement. The theory I construct in the following chapter outlines a very different relationship between police enforcement and governance, though Zaluar's focus on the security environment in determining these outcomes is one that this project shares.[43]

Alternatively, Dowdney (2003, 64) suggests that gangs engage in less violence and threats when they lack both the capacity and the desire to implement more intensive governance. Some gangs control enormous swaths of territory, include hundreds of members, and have access to huge arsenals of weapons. Others may hold very small territories, have only a handful of members, and lack high-powered weaponry. The difference in coercive capacity across these

---

[43] Conversely, Wolff (2015) suggests that violent and abusive police operations will lead gangs and residents to find "common cause" though it's unclear what, if any, impact this has on governance activities.

organizations is manifest. This book attempts to understand variation across gang organizations of similar size and with similar coercive capacities. Why some gangs do not engage in highly coercive governance practices when they have the capacity to do so remains a puzzle.

Numerous scholars have described how gangs can provide significant goods and services to favela communities yet there is little consensus as to why. Some argue that the degree to which a gang provides benefits is largely idiosyncratic, dictated entirely by the leadership style and personal philosophy of the Dono or gang leader (Arias 2006b; Arias and Rodrigues 2006; Dowdney 2003; Leeds 1996). Within this perspective, some gang leaders are "good" while others are "bad." Meio Kilo from Jacarezinho, Flavio Negão from Vigário Geral (Ventura 1994), Escadinha from Juramento (Amorim 1993; Leeds 1996), Orlando Jogador of Complexo do Alemão (Barcellos 2003; Magaloni, Franco-Vivanco, and Melo 2020), and Lulu and Nem of Rocinha (Glenny 2016) were all famously "good" gang leaders. Why, we must then ask, are some gang leaders good and others bad?

In many cases, a Dono that grew up in the community and has significant connections with the community will attempt to redistribute wealth and be more responsive to resident demands. In other cases, however, "bad" Donos are also from the community and seek only their personal enrichment. This explanation is unsatisfying for two reasons: first, this argument overlooks the surprising continuity in benefits that certain gangs provide over many years despite multiple changes in leadership; second, some gang leaders have shifted their own governance philosophy considerably, moving to provide more or less benefits and becoming more or less coercive over time. Why Donos do so has yet to be explained.

To explain variation in the benevolence of gangs, Dowdney (2003) offers a political–economic account, in which highly profitable gangs can overcome the "butter-or-guns" trade-off by purchasing the loyalty of residents while not diminishing their security expenditures. He quotes a member of one such profitable gang: "Here we're all about strengthening [the community]. If a resident needs a gas cylinder, we get it for them, if another resident needs a place to live because the rain has destroyed their house, we support them" (p. 62). However, not all highly profitable gangs provide significant goods and services to local populations. In fact, as I document in the case studies of this book, similarly lucrative gangs can provide very different levels of benefits.

The final and perhaps most compelling explanation for why some gangs provide more benefits focuses on the gang's illicit connections with the local AM. These informal democratic institutions represent the interests of favela communities to state agencies and political parties. By the 1990s, after Rio's gangs had consolidated their territorial control and become the dominant political authority in favelas, they quickly co-opted the AMs by assassinating or expelling intransigent leaders and replacing them with representatives more amenable to gang influence. Since then, many gangs have used the AM to provide various services to the community. For instance, Arias has described how traffickers often "enlist the help of the [AM] in hiring performers, purchasing presents for attendees, and running the party" for large-scale festivities in favelas (2006b, 310). The gang can also use the AM as a more legitimate organization through which to negotiate with political parties, state agencies, or the police outside of the favela (Arias 2006a, 2013; Gay 1990; McCann 2014). Finally, gangs can delegate certain tasks to the local AM, such as resolving disputes arising from housing, electricity, water, and other problems that the gang does not want to deal with. While this offers a plausible explanation for how the provision of benefits varies across communities – gangs with closer connections to AMs provide more and better services – it is not true that all gangs that offer significant goods and services do so primarily through the AM. In fact, as I will show in the case studies, some gangs provide significant benefits while sidelining the AM even as other gangs offer few benefits while retaining close connections.

One final existing study of governance in Rio de Janeiro is necessary to mention. Magaloni, Franco-Vivanco, and Melo's (2020) research on Rio's gangs shares much in common with the framework I develop in this book as they also outline a typology of "criminal regimes." There are several key differences, however. First, they conceptualize the relationship with communities as simply abusive or cooperative. This book complicates and broadens our understanding of these arrangements as I argue that criminalized governance is not just an either/or but can also be both or neither abusive nor cooperative. Put more simply, coercion and benefits operate independent of one another. Moreover, Magaloni, Franco-Vivanco, and Melo are not seeking to explain governance or how or why these relationships emerge or vary over time. In fact, in their framework (p. 558), relations with rivals and with the police have no bearing on the relationship with the community. The theory developed in Chapter 3 demonstrates how these relationships, with rivals and the police, systematically shape the dynamics of governance. That said, our work can be usefully be read together as we come to some of the same conclusions, especially pertaining to the consequences of public security interventions (see Chapter 8; Barnes 2022b).

Overall, while the existing literature has provided several plausible explanations for how and why gangs employ coercion and provide benefits, there have been no attempts to systematically study these phenomena together or to explain their variation within a governance framework. Developing such a theory is the task of Chapter 3.

3

A Theory of Criminalized Governance

...political actors would rather be disliked but feared than liked but not feared
when their rival is feared.
    —Stathis Kalyvas, *The Logic of Violence in Civil War* (2006, 114)
We lived with the state. For us the state had to exist...
    —Carmine Schiavone, a powerful Camorra boss, quoted
        in Roberto Saviano, *Gomorrah* (2008, 190)

INTRODUCTION

By mid-October 2013, I had been living in Nova Holanda for nearly four
months. On an otherwise ordinary Wednesday, I had arranged to speak with
the director of the Lona Cultural Municipal Herbert Vianna, an NGO located
in the heart of Maré. The Lona, as most locals refer to it, sits on the border
between the territory controlled by the CVNH gang, where I lived, and the
adjacent set of neighborhoods controlled by a gang connected to the TCP faction (see Figure 3.1). Over the course of my first few months in Maré, I had
already visited the Lona several times. It was only a five-minute walk from my
apartment. So just before noon, I turned onto Rua Principal (Main Street),
and headed in the direction of the *divisa* (border), as residents refer to it. Like
nearly every other day, the traffic was heavy. Cars and trucks slowly squeezed
past one another as young men and boys, many of whom were affiliated with
the gang, zigzagged in and out of the traffic on their motorbikes.

On my way, I passed two bocas where I could see the drug trade already
operating at full tilt in the midday heat. At the first, a handful of well-armed
gang members sat next to two tables they had placed in the shade. Several customers perused a dozen or so plastic bags of different quantities of marijuana,
cocaine, and crack that were haphazardly arranged on the table alongside a

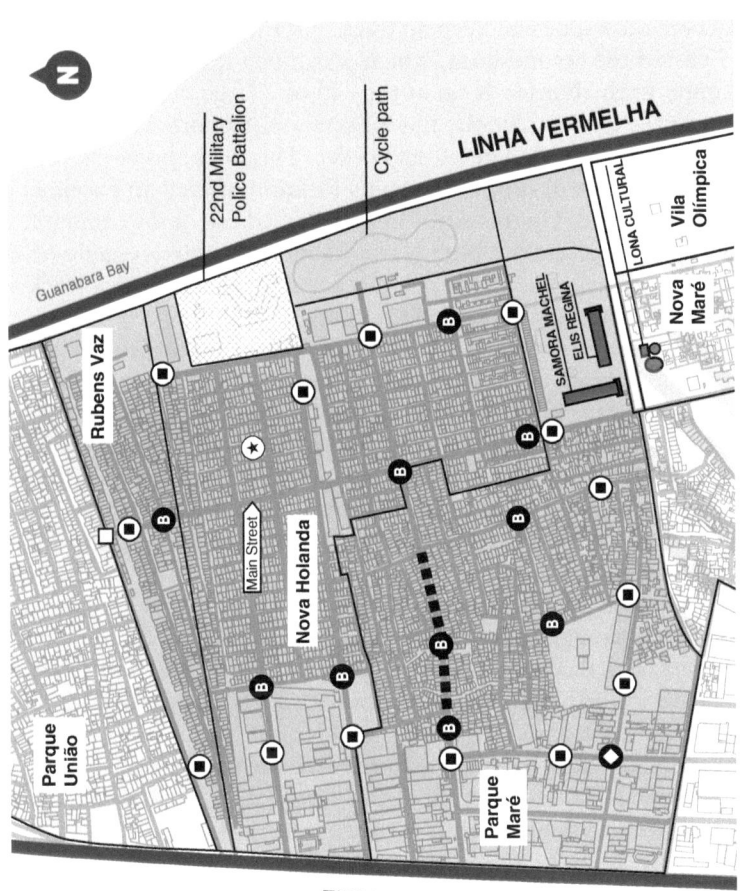

Comando Vermelho
Parque União (CVPU)

Comando Vermelho
Nova Holanda (CVNH)

Terceiro Comando Puro
(TCP)

Bridge of Friendship

Olheiro
(lookout)

Boca de Fumo

Residence during
fieldwork

Baile Funk

Drug users
community

FIGURE 3.1 Map of CVNH territory during fieldwork
Visualization by Bruna Montuori.

57

notebook where the vapor was keeping track of the accounts. A couple of minutes later I passed the second boca, which was much less busy, likely because of its proximity to the border. It sat at the end of a large plaza, which opened onto the entrances to two schools, Elis Regina and Samora Machel, both situated on the Nova Holanda side of the border. This boca, however, served as more than just a source of drug revenue; its location offered an excellent vantage point of the border. On this day, nothing seemed out of the ordinary. Two adolescents sat lazily around a blue plastic table with only a couple of sacks of drugs on it. Their semiautomatic rifles leaned against the nearest brick wall. They did not even look up as I passed.

The actual border between the CVNH and TCP gang territories is constituted by a single narrow street, Evanildo Alves. Compared to similarly sized streets in other areas of Maré, it had far fewer bars and shops. Residents often refer to this street and the surrounding streets as the *Faixa da Gaza* (Gaza Strip) because of the significant violence that has occurred there over the years. I had heard numerous stories of gang shootouts and invasions along this border but, since I had moved to Maré, there had been no such intergang violence. In fact, according to residents and gang members, there had been no serious shootouts or invasion attempts for at least the last year. The two gangs were in a period of détente though each continued to monitor the border and maintain a presence there. For their part, residents could cross over with little concern for their safety. I, myself, had crossed the border dozens of times since moving to Maré. In fact, most days I ate lunch in the home of an older couple and spent many evenings at a bar that featured live shows by local bands, both of which were in TCP's territory. In all those crossings, I had never felt gang members on either side paying particularly close attention to me. This day was no different.

The Lona is comprised of three main buildings – an auditorium, a small library, and a kitchen and offices – all surrounded by a ten-foot brick wall. I walked through the open double metal doors and was immediately greeted by several children that regularly hung around the NGO. The director welcomed me, and we made our way to his office in the back of the compound. After our interview, which lasted about an hour, he left for another meeting and I stuck around to chat with two of the staff, Clara and Breno, with whom I had become acquainted on my previous visits. As the three of us were talking at the threshold of the entrance, three gunshots rang out. *Pop pop pop*. We instinctively ducked our heads and stepped back from the doorway. Frozen, we waited for what came next. A couple of moments passed before a return volley came from the CVNH side of the border. From there, the shootout quickly escalated. Multiple shots came from all around us. Breno and I quickly closed and locked the double metal doors and the three of us rushed to the back of the compound. On our way, we looked for the children but, thankfully, they had gone home for lunch. We made our way to the director's office, effectively putting several brick and concrete walls between us and the bullets. It seemed as good a place as any to wait it out. We laid down on the floor and listened to the shootout unfold around us. Dozens of shots came from every direction. Some could be heard further off in the distance, others from right outside the Lona's walls. I don't know whether it was the cool tile floor or the adrenaline coursing through my body, but I vividly recall all the hairs on the back of my neck standing on end and shivers running down my spine.

For several years, I had read and heard numerous accounts of the incredible violence between Rio's gangs but had never experienced it up close. I was stunned by how long the shootout stretched on. It was a full half an hour of constant shooting before we heard a loud explosion. *Boom!* All the windows in the office shook. I didn't understand what had happened. I looked to my companions. Breno, who had grown up in Maré and was now in his early thirties, howled, "*Caralho! Foi uma granada!*" (Fuck! That was a grenade!). I knew that many of Rio's gangs had access to such weapons but, still, their use came as a shock. Another grenade exploded several seconds later, shaking the windows again. More gunfire. Then a string of grenades, four or five in quick succession, that reverberated through the building and in my chest. Clara took out her computer, opened Facebook, and began writing messages to her friends and family about where she was and what was happening.[1] It was another half hour of unbroken gunfire before the shots eventually became more sporadic then ceased entirely. Later, in interviews with gang members, I learned the shootout was the result of an invasion attempt by TCP (see Figure 3.2).[2] More than two dozen heavily armed TCP members had tried to cross into CVNH's territory at several strategic points. CVNH members had detected the invasion immediately and successfully repelled it. TCP did not end up getting very far that day and the shootout had mostly occurred along the border.

We waited an hour after the last gunshot before emerging from our hiding place. We opened the main doors, peeked out, and cautiously exited the building. There was a strange smell in the air. The exterior wall of the Lona was riddled with bullet holes and the school just across the border as well (see Figures 3.3 and 3.4). It was difficult to tell which ones were new and which had been there for some time. I looked around for larger signs of damage but couldn't see exactly where the grenades had gone off or which side had used them. They were likely *granadas de atordoamento* (stun grenades), used to disorient and incapacitate an enemy with a loud burst and flash of light. My only thought at the time was to get away from the border area. Breno and I lived in CVNH's territory, Clara in TCP's. We said our goodbyes and headed

---

[1] This is a common way for favela residents to communicate about such violence. Shootouts like this can be heard from anywhere in the surrounding neighborhoods but word also spreads quickly through social media, alerting those planning to visit or return to Maré from other areas of the city.
[2] Severino 5/15/2014; Inácio 3/26/2014; Everton 4/24/2014.

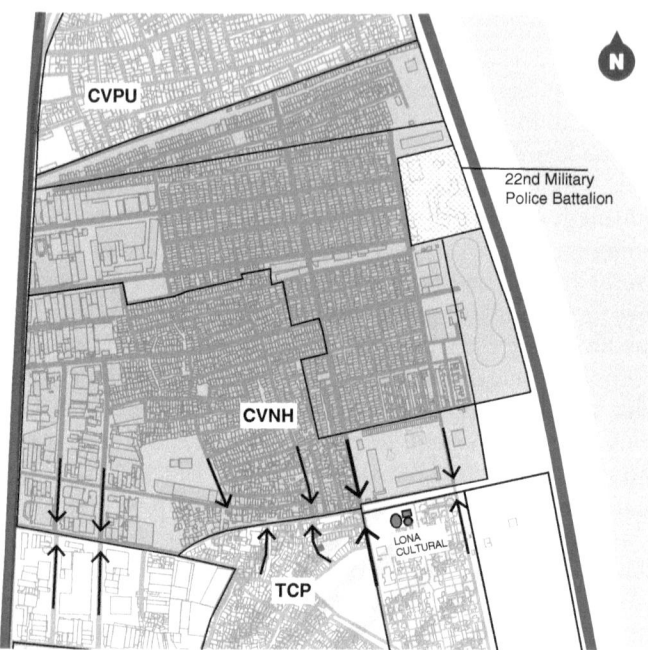

FIGURE 3.2 Map of gang invasions in CVNH territory
Visualization by Bruna Montuori.

FIGURE 3.3 Photograph of bullet holes in the side of Samora Machel School in
CVNH territory
Photograph by author.

FIGURE 3.4 Photograph of bullet holes in the side of houses in TCP territory
Photograph by author.

in opposite directions. Breno and I turned down Main Street, moving quickly but not running because we did not want to draw the attention of any lingering gang members. The last boca that I had passed on my way was now empty. The two gang members and the sacks of drugs were gone, the plastic table and chairs had been cast aside and were laying in a heap. I spotted hundreds of shell casings on the ground.

Nova Holanda was a ghost town. There were no cars, trucks, or motorcycles on the roads. The *barracas* (carts and stalls) that lined the streets were empty and all the shops were closed, their metal grates pulled down and locked. I noticed several residents peeking out from doorways or from windows, appraising the situation, wondering if it was safe to move around. There were likely hundreds of residents still waiting at bus stops, restaurants, and snack stands along Avenida Brasil until they were sure it was safe to return to their homes. I said goodbye to Breno, turned the corner to my street, and suddenly felt very tired. I climbed the four flights to my apartment and immediately threw myself on the bed. Before I fell asleep, I remember hearing the dull thumping of a police helicopter somewhere in the distance.

A THEORY OF CRIMINALIZED GOVERNANCE

In this chapter, I employ ethnographic insights garnered during my time living in CVNH's territory to develop a theory of criminalized governance. It accounts for how and why gangs implement the governance regimes typologized in Chapter 2. The principal theoretical insight of this book is that the security environment in which a gang finds itself determines the type and degree of support it needs from the local population as well as the incentives and opportunities residents have to shape gang behavior.

All gangs the world over face two primary security threats: from rival gangs and the police. I argue that these threats impact governance in divergent ways. First, gangs can face threats from rivals that vary from *active* to *absent* (see Table 3.1). An *active* threat means that an incumbent gang faces a belligerent rival trying to invade and take over their territory. Active competition can include everything from all-out invasions like the one I witnessed to drive-by shootings, targeted assassinations, as well as more surreptitious attempts to infiltrate a territory. An active rivalry constitutes an existential threat to any gang organization because, if they lose control of their territory, the gang basically ceases to exist. All incumbent gang members will be killed, expelled from the area, or, if they are lucky, absorbed into the newly dominant gang. Such an existential threat produces short time horizons for the incumbent gang as it must ensure its territorial control at all costs. The gang will quickly shift all available resources to securing their territory, increasing its use and threat of violence not just against its rival but also toward the local resident population. With enemy gang members invading and infiltrating their turf, governance quickly deteriorates, and disorder pervades. The gang will break any existing agreements or limits on their behavior. In these circumstances, the gang cares less about being liked by the local population, and instead prefers to be feared (see Kalyvas' quote earlier). Active threats can sometimes last for just a few hours or several days but can also stretch on for much longer. Periods of warfare between gangs have been known to last for months or, in some cases, even years. The longer the period of active threat persists, the more erratic and paranoid gang behavior will become. They will use violence indiscriminately and coercion often becomes extreme. Not every gang, however, faces such an active rival threat.

On the other end of the spectrum, an *absent* rival threat means that a gang faces no competitors for territorial exclusivity. This is often due to the gang having successfully defeated and absorbed all local rivals or because of its relative geographic isolation. Another possible reason for the absence of territorial threat is due to stable alliances or arrangements with surrounding gangs or other OCGs. When gangs face little or no rival threat, they will not fear invasions or the infiltration of their territory, nor will they be concerned with residents collaborating with an enemy. As a result, they will not be as physically present nor ostentatiously display themselves within their turf, will rely less on

TABLE 3.1 *A theory of criminalized governance*

Police enforcement	Rival competition		
	Active	*Latent*	*Absent*
Active		Benevolent dictator	Social bandit
	Disorder	High coercion	Low coercion
	Extreme coercion	Responsive benefits	Responsive benefits
Absent	No benefits	Tyrant	Laissez-Faire
		High coercion	Low coercion
		Unresponsive benefits	Unresponsive benefits

threats and violence to punish residents for disobedience, and will refrain from intensively monitoring their borders.

Between these two poles exists a third type of rival threat, which I refer to as *latent*. A latent threat applies to contexts where a gang does not face a rival that is actively trying to take over their territory but due to their proximity or a history of conflict and territorial turnover, the possibility of contestation is still present. This category encompasses a broad array of situations, including when active competition has just ended or is about to begin but can also apply to situations in which the possibility of intergang violence remains present for longer periods. In these contexts, the gang will put limits on their coercive behavior but continues to maintain a heavy physical presence on the streets, rely on violent punishments to remind residents that disobedience comes with a price, and intensively monitor the local population.

Police enforcement also varies from *active* to *absent*, but produces a very different set of governance dynamics (see Table 3.1). Active enforcement applies to situations in which a gang faces consistent police efforts to investigate and arrest them. Some active enforcement can even be highly aggressive and militarized, where police are authorized to use lethal force against gang members.[3] And yet, even at their most competitive, gang–police relations do not have the same zero-sum quality as intergang rivalries. Police do not seek to conquer gang neighborhoods and develop social relations with these communities, nor do they want to regulate illicit markets. As such, they lack the information and capacity to truly threaten gang territorial control. Even anti-gang operations specifically designed to "defeat" or "eradicate" gangs and "take back territory" for the state, which can include the military or other branches of the state security apparatus, seldom constitute an existential threat to these organizations. In fact, it is difficult to find many cases where the police or any other security arm of the state have effectively removed the presence of a gang organization from a territory through traditional or even highly militarized

[3] This is the modal form of police enforcement in Rio de Janeiro.

techniques while there are numerous examples of rival gangs accomplishing this. For these reasons, I argue that active enforcement represents only a transient threat to gangs.

For their part, gangs, like virtually all other criminalized groups the world over, are ambivalent about the state (see Schiavone quote earlier).[4] They never aim to exclude the state and its personnel from their territory entirely.[5] Instead, gangs prefer to avoid violent confrontations with the police both because they do not fear losing control of their territory in the same way as to a rival, but they also lack the capacity to directly confront often better armed and trained police. Moreover, direct confrontation with the police will only encourage further enforcement. As a result, gangs seldom respond to even the most aggressive police operations with violence.[6] Instead, they prefer to hide from police and attempt to evade enforcement. To do so, the gang needs residents to not inform the police as to their whereabouts and may seek resident assistance more directly. Gang members may need residents to alert them to police presence, offer them clothing to disguise themselves, or allow them to shelter in their homes or businesses during police operations. As a result, the gang is incentivized to develop more responsive and beneficial relations with residents. They do so by resolving disputes, offering financial assistance, and organizing forms of recreation.

Not every gang, however, encounters such active enforcement. Many gangs the world over face little possibility of enforcement, either due to a lack of police capacity or because enforcement has proven too difficult or even counterproductive. Other gangs avoid enforcement by developing collaborative arrangements with the police, which can include tacit or even formal agreements concerning the gang's illicit activities and may even involve ongoing bribery or corruption schemes.[7] Through either neglect or collusion, such gangs face little likelihood of enforcement and, therefore, need less support from the community. I argue that gangs experiencing absent enforcement will be less responsive to resident demands for dispute resolution, provide little financial assistance, and organize few opportunities for recreation.

Like intergang relations, enforcement can shift significantly over time as administrations and personnel turn over, new security initiatives are implemented or cast aside, or when gang–police collaboration breaks down or emerges. Gang–police relations, like competition between rivals, may also not exist solely at the polar ends of the spectrum but lie somewhere between. In

---

[4] This is not to suggest that gangs do not have a deep hatred of the police, but their primary battle is not with the state, a distinction from some other more "politically motivated" non-state armed groups.

[5] Doing so would make them more akin to a rebel group or insurgency.

[6] Although still rare, the phenomenon of OCGs directly confronting the state has become more common in recent years (Lessing 2017). I argue that most contexts in which gangs and other criminalized groups confront the state directly coincide with active competition with rivals.

[7] See Lessing (2017) and Misse (1999) for a description of these dynamics in Rio de Janeiro.

such cases, the resulting governance regime will fall between these ideal-typical categories.

So far, I have outlined a theory of criminalized governance revolving primarily around the external threats that gangs face from their rivals and the police. Although gang-level motivations and behaviors may seem to predominate, the role of residents is crucial in shaping these governance outcomes. This insight has already been baked into the theory as gangs are incentivized to: (1) use higher levels of coercion to deter residents from collaborating with a latent or active rival and (2) provide more responsive benefits to gain the silence and support of residents in avoiding active police enforcement. Building on these assertions, I argue that residents can influence criminalized governance through two strategic behaviors, *denunciations* and *demands*.

First, most residents living in gang territories have vital information regarding gang activities and their whereabouts.[8] They know where gang members live, the location of their security positions, and where they engage in illicit activities. They are familiar with the gang's schedule, the location of bocas, their hiding places, where they store guns and drugs, and when and where they are likely to engage in violence. In the hands of rivals and the police, this information can spell disaster for a gang. Rivals can use this information to invade weak points in the gang's defenses or when the gang is less vigilant or undermanned. Police can use information provided by residents to target specific gang members or strategic locations in the community. Thus, denunciations are a key mechanism shaping the type and degree of threats a gang may face.[9]

Although any individual denunciation may be motivated by a very personal and idiosyncratic grievance, I argue that denunciations largely revolve around the opportunities and incentives residents may have to denounce, which are primarily dictated by the local security environment.[10] In contexts of active

---

[8] This definition of denunciation differs from some existing work. For Kalyvas (2006), denunciation refers to civilians informing on fellow civilians and not civilians providing information about the armed group itself, which he defines as *defection*. I use the term denunciation for the latter because it is how residents and gang members in Rio de Janeiro's favelas describe this phenomenon.

[9] Denunciation is merely one of several strategies that residents have for resisting gangs. How residents resist criminalized governance has been the subject of growing scholarly interest in recent years, though the vast majority of research focuses on the most visible and collective forms (Bateson 2013; Berg and Carranza 2018; Goldstein 2004; Ley, Mattiace, and Trejo 2019; Moncada 2019a; Phillips 2017; Smith 2019; Starn 1999; Zizumbo Colunga 2015). In Rio, favela communities have largely been unable to collectively mobilize to prevent or directly influence criminalized governance (see Arias 2019 for exceptions).

[10] There is a huge range of motivations that may drive these behaviors. According to Kalyvas, relationships between civilians and armed groups are the result of "variable and complex sets of heterogeneous and interacting motivations, which are affected by preferences over outcomes, beliefs about outcomes, the behavior of others, and the networks into which people are embedded, and security considerations in an environment where chance and contingency cannot be

or latent threat from rivals, some residents will provide information to a rival despite the gang's best efforts to prevent this. In this regard, a gang that faces an active threat and uses extreme forms of coercion may find residents are even more willing to collaborate with their rival to punish them for their bad behavior especially if they are likely to be targeted either way.[11] In contexts of latent threat, although the gang will refrain from such extreme and indiscriminate forms of coercion, they still try to prevent collaboration with their rival through the use of coercion. Some residents will nonetheless find ways of providing information: they may be drug customers that want to curry favor with a rival, residents with contacts to a rival (perhaps through extended family networks or other social relations), or residents that hold a grudge against the local gang for past violations or abuses. When territorial competition is absent, however, denunciation to rivals is unlikely because there is little or no opportunity to do so.

In contexts of active enforcement, gangs also fear denunciation to police, but their response is very different. Because enforcement constitutes a transient threat, not an existential one, there is less need for the gang to respond with the same levels of violence and coercion. Moreover, unlike denunciation to rival groups, which is extremely difficult and dangerous, residents can easily and safely provide information to the police through emergency numbers or anonymous hotlines.[12] Gangs could try to deter denunciation to the police by using threats and violence but because of the often-anonymous nature of these denunciations, they would need to punish the community more indiscriminately. Such indiscriminate forms of coercion would only anger residents and likely lead to further denunciations and more enforcement. Coercion is also not going to produce the type of "spontaneous support" that gangs need if they are to evade enforcement.[13] Thus, to combat this type of threat, gangs

---

underestimated" (2006, 96–97). Although Kalyvas is describing contexts of civil war here, the insight can be equally applied to areas of criminalized governance.

[11] Arias (2006a) describes how one community organized the takeover of their own neighborhood by a rival gang to remove a paranoid and violent gang from power. Dowdney (2003) and Arias and Rodrigues (2006) describe similar efforts by residents to replace an extremely violent and coercive incumbent with a rival.

[12] In almost every city throughout the world, citizens can report crimes and violence directly to the police through emergency numbers. Many cities also now have anonymous hotlines, such as *CrimeStoppers* in the US and UK, and DD in Rio de Janeiro. It is largely due to the anonymous nature of DD that Rio's favela residents have been able to denounce gangs to the police without the fear of gang retaliation. Denouncing to rival gangs, on the other hand, is seldom anonymous, extremely dangerous, and, therefore, less common. This difference mirrors Kalyvas' assertion that anonymity determines the willingness of civilians to engage in denunciation because, otherwise, they cannot be sure that they will go unpunished (2006, 193–94).

[13] Arjona defines "spontaneous support" as "volunteering to do specific tasks that favor the armed group short of joining, without the latter having given the civilian, either explicitly or implicitly, the order to do so" (2017, 762). In this case, I am referring to residents assisting the

turn to the carrot instead of the stick. Providing benefits is the most reliable way for gangs to gain the silence and support of the community when they face active enforcement by the police. When enforcement is not forthcoming, however, gang members do not need the silence or support of the community, have little fear of denunciation, and thus are not incentivized to provide benefits in the same way.

Demands also matter to governance outcomes because gangs cannot provide benefits if residents do not ask for or accept them. Although demands do not directly influence the security environment and, thereby, governance like denunciations, I include them here because, ultimately, gang–resident relations are *"um a um"* (one-to-one), as one of my interlocutors put it. That is, criminalized governance is always constituted by face-to-face interactions. It is never bureaucratic or impersonal in the way that states or perhaps some other armed groups govern. "If one of the gang members is known to be unlikable or treats people poorly then everyone will stop going to that person for favors or help. …At the end of the day, it falls to the community how the gang is going to treat them," Fausto concluded.[14] In this way, criminalized governance should be considered a joint production rather than a set of practices that gangs impose on the community.[15] The various governance outcomes are the result of repeated and strategic interactions between gang members and residents within specific security environments.

For instance, the gang does not suddenly decide to provide benefits and the community automatically accepts. Some residents will categorically refuse to accept any goods or services from gangs. That said, favelas are communities of precarity. At some point in their lives, many residents will lack access to affordable or safe housing, enough food to feed their family, or mechanisms for dispute resolution. While not every resident will seek out the gang in such circumstances, many do, especially when the gang is responsive to them, (i.e., when the gang and its members find themselves being pursued and investigated by the police and are actively seeking the support of the community). Gang members will tell residents to come talk to them if they have problems, offer welfare to residents if they hear about their hardship, and make sure that residents are pleased with the benefits they provide. Through word of mouth and the tight social networks that permeate these neighborhoods, residents come to understand that gang members are willing to help. If the gang solves

gang in more direct ways: providing information, allowing them to use their homes or businesses to hide during police operations, and so forth.

[14] Fausto 7/30/2018.

[15] Such an analytical framework borrows heavily from Kalyvas (2006) in his theory of violence in civil war but also builds on existing work by Venkatesh (1997) and Sánchez-Jankowski (1991), who both argue that gangs are thoroughly integrated within the local and larger community, and that this "integration" must be continually reconstituted through social interactions. In the end, the "gang and those actors with whom it interacts mutually determine each other's status and identity in local community social organization" (Venkatesh 1997, 87).

these problems or provides meaningful assistance, other residents will hear about it and be more likely to seek out gang members as well. If gangs do not provide these much-needed goods and services even when police are pursuing them, residents can punish them through denunciation. When enforcement is absent, however, gangs are not incentivized to provide benefits in the same way. Through the same dense social networks, residents will know that the gang is unwilling to provide benefits and are, therefore, unlikely to demand them. And when enforcement is not forthcoming, residents have little leverage over gang behavior.

In the rest of this chapter, I describe how the shifting security environment in CVNH's territory shaped the behavior of gang members and residents during my fieldwork. I first address each threat as distinct and separate phenomena before theorizing how they interact within each of the governance regimes. The later section relaxes some of the assumptions embedded within this framework by addressing three additional factors that may impact criminalized governance: the drug trade and other illicit markets, the state (other than the police), and the specific characteristics of favela communities.

RIVAL THREAT AND COERCION

I awoke several hours later. It was already dark and I was ravenous. After the incredible violence I had witnessed that day, I was unsure if any restaurants would be open but decided to look anyway. To my surprise, Main Street had seemingly returned to normal. The bocas were up and running, cars and motorcycles filled the street, most of the shops and restaurants were full, and residents were busily going about their evening. I spotted Severino standing at his intersection. I could immediately tell he was not in the mood to chat but he smiled nonetheless and we exchanged greetings. Not wanting to disturb him, I said I was looking for food. He suggested the pizza restaurant down the street. Before I walked away, he grabbed my arm and said, *"Tem cuidado, cara, e evita a divisa"* (Be careful, man, and avoid the border). In all of our conversations and exchanges, he had never said anything so direct and serious to me. At the time, I thought he was simply referring to the possibility of more shootouts. I nodded and thanked him. My mind was already on pizza.

I took a seat at one of the plastic tables outside the pizza place and the server came over and took my order. I turned my attention to the street. After a few minutes, I recognized a couple of university students walking in my direction. I waved and they came over. I immediately noticed they both looked a little peaked. They explained that they had just returned from teaching *prevestibular* (the equivalent of a General Education Development course in the US) at one of the NGOs in TCP's territory and had been stopped by a CVNH gang member coming back across the border. He had pointed his rifle in their faces and shouted at them. He demanded to know why they were crossing over. They told him about the classes and explained that they were both from Nova

Holanda. He had eventually let them pass but they were visibly shaken by the encounter.[16] This was the first time I had heard of the gang directly threatening residents along the border since I had been living in Maré. Although such threats were said to be common in the distant past, residents and gang members alike told me they were no longer used.

The temporal connection between the invasion attempt, Severino's warning, and this more coercive approach to controlling their territory was noticeable. Over the ensuing days and weeks, tensions remained high. The activation of the rival threat, although brief, changed CVNH's approach to governance. Most obviously, the gang shifted even more of its attention and resources to defending the border. The security checkpoints and bocas in that area became heavily militarized. Instead of just a couple of gang members, larger groups of adolescents and young men manned these stations around the clock. Marcos, a nineteen-year-old gang member, was assigned to the night shift at one of these checkpoints and was responsible, along with several colleagues, for closely monitoring the border from 6 pm to 6 am. According to Marcos, there were at least twenty-five soldados monitoring the border at any given time, and the Dono and his gerentes were holding regular meetings in which they discussed their available armaments, and stressed "*vigiando*" (keeping watch) for the TCP gang.[17]

In addition to looking for any signs of an impending invasion by their rival, CVNH feared infiltration of their territory by TCP informants and the possible collaboration of residents with their enemy. They began to monitor resident movement across the border more closely. Gang members stopped, questioned, and sometimes threatened residents crossing over. Bernardo, a resident in his twenties, recalled being stopped by several CVNH gang members that wanted to check his afro for a camera. They told him they were concerned he was spying for their rival. He was only allowed to pass when one of the gang members recognized him as being from the area.[18] Breno also recounted how a CVNH member had pointed his rifle at the car he was driving and ordered him to get out. He said he did not know why the gang member was suspicious of him but the young man didn't stop pointing the gun at him until he explained that he was from the neighborhood and was on his way home.[19] David, a manual laborer, recalled gang members grabbing him by his backpack, pointing a pistol in his face, and bringing him to a boca, where he was interrogated by a gerente.[20] Upon being asked what he was doing in the community, he said he had grown up in Maré and told them where he lived. They only let him go

---

[16] Field notes 10/16/2013.
[17] Marcos 11/3/2014.
[18] Bernardo 1/16/2017.
[19] Breno 3/26/2014.
[20] David 1/2/2017.

when someone waiting in line to buy drugs vouched for him. As David walked away, he heard the gerente instruct his men, "Don't let anyone in!"

In all the time I lived in Maré, I was only stopped and questioned by gang members once. It was in February 2014, several months after the invasion attempt I witnessed and shortly after another subsequent shootout between the gangs. It was my custom to jog in the evenings after the heat of the day had subsided. I ran in an area called the *ciclovia* (cycle path), a short, mostly dirt trail that surrounded a couple of football (soccer) fields next to the Linha Vermelha highway (see Figure 3.1). The area was heavily used by walkers and joggers in the mornings and by football teams on the weekend. The ciclovia also straddled the border between the CVNH and TCP territories though gang members were seldom present in the area because there were no buildings or places to hide. It was too vulnerable an area for them to spend much time.

One night as I jogged, two young men called out to me and waved me over. I had not even noticed their presence because there were only a couple of lights along the path leaving much of the rest of the area in near total darkness. As I approached, they stepped out of the shadows. Both were holding semiautomatic rifles. I immediately became very nervous because there was no one around. Although I did not recognize them, I knew they were CVNH. TCP members would never come this far into the CVNH area and behave so casually. By my estimation, one of the men was in his early twenties, the other in his late teens. I was a full head taller than both of them. The older one asked, "*Com tudo respeito, não te reconheço. Por quê está aqui?*" (With all due respect, I don't recognize you. Why are you here?). I explained that I was conducting research in Maré and working with some of the local NGOs. I told them where I lived, using the older name of the street that only longtime residents would be familiar with. They looked at each other. "*Lembro dele, sim*" (Yeah, I remember him), the younger one mumbled. "Okay," the older one said and he waved me on.[21]

These sorts of incidents are not uncommon when gangs feel threatened by a rival. If a resident does not have a good enough answer to their questions, they might interrogate them further and, depending on their answers, refuse them entry, threaten them, or even use violence against them. If their rival had still been actively trying to take over their territory, the two gang members that stopped me may not have even asked questions. Gang members have been known to preemptively shoot at cars or people they find particularly suspicious.[22] I asked Severino why the gang was so concerned with residents who were crossing over. "Some people who go back and forth [across the border] will tell us how the other side is preparing for an invasion or when they are

---

[21] Field notes 2/4/2014.
[22] For this reason, it is a norm in every favela in the city to roll the windows down and turn on the interior lights so that gang members do not become suspicious.

weak. They tell us what the other side is doing so they must do the same for them," he said.[23]

When gangs face the possibility of such invasions, they try to reduce the number of people who might provide information to their enemy. Preventing movement between these neighborhoods is one of the best ways to accomplish this. Although the gang cannot be sure who might collaborate with their enemy, they mostly focused their surveillance efforts on young men of trafficking age and any other individuals they suspect might have interactions with rival gang members. For this reason, most youth who grow up in these neighborhoods seldom cross over gang boundaries.[24] Many other residents also stopped crossing the border entirely following the brief activation of the rivalry between the two gangs. Those that continued to cross tried to do so during the day or with female relatives.[25] On several occasions, when I was crossing the border with groups of other men, we decided to break into pairs and cross separately to not arouse suspicion. At night, when I attended music shows or went to meet friends or colleagues in the TCP territory, we walked all the way to Avenida Brasil and around the border – lengthening the trip from several minutes to half an hour – to avoid the possibility of a threatening or violent encounter. According to several of my informants, young men with darker skin, certain kinds of haircuts, or anyone wearing particular kinds of clothes or colors associated with the gangs (naturally, red is the color associated with CV, the Red Command) were also more likely to be stopped.[26] One colleague categorically refused to cross the border because he had been stopped and harassed by gang members so many times in his life.[27]

Following the activation of competition, I also observed more gang members visible in CVNH's territory, many of whom were not native to the area. CVNH was receiving reinforcements from several other CV gangs around the city. The number of gang members eventually swelled to an estimated 250, almost double the gang's normal size.[28] By early 2014, heavily armed gang members could be observed ostentatiously displaying their weaponry along all the major streets of the CVNH territory. The presence of so many foreign gang members added to the more coercive profile of the gang. Foreign members

---

[23] Severino 7/4/2018.
[24] Numerous residents said that they had never crossed over a gang border. One local NGO project, *Maré Sem Fronteiras* (Maré without Borders), even organized bike rides across gang territories to show local youth that their own neighborhoods were not that different from the ones on the other side of the border.
[25] Women have far fewer concerns with gang members stopping them along the border, "unless they look like a trafficker's girlfriend," Julia said (7/24/2015).
[26] This resembles contexts of civil war where armed groups rely on "collective targeting" or profiling of populations to estimate the probability that someone will collaborate with their enemy (Balcells 2017; Steele 2017).
[27] Field notes 7/7/2013.
[28] Severino 5/15/2014; Bruno 10/27/2014.

often have low information about the community, maintain weak connections to residents, and experience higher levels of insecurity as a result. Therefore, they are more likely to engage in violent or threatening behavior.[29]

Numerous residents related stories of abuse and threats that were not common before their arrival. For instance, at one community meeting in early 2014, residents complained that nonnative gang members were shooting off their weapons for no reason or just to frighten residents.[30] In another incident, a gang member intimidated a couple of adolescent girls by verbally insulting them, lifting his shirt, and showing them the pistol that was tucked into his shorts.[31] Even CVNH's own gang members recognized how problematic this behavior was. Bruno, a longtime CVNH member, said nonnative gang members were *"bagunçando a comunidade"* (messing up the community) by not respecting and mistreating local residents.[32] When I asked Severino about these incidents, he told me they were true. He said they were occurring regularly, at least once a week in his estimation. "The Dono was asked to resolve a couple of these problems but there was nothing to be done. He can't discipline a gang member from another community unless he wants to start a conflict within the faction," he said.[33] Some CVNH members were even critical of their own Dono for allowing so many foreigners into their community and causing so many problems.[34] "If I were the Dono, I wouldn't let any foreign members in my territory," Everton told me emphatically.

Gang members and residents also described how the normal rules do not apply during periods of active competition. One example illustrates this dynamic well. As part of the existing social contract between the CVNH gang and residents, members are not supposed to enter or use a resident's property without their permission.[35] Naldo, who lived close to the border, recalled that he had denied a gang member the use of his roof to watch for a rival gang invasion following the activation of competition.[36] The gang member ignored Naldo's refusal and used the roof anyway. Subsequently, Naldo built a wall to prevent such easy access. He confessed that he was afraid of what would happen if that gang member found out he could no longer get to the roof during a shootout. "He may want to punish me," he said. Under less conflictual circumstances, this would be well within the rights of the resident, but may

---

[29] A similar argument concerning nonlocal militia members is made by Daly (2016) and Carey and Mitchell (2017, 135–37), while also supporting Olson's (1993) distinction between the treatment of a population by a stationary versus roving bandit.
[30] Meeting #8.
[31] Eduardo 2/11/2014.
[32] Bruno 10/27/2014.
[33] Severino 5/15/2014.
[34] Márcio 4/17/2014; Everton 4/17/2014.
[35] This rule exists for most gangs in Rio and distinguishes them from the police, who seldom ask for permission before entering favela homes, even though they are required to by law.
[36] Naldo 12/17/2014.

lead to violence when rival threat is active and the possibility of invasion is high. Eduarda described the dynamics of intergang violence in this way: "The violence between the gangs… doesn't just stay between groups, it overflows. I've seen a resident beaten because he didn't let a gang member use his rooftop when he needed it. The violence against the resident grows a lot when the gangs are fighting."[37]

For gang members, the use of such violence is viewed as necessary. When they face an enemy intent on killing them and taking their territory, they demand higher levels of obedience. They cannot be concerned about resident welfare in such circumstances.

To conclude, the invasion attempt by TCP reminded CVNH of the possibility of losing its territorial control. If the TCP invasion had succeeded, all CVNH members would have either been killed or forced into exile, scattered throughout the city, and left to fend for themselves. TCP would have further consolidated their control over the territory by finding, expelling, or killing any known associates or family members of the gang. Every CVNH member understood the existential nature of this threat. Severino put it this way: "We will defend our territory at all costs. We have to. Our lives, our family, our houses, everything depends on us staying here. We have to stay. If we run, our families will be expelled. …With a rival, we can lose everything."[38] Although the activation of the rival threat I witnessed was brief and neither residents nor gang members considered it a period of *guerra* (war), skirmishes and shots along the border in the subsequent weeks and months kept tensions high. CVNH implemented a set of coercive practices throughout their territory as described earlier. While coercion is, by its nature, a shortsighted strategy, the gang had limited options in this respect. Providing more responsive benefits would not have prevented TCP from invading again and trying to take over their turf. In the face of such an existential threat, CVNH needed to prevent infiltration and collaboration with their enemy at all costs. Ramping up coercion was the most reliable and expedient way to achieve this.

ENFORCEMENT AND THE PROVISION OF BENEFITS

I had originally planned to move to Maré on the morning of June 25th, 2013. A truck was supposed to pick me up in the Zona Sul (Southern Zone) favela in which I was living and take me and all of my belongings – a bed frame and mattress, a small table and lamp, a couple of boxes with kitchen supplies and toiletries, and several suitcases full of clothes – across the city to Nova Holanda. As I waited for the truck, I received a call from one of my local contacts who informed me that a massive police operation was happening and my move would have to

---

[37] Eduarda 9/19/2013.
[38] Severino 7/4/2018.

wait.[39] The previous afternoon, a public protest that began in Bonsucesso, a working-class neighborhood just on the other side of Avenida Brasil from Maré, culminated with protestors shutting down several lanes of rush hour traffic. This particular protest was relatively small, with just a few hundred activists and local residents decrying the increase in bus fares, corruption, and police violence.[40] Although the protest itself was a peaceful one, according to police, several youth took the opportunity to rob motorists in the stopped traffic.

A small group of nearby BOPE, an elite counter-gang police unit akin to SWAT in the US, were alerted and pursued the fleeing youth into Nova Holanda.[41] Upon entering the favela, gang olheiros and soldados were likely surprised to see BOPE invading their territory on foot (an almost unheard of occurrence) without the militarized vehicles and helicopters that would normally accompany them. A brief shootout ensued in which the sergeant in command of the unit was shot in the head and instantly killed. BOPE police retreated and quickly called for reinforcements. Over the course of the next twenty-four hours, two dozen militarized vehicles and more than 140 BOPE police scoured Nova Holanda and Parque União for CV gang members.[42] They knocked out power to the area, invaded homes, shouted threats from the streets, and eventually killed eight adolescents and young men allegedly involved with the gang.[43] Their bodies were mostly found in apartments, some with multiple gunshot wounds. It is unclear whether they had tried to defend themselves or surrendered and were summarily executed.[44]

This was, by far, the most violent operation in the history of Maré and perfectly encapsulates the logic that Rio's public security apparatus has used to combat gang organizations for the last several decades. If gangs choose to confront them, and especially if any police are killed or wounded, they respond by

---

[39] The description of these events have been compiled from a large number of interviews with residents, gang members, and two Homicide Division detectives.

[40] Such protests were commonplace in June 2013. Hundreds of large and small protests against rising transportation costs, corruption, and the vast amounts of public money being spent on preparations for the World Cup were occurring across much of Brazil (Alonso and Mische 2017; Barnes 2013).

[41] According to police, several shots were also fired in the direction of Avenida Brasil which precipitated the initial invasion (Meeting #40).

[42] Delegado I 1/12/2015; Delegado II 1/12/2015.

[43] A ninth victim, a waiter working in local restaurant, was killed by a stray bullet fired from inside one of the police vehicles (*Extra* 11/9/2013).

[44] Even if these individuals had been summarily executed, they were categorized as "resisting arrest killings" (*autos de resistência*). Such police killings are only rarely investigated. In fact, it is almost impossible for police to be prosecuted for killing someone suspected of being a "criminal" (Misse et al. 2011, 120–30). The Homicide Division of Rio's Civil Police did not even consider police killings to be homicides until recent years (p. 83). From 2001 to 2011, police accounted for roughly 22,000 killings in Rio de Janeiro, roughly half the total (p. 37). The documentation of police killings in Rio is extensive (Acebes 2016; Andreoni and Londoño 2020; Delgado 2009).

dramatically escalating.[45] It is a strategy intended to instill fear in the hearts of gang members and deter them from confrontation. And yet, even these incredibly aggressive and deadly operations constitute a very different type of threat to gangs. No matter how many militarized vehicles, helicopters, and police the state brings to bear, it is incapable of truly threatening a gang presence within a territory. Police will not embed themselves in favela territories permanently (by living and developing social relations there) nor do they intend to take over illicit markets for themselves. Police may kill or arrest numerous gang members but they do not constitute an existential threat like a rival.[46] The threat from police is only a transient one. Therefore, I argue, gangs do not require the same violent and coercive response. Instead, aggressive enforcement by the police incentivizes gangs to develop more responsive and beneficial relationships with local communities because they need their support to evade such enforcement efforts.

By the time I moved to Maré, several days after the *chacina* (massacre), as many residents came to refer to it, Nova Holanda and the rest of Maré had been subject to hundreds of BOPE operations over the preceding years. In fact, in August 2011, BOPE had moved its headquarters to the defunct 24th Armored Infantry Battalion military base on the edge of Maré (see Figure 1.1). The two CV-controlled areas of Maré were a particular focus of BOPE operations because combatting and weakening CV was at the core of the city's once-heralded UPPs.[47] Begun in 2008, the UPPs were a public security initiative, designed "to break the paradigm of territories that are controlled by traffickers with weapons of war," according to then-Public Security Secretary Mariano Beltrame.[48] Because of its location near the international airport and at the confluence of the city's three busiest highways (Avenida Brasil, Linha Amarela, and Linha Vermelha), Maré was an essential component of the project. It was so important that when it was finally "pacified" in April 2014, just two months before the kickoff to that year's World Cup, it was in the form of a military occupation by 2,500 Marine and Army soldiers (see Chapter 8). The Brazilian military would occupy Maré for fifteen months but it was BOPE that was tasked with combatting Maré's gangs in the years leading up to it.

In the nine months I lived in Nova Holanda prior to the arrival of the military, BOPE operations were a regular part of life. According to my field notes, I witnessed a BOPE operation at least once a week over this period. Most lasted just

---

[45] In May 2021, the most violent police operation in the history of Brazil followed a similar pattern. After the killing of a police officer in the Zona Norte favela of Jacarezinho, elite counter-gang units proceeded to kill twenty-four residents, almost all of whom were young men and adolescents suspected of gang involvement (*O Globo* 5/6/2021).

[46] Nearly every gang member I interviewed described this difference. Some even noted that the police could kill more gang members but they weren't as much of a concern. "They don't stress you out as much," Lucas said (9/20/2013).

[47] Of the roughly 250 favelas to eventually receive a UPP, only a handful were not controlled by CV.

[48] *The Guardian* 4/12/2010.

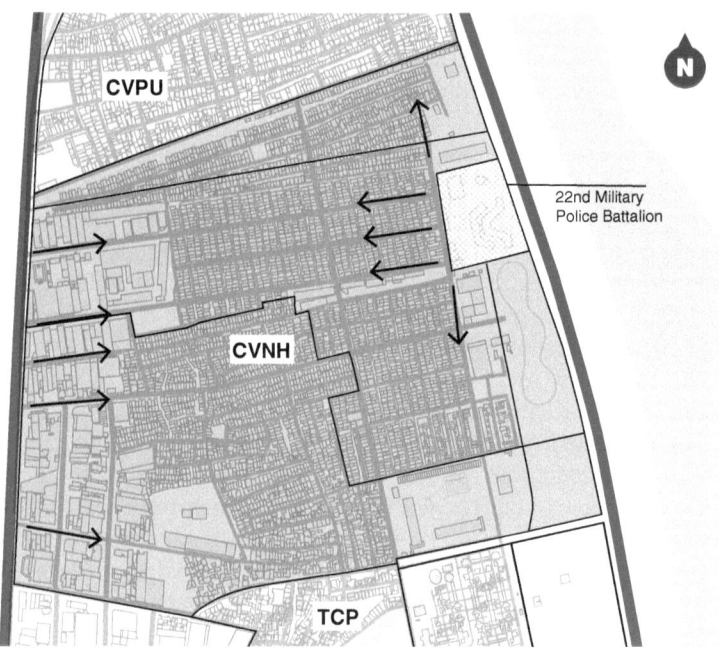

FIGURE 3.5 Map of police operations in CVNH territory
Visualization by Bruna Montuori.

an hour or two and involved little or no violence though a couple, like the operation described earlier, turned more violent. BOPE always invaded Nova Holanda
in one of two ways: either directly from the 22nd Military Police Battalion along
Linha Vermelha or from one of several streets along Avenida Brasil (see Figure
3.5). When BOPE operations began, gang olheiros, stationed at all the entrances
to CVNH's territory, would shoot off firecrackers to signal an impending police
operation.[49] Upon hearing the firecrackers, gang members and residents alike
would quickly find places to hide. Nova Holanda's streets, normally bustling with
activity, would become almost entirely vacant for the duration of these operations.
    BOPE operations always involved one or more enormous, armored trucks
called *caveirões* (big skulls, literally), designed to withstand gunfire from assault
rifles as well as high-powered explosives (see Figure 3.6). These vehicles often
include a 360° gun turret, multiple firing ports, and can transport as many as
a dozen police in and out of favelas. Joining the caveirões were helicopters that
flew low over the community to prevent gang members from using the rooftops
as escape routes or as locations from which to fire on the police below. The sight
and sound of the caveirões' diesel engines rumbling on the streets combined with
the deafening sound of the helicopters overhead created the sensation of being

---

[49] This is an old technology that has been replaced by radios and cell phones by some gangs but
    the local CVNH gang still used firecrackers as of the end of my fieldwork in 2015.

FIGURE 3.6 Photograph of caveirão
Photograph by Douglas Lopes.

under siege. Most BOPE operations occurred in the early mornings. If they were in my area of Nova Holanda, it was impossible to sleep. For the first few months, I lived in Maré, I would make a cup of coffee and watch the helicopters circle low over the community from my rooftop patio during BOPE's dawn operations (see Figure 3.7). Then, one morning, my neighbor across the street saw me and yelled, "*Eles atiram!*" (They shoot!), pointing at the helicopter, and holding her hands out like she was holding a rifle. She later explained that police had been known to shoot and kill innocent bystanders, not just gang members. I stopped watching the helicopters from my patio after that.

On the streets of Nova Holanda, the caveirões were restricted to the main thoroughfares because the neighborhood's numerous alleys and side streets are not wide enough for the massive vehicles to maneuver. BOPE police would often exit their vehicles to pursue gang members or carry out searches in these areas. BOPE typically wear all-black tactical uniforms and *touca ninja* (balaclava) to cover their faces.[50] Many of them do not even have their names or badges showing on their uniforms. One of the only visible markers of BOPE police is their insignia – *faca na caveira* (knife in the skull) – embroidered on their sleeves and emblazoned

---

[50] Some of these masks have skulls printed onto them, making BOPE's presence even more ominous. Public Security Secretary Mariano Beltrame officially legalized their use in 2015 (*O Globo* 8/25/2015).

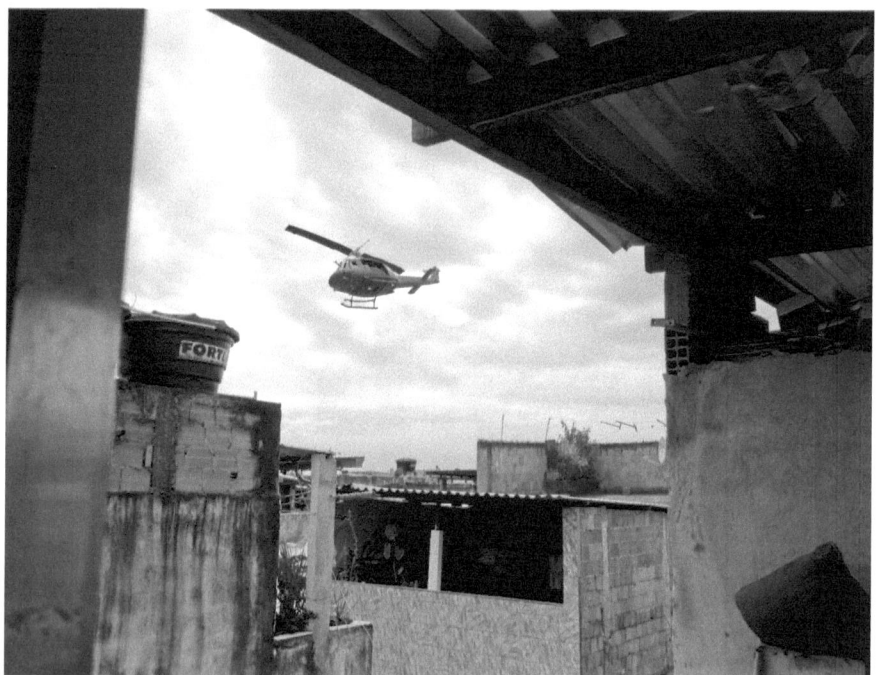

FIGURE 3.7 Photograph of helicopter from author's residence
Photograph by author.

on the sides of all their vehicles. BOPE police are well-trained in urban counterinsurgency tactics. Their movements are highly coordinated, and they seldom
make much noise as they move through the streets on foot. On several occasions,
I watched them use hand signals to navigate around corners, through alleyways,
and in difficult urban spaces. BOPE operations would occasionally yield tangible
results – the seizure of drugs or weapons or the arrest or death of a gang member – but most occurred without incident and were short-lived.

Even if CVNH gang members had wanted to confront BOPE, they were
little match for the elite police unit. Despite their significant armaments and
manpower, gang members are largely untrained, and the gang had no defense
against the caveirões. Gang members also understood that confrontations with
BOPE would only increase the severity of operations and the likelihood of
enforcement against them.[51] According to Inácio, one of the gang's managers,
"They [BOPE] don't scare us ... but we don't want confrontations. That's the

---

[51] This is not just a Rio phenomenon. The clear majority of gangs and other OCGs the world
over have chosen not to respond to even the most aggressive state enforcement efforts with
direct violence. In Mexico, for instance, just a small percentage of the hundreds of thousands of
homicides committed since 2006 are the result of direct confrontations between the state forces
and cartels (Heinle, Molzah, and Shirk 2015). More often, Mexican cartels will seek to hide
or limit their use of violence to avoid further enforcement (Durán-Martínez 2018; Rios 2013).

Dono's call. He doesn't want confrontations with them when they come in because it'll only make things worse."[52] Moreover, gang members knew that BOPE was never going to take their territory permanently and that their presence would always be brief. Therefore, instead of running to defend their territory, like they would for a rival, the gang melted into the population during BOPE operations. Gang members quickly found places to hide, often in the homes and businesses of family, friends, girlfriends, or other residents, and waited for the operation to conclude. CVNH members often placed several steel I-beams in deep holes at the various entrances to the neighborhood, which forced BOPE police to exit the caveirão and remove them before resuming the operation. This simple tactic gave gang members valuable seconds to find sufficient hiding places. While BOPE was in the area, residents and gang members stayed off the streets but within minutes of the operation concluding, gang members would reemerge and resume their activities.

Despite not being an existential threat to the gang, if members were to avoid arrest and possibly death at the hands of police and limit the confiscation of guns and drugs, they required the help of residents. In interviews with current and former members, they described how they had sometimes needed residents to hide them, their weapons, or drugs during an operation, to warn them of police in the vicinity, to use their house to escape, or to give them different clothes (often a school or work uniform) so they could disguise themselves. According to Francisco, "We bought things for them so they would help us. We bought gas or medicine or food and they would hide us or give us clothes."[53] Beyond these spontaneous forms of support, gang members also wanted residents to not denounce them to the authorities. Since the mid-1990s, favela residents have been easily able to provide information to the police through DD, the anonymous hotline. First created to stop a spate of kidnappings, DD quickly expanded to include every type of crime and, since then, has received more than 2.5 million denunciations from across the city, the majority of which concern gang activities and whereabouts. Information provided to the hotline is regularly used by BOPE and other police units to carry out operations and investigations in gang territories.

Nearly every gang member I interviewed was concerned about denunciations to the police. For instance, Fulton reminded me several times throughout our interview – even making sure I wrote it down in my notebook – that gang members must "*usar inteligência*" (be smart) and treat residents with respect to avoid arrest or possible death because "one resident talks to

---

Even Rio's CV, renowned for its supposed willingness to confront police, seldom actually does so and, if possible, prefers to avoid direct encounters with police.
[52] Inácio 4/24/2014.
[53] Francisco 7/17/2013.

another, talks to two, to three, and so on."[54] Others told me that they must be responsive to residents when they ask for help or they can become angry and denounce them.[55] Luiza, a former *avião* (messenger) for the CVNH gang, said, "I was always afraid someone would denounce me. We were all afraid of being denounced."[56] I asked her if there was any way to avoid denunciation. "Don't mistreat residents," she said immediately then thought for a moment. "And sometimes the boys ride around in a van and hand out food baskets to people. They give out hundreds each month."[57] Another former gang member, Natan, told me, "You gotta treat the community well. You could be the baddest dude in the world, but you'll live a short life if you don't have the community on your side."[58]

Gang members also described when and why residents might denounce. "Sometimes, there's nothing to be done. Like when they punish a kid for stealing. The mother or father of the kid won't stand for it," Luiza said.[59] Bruno reiterated this point. "Imagine you have a son or a cousin and he makes a mistake and the gang punishes him. You will never accept it. Now let's say you live close to a *boca*. You will wait until the moment when you can get revenge."[60] Natan described the same dynamic with regard to the timing of denunciations. "It's just logical. If you mistreat someone and that person knows what you're doing, the first opportunity they have they're gonna betray you. They'll denounce you when there's an operation. They may even silently cheer when you get arrested."[61]

The importance of denunciations was further brought home to me in mid-November 2013, when I ran into Flávio, CVNH's *gerente de crack* and Severino's boss, at a popular restaurant around lunchtime. We had already spoken several times before and he was familiar with my research project. He asked if I wanted to join him for lunch and I readily agreed. We sat down at one of several outdoor tables. A few minutes later, a couple of men on motorcycles pulled up next to our table. One of the men with an AK-47 strapped to his back hopped off his bike and looked me over before whispering something into Flávio's ear. The two of them spoke in hushed tones for several minutes. After the men had sped away on their bikes, Flávio turned back to his meal. I asked him if everything was okay. He said that there had been a large police operation the day before and that a couple dozen CVNH members had been

---

[54] Fulton 7/3/2014.
[55] Inácio 3/26/2014; Severino 10/16/2013; Bruno 10/27/2014.
[56] Luiza 10/2/2014.
[57] Venkatesh also argues that familial connections and social networks serve to shield gang members from denunciation (1997, 95).
[58] Natan 8/22/2013.
[59] Luiza 10/2/2014.
[60] Bruno 10/27/2014.
[61] Natan 8/22/2013. According to Zaluar, before Rio's gangs became militarized, gang members that mistreated residents were likely to end up lynched by the local population (1985, 148).

arrested.[62] It was one of the most successful operations he could remember. "They used information from months of denunciations," he said.[63]

Due to the anonymous nature of these denunciations, however, the gang had a very difficult time knowing who was responsible for providing the information. Especially since the advent of the cell phone, nearly anyone can easily make a call to DD, which neither asks nor records any information about the caller.[64] Although some gangs have been known to force all favela shops to close for short periods following the death of a gang member at the hands of police (Lessing 2017; Penglase 2008), they mostly refrain from more indiscriminate forms of coercion against favela communities in response to police enforcement. They understand that the support and silence of the community would quickly erode if they punished residents indiscriminately.[65] Therefore, in contexts of frequent enforcement, I argue that gangs will attempt to develop more reciprocal and beneficial relations with residents. They will provide more responsive dispute resolution services, offer greater access to welfare and informal economies, and organize more forms of recreation. I observed many of these behaviors in the local CVNH gang in the nine months before the military occupied the area in April 2014.

First, CVNH was highly responsive to community demands for dispute resolution. They dealt with numerous resident issues and were willing to intimately involve themselves in their personal lives. Nearly all the CVNH members I interviewed reported that they frequently resolved domestic disputes and small conflicts that arose between families, lovers, neighbors, and friends. Some suggested that they dealt with several such cases each week while others said that they addressed as many as fifty.[66] They also nearly unanimously told me that they must try to resolve these disputes amicably if they wanted to avoid some residents becoming angry with the result.[67] Given the complicated and deeply personal nature of many of these conflicts, resolving disputes is no easy task. Nonetheless, CVNH members were clearly interested in resolving them in a mutually agreeable way and to avoid angering either of the parties, if possible. Inácio described it in this way: "Residents get mad if we don't solve their problems and we want everyone to be happy with

---

[62] And yet, the number of gang members in the CVNH area continued to increase over the ensuing weeks and months due to the influx of foreign members. Perhaps the CVNH gang leader allowed so many foreign CV members into his territory to bolster his own gang, which had, over time, been weakened by constant police operations.

[63] Flávio 11/14/2013.

[64] The DD number is plastered on almost every city bus and in many public places throughout the city. Most people living in Rio know the number by heart: 2253–1177.

[65] This is reminiscent of Kalyvas' (2006) assertion that indiscriminate forms of violence against civilians in civil war are counterproductive because they lead to the loss of civilian support and defection.

[66] Marcos 11/3/2014; Severino 10/2/2013; Everton 4/17/2014.

[67] Inácio 3/26/2014; Severino 10/16/2013; Bruno 10/27/2014.

the solution."[68] Such a responsive form of order was founded on the under-standing that the gang needed the residents and that their relationship was reciprocal. Bruno summed it up like this: "Everything is a conversation. You have to go and listen to both sides of the story. We help them because they help us. They give us food and water while we're working or help us when a police operation is coming."[69]

Some gang members even reported that they received complaints concerning the behavior of the gang itself. Many of these grievances were about nonnative members (see earlier) but others concerned *cria*, members who were born and raised in Nova Holanda. Reinaldo, for instance, told me that a woman had recently accused a CVNH member of sexually assaulting her daughter.[70] The Dono eventually sided with the woman and punished the accused gang member because he was concerned about what the community might think, Reinaldo reported. When police attention and enforcement is active, these decisions take on added significance because both gang members and residents know that the outcome can determine whether this resident and possibly others are willing to stay silent. Without active enforcement by the police and the presence of an implicit threat of denunciation, a gang will likely be less concerned how residents feel about them. Moreover, residents may think twice about demanding justice or going to the gang to resolve disputes if they fear the gang is unlikely to be responsive.

CVNH also provided significant welfare and economic stimulation to residents in their territory. In dozens of interviews, gang members frequently spoke of welfare as a major component of the gang's governance strategy. Severino said that the gang continued to provide some 200 families with a monthly food basket through local shops that sold these baskets and also paid for gas cannisters and medicine for the neediest residents.[71] The Dono also autho-rized numerous residents to use the sidewalks and various areas of the com-munity to put up barracas to sell various informal and unregulated goods and products.[72] In fact, Nova Holanda was chock-full of these informal vendors. Barracas crowded most of the major streets to the point that cars, motorcycles, and pedestrians were forced to share increasingly narrow streets. "Teixeira Ribeiro [Nova Holanda's largest thoroughfare] has become an alley again!" Severino chuckled.

While some forms of economic stimulation and welfare were only provided by the Dono or other senior members of the organization, many rank and file also provided financial assistance, which they referred to as the *custo de ajuda* (cost of help) or just *favores* (favors). They understood such activities as essential

[68] Inácio 3/26/2014.
[69] Bruno 10/27/2014.
[70] Reinaldo 10/28/2013.
[71] Severino 10/2/2013.
[72] Inácio 3/26/2014.

to avoid denunciation and possible police enforcement. For example, during one of our conversations on his corner, a middle-aged woman approached Severino to ask him if he could spare some cash for her kids. He handed her a R$50 note ($20, at the time). While this assistance may not seem like much, for the poorest residents it can be the difference between their children eating or going hungry. Thus, it is an important way that many gang members keep on good terms with the community. When I asked him about this, Severino said residents know he is a member of the gang and, therefore, how he responds to such requests may matter in important ways for his future.[73]

In addition to economic stimulation, CVNH also created numerous opportunities for recreation and leisure. First, CVNH continued to throw massive baile funk parties even as BOPE operations and police enforcement became more intense in the months leading up to the arrival of the military. Each Saturday night, the gang would close off a long stretch of Teixeira Ribeiro Street, the commercial hub of Nova Holanda, by parking two "borrowed" city buses at each end of the street. This was done to ensure that police vehicles would not be able to pass.[74] The gang then hired an event production company to build huge walls of speakers at three points along the street and booked popular DJs to perform. The gang set up a long line of tents for dozens of vendors, who made significant income selling food and alcoholic beverages to the partygoers each week.

While the bailes provided CVNH an opportunity to sell even more drugs, they were also an important way to bolster its popularity, especially among local youth.[75] I attended dozens of bailes during my time in the field. At that time, the Nova Holanda baile was considered one of the best and most popular in the city. They were a sonic and visual spectacle with several thousand tightly packed youth (mostly in their teens and twenties) moving to the *batidão* (heavy beat). The deep bass track could be heard from most parts of the Nova Holanda territory but within the enclosed baile area, the sound was deafening. I could feel the vibrations from the speakers inside my chest, like someone was rattling my internal organs. If I was near one of the walls of speakers, all the hairs on my body would stand on end. For many of the *funkeiros* (regular attendees), the experience must be transcendent. Nowhere else can they escape the oftentimes difficult reality of their lives by engaging in such unbridled fun and collective effervescence that accompanies these parties. Most partygoers will know all the explicit and highly provocative lyrics by heart and participate in the sexually suggestive and intricately choreographed dance routines. Many youth will meet and form close friendships and romantic partners at these parties. The gang is

---

[73] Field notes 10/21/2013.
[74] Police seldom engage in operations during these parties because of the chaos, violence, and casualties that would inevitably result. Many gangs also pay bribes so that these parties remain undisturbed.
[75] See Chapter 5 for an estimate of these revenues.

seen as the host and providers of this experience. In this way, the bailes helped shape the image of the CVNH gang as a benevolent force within the community. CVNH members also attended these parties though they did not seem to enjoy the scene as much as the rest of the attendees. The gang generally had a VIP tent or designated area with food and drink just for them and their guests. I seldom observed the more senior members of the gang at these bailes though perhaps they were keeping a lower profile and I just did not see them. Most of the gang members I did observe appeared more serious and professional, often carrying or handling their weapons, or being involved in the sale of drugs. According to Fausto, "The baile is not a place for them to enjoy themselves but more of a place to present themselves to the community."[76] That said, these parties are good opportunities for gang members to expand their social networks as there are many youth and women trying to get to know them.[77] Bailes are serious business for the gang both in terms of the revenues they can produce but also for the image and popularity of the gang within the community. Especially when the gang is concerned about its image, they will make every effort to attract as many people as possible to these parties and make sure they run smoothly.[78]

Bailes were not, however, the only parties that CVNH threw. During the height of police operations in early 2014, one of the two acting Donos of CVNH organized a large birthday celebration.[79] The party included a float decorated with hundreds of balloons and an electric sign that read, *"Feliz Aniversário Ninho!"* (Happy Birthday, Ninho!). At the end of the short parade, a stage with live music was set up in the middle of the street with free food and drink provided to the attendees. The live music and food was followed by an Evangelical religious ceremony.[80] Ninho's birthday took place during a period of significant police attention and a deteriorating relationship with the local community in part due to the presence of numerous nonnative gang members and the more coercive behavior of the gang (see earlier). According to several CVNH members, the Dono was seeking to shore up support during a difficult period, with the gang suffering from frequent police operations.[81] Inácio, a manager in the organization, attributed this same motivation for why he threw an enormous birthday party for his daughter to which he invited hundreds of his neighbors and other residents, provided free food and drink, and gave presents to all the attendees. He said he spent an estimated R$10,000 on the party ($4,000 at that time).[82] While throwing such parties and offering these forms of recreation may not seem like significant benefits, they remain an important

---

[76] Fausto 6/16/2014.
[77] Gabriela 12/10/2014.
[78] Fausto 6/16/2013.
[79] The CVNH gang had one Dono in prison and another in the community during the period I lived in Nova Holanda (see Chapter 5).
[80] Breno 3/26/2014.
[81] Inácio 3/26/2014; Bruno 6/10/2014.
[82] Inácio 3/26/2014.

way that gang members maintain their popularity and the support, or at least the silence, of the community.

Overall, the active and frequent enforcement efforts by BOPE against CVNH produced an organization that was deeply committed to providing responsive benefits to the community. The gang spent significant resources attempting to gain the silence if not the direct support of residents. They resolved many personal matters that residents brought to their attention. CVNH offered significant financial assistance and economic stimulation to residents through cash handouts, food baskets, and by providing numerous opportunities for residents to make money. The gang also hosted one of largest and most successful bailes in the city and promoted a series of other parties and opportunities for resident recreation. All these activities should be viewed not just as a gang interested in their reputation for its own sake but as a strategic response to the active threat of enforcement.

CRIMINALIZED GOVERNANCE REGIMES

Before describing how variation in the two threats combine to produce a distinct set of dynamics within each of the criminalized governance regimes, I will briefly note on the temporal dynamics of the theory. As outlined earlier, when a gang's security environment changes, so too will their governance activities but how long it takes for these changes to emerge vary. Some shifts in the security environment are obvious straightaway and will quickly change the governance regime. The activation of a rival threat, for instance, demands immediate action from the gang and will quickly translate into a more coercive regime. However, when an active threat from a rival or the police ends, it may take some time for the organization to realize that their rival is no longer invading their territory or that the police do not intend to enforce against them so consistently. Even after the change in security environment is fully internalized, it can take time for a gang to implement a new set of governing policies. It may take weeks, months, or even longer to curtail the more coercive behavior of a gang's rank and file following a long period of warfare. Alternatively, to establish more responsive relations with the community after the activation of police enforcement (i.e., following the installation of a new police post near a gang territory, the commencement of a new public security initiative to combat gangs, or the arrival of a more truculent local commander who orders more frequent operations), it may take some time for gang members and residents to learn the contours of these more responsive policies and practices. Nonetheless, if the change in the security environment persists, these changes should eventually manifest.[83]

---

[83] In the case study chapters to come, I have attributed governance regimes to specific years though, where possible, I have documented the more exact beginning and end dates within the text.

Disorder

I argue that disorder emerges whenever a rival is actively trying to invade a gang's territory. During these periods, the rules and agreements which normally govern gang behavior no longer apply. The gang cannot restrict their behavior for the sake of resident well-being or in the interest of the long-term relationship with the community because gang members cannot be certain that they will be around for long. The gang will immediately reduce their provision of benefits – they will no longer resolve disputes between residents, provide welfare or economic stimulation, or throw parties, or organize other forms of recreation. Both gang members and residents of Rio's favelas often refer to these periods as guerra. The gang whose territory is under threat will be much more likely to engage in extreme violence and coercion against local residents.[84] They may execute or publicly torture residents, shoot at unidentified people coming into their territory, and become threatening and disagreeable more generally. Some of this behavior may be caused by the stress of war – the psychological toll on gang members should not be discounted – but it is also a natural, "shoot first, ask questions later" type of response to an existential threat of this kind.

In many contexts of disorder, police enforcement often becomes active if it was not already due to the high amounts of violence caused by warring gangs. Even if more collaborative relations between the gangs and police preexist these arrangements, it is seldom the case that the public security apparatus will ignore intergang violence and refrain from actively enforcing for long. Moreover, disorder makes existing bribery schemes with the police more fragile as local precincts and battalions face more scrutiny from senior officials and political elites amid extreme levels of violence. Gang leaders may also choose to end collaborations with police if they feel they are not receiving the protection promised. In many cases, however, strong links with the police will prevent a rival threat from becoming active as a rival knows that a gang supported by the police is unlikely to be conquered.

If and when enforcement becomes active in the midst of disorder, police operations can sometimes limit or prevent warfare between gangs. Other times, gangs will continue to engage in invasions and shootouts, not refraining from confronting police directly especially if an operation coincides with a rival invasion. The incumbent gang may even decide to seek out confrontations with the police as a last ditch effort to provoke further enforcement in the hope that it will prevent a rival gang from wresting territorial control from them. The invading gang may also engage with police in their effort to weaken the incumbent by bringing even higher levels of police attention and enforcement within their territory.[85]

---

[84] Sometimes both gangs are invading each other's territories, in which case they will both be experiencing active rival threat. In others, one gang is the primary aggressor. I distinguish between these scenarios in the case studies to follow.

[85] Lessing (2015, 2017) refers to this as "*calentar la plaza*" (bringing down the heat on rivals).

Disorder will quickly take its toll on a gang. Members must always be ready to drop everything at a moment's notice and run to defend their territory. They will suffer severe psychological trauma. They will witness, engage in, and be victimized by extreme forms of violence. They will lose friends, colleagues, and perhaps family members. Some members will become withdrawn and are more likely to use drugs, making their behavior even more erratic. The longer disorder continues, the greater tendency there is for a breakdown within the gang organization itself. It is often these moments that lead to fragmentation and internal disputes, which may turn one gang into two or in which coup attempts may occur. That said, such schisms and internal disputes can occur outside of active rival competition and could be another cause of disorder.

As for residents, disorder presents a number of difficulties. First, the social and economic consequences can be huge as residents are hit by stray bullets, children are unable to attend schools, parents cannot get to work, and businesses are unable to open. Moreover, the unpredictable and violent behavior of the gangs will lead most residents to eschew encounters with gang members. They will avoid making any demands or providing any assistance to the gangs unless absolutely necessary. Those who can separate themselves from the gang will do so out of fear of a rival takeover and possible persecution if they are known to have aided the incumbent gang. Only the closest relatives and those who rely directly on the gang will continue to provide support, due to natural allegiances and affinities but also because they understand that they will likely be expelled from the territory should the gang lose the war with its rival.

Benevolent Dictator

Benevolent dictator gangs experience both latent threat from rivals and an active threat of enforcement from the police. The combination encourages them to remain constantly vigilant. They must be prepared for the latent threat from their rival to immediately turn active and to be forced to defend their territory at a moment's notice. At the same time, they must remain ready to run and hide when police engage in operations. The mix of these two threats produces a gang that seeks to be both feared but also loved by the community.

In response to the latent threat presented by their rival, benevolent dictator gangs will employ high though not extreme levels of coercion. They will continue to use some threats and violence to punish residents, ostentatiously display their firepower and weaponry, and closely monitor their borders. However, the gang will avoid indiscriminate violence toward residents both because their rival is not actively invading their territory and high levels of police attention and enforcement encourage the gang to worry about how they are viewed within the community. Unwarranted or extreme forms of coercion will risk alienating the local population, encourage denunciations against the gang, and further provoke police enforcement. Overall, the combination of latent competition and active enforcement will mitigate some of the incentives for gangs to engage in the most coercive behaviors.

In the face of active enforcement from police and, partially because of their more coercive posture, benevolent dictator gangs must cultivate even higher levels of resident support if they are to survive. The gang will be responsive to resident demands by resolving a variety of disputes. They will encourage residents to come to them for various problems. If financially possible, they will expand their provision of welfare and access to economic benefits. Their efforts to intensively control space by being more physically present on the streets and monitoring resident behavior will also increase the capacity of the gang to provide benefits by increasing their interactions and information gathering about the community. Benevolent dictator gangs will also use forms of culture and recreation as avenues to further gain resident support.

Not every benevolent dictator gang, however, will manage to maintain sufficient support or obedience from the community. Because of their continued use of high levels of coercion, some residents may refuse to accept their benefits while others, particularly those that have suffered from said coercion, may take the opportunity to denounce the gang. Because enforcement is active, such denunciations are much more likely to lead to arrest or possibly even death for gang members. In this way, the relationship between the gang and some parts of the community may deteriorate. If enforcement activities are particularly intense and effective, they may even weaken the gang sufficiently to incentivize the activation of competition by a rival.

Alternatively, benevolent dictator gangs which manage to effectively balance their response to these two threats can present a formidable and resilient organization, capable of governing for long periods within this security environment. If they can sufficiently manage their more coercive tendencies while providing responsive benefits (resolving disputes, offering economic benefits, and providing forms of recreation), many residents will be supportive of the local gang. Benevolent dictator gangs often expand their organizations as they require significant human resources to defend their territory and provide such responsive benefits. Such a large organization will be deeply embedded within its territories and the local population. During my fieldwork prior to the military's intervention, CVNH was just such a benevolent dictator gang.

Tyrant

The tyrant gang faces a latent threat from a rival but absent enforcement by the police. In these contexts, gangs will implement a more coercive form of governance due to the possibility that the threat from their rival will become active. Like benevolent dictator gangs, they will expand their organization, intensively monitor entry and exit to their turf, and ostentatiously display their firepower as a reminder to residents that they are in complete control. Also, because tyrant gangs face little possibility of enforcement from the police, tyrant gangs will not reduce their coercive profile as a benevolent dictator might. The lack of police enforcement means they have little reason to moderate their behavior in this regard.

Tyrant gangs are especially common in areas of a city where the police have little presence – the periphery – but can also exist where a gang has developed collusive relations with the police. These arrangements may influence the exact degree of latent threat these gangs feel. For instance, a gang supported or protected by the police is less likely to be worried about a latent threat from a rival but may also be more willing to engage in coercive behavior if they are sure enforcement will not be forthcoming. Either way, the gang's focus in these contexts is almost exclusively on the defense of their turf, providing little in terms of benefits to the community. Because enforcement is not forthcoming, the tyrant gang does not need the community to evade the police and, as a result, is unresponsive to demands from residents and provides few benefits to the community overall. Gang resources will mostly be spent on weapons or personal luxury goods, relatively less on stimulating the local economy and welfare.

Residents have little leverage over a tyrant gang. If the tyrant gang becomes too coercive and indiscriminate in their use of violence, residents may even turn to the potential rival in the hope that they will invade, take over, and govern the community more responsively. That said, most residents will not risk getting caught providing information or support to a rival because of the severe consequences should they get caught. Moreover, tyrant gangs, although generally unliked by most residents, may provide at least some form of order, which would quickly deteriorate if territorial competition between the rivals becomes active. If and when enforcement does become active, however, tyrant gang members may suffer as residents will seek to punish them for their past behavior. Because a latent threat encourages short-term thinking, however, many gangs in this situation will not have the foresight to develop more responsive and beneficial relations.

Social Bandit

Social bandit gangs face little or no threat from rivals but active enforcement efforts by police. As a result, they will seldom use or threaten violence within their turf while also providing substantial benefits to residents. For the most part, the gang will not feel the need to monitor entry and exit to their territory, ostentatiously display their weapons, or rely on threats and punishments to elicit obedience from residents. The lack of an existential threat means the gang has longer time horizons and thus can engage in more reasoned and deliberate policies. The lack of intergang violence, which often constitutes most of the violence in urban contexts makes living in a social bandit gang territory an altogether different experience than either of the two previous regimes.

Enforcement efforts, however, can be significant and, as a result, the gang will seek high levels of resident support to avoid arrest or death at the hands of the police. Social bandit gangs will offer responsive forms of dispute resolution, significant welfare and various forms of economic stimulation, as well as a variety of recreational activities. Residents will have little fear of going to the gang to resolve problems because it has a more relaxed and welcoming posture overall. However, because the gang does not need to defend and control their territory intensively, their organization is likely to be smaller, and, therefore, the capacity to provide these benefits may not be as great as benevolent dictator gangs, which have expanded their organization accordingly. If and when a social bandit gang behaves outside of the established social contract, residents can punish the gang by denouncing them to the police. I predict a social bandit gang will only engage in higher levels of coercion or violence if a resident is caught providing information to the police. Even then, the gang may refrain from the more gruesome and extreme forms of coercion used against someone collaborating with a rival. Overall, social bandit gang territories should be better contexts in which to live because of the lack of intergang violence and the absence of high levels of gang coercion. However, these territories can also suffer from aggressive, violent, and indiscriminate enforcement efforts as the police may view the community as largely supporting the local gang.

Laissez-Faire

Laissez-faire gangs face no threat from rivals and minimal or no enforcement efforts by the police. As a result, the gang will engage in a largely noncoercive approach to governance while also providing little to the community in terms of benefits. The laissez-faire gang refrains from using violence directed toward residents and does not seek to intensively control movement or dominate territory in the same way as gangs experiencing higher levels of rival threat. In some cases, the boundaries of laissez-faire gang territories may even be difficult to distinguish because the gang feels no need to monitor or demarcate their turf. Because police enforcement is absent, the gang is not incentivized to resolve disputes, stimulate the local economy, or provide forms of recreation. That said, a laissez-faire gang will nonetheless maintain a minimal level of governance necessary to regulate the local drug trade and maintain the functioning of the organization (recruit new members, punish indiscipline, etc.). A laissez-faire gang regime should not be confused for a lack of governance but, rather, is emblematic of a controlled and secure gang that neither seeks to dominate nor offer much in return to local populations.

For residents of these territories, the situation is much better than living under more coercive gangs. Most residents will not mind the gang's presence and may even consider gang members to be a natural part of the landscape so long as its members refrain from predation and other forms of violence. The laissez-faire gang allows residents to move around freely and does not restrict social and economic life. That said, there are a variety of needs and demands from the community which the gang is unwilling to meet.

In practice, a laissez-faire regime can emerge in one of two contexts. Laissez-faire regimes are most likely in less densely populated areas on the periphery of cities where fewer gangs are present and the drug trade or other illicit markets are less profitable. A more robust illicit market would likely attract at least some competition from rivals. The periphery of cities are also often areas of lower state capacity and, therefore, a more limited police presence. Other laissez-faire gangs can emerge amidst denser populations and more lucrative illicit markets if they are surrounded by allies and maintain more collusive relationships with the police. In this way, a laissez-faire regime can exist for very different types of gangs.

ADDITIONAL FACTORS

There are several additional factors that have so far been mostly ignored in this theory of criminalized governance: the drug trade and other illicit markets, the state (other than the police), and the specific characteristics of favela neighborhoods. In this section, I discuss how their inclusion might impact the theoretical model.

The Drug Trade and Other Illicit Markets

For the most part, this theory of governance holds the economic activities of gangs constant. First, the structure of the drug trade in Rio de Janeiro varies little. All of city's gangs have developed a franchise model, where the gang itself directly engages in the retail drug trade by packaging and selling marijuana, cocaine, and crack at bocas within their turf.[86] Their members make salaries and do not directly earn the profit from sales.[87] This model has been in place since the 1980s, when cocaine arrived to the Rio de Janeiro and, since then, has evolved very little. In the case studies to follow, I show how each of the gangs in Complexo da Maré has slightly modified the standard franchise model to match local dynamics. I argue these modifications are as much a result of the security environment and the dynamics of governance as they are an effort to maximize the profits of the drug trade. Overall, there is good reason to believe that the structure of the drug trade does not shape the existing variation in criminalized governance outcomes across the gangs studied in this book.

Although the structure of the drug trade differs little across Rio's gangs, there are large disparities in drug revenues. The most profitable gangs will

---

[86] The other two primary models are *freelance*, in which the gang would sell wholesale to individuals that then package, sell, and retail the drugs themselves, and *consignment*, in which the gang loans the drugs to sellers that are then expected to pay them back after they have sold the drugs (Lessing and Denyer Willis 2019, 592).

[87] Vapores do earn a commission depending on the quantity they sell.

generate tens of millions of *reais* (Brazilian currency) annually while the poorest gangs perhaps only hundreds of thousands. Much of this difference is determined by geography. Gangs located near wealthy neighborhoods, touristy areas, bustling commercial hubs, or along busy highways will produce much higher revenues than gangs located on the outskirts of the city. The economic capacity of the richest gangs is significant indeed. They can more easily develop lucrative bribery schemes with the police, spend more on the economic stimulation of the local economy, and fund larger parties. Therefore, some gangs may have sufficient resources to easily maintain *both* highly collaborative relations with the police while also providing significant benefits to the community (an outcome my theory suggests should not happen). While a resource-rich gang may easily provide some extra benefits due to their surplus, a gang that really needs the support and silence of the community will not just offer financial benefits but also nonmaterial, labor-intensive ones like resolving disputes and implementing a responsive form of social order. A gang that faces little likelihood of enforcement will not be incentivized to do so in the same way.

Drug revenues can also generate incentives for competition between gangs. The more profitable the gang, the more likely rivals will see their territory as a desirable one to control. Territorial competition is, therefore, more likely for resource-rich gangs. That said, a gang with access to substantial resources can purchase larger arsenals and hire more personnel to monitor and defend their territory, deterring would-be rivals. In this way, it is difficult to predict, a priori, how resources alone produce more or less coercive gangs. In the rest of this book, I compare across similarly resource-rich gangs, not all of which are equally coercive or responsive, suggesting that revenue does not automatically produce coercive or benevolent gangs. I also pay close attention to how and why their profitability changes over time, which gives us some insight into the relationship between drug revenues and governance.

Second, although they continue to generate most of their revenue from the drug trade, Rio's gangs have diversified their economic portfolio in recent years. Many gangs now engage in housing speculation, informal transportation, and internet and cable TV services. While these activities produce just a small portion of most gangs' overall revenue, many other gangs throughout the world may rely less on the drug trade and instead sustain their organizations through extortion, robbery, prostitution, illegal gambling, or a variety of other illicit or informal economies. The demands of these industries may shape the competition for territory, the dynamics of enforcement by the police, and the specific governance activities involved.

For example, when gangs run protection rackets, there are likely different governance dynamics at work because residents and business owners are directly paying the gang for a service (though the quality of that service may vary). Such a financial exchange may influence how much a gang needs to use and threaten violence, what if any benefits the gang provides, and how their clients (victims?) and other residents may respond.[88] In addition, the need for exclusive territorial control may differ according to the exact illicit market from which a gang profits. Without the need for exclusivity, the dynamics surrounding competition would change and there may not be such a tight connection between coercion and competition. That said, regardless of their economic activities, gangs the world over nearly always desire an exclusive turf. This is as much for the security of their own members as it is to ensure their economic base. In the end, I argue that all gangs will seek to maintain territorial exclusivity regardless of their specific economic activities. I predict that the dynamics of competition and enforcement will provoke similar governance reactions in gangs even when they engage in a very different set of economic activities.

The Role of the State

The theory developed here focuses exclusively on the security arm of the state in shaping criminalized governance outcomes. The police (and military) are not, however, the only representatives of the Brazilian state that exist within Rio's favelas. Beginning in the second half of the twentieth century and increasing since the end of the military dictatorship in the 1980s, the Brazilian government has taken a more active developmental role in hundreds of favelas throughout the city. Through a series of massive development projects, the municipal, state, and federal governments have attempted to upgrade infrastructure (sanitation systems, roadways, electrical grids, etc.) and increase access to social services, including the building of schools and public health posts.[89] Despite significant improvements in some communities, the successes of these programs have been uneven at best. To my knowledge, no favela has ever been fully incorporated within the formal urban grid (without, that is, the removal of their residents) nor have these projects provided residents access to all the rights and privileges of full citizenship. Most glaringly, favela urbanization projects have had little to no impact on the lack of access to the criminal justice system nor the abusive and corrupt behavior of the police in these communities. Thus, despite important gains, favelas can be considered areas where the state is either unable or unwilling to enforce order and the rule of law. Given these conditions and the fact that the police are always one of the primary concerns of any gang, narrowing the role of the state to the variation in police enforcement is justified.

[88] See Moncada (2022) on the dynamics of these arrangements.
[89] The most prominent and well-funded of these projects were Promorar (1978), Project Rio (1979–81), Favela-Bairro (1994–2008), the Growth Acceleration Program or PAC (2007), and Morar Carioca (2010), among others. The actual design, implementation, and effectiveness of these projects varied considerably (Burgos 2006; Perlman 2010).

Another way that the Brazilian state is at least partially present in favela communities is through politicians and their parties. Favela residents constitute roughly 20 percent of the city's population, a considerable voting bloc. In the lead-up to elections, gangs offer access to politicians through local representatives (usually the AM), in exchange for some limited, one-off benefits or favors, such as building materials for community construction projects or perhaps some other public or club goods for residents (Albarracín 2018).[90] That said, overall, Rio's gangs maintain weak connections to politicians and political parties and these exchanges involve relatively few real benefits for either gangs or residents. Unlike Rio's milícias, which have developed highly collusive and interdependent arrangements with political parties, in some cases becoming politicians themselves, gangs and their leaders have never truly inserted themselves into the politics of the state directly nor have they gained any leverage over the policies these politicians adopt.[91] Moreover, the illicit networks connecting gangs, politicians, and AMs have only become weaker since their height in the 1990s. I document the evolution of these connections in the case studies to come and show that the dynamics of territorial competition and police enforcement supersede and, in some cases, drive these political arrangements.

Neighborhood Characteristics

Finally, although I have left the specific characteristics of favela communities out of this theory, the governing relations between gangs and communities are shaped by local circumstances in myriad ways. For example, favelas can range in size from just a few hundred residents to as many as 70,000. The largest are brimming with shops and restaurants, high-rise apartment buildings, theaters, soccer fields, and schools, while others lack even the most basic infrastructure such as paved roads, sewage, or electricity. Also, unlike some cities where informal neighborhoods are primarily located on the periphery, Rio's favelas can be found in every corner of the urban space. They are in the bustling city center, on the steep hillsides surrounding Rio's iconic beaches, in swamps or tidal plains next to middle- and working-class neighborhoods, and on defunct estates or unused lands on the edges of the vast municipal boundary. Most of Rio's favelas were settled gradually and haphazardly by migrants arriving from the rural hinterlands, although some were created by highly organized land invasions. Still, others were built by the municipality as housing projects but, with little continuing investment, can be considered

---

[90] The pervasive stigma and criminalization of gangs and their members in Rio de Janeiro likely inhibits the creation of more durable and overt partnerships between drug traffickers and politicians.

[91] One exception to this would be Nem, the Dono of Rocinha, Rio's largest favela, in the 2000s (Glenny 2016).

more favela than *asfalto* (literally, asphalt, or the formal city).[92] Some favelas also contain significant social and political movements, lucrative businesses, active NGOs, and a huge variety of churches and other religious organizations within them while others may lack such robust forms of association and mobilization. How each of these factors impact criminalized governance is difficult to predict because of the sheer number of variables and the diversity of favela contexts.

In this regard, one of the significant advantages of this book's research design, is that Complexo da Maré contains much of this variation within it. Among Maré's fifteen neighborhoods, there are different geographies, settlement patterns, demographics, and levels of development. There is also a huge range in the number and makeup of social and religious organizations within each of these neighborhoods. Throughout the empirical chapters, I pay close attention to these differences while demonstrating how the theory I have developed applies to these specific circumstances and, in the long run, may even shape the characteristics of these neighborhoods.

CONCLUSION

In this chapter, I have developed a theory to account for why criminalized governance regimes vary across space and time in Rio de Janeiro. Through ethnographic insights garnered from long-term fieldwork in one gang's territory, I argue that the different security threats that gangs face – from rivals and from the police – determine the degree to which they use coercion and provide benefits to residents. For their part, residents are integral to these governance outcomes as they shape gang behavior through denunciations to rivals and the police and through the demands they make of the gang. Building on these insights, I then described the dynamics that should be observed in each of the criminalized governance regimes. The combination of active, latent, or absent rival competition and active or absent police enforcement determines what gangs need from the local population and the opportunities and incentives residents have to respond. Finally, I addressed three additional factors that may also shape criminalized governance but which are not explicitly included in the theory: the drug trade and other illicit economies, the role of the state beyond the police, and the specific characteristics of favela neighborhoods.

In the following chapters, I expand the temporal and geographical scope from just one gang within a short period of time to three separate gang organizations over nearly forty years. In Chapter 4, I analyze the origins of three of Maré's gangs, noting on how the dynamics of competition and enforcement can also help explain their emergence and their first forays into governance. In

---

[92] *Conjuntos habitacionais* (housing projects) are seldom classified as favelas though gangs are present in a great many of them.

Chapters 5–7, I then trace the evolution of each of these gangs from the early 1990s, when they integrated into the prison-based factions until the occupation of Complexo da Maré by the Brazilian military in April 2014. Chapter 8 describes this period of occupation and traces how each of the three gangs responded to the loss of overt territorial control and the ability to provide significant benefits to these communities. I show how the theory developed here helps us understand the dynamics observed during this period as well.

4

The Origins of Criminalized Governance

> By gathering a powerful means of physical coercion, that is, firearms, and by enriching themselves, gangs end up becoming a political force and setting up a system of local power.
>
> —Alba Zaluar, *A Máquina e a Revolta* (1985, 166)

INTRODUCTION

Hundreds of drug-trafficking gangs have governed favelas in Rio de Janeiro for more than four decades. While most scholarship focuses on the emergence of prison-based factions during Brazil's military dictatorship (1964–85) as the starting point of these arrangements, the real history of Rio's gangs begins long before, on the streets and in the alleyways of these neighborhoods. This chapter traces the origins of Complexo da Maré's first embryonic gangs. In doing so, I seek to answer a series of interrelated questions: Where do gangs come from? How and why did they begin to govern? And what did those first forms of governance consist of?

These are important questions because we continue to lack a systematic understanding of gang formation and evolution in Rio de Janeiro. While today's drug-trafficking gangs look little like the small groups of young men that began to organize themselves more than a half century ago, several of these organizations can be traced directly from these initial groups to their modern incarnations. Most studies of gangs, however, deal little with their origins. This is for good reason. Gang formation is mostly lost to history. The lives and activities of their members are almost never written down or recorded, only existing in the memories of those involved or the residents living in these neighborhoods at the time. In this chapter, I combine dozens of oral histories conducted with former gang members and longtime favela residents, reports from local newspapers, and documents from community archives to reconstruct the origins of Complexo da Maré's gangs. In doing so, I make several interrelated arguments concerning gang emergence and governance.

First, gangs formed in Complexo da Maré's favelas at very different times and only after previous governance arrangements had broken down.[1] Increasing migration over the course of the 1960s and 1970s led to worsening conditions in Maré. Without sanitation, electricity, or basic infrastructure, Maré's favelas became downright squalid. A variety of other non-state actors that had previously maintained order and provided some services to residents could no longer effectively govern this burgeoning population. Rio's favelas were also increasingly marginalized during Brazil's military dictatorship (1964–85) as the abusive and violent practices of the police became more widespread. These combined factors led to spiking levels of crime and violence and, eventually, the emergence of several gangs in the early 1970s in Nova Holanda, where the conditions deteriorated most quickly. In Maré's other favelas, gangs would only emerge more than a decade later as existing governance arrangements more effectively controlled violence and crime and, thus, delayed the formation of gangs. Eventually, however, they too would be incapable of preventing gangs from forming.

I also seek to explain how and why these gangs began to govern. I argue that competition between rivals, police enforcement, and governance were inextricably intertwined from the very beginning. Quickly after their emergence, several nascent gangs began to compete over increasingly valuable drug-selling turf. The more successful gangs destroyed or incorporated their rivals through conquest or alliance and extended their turf to these areas. The expansion to governance activities was, in some sense, inevitable. Residents and all local political and economic actors became subject to gang authority as they demanded obedience amid increasingly competitive dynamics with their rivals. Gangs also sought the protection and cooperation of residents as police began to focus their attention on these organizations. In Nova Holanda, multiple fledgling gangs violently competed for dominance over the course of the

---

[1] This finding builds on a large literature within sociology, in which poverty, broken homes, and residential mobility are seen to hinder the ability of communities to control crime and violence through informal mechanisms (see Morenoff, Sampson, and Raudenbush 2001; Sampson 2012; Sampson and Groves 1989; Sampson, Raudenbusch, and Earls 1997; Shaw and McKay 1942; Suttles et al. 1968). In these contexts, the state is viewed as either failing or deciding not to provide stable institutions (adequate social services, functioning schools, and avenues for employment) that allow youth to make the jump to adulthood. Gangs fulfill this role by providing young men and women with social identities and self-esteem (see Bourgois 2002; Horowitz 1983; Shaw and McKay 1942; Thrasher 1927; Vigil 1988; Vigil 2002; Whyte et al. 1993), while offering opportunities for these individuals to gain access to resources, security, and material benefits (see Cloward and Ohlin 1960; Sánchez-Jankowski 1991; Suttles 1968; Venkatesh 1997, 2008; Whyte et al. 1993). This approach to gang formation and proliferation, developed in the US, has been increasingly applied to the Latin American context (Escobar 2012; Núñez, Tocornal, and Henríquez 2012; Villarreal and Silva 2006).

1970s and early 1980s. After several years of gang warfare, one gang would eventually win out and, in the process, develop the capacity to engage in more significant governance activities. For the other two case studies investigated in this chapter, a single gang would emerge from Parque União and another from Morro do Timbau. Unlike Nova Holanda, there would be no such violent competition for territory, at least initially. These gangs would only begin to exert territorial control and govern like their Nova Holanda counterpart after they integrated into the prison-based drug-trafficking factions in the 1990s.

The final point I will make concerns the role of residents. Favelas were not, as has often been argued, places of rampant criminality or anarchic environments from their beginnings. On the contrary, favela communities often developed highly cohesive and stable governance mechanisms even amid contexts of precarity. Before gangs emerged and began to govern, a mix of other favela actors provided governance services that resident populations desired: a stable form of order, crime fighting, dispute resolution, and some access to welfare. In many cases, it was the AM president, local strongman, or prominent businessman, through their connections to the police or military that took on this role. Although the emergence of gangs would not be a positive development within these communities, gangs did take over this pivotal function within the community. They imposed an essential, if perhaps violent, form of order while variously providing certain benefits that favela residents sorely needed. In return, residents offered gangs their tacit or explicit support by not denouncing them to their rivals or the police. This exchange formed the foundation of a social contract that still exists to this day.[2]

This chapter is organized as follows. The below section provides a brief overview of the early history of Rio's favelas and the predecessors of gangs in the city. The rest of the chapter focuses more intensively on Complexo da Maré and the cases that form the empirical backbone of this book. I first trace the pre-gang history of Maré's favelas, focusing on the settlement patterns and the various actors that provided governance prior to the emergence of gangs in the area. I then offer a detailed account of the deteriorating living conditions, increasingly abusive and repressive behavior of the public security apparatus, and the breakdown in preexisting governance arrangements that eventually led to the emergence of the gangs. I take considerable care to outline the diversity of these pre-gang governance arrangements that would impact when and where gangs formed and eventually governed. I conclude with a

---

[2] Like Arjona, I do not use the term "social contract" in the strict political sense but rather to signify a shared expectation of behavior and exchange (2016, 26). For Zaluar, this alliance (*aliança*) is based on residents not informing on the gang and the gang defending the area against other gangs, respecting residents, and stopping rape and theft within the community (1994, 139). In the American context, Sánchez-Jankowski describes a similar agreement between communities and gangs so long as the gang: (1) avoids antagonizing residents by not predating on them or harassing them and (2) provides help to residents when the occasion arises (1991, 31–32).

short description of the emergence of the prison-based factions in the 1970s, their eventual spread from the prisons into Rio's favelas, and the integration of Maré's gangs into these larger networks.

A SHORT HISTORY OF CRIME AND GOVERNANCE IN RIO DE JANEIRO'S FAVELAS

According to a popular myth, Rio's first favela was established in 1897 by veterans of the Canudos War who pitched their tents on a hillside in the center of Rio de Janeiro to await payment for their service from the federal government (Valladares 2008, 28–30). The ex-soldiers, many of whom were former slaves, called the hill *favella*, after Monte Favella, a small mountain in a remote region of Bahia where they had fought – and many died – during the war.[3] The real birth of this community, however, was several years earlier, in January 1893, following the destruction of Cabeça do Porco (Pig's Head), a massive *cortiço* (tenement) in the center of the city. Cabeça do Porco, which housed roughly 4,000 urban poor, was one of hundreds of tenements that provided unsanitary and cramped living quarters for many of Rio's newly freed slaves and recent migrants from Brazil's hinterlands and parts foreign.[4] After demolition by municipal workers, former residents gathered what few belongings they managed to save and began constructing ramshackle huts on a nearby hillside (Chalhoub 1996, 15–20). The ex-soldiers would join them on that hill several years later.

Tenement removals were common around the turn of the twentieth century as Rio began to model itself after major European cities by carrying out massive public works and urban reforms to realize this self-image.[5] After being suddenly and, in many cases, violently dispossessed of their housing, residents were forced to search for alternative accommodations. The steep hillsides in the center of the city, difficult terrain though they were, had available land on which they could build homes and these fledgling communities grew from a smattering of huts into permanent settlements with hundreds of domiciles and thousands of residents. Just as the tenements were viewed as public health risks and dens of vice and iniquity before, favelas would take up this mantle. They faced an increasingly threatening and invasive government. Many politicians, urban planners, and numerous government agencies collaborated in favela eradication and removal campaigns. It was often Rio's Military Police that was responsible for evicting residents and sometimes burning down these settlements. These policies were largely driven by pervasive prejudice and

---

[3] See Perlman for a description of Rio's first favela (2010, 25).
[4] Brazil was the last country to outlaw slavery in 1888.
[5] It is estimated that some 37,000 people were left homeless due to tenement demolitions in the first decade of the twentieth century alone (Vaz 1985, 226).

racism toward the inhabitants of these communities, assisted by sensationalized media accounts.[6]

The reality was that favelas were neither as violent nor as full of criminals as was commonly believed though some types of criminality existed in these communities. Favelas of the period probably contained some low-level drug dealers, neighborhood *capoeira* (a Brazilian form of martial art combining music, acrobatics, and dance) groups called *maltas* that may have engaged in some violence, as well as possibly some *cangaçeiros* (bandits and thieves) that had migrated from the Northeast of Brazil where banditry was common. Misse has argued that favelas of the era had *malandros* (scoundrels), *valentes* (warriors), and *malfeitores* (wrongdoers), three categories of low-level criminals that engaged in theft and robbery, smoked marijuana, and were considered, to varying degrees, dangerous and antisocial (1999, 251–62). Notwithstanding such different understandings of what constituted a criminal, more organized forms of criminality were little present in Rio's favelas in the early part of the century.

By the 1920s, only a couple dozen favelas dotted the hillsides in and around the city center but by 1940 there were at least 116 such informal settlements in the quickly expanding city (O'Hare and Barke 2002, 228). In this second phase of favela development, a host of other actors would participate in land invasions and squatting, not just the indigent freedmen and women who could not afford formal property or lodging. Wealthy land speculators, politicians, lawyers, the middle class, traditional rural poor, foreign immigrants, and farmers seeking land to raise crops and livestock, among many others all vied to get a piece of the highly valuable real estate market.[7] Many of the favelas from this era would look little like their predecessors. The lands these assorted groups occupied were no longer solely on steep, almost uninhabitable hillsides; they were defunct estates, unused church or state property, unoccupied land, and even swamps that residents would fill in over time. Many of these areas were far from the city itself but within the vast municipal territory.[8]

Complexo da Maré would emerge in this second phase of favela development. At the end of the 1930s, several miles north of Rio's bustling city center, an immigrant couple from the neighboring state of Minas Gerais built a small hut on a hill surrounded by Guanabara Bay's massive tidal plain.[9] The area

---

[6] Benjamin Costallat, a journalist and chronicler of favelas at the time, described how a favela he visited in the early 1920s was "all about violent crime, stabbings, violence, vengeance, and bravado…" and that in the areas surrounding the favela "the deal is robbery, it's cunning, it's the professional picklock who knows how to use a file and crowbar" (1995, 33–34).

[7] For a detailed description of these dynamics, see Fischer (2008, 211–93).

[8] Perlman described the process this way: "The first favelas developed at the bottom of hillsides and the edges of the bay, but as those prime locations (as it were) began to fill up, the newcomers went further up the hillsides, further out into the water, and further away from the city's[sic] core" (2010, 27).

[9] The word *maré* directly translated from Portuguese means "tide." Guanabara Bay would almost completely cover this area at high tide then reveal a muddy shrubland at low tide.

FIGURE 4.1 Aerial photograph of Morro do Timbau and Baixa do Sapateiro, 1960s
Morro do Timbau is in the foreground and the palafitas of Baixa do Sapateiro can be
seen at the top left. Source: Archive of the Brazilian National Library Foundation.

was almost completely unsettled except for a colony of local fisherman who
used the area to tie their boats at night (Santo, Gonçalves, and Silva 2013, 21;
Santos 1983, 44). Slowly, other immigrants followed and by the middle of the
1940s, a small community had taken shape on Morro do Timbau, Maré's first
favela.[10]

Several years later, in the late 1940s, Avenida Brasil, a major highway connecting the center of Rio to surrounding suburbs would spur migration to
the area. Other industries would quickly follow, including a petroleum refin-
ery. Many of the male residents of Morro do Timbau found steady but gru-
eling work in these factories. Two other favelas quickly materialized: Baixa
do Sapateiro (1947) and Parque Maré (1950). These communities would be
located on the only other two surrounding areas of land that were permanently
dry. When these areas were settled, other migrants began to build *palafitas*
(shacks on stilts) above the tidal plain (see Figure 4.1).

---

[10] The name Timbau comes from the Tupi-Guarani word *thybau*, meaning "between the waters."

Parque Rubens Vaz (1951) and Parque União (1954), Maré's next two communities, followed a slightly different pattern of settlement in which one resident dictated much of the organization and migration to the area.[11] Margarino Torres, a lawyer and member of the Communist Party, came to Parque Rubens Vaz in 1958 to protect the community from removal by the police and quickly became the undisputed community leader (Vaz 1994, 158). He would eventually organize the occupation of an adjacent area, where a local industrial firm, Tekno, had already filled in some of the low-lying swampland. This area would later become known as Parque União.

As the percentage of the municipal population living in favelas steadily increased, so too did the possibility for these communities to influence public policy. The most important politician of this era, Getúlio Vargas, sought greater support from the burgeoning lower classes and favela residents. During his tenure as dictator (1930–45) and then President (1951–54), Vargas helped found the Fundação Leão XIII and the Municipal Guard, two government agencies that transformed the way the government dealt with favelas. Public policy shifted from being exclusively focused on removing favelas to improving their infrastructure and providing services while simultaneously attempting to control the social movements emerging from within them. President Juscelino Kubitschek (1956–61) would also promote more development-oriented policies, even sponsoring a law that placed a two-year ban on all favela evictions while supporting vocational training programs for industrial workers, which largely benefitted favela residents. In addition, the Catholic Church, amid transformations of its own in the Second Vatican Council (1962–65), began promoting democratic principles and services for the poor, inserting itself into favela communities with vigor.[12] As these progressive changes were occurring, favela communities including those in Maré began to form AMs to represent their interests to government agencies and political parties. Across the city, these informal democratic institutions elected local leaders, formed coalitions, petitioned the municipal government, and carried out many essential functions for residents. In some favelas, AMs managed to bring significant public services and infrastructure to the community.

And yet, the outcome of this period for favela residents was ambivalent. Forced removal remained an important municipal policy when it came to favelas. The 1938 Building Code was the first official document to recognize the existence of favelas though it simultaneously declared them illegal and prohibited their creation or expansion (Perlman 2010, 26–27). In addition, residents of favelas faced increasing violence from the police in the middle decades of the twentieth century. Extortion, detention, mass arrest, illegal invasions, and even dispossession

---

[11] The date of Parque União's founding is contested. Initial settlement of the area began in 1954 but the more organized occupation began in 1958 (Vaz 1994, 163–64).
[12] See Mainwaring (1986) for an analysis of this shift in Catholic Church policy and its repercussions for Brazilian politics and favela communities during the dictatorship era.

became standard police procedures and, by the 1960s, some precincts were even engaging in torture and murder of suspected criminals (Fischer 2008, 204–8). In many favelas, residents seldom cooperated with police during investigations and refused to make statements or offer testimony of any kind. For these reasons, "many poor communities began to effectively remove themselves from police jurisdiction for all but the most serious of crimes" (p. 206).

Favela communities used whatever means were at their disposal to prevent removal and provide themselves with services. Through local community leaders, they created complex client-patron networks with various state and non-state actors: the Catholic Church, Fundação Leão XIII, political parties, and the Ministry of Justice, just to name a few. For more local matters, such as crimes and disputes within the favela itself, residents sometimes sought out the police. Knowing that police would likely detain and possibly abuse those accused of crimes even without evidence, residents began to use the police as a coercive tool to resolve disputes and exact revenge (Fischer 2008, 207; Kant de Lima 1986). In other cases, residents sought out respected community leaders who could be called upon to arbitrate disputes. Finally, residents could sometimes turn to emerging organized crime networks, represented by the *jogo do bicho* (animal game, akin to the numbers racket in the US), drug dealers, or other bandits whom residents "respected," either because their verdicts were just or because they had the means to enforce their decisions.[13] The cumulative effect of this piecemeal rule of law was that traditional forms of justice and citizenship would become even more difficult to find in Rio's favelas.

Complexo da Maré's evolution closely maps onto these larger citywide dynamics. In the early 1960s, two other communities were inaugurated in Maré that were temporary housing projects built by the municipal government for residents who had been removed from other favelas in the city. One of these housing projects, *Centro de Habitação Provisório de Nova Holanda* (Provisional Housing Center of Nova Holanda), was constructed in the low-lying swampland between Parque Maré and Parque Rubens Vaz in 1962 (see Figure 4.2). Conjoined single and two-story wooden homes were built with straight wide streets and a more "rational" checkerboard design (see Figures 4.2 and 4.3). What was intended to be a "temporary community," turned into a permanent settlement, and with only minimal investment, Nova Holanda quickly came to differ little from the surrounding favelas.

In 1964, a military coup overthrew the democratically elected President, João Goulart, and instituted a twenty-one-year dictatorship during which favela policy would be characterized even more by removals and repression. The influence of the AMs waned as petitioning authoritarian institutions became more difficult. The military regime created new government agencies with the purpose of eradicating the favelas from the urban landscape. From

---

[13] See Chazkel (2011) for a description of the jogo do bicho's origins and evolution.

FIGURE 4.2 Aerial photograph of Complexo da Maré, 1979
Notice the checkerboard layout of Nova Holanda in the background and the palafitas
extending into Guanabara Bay in the foreground. Source: Vieira Archive, Museu da
Maré, available at www.arquivomuseudamare.org.

1968 to 1975, the city of Rio removed seventy favelas and more than 100,000
residents (Perlman 1976, 258–60). Most of these evictions were from highly
desirable locations in and around the famous beaches, wealthy neighborhoods,
and the city center where property values had already begun to skyrocket.
When and if AMs attempted to intercept such forced removal, they were dealt
with harshly by public security and military forces (Gay 1994, 20).

For residents of Maré, life progressively became more difficult during the dictatorship. Continued migration to the area led to a swelling population and with very little investment in public infrastructure, the living conditions became unequivocally terrible. By 1980, some 68,000 residents were living in Maré's nine favelas, increasing to nearly 80,000 by 1987 (Ribeiro da Silva 2006, 194) (see Figure 4.3).[14] Roughly a quarter of those residents lived in palafitas, which generally consisted of one room with no running water, electricity, or sanitation. The palafitas were connected by a series of precariously constructed planks (see Figure 4.4), which led to many accidents, sometimes proving fatal when small children fell into the water or mud below (Vieira 1998, 72). In interviews with longtime residents, they recalled how unsanitary and dangerous it was to live in Maré at that time. According to one resident, "The situation was really bad. The community kept growing. Lots of people from the Northeast [region of Brazil] kept coming and there were no services. The standard of living was really terrible."[15] One of the most difficult aspects of local life was that there was no source of fresh water in the community. Residents had to carry buckets or roll barrels across the busy Avenida Brasil highway. "I saw many people die getting hit by trucks trying to cross over," João told me.[16]

In addition, the public security apparatus' tendency for violence and abuse only increased during the dictatorship. Of Maré's nine existing favelas during the 1970s, four had a *Destacamento de Policiamento Ostensivo* (Ostensive Police Detachment, hereon DPO), or a *Posto de Policiamento Comunitário* (Community Police Post, hereon PPC), often just a small building with an office and a cell, located within the community (Ribeiro da Silva 2006, 202). By this time, police had been carrying out periodic violence and removals of residents for several decades. They had even managed to expel and destroy a handful of embryonic communities from the area (pp. 190–92). Moreover, the use of torture by the police was widespread, especially following Institutional Act number 5, issued by the military regime in 1968, which suspended some civil and political rights including *habeas corpus*.

In some of Maré's favelas, the relationship between residents and police deteriorated to the point that police seldom left their post and residents refused to enter. In interviews with longtime Nova Holanda residents, they described the horrifying brutality with which the police carried out their job. Artur recalled living across the street from one of the police posts. He explained how police would round up the extremely poor who were accused of *vadiagem* (vagrancy). "Sometimes they would arrest up to ten people at a time and lead them in a line by rope back to the post. My house was across the street and

---

[14] *União da Maré* 5/1980.
[15] Eduardo 10/11/2013.
[16] João 10/16/2013.

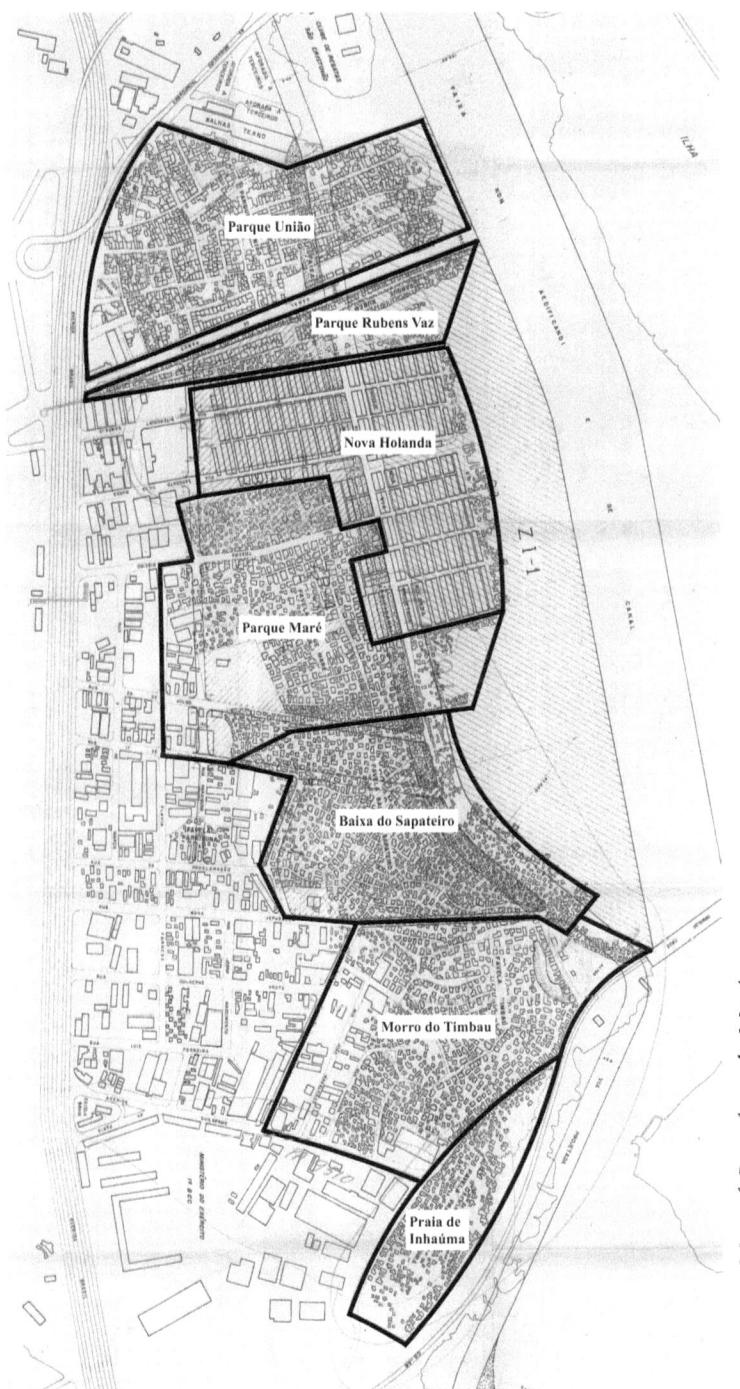

Labels on map:
- Parque União
- Parque Rubens Vaz
- Nova Holanda
- Parque Maré
- Baixa do Sapateiro
- Morro do Timbau
- Praia de Inhaúma

FIGURE 4.3 Map of Complexo da Maré, 1974
Not pictured are Praia de Ramos and Roquete Pinto. Praia de Inhaúma was demolished in 1974. Source: PCRJ/SMPU, available at https://acervoimagens.rio.rj.gov.br/.

FIGURE 4.4 Photograph of palafitas in Complexo da Maré, 1969
Source: Vieira Archive, Museu da Maré, available at www.arquivomuseudamare.org.

we could hear them scream when they tortured them. All these tactics were approved by the dictatorship," he said.[17]

In other areas of Maré, however, the relationship with police had not deteriorated so precipitously.[18] In Praia de Ramos, for example, where another of the era's PPCs was located, resident reactions were not so uniformly negative. Few recalled episodes of torture and generally considered relations with the police decent to the point where residents would still enter the post to make

---

[17] Artur 3/17/2014.
[18] This is emblematic of favela–police relations throughout the city. As Fischer argues, police institutions varied enormously across the city and "the police were too linked to too many aspects of poor people's lives to conform to any single description" (2008, 208).

complaints and fill out reports.[19] In Morro do Timbau, where the AM worked closely with the military, and Parque União, where the AM maintained connections to the police, residents continued to report crimes and ask for dispute resolution from public authorities until the 1980s.[20]

During this middle period of the twentieth century, with the exponential growth of Rio's favelas and the dramatic change of the urban landscape, drug traffickers began to emerge as major players in favelas and urban politics. Misse (1999) traces the beginnings of o movimento (the movement), or the initial forms of drug trafficking, to two of the city's oldest favelas in the 1940s: Providência (formerly Morro da Favela) and Mangueira. By the 1950s, several other favelas were known to have drug trafficking and by the 1960s it was in most favelas. Despite the single term, drug trafficking did not have a uniform expression on the ground. Drug traffickers had no specific organizational structure and the individuals and groups involved were often not interconnected (p. 319). In most cases, it was only a local boca de fumo. Even before the retail drug market arrived, however, the role of the Dono was already well-established through the presence of the jogo do bicho or through a local group of bandits and thieves who organized themselves as a unit (pp. 313–15). The relations that Donos maintained with favela communities varied incredibly but were founded on his – they were exclusively male – ability to control the abuse of residents, defend the community from bandits or thugs, and the mediation of disputes or help in times of need that allowed him to maintain his dominion (p. 343).

At the beginning of Brazil's military dictatorship, gangs did not exist in Maré, but by its end, they would be present in every one of the Complexo's favelas. In the sections to follow, I detail the emergence and eventual ascendance of three gang organizations from different favelas in Maré: Nova Holanda, Parque União, and Morro do Timbau. Across these cases, several factors helped incentivize the formation of gangs and facilitate their expanding influence and power. First, these were difficult times in Maré. Migration to the area continued and the population swelled but with little investment in infrastructure, living conditions deteriorated. The burgeoning drug trade, armed robbery, and theft became important sources of income for families who had a difficult time making ends meet. In addition, increasing numbers of young men were being excluded from the formal labor market as they became the focus of police enforcement. Arrest, imprisonment, and powerful social stigma often prevented them from acquiring decent and stable employment, thus expanding the number of men willing to engage in crime for a living. Finally, increasingly repressive and indiscriminate policing tactics and the marginalization of previous forms of governance, a former source of stability and order in these communities, led to growing distrust of state institutions. By the 1980s, residents

[19] Beto 10/8/2013.
[20] Ademir 11/19/2014; Artur 1/9/2017; Vinícius 11/9/2014; Gustavo 11/19/2014.

seldom reported crimes to the police. The informal governance arrangements that existed previously were incapable of dealing with rising levels of crime and violence.[21] What each of the following cases makes clear, however, is that gangs emerged and began to govern at very different times across Maré that corresponded to these local conditions. This temporal variation provides initial evidence as to the dynamics influencing how and why gangs govern.

THE EMERGENCE OF CRIMINALIZED GOVERNANCE IN COMPLEXO DA MARÉ

Nova Holanda

In January 1962, the municipal government of Rio de Janeiro began relocating several thousand residents that had been removed from a handful of favelas (Praia do Pinto, Morro da Formiga, Esqueleto, Macedo Sobrinho, and Morro de Querosene) in more desirable areas of the city to the temporary housing project known as Nova Holanda.[22] Many of those eventually relocated were residents who could not afford the cost of monthly payments for properties in more permanent housing projects, such as Cidade de Deus, Cidade Alta, or Vila Kennedy (Ribeiro da Silva 2006, 99). For some, Nova Holanda represented an improvement in living conditions, at least initially, with mostly stable multiroom houses that had electricity, sanitation, and running water. For many others, the experience was an incredible trauma, having been violently removed from their former homes, loaded onto trucks with what few belongings they could gather, and unceremoniously left in unfamiliar territory. Fabiene described how her family arrived to Nova Holanda:

My grandfather was a bricklayer so their house in Macedo Sobrinho [in Humaitá] was one of the few brick houses on the hill and it was a very big, comfortable house. There was a whole support network of family and friends close by and my grandmother ran a *birosca* [bar and convenience store] out of the house so she could work and stay home to take care of their six children and her brother who had a disability. But my grandfather died and when a social worker came to assess my grandmother's economic level, they decided that she was one of the poorest because she was a widow with six children. So instead of Vila Kennedy or Cidade de Deus, they threw her in a wooden shack with a dirt floor in Nova Holanda. She didn't have any support structure, no place to work,

---

[21] Skarbek (2014) makes a similar argument about informal institutions and social norms being unable to govern behavior among prison inmates once overcrowding becomes a problem.

[22] The close connection between the construction of housing projects and the emergence and persistence of gangs has been addressed at length in the Chicago context (Aspholm 2020; Hagedorn and Rauch 2007; Venkatesh 2000, 2008). For other work on the relationship between housing projects and gangs, see Vigil (2007) on Los Angeles, Dubet (1987) on Paris, and Pinnock (1984) on Cape Town.

and six children, the youngest of which was six months old. It was a very, very difficult history. ...My grandmother never spoke of it because it was too painful.[23]

Fabiene's family story is supported by the historical record. In fact, many of Nova Holanda's wooden homes were not finished when residents arrived – the floors were still dirt and there were no faucets or electrical outlets (Vaz 1994, 129–33). In some cases, like those of Fabiene's grandmother, these living conditions were far worse than the favelas from which they had come. Moreover, after only a couple of years, the sanitation, water, and electrical systems ceased to function in most of the houses and most of the wooden structures would eventually be at risk of collapsing.

Nova Holanda was initially placed under the supervision of Fundação Leão XIII, an organization born of a partnership between the Catholic Church and the municipal government. Although Leão XIII represented a shift to less repressive public policy toward favela inhabitants, its larger motive was to suppress popular unrest, prevent Communist influences, and control much of community life with the threat of expulsion (Valladares 2008).[24] Leão XIII did not allow residents to make any improvements to their homes even as the living conditions deteriorated (Vaz 1994, 125–27). Leão XIII did, however, provide some governance services to residents, at least for a while. They mediated disputes, punished and prevented crime through their connections to the police, and offered education and hygiene classes to "civilize and urbanize" a population that the state thought was unprepared for permanent apartments (Varella, Bertazzo, and Jacques 2002, 40). In addition, through their connection to Leão XIII, police began to extort local residents by making them pay to move into the community in the first place (Vaz 1994, 128). Many of Nova Holanda's original inhabitants almost immediately turned away from Leão XIII because of its corrupt behavior and intransigence to local realities. Moreover, the memories of their violent expulsions from their former homes often led to powerful grievances. Thus, when problems arose between residents or someone needed help within the favela, most residents sought out informal leaders and not Leão XIII.[25]

The drug trade likely arrived to Maré with the inauguration of Nova Holanda. The temporary housing project received thousands of residents from much older favelas where "the movement" was already active. At first, it was just a few residents, mostly women, in fact, that grew marijuana in their houses and sold it to their neighbors to help make some extra income to support their family.[26] For many residents from the Northeast of Brazil, this was a familiar practice. Nova Holanda residents from this period also remember some *bandidos* (bandits) who lived in the neighborhood but there were no organizations

---

[23] Fabiene 7/25/2018.
[24] Eduardo 10/11/2013.
[25] Eduardo 10/11/2013; João 10/16/2013.
[26] Josie 7/10/2018.

or groups yet operating. According to Vicente, "One guy or another would have a small pistol that he would use to rob people outside of the favela but crime was very underground at the time."[27] Other longtime residents told me that if there was ever violence in the community during this period it involved knives and not guns.[28] Beto remembered that there were a couple of older men with pistols in the 1960s but they didn't display them and almost never used them. "It was all hidden," he said.[29]

Longtime residents could not recall very much violence in Nova Holanda before the 1970s and no one could remember the presence of gangs until at least a decade after the neighborhood's creation.[30] By the late 1970s, however, six different gang-like groups had emerged and began laying claim to small pieces of turf within Nova Holanda. Each operated within just a couple of blocks or streets and their members were generally all from the same favelas from which they had been removed. According to Vaz:

> The immense ruptures created by the loss of their former homes (as well as friends and relatives) traumatized the removed who, upon arriving to [Nova Holanda], were divided into groups according to the favela of origin. These became demarcated territories in which, for example, a resident of Praia do Pinto could not walk in the 'territory' occupied by residents from Esqueleto (1994, 136).

It is difficult to say with certainty because we have no systematic documentation of these initial groups, their membership, or the exact activities in which they were engaging, but it is likely that the gangs initially formed in response to local prejudices and fears.[31] Young men turned to forming groups to prevent physical and verbal abuse by others.[32] After forming for mutual protection, these groups then began to use their organization to make money by developing the drug trade or engaging in daring robberies and assaults outside of the favela.[33] By all accounts, the gangs coexisted relatively peacefully until the end of the 1970s when small conflicts and physical confrontations gradually grew to include gunfights and revenge killings.[34]

---

[27] Vicente 11/6/2013.

[28] João 10/16/2013.

[29] Beto 10/8/2013.

[30] Lino 11/3/2014; Artur 3/17/2014; Eduardo 10/11/2013.

[31] Hagedorn points to similar tensions within and among Hispanic communities as key to the formation of Puerto Rican and Mexican gangs in Milwaukee (1988, 66).

[32] For example, one area of Nova Holanda became referred to as *Vietnã* (Vietnam) because it was thought to be full of *ladrões* (thieves) that had come from Praia do Pinto (Vaz 1994, 136).

[33] *O Globo* 7/24/1967; 6/12/1969; 5/26/1973; 6/26/1976; 4/10/1979.

[34] This process is remarkably similar to that proposed by some scholars of US gangs, which form to protect themselves from abuse, harassment, and violence (Brenneman 2011). The more violence and abuse, the more necessary it will be for young men (and women) to form or join gangs. Moreover, the emergence of one gang often leads other gangs to form as youth become even more susceptible to harassment and violence, what Klein has referred to as the "tipping

By the early 1980s, intergang violence began to seriously disrupt community life. The *Irmãos Metralha* (Beagle Boys), named after the Disney cartoon characters, were the most powerful gang in the area. They were led by the youngest of five teenage brothers, Wanderlei, referred to as Lelei. Through direct conflict with some of the other local gangs, the Irmãos Metralha had won control of roughly half of Nova Holanda. The other half was contested by a handful of less powerful gangs: Candinho's gang, Vavá Rosalvo's gang, Tiãozinho's gang, Juarez's gang, and the 8th Street gang.[35] Candinho's gang would eventually become the most powerful of these and initiate an all-out war for control of Nova Holanda with the Irmãos Metralha. Although some of the other gangs persisted, they were quickly destroyed or incorporated by Candinho's gang during the conflict.

At this time, neither of the two gangs yet had high-powered rifles. Most of the members had pistols of varying calibers and one or two of the members possessed a submachine gun.[36] Despite their lack of high-powered weaponry, because of their relatively equal size and strength – roughly twenty members, ranging in age from late teens to early twenties – these two gangs remained in a constant state of violent conflict for several years (Silva 2012, 106–9). One gang would routinely invade their rivals' territory in the early morning and kill as many members of their rival as they could find.[37] Despite the presence of a DPO in Nova Holanda and police efforts to find and apprehend gang members, the police lacked the capacity (and perhaps desire) to effectively pursue and capture the gang members or put an end to the violence.

During the two-year gang war, the Irmãos Metralha and Candinho's gang began to intensively control space by patrolling the border with their rival and preventing residents from crossing over. Each gang also began to engage in extreme forms of punishment for anyone suspected of cooperating with their rival (Silva 2012, 106–9). There were few limits to what either of the gangs would do to try to defeat their rival: They tortured their victims by cutting off limbs, mutilating their bodies, and leaving them in the street. No one was beyond suspicion. In 1983 alone, more than fifty people were murdered in Nova Holanda.[38] The violence became so bad that residents stopped crossing over the border between the two gangs' territories and began referring to the two sides of the community as Nova Holanda I and II.[39]

point" (1995, 29–32). Overall, instead of viewing gangs as the embodiment of violence, much work in this area understands them more as a response to violence (see also Melde, Taylor, and Esbensen 2009; Sánchez-Jankowski 1991; Sobel and Osoba 2009).

[35] Josie 7/10/2018; *O Globo* 5/26/1973; 7/26/1983.

[36] The first semiautomatic rifle, an AR-15, arrived to Maré in 1991 and was owned by Thaíris until his death (Josie 7/10/2018).

[37] *O Globo* 7/26/1983.

[38] *O Globo* 12/28/1983. If true, this is a staggering number, which equates to a homicide rate of roughly 500 per 100,000, which would be among the highest ever recorded.

[39] *O Globo* 12/16/1983.

Overall, favela residents had little recourse to stop these battles for outright supremacy. The history of Maré does, however, contain one prominent example of community collective action to try to bring an end to gang turf wars. Amid the conflict between the Irmãos Metralha and Candinho's gangs, several local social movements and community institutions, including members of the Catholic Church, a women's group, community health workers, the local samba school, and members of Maré's *União das Associações de Moradores da Maré* (an association of various AMs in Maré) decided to try to put an end to the violence. They organized several protests, hung a massive banner spanning the border between the gangs that read *"Vamos Acreditar na Paz"* (Let's Believe in Peace), and met with the two gangs' leaders, individually, demanding an end to the war (Silva 2012, 106–9). Lelei and Candinho eventually agreed to a truce.[40] In a historic scene, the two fully armed gangs met at a predetermined time on the border between their territories. In front of a large crowd, gang members threw their weapons on the ground, thus bringing an end to their yearslong conflict.[41] Although each gang retained control of their respective turf and continued to engage in a variety of illegal activities, their war and all its associated violence came to an end. This, however, would be the last time residents managed to collectively demand an end to gang violence in Maré. The territorial disputes and intergang conflict that would arrive to Maré in the 1990s would be of an entirely different magnitude.

Despite the truce, the rivalry between the two sides continued. At the end of 1983, the Irmãos Metralha side of the community, which contained many of the palafitas, was destroyed by the municipal authority and all of the residents were removed to housing projects in other areas of Maré (see Chapter 7).[42] Without a reliable base of operations, several of the Irmãos Metralha were quickly imprisoned and their leader, Lelei, was eventually killed in 1985 (Silva 2012, 103).[43] Candinho's gang immediately took over the Irmãos Metralha territory. Around this time, Candinho was arrested and his second in command, a man known as Jorge Negão (Big Black Jorge), became the gang's new leader. For the next decade, Jorge Negão would be the most powerful gang leader in Maré. He developed an intensive and personalistic form of governance in Nova Holanda, in which he became the local arbitrator of disputes, punisher of criminals, and distributor of benefits.

---

[40] According to one resident at the time, the key motivating factor behind the gang leaders agreeing to the truce was the threat by Escadinha (José Carlos Encina, one of the most feared and well-known CV leaders) that he would invade Nova Holanda and take the area over if the gangs did not end their war (*O Globo* 11/16/1986).

[41] In a similarly successful act of collective and public resistance, the residents of Vigário Geral demanded the removal of the local gang following a particularly violent episode (Ventura 1994). These moments are incredibly rare in the history of the city.

[42] *O Globo* 12/16/1983.

[43] Lino 11/3/2014; Josie 7/10/2018.

Shortly after becoming Dono, Jorge Negão distributed pamphlets to residents explaining that any violence within his territory would no longer be permitted.[44] He showed residents that he was true to his word by harshly punishing those that disobeyed. Over the years, Jorge Negão would become renowned for his adherence to this rule.[45] He and his gang often turned to brutal forms of punishment, including execution, for crimes committed within the community, such as stealing or rape.[46] While such spectacular forms of punishment would seem to indicate a more disordered and competitive environment, residents of the era welcomed the harsh form of justice. Many long-time residents described Jorge Negão's tenure as idyllic and peaceful.[47] In an interview from that era, one resident reportedly said, "Here in the favela no one steals. If you steal, you are expelled or killed. These guys [the gang] give us protection. We get more protection from them than we do from the police."[48] Another resident described Jorge Negão's regime in the following way: "There are people who think they can come out of nowhere and stab each other... and there are lots of feuds between families. If it weren't for the gang, there would be a lot of death here."[49]

Especially following several years in which crime was mostly uncontrolled within the community and levels of violence reached incredible levels, Jorge Negão's strict form of order was welcomed by many. Homicides fell from an astonishing fifteen per month in 1984 to less than one per month in 1986.[50] Jorge Negão was especially popular among shop owners as he implemented a security patrol in which gang members would ride bicycles around the community to ensure there were no crimes occurring.[51] Other than the brutal punishments – directed mostly at young men caught stealing or engaging in other prohibited activities within his territory or gang members accused of *vacilação* (disloyalty) – Jorge Negão and his gang refrained from using threats and violence more indiscriminately. Residents were able to move freely and the gang did not monitor their borders like during their war with the Irmãos Metralha.

The principal reason why Jorge Negão could maintain a less coercive posture was that he and the other existing Donos in Maré refrained from violent competition. After the truce between the Irmãos Metralha and Candinho's gang, no one could remember any intergang violence occurring until the arrival

---

[44] *O Globo* 7/2/1992a.
[45] By the time of his death in 1992, Jorge Negão was sought for the murder of no less than thirty people (*O Globo* 7/2/1992a). According to numerous residents, he commonly wore his baseball cap backward when he was going to punish someone (Mattos 2016).
[46] Claudio 10/28/2013; *O Globo* 11/16/1986.
[47] Osvaldo 1/7/2015; Reinaldo 10/28/2013; Angelo 3/12/2014; *O Globo* 11/16/1986.
[48] *O Globo* 11/16/1986.
[49] *O Globo* 11/16/1986.
[50] *O Globo* 11/16/1986.
[51] *O Globo* 7/2/1992a.

of the factions in the 1990s.[52] There were no invasions or other gang confrontations for the better part of a decade.[53] According to gang members of this era, the Donos from Nova Holanda, Morro do Timbau, and Parque União respected each other and allegedly even attended baile funk parties in one another's turfs, something that would become unimaginable after the arrival of the factions.[54]

In addition, with the arrival of cocaine to Maré in the 1980s and the increasing profits of Jorge Negão's gang, many residents began to seek the gang leader out to help pay for medicine, food, or other expenses. On the one hand, as one of the wealthier members of the community, and given the degree of poverty among some residents, it was seen as his duty to help those in need. This was probably the case for other more economically stable members of the community as well but there was a quid pro quo nature to these exchanges that likely did not exist for other more licit enterprises. Jorge Negão was a wanted man, and the police regularly scoured the area for him.[55] The Dono would have suffered greatly – he eventually did – should he have been captured. Both he and Nova Holanda's residents knew this.

Jorge Negão was a famously popular and well-liked Dono. He often bought snacks for kids, medicine for the elderly, and occasionally paid for holes in the street to be filled.[56] His gang regularly stole trucks full of chickens or robbed rice, beans, and other staples from grocery stores that they then distributed to residents in what Osvaldo referred to as "a Robin Hood thing. ...If you asked my mother straight up, she would still say Jorge Negão was the best gang leader ever."[57] The Nova Holanda gang also organized weekly baile funks, where DJs would play an emerging, underground style of music that combined explicit lyrics with a heavy bass track.[58] Jorge Negão and his gang also threw holiday parties on Easter, Mother's, Father's, and Children's Day, and for the *Festa Junina* (June Festival), a Brazilian holiday celebrating the harvest and rural life. Jorge Negão even funded drag shows called *Noite das Estrelas* (Night of the Stars), in which trans and queer members of the community would perform to large audiences (Noite das Estrelas 2021). Jorge Negão also often set up a television in the street so that everyone could watch the very popular *novellas* (soap operas) of the era.[59]

---

[52] One exception was the murder of Thaíris, who had taken over the remnants of the Irmãos Metralha gang after most of the brothers had been killed or imprisoned (*O Globo* 7/2/1992a). Allegedly, Thaíris stole money from a boca in Nova Holanda and Jorge Negão ordered his murder (Josie 7/10/2018).

[53] *O Globo* 7/2/1992a.

[54] Lino 11/3/2013; Claudio 10/28/2013.

[55] In Nova Holanda, a PPC replaced the DPO in 1986, which was used as a local base to pursue gang members. Residents remained unwillingly to enter the premises (Artur 3/17/2014).

[56] Reinaldo 10/28/2013; Lino 11/3/2014; Breno 12/16/2014; Wagner 1/2/2017.

[57] Osvaldo 1/7/2015; *O Globo* 9/10/1983.

[58] *O Globo* 7/2/1992a.

[59] Lino 6/18/2014.

Decades later, men and women who grew up during this period recounted how they had idolized Jorge Negão. Some of the men I interviewed admitted to pretending to be him when they playacted with their friends, shooting at police or other bandits with his characteristic submachine gun.[60] When Jorge Negão was finally killed by a Federal Police agent in 1992, hundreds of residents put candles in their windows and along the streets to commemorate his death.[61]

Jorge Negão was not the first Dono in Rio to engage in the provision of benefits – such practices were one of the primary ways that Donos throughout the city could popularize their authority and maintain the support of the community. Like other Donos of the era, Jorge Negão's relationship with residents of his territory was always a proprietary and personalistic one. This was Jorge Negão's gang and *his* community. He was the one on the streets doing the punishing, arbitrating disputes, and providing benefits. His incredible popularity likely delayed the integration of the Nova Holanda gang into the expanding prison-based factions by several years (see Chapter 5).[62] Although the role of the Dono would continue to be an important element in future criminalized governance regimes, no longer would the Dono be so visible or at the forefront of governance. Such highly personalistic rule would mostly come to an end. Instead, governance activities would be implemented by an expanding organization.

Parque União

The gang that would eventually emerge and govern Parque União followed a very different trajectory. Unlike in Nova Holanda, Parque União had little to no crime during its initial stage of development. Residents could not remember any thieves, robbers, or drug dealers living within the quickly growing favela for the first two decades of the community's existence, until the end of the 1970s. Tight control of the community, initially by Margarino Torres, a Communist lawyer, then by other community leaders, likely prevented crimes from occurring and gangs from emerging. In addition to organizing the settlement of the area and prohibiting the entrance of "bad elements," Torres charged all residents a tax, prohibited prostitution and gambling, and burned down houses that were built without his authorization (Vaz 1994, 167). Through his legal expertise and connections, Torres also helped consolidate the area as a permanent settlement by preventing police from entering the community without search warrants (Ribeiro da Silva 2006, 88–89).

---

[60] Breno 12/16/2014; Wagner 1/2/2017.
[61] Eduarda 9/19/2013.
[62] Jorge Negão also allegedly began paying the CV faction for protection near the end of his tenure (*O Globo* 7/18/1992).

In 1961, just a few short years after the initial occupation, Torres abandoned Parque União and Antônio Azevedo took over the administration of the area. Azevedo would continue many of Torres' practices and was instrumental in the organization of an AM (Vaz 1994, 167). Parque União continued to rapidly grow during the 1960s as the settlement's wooden shacks were gradually replaced with brick-and-mortar houses. In the coming decades, many residents managed to build multiple levels to their homes and Parque União would become the most populous neighborhood in Maré.

In the 1970s, a PPC was installed along Avenida Brasil, on the edge of Parque União. Residents remembered that, initially, police in the PPC worked with the AM to resolve problems and fight low-level crime within the community.[63] One longtime resident recalled that the police would sometimes arrest or detain *"vagabundos"* (bums), take them to the PPC, and force them to clean the bathroom or just check to make sure their papers were in order.[64] No one I interviewed from Parque União, however, could recall the police engaging in the kinds of torture and abuse that I commonly heard from Nova Holanda residents.

There are several possible explanations for this disparity. First, the PPC in Parque União was located on the edge of the favela and not in the very heart of the community like in Nova Holanda; torture could have been occurring and residents were just unaware. An alternative explanation is that the police in the two posts behaved differently. According to Bernardo, for instance, the police in Nova Holanda felt like they needed to deal with criminals in a more violent and coercive manner because they were failing to control violence and criminality.[65] Moreover, the population in Nova Holanda was inhabited overwhelmingly by descendants of slaves who had lived in Rio's older favelas for generations whereas Parque União was mostly settled by mixed race migrants from the impoverished Northeast region of Brazil.[66] The different practices of the police could have also been driven by their perceptions of and prejudices toward these two communities. Finally, it may have been that the levels of abuse and torture were similar in the two communities but that due to the histories of removal and their disdain for the police, residents of Nova Holanda remembered this violence as excessive and unacceptable. Whatever the explanation, residents recalled that the relationship with the police in Nova Holanda had always been more precarious than in Parque União. Nonetheless, over time, the relationship with the police in Parque União would similarly deteriorate and, as drug traffickers and groups of robbers became more common, the behavior of the police became as aggressive and abusive as other areas of Maré.

---

[63] Vinícius 11/9/2014; Gustavo 11/19/2014.
[64] Gustavo 11/19/2014.
[65] Bernardo 1/16/2017.
[66] According to a recent Maré census, roughly 18 percent of Nova Holanda identifies as *preta* (black) while only 5 percent in Parque União (Redes da Maré 2019a).

By the late 1970s, several individuals and small groups began to engage in crime and violence in Parque União. Vinícius, who moved to the area as a child in 1963, recalled that Lulu, a local musician who played in a *Música Popular Brasileira* (Brazilian Popular Music) or MPB band, and who would later become the leader of the gang, sold marijuana on the side during the 1970s.[67] His drug dealing was clandestine and he did not carry any weapons at first. In addition, the jogo do bicho was also active in the community and there were several groups of young men who were known as robbers and thieves.[68] Importantly, none of these small groups were part of larger organizations and they lacked the capacity to monopolize criminal activities and violence within the community.

Lulu would eventually be arrested in the mid-1970s and sent to prison where he made connections with elements of what would later become CV. Upon his return to Parque União several years later and with access to CV's trafficking networks, Lulu started selling cocaine and slowly expanding his gang. Residents began to refer to him as the Dono.[69] Despite the use of this moniker, Lulu still wielded relatively little authority within Parque União. Unlike Nova Holanda, where multiple gangs emerged and began to compete for control of the drug trade, forcing them to become cohesive and militarized units, there was no similar process in Parque União. Residents said that Lulu controlled the drug trade with only a pistol and that although he had a bunch of friends who were also involved in drug dealing, "they weren't really an organization."[70] Without a rival threat, Lulu and his gang were not incentivized to militarize nor to create a more cohesive organization such as Nova Holanda's gangs.

For the duration of the 1970s, Lulu threw some parties and organized the occasional soccer tournament but did not provide much in terms of resources to help people in the community. He did little to control violence within the community and mostly did not mediate disputes between residents. As an example of the relative lack of power of Lulu and his fledgling gang, residents retained the right to have and use firearms until the 1990s. Evaristo, for instance, remembered that his grandfather, a local bar owner, used to have a gun behind the bar just in case there would be any problems with customers.[71] He recalled that his grandfather would shoot his gun in the air when customers got into fights to calm a situation down.

---

[67] Vinícius 11/9/2014. It is also interesting to note that there are incredibly diverse origins of what would eventually become the gangs. In Maré, some founding members of local *quadrilhas* (gangs) were bandits and thieves, others musicians, or even construction workers. Perhaps the most common origin was just a group of friends that hung out on a street corner. This matches existing work from the US (Hagedorn 1988; Thrasher 1927).

[68] Vinícius 11/9/2014.

[69] Vinícius 11/9/2014.

[70] Vinícius 11/9/2014.

[71] Evaristo 12/23/2014.

There are two interesting things to note in Evaristo's recollection. First, it is almost unheard of for residents not involved with the gang to have or use firearms. Once a gang takes control of a community, they will never allow residents to have or use weapons. The fact that Evaristo's grandfather continued to have a firearm signifies that the local gang still had not monopolized violence within their turf. Second, the fact that there were fights and problems within the community serious enough that a firearm was necessary also means that the gang remained relatively weak. Serious fights and destruction of property other than if sanctioned by the gang itself is almost nonexistent in favelas with a powerful gang because everyone knows that severe forms of punishment await anyone engaging in such behavior. Moreover, Evaristo recalled that even in the early 1980s, police would still frequent his grandfather's bar during the day and then the gang members could be seen at the same bar in the evenings. In the coming decades, this would become an impossibility. Police would no longer enter favela territories so casually nor spend much time in them.

At the beginning of the 1980s, the AM in Parque União still maintained significant authority within the community. One president, Custódio Belardino, was particularly active, resolving disputes between residents, offering a variety of services through the AM, and successfully demanding a series of infrastructure projects from the municipal and state governments.[72] In addition, the Catholic Church as well as several Evangelical Churches already maintained a strong presence within Parque União. Residents also sought out these organizations to resolve disputes and gain access to services.[73]

In the early 1980s, crime and violence began to increase in Parque União. The archive of *O Globo* newspaper contains dozens of articles detailing the activities of criminals, mostly thieves, robbers, and kidnappers, who used Parque União as a home base, yet another example of the weakness of Lulu's embryonic gang.[74] A stronger, more cohesive gang would not have allowed such unaffiliated individuals to use or live in their turf for fear of attracting attention to their own activities.[75] Such forms of violent crime, naturally, led to increased police attention, which eventually forced Lulu to start imposing a more responsive form of order.[76] According to Gustavo, after the police started conducting more operations, Lulu made sure that people did not steal within the neighborhood and expanded his governance activities by resolving a lot of the residents' problems.[77] In this way, it appears that the gang's first forays into governance were less driven by competition with rivals and a need

---

[72] *O Globo* 10/20/1982; 12/28/1984; 8/13/1989.
[73] Patrício 6/27/2014.
[74] *O Globo* 1/15/1979; 4/10/1979; 7/18/1980; 7/19/1980; 5/21/1981; 10/20/1981; 2/8/1982; 4/1/1982; 12/21/1982; 1/9/1984; 3/26/1984.
[75] Also part of the reason why Jorge Negão fought crime so assiduously in his area (*O Globo* 11/16/1986).
[76] Vinícius 11/9/2014.
[77] Gustavo 11/19/2014.

to assert their dominance, as in Nova Holanda, and more incentivized by a need to avoid enforcement.

Over the next few years, Lulu treated the community very well, avoided antagonizing the police, and prevented crime and violence within the neighborhood. He was eventually killed in 1986 by a member of his own gang, Djalma Negão, who then tried to take over leadership of the gang.[78] Lulu's brother, Joãozinho, however, ended up winning the support of the rest of the gang, forcing Djalma to flee. One month later, Djalma returned with a gang of his own, and attempted take the community back by force, the only time anyone could remember that a gang tried to invade Parque União. He was killed by police in the ensuing shootout between the two gangs.[79] According to Vinícius, Joãozinho was a very social and benevolent Dono but he also died at the hands of police a short time later.[80] The leadership of the gang then passed to Leandro, Joãozinho's nephew, who was only a teenager at the time. According to Vinícius, "Leandro was a cruel and wicked kid."[81] He disrespected residents, refused to mediate disputes, failed to combat crime, and provided few services. This was one of the worst periods for residents in Parque União because they were still unable to go to the police for fear of retribution but Leandro had little sense of what he should provide to the community in return.[82] Continuing enforcement efforts should have incentivized Leandro to provide responsive benefits to the community as Lulu and Joãozinho had done before but he failed to understand this fundamental relationship and what he needed from the community (perhaps due to his age). Overall, this meant that Leandro never gained the authority or fame of some of his counterparts in other areas of Maré (longtime residents of Parque União seldom even remembered his name) and perhaps explains why he would also eventually be murdered by a member of his own gang.

Despite Leandro's deviation from expectations in terms of his treatment of the community, the case of Parque União, like Nova Holanda, supports the theory developed in Chapter 3. One of the unique qualities of Parque União during this period was its relative calm. By the late 1980s, most other communities in Maré had already experienced violent turf wars for control of the drug trade. Parque União was an exception. The primary reason for this lack of competition was that a large drainage canal separated Parque União from the rest of Maré. To enter the community, residents had to pass by the PPC along Avenida Brasil, likely preventing other gangs from invading. Conversely, the canal also prevented the Parque União gang from attempting to expand their own territory. This lack of rival competition meant that the gang did not

[78] Vinícius 11/9/2014; *O Globo* 2/20/1986.
[79] *O Globo* 2/20/1986.
[80] Vinícius 11/9/2014.
[81] Vinícius 11/9/2014.
[82] Vinícius 11/9/2014.

need to expand the organization by increasing its manpower and weaponizing to the same degree as in Nova Holanda. Without the incentive to monitor and control their territory more intensively, the gang did not monopolize violence until almost a decade after Jorge Negão and his gang in Nova Holanda. And yet, due to increasing pressure from the police, the Parque União gang and its leaders (other than Leandro) began to resolve disputes and provide a more responsive form of order within the community. In these ways, the Parque União gang demonstrates the close connection between enforcement and the provision of benefits.

Morro do Timbau

The gang that would eventually emerge from Morro do Timbau followed yet another path of development. From the very beginning of Maré's first settlement, the military controlled migration to the area and dominated resident life with the threat of expulsion. Residents eventually formed a close relationship with the military that helped to prevent gangs from forming until much later than in either of the other two cases detailed earlier. A single gang would eventually emerge on the Morro, more than a decade after Nova Holanda gangs had begun to violently compete with one another and after Lulu's drug-trafficking operation had already formed. As a result, despite the Morro predating the other favelas in Maré by several decades, the Morro do Timbau gang's governance activities began much later than the other two cases.

Shortly after the founding of Morro do Timbau, an adjacent area was selected for the Brazilian Military's 1st Regiment of Combat Vehicles (*1° Batalhão de Carros de Combate*) and a base was built in 1947. An army Sergeant named Adauto quickly appeared on the Morro, telling residents that the entire area was the property of the military, and that they had to pay a monthly fee to avoid expulsion (Santos 1983, 44). Because they were squatting on land they did not own, the residents had no legal recourse. According to military personnel, this was unsanctioned behavior, and the senior officials had no knowledge that Adauto was engaging in this activity (p. 44). Nonetheless, Adauto allowed the residents to remain on the Morro and even helped the community expand. This began a symbiotic if unequal relationship between the community and the military that remained in place for most of the next four decades.

For the first several decades, control of life by the military was near absolute. Adauto required residents to sign a contract that stipulated that the lands on which they lived belonged to the Armed Forces and that they would behave and organize their homes as if they were in the military (Ribeiro da Silva 2006, 205). Anyone who wanted to move to the area was forced to pay a fee and meet several standards of respectability and financial security.[83] In the 1950s, the military implemented even stricter rules under a new sergeant's (Julio)

---

[83] Ademir 11/19/2014.

tenure by prohibiting any new constructions or renovations and limiting entry and exit to the favela, while continuing the protection scheme (Ribeiro da Silva 2006, 77). When Sergeant Julio found that new houses had been built without his authorization or that renovations to existing homes had been made, he destroyed them immediately with no regard for families or possessions. Military personnel even carried out curfew checks at 10 pm to ensure residents were in their homes (Santos 1983, 7–8). If there were interpersonal conflicts or problems within the community, Sergeant Julio or one of the Commanders at the base would resolve the dispute.[84] Finally, they even built a barbed wire fence around the Morro with a guard post where residents were forced to present documentation to enter and exit and which prevented them from having visitors outside of the specified hours (Santos 1983, 8).

On one hand, the military's imposition of this extremely strict form of order had several benefits. First, the Morro became the least densely populated favela in Maré because many would-be migrants to the area were turned away and others expelled. Also, by controlling entry and exit and by imposing curfews, much crime and violence was likely prevented. Those with the need or desire to engage in illegal activities were wary of doing so through the credible threat of expulsion. In this regard, the Morro differed considerably from the neighboring favelas of Baixa do Sapateiro and Parque Maré, which were not supervised by the military and lacked a significant form of organization. Settlement of these areas was totally unplanned. Criminality emerged much sooner in these areas and they were considered by residents to be, "a very dangerous place... full of bandits" (Vaz 1994, 9). Though this description is likely hyperbolic, the presence of thieves and bandits in other areas of Maré significantly predates their emergence in Morro do Timbau.

Such absolute control by the military, however, made life difficult for residents. Although the community was highly organized, residents were unable to improve their housing situation, lacked the resources to improve the infrastructure of the community, and the military often dealt with them in a rather violent and brutal fashion.[85] With the prospect of eviction and removal constantly hanging over them, residents lived in a precarious and untenable situation. They eventually began to push back. First, residents became increasingly distrustful of the military's claim to their land. Groups of residents disseminated lists with hundreds of signatures to various authorities demanding property rights, even inviting several political party members and local politicians to visit the Morro (Vaz 1994, 11). In return for promised support during elections, these politicians became highly critical of the military's treatment of residents.[86] The response of Sergeant Julio and the base Commanders was initially retaliatory but, by the 1960s, the residents and the military came to

[84] Ademir 11/19/2014.
[85] Ademir 12/4/2014.
[86] *O Globo* 6/17/1954.

an agreement. The military could maintain their security regime but residents were allowed greater freedom of movement and, with the authorization of the Commander, the ability to renovate and improve their homes (Santos 1983, 13). This led to several public works projects, the first of which was the installation of three huge water cisterns followed by the inauguration of a Light Commission in 1967 that provided electricity to many of the residents (pp. 14–15). Finally, residents acquired guarantees that any existing homes would not be demolished or evicted (Vaz 1994, 10–12).

In the late 1960s, Agamemnon, a young student activist, became president of the AM, founded in 1954, which began a period of infrastructure development and an even closer partnership with the military. Agamemnon worked to improve the water networks, extend the electrical grid, pave streets, and build retaining walls and sewage drains (Santos 1983, 20). All of this was done under the watchful eye of Sergeant Cruz, who began his tenure of control in 1970. He made sure that all infrastructure improvements did not impede military access to any part of the community and conformed to the security specifications of the base. Sergeant Cruz even lived on the Morro, in housing built for military personnel, which further solidified the close relationship between the Morro and the military (p. 19).

If any problems within the community arose – such as disagreements between community members – "Agamemnon gave the verdicts and the Sergeant legitimized them" (p. 20). Occasionally, soldiers from the base would get drunk on *açucana* (sugar cane liquor) and abuse or threaten residents. In these cases, Agamemnon went to Sergeant Cruz or the base Commander to complain and the soldiers were disciplined.[87] Many residents also used to go to Agamemnon to resolve their problems; couples, neighbors, virtually anyone who needed something to be done went to Agamemnon.

For the entirety of the 1960s and 1970s, no one could remember any thieves, bandits, or drug traffickers being present in Morro do Timbau. Beginning in the mid-1980s, however, important changes were taking place. First, the military began to extract itself from the daily governance of the community. After years of investigation, the property claims of the military were found to be spurious and, after residents gained property rights, the governance arrangement between Sergeant Cruz and Agamemnon collapsed (Santos 1983, 147). As this relationship broke down, a group of residents challenged Agamemnon's authority, arguing that only he and a small group of friends were profiting from his "despotic" and "violent" methods (Santos 1983, 23). In 1984, another candidate won the AM elections and the close relationship between the military and residents of Morro do Timbau finally came to an end.[88]

Without the threat of eviction and punishment by the military, some young men began to engage in criminal activities. In the mid- to late-1980s,

---

[87] Ademir 12/4/2014.
[88] Ademir 12/4/2014; 11/19/2014; Silvia 11/19/2014.

several high-profile bank robberies were carried out by residents of the Morro.[89] Eventually, a man nicknamed Kito emerged as the leader of this group of bandits.[90] He was initially more interested in robbing banks and armored cars than developing the drug trade but eventually took over the drug business from a man known as Rene do Pô (Powder Rene) in a "*golpe sem sangue*" (bloodless coup).[91] Although he did not dominate the area like Jorge Negão in Nova Holanda, he was able to slowly expand his organization, eventually taking over the drug trade in neighboring Baixa do Sapateiro from a man nicknamed Paulo Brasil.[92] Residents of the area began to refer to Kito as the Dono.

For several years, Kito's group of bandits engaged in no violent competition with other gangs and, as a result, they remained uncoercive.[93] They were little present on the streets and did not monitor the borders of their turf. If and when Kito dealt with crime in the area, residents remembered him preferring to expel those involved instead of employing violence.[94] Kito and his men provided few other benefits to the community initially. The attention of the police to the emerging drug trade on the Morro and Kito's fledgling gang seems to have remained far below what Jorge Negão and his Nova Holanda gang experienced. This difference in enforcement is perhaps because Kito's gang were less violent and only engaged in theft and robbery outside of the favela itself.[95] In addition, unlike Nova Holanda, many residents still reported crimes and dealt with disputes by going to the PPC stationed in Baixa do Sapateiro.[96] Like Parque União, the relationship with the police was not nearly so bad on the Morro as it was in Nova Holanda. It is curious, then, that the police did not receive more complaints about the gang and its behavior though perhaps so long as Kito and his men did not engage in violence and crime within the community itself, residents did not mind their presence. It was only after Kito and his gang integrated into the TC faction, that they became a significant focus of police enforcement efforts. Thereafter, the gang would quickly become more responsive to resident demands to resolve disputes, provide economic stimulation, and organize parties. This integration also coincided with higher levels of rival threat and the increasing use of coercion to control these communities (see Chapter 7).

---

[89] *O Globo* 11/26/85; 12/6/1985; 4/10/1986; 9/1/1990.
[90] Kito's real name is disputed, variously being referred to as José Ferreira de Almeida, Greik Santos da Cunha, and Francisco de Assis Santos.
[91] *O Globo* 4/10/88; 6/5/1988.
[92] Bruno 10/27/2014.
[93] Paulo 10/2/2013; Claudio 10/28/2013.
[94] Ademir 11/19/2014; Márcio 4/17/2014; Everton 4/17/2014.
[95] Dozens of news articles focus on crime and violence in Nova Holanda in the 1980s. There are extremely few from the Morro and mostly from the end of the decade.
[96] Ademir 11/19/2014.

THE BIRTH AND EXPANSION OF RIO DE JANEIRO'S
PRISON-BASED FACTIONS

At this point, it is necessary to address the other side of the organizations that would come to govern Rio's favelas. While small and fledgling street gangs were slowly developing in Maré and hundreds of other favelas across the city, another type of gang was emerging from within Rio de Janeiro's prisons. The marriage of these two organizational forms (prison and street gangs) would eventually change the nature of violence, crime, and politics in the city. In this section, I provide a brief history of the birth and expansion of CV and Rio's other prison-based factions.

The first modern gang faction, CV, was born in the 1970s during Brazil's military dictatorship (1964–85). In 1969, after a series of bank robberies by leftist revolutionaries, the Brazilian congress passed Decree No. 898 or the *Lei de Segurança Nacional* (National Security Law) through which the government could try political dissidents in military courts. Article 27 of that law stipulated that any attempt to rob a bank would lead to a sentence of 10–24 years or longer if anyone was killed (Gay 2015, 81–84). This meant that not only were revolutionaries tried in military courts but also many less ideologically inclined, "common" bank robbers and bandits. All these men were then incarcerated together in the Penal Institute of Cândido Mendes, the famed *Caldeirão do Diabo* (Devil's Cauldron) on Ilha Grande (Big Island), a former leper colony.

In Cândido Mendes, the revolutionaries and common prisoners were housed together in Cell Block B. The relationship between the common criminals and the revolutionaries was fraught from the beginning (Amorim 1993). This was not the meeting of two groups of equals with a common cause of ending the state's brutal, racist, and repressive behavior. Rather, it seems that the political prisoners always sought to distinguish themselves from their fellow cell-block mates. They saw these mostly dark-skinned men from favelas as real criminals and incapable of understanding their ideological movement. From the beginning, there were conflicts between the two groups and the political prisoners resorted to using violence when they thought one of their cellmates was out of line (Amorim 1993, 77; Misse 1999, 357). The political prisoners eventually demanded the prison administration separate the two groups and a brick wall was hastily constructed (Amorim 1993, 66; Misse 1999, 357).

There is still significant controversy concerning the role of the revolutionaries in the eventual creation of CV.[97] According to Amorim (1993), the presence

---

[97] Some of the prisoners had already become politicized over the course of the 1960s, in the first years of the military dictatorship (Amorim 1993, 74). Many of the rest, in addition, to contact with the revolutionaries, had access to books about guerrilla warfare and leftist thought that were passed back and forth among the prisoners, including works by Debray, Guevara, Marighela, Marx and Engels, Hubberman, and Hannecker, among others (pp. 70–74).

of the revolutionaries was instrumental in CV's creation while Misse (1999) argues that the connection between the political and common prisoners was weak and that the prisoners would have likely organized on their own. Either way, the political prisoners created a highly structured organization within Cândido Mendes.[98] Each member had a role (secretary, manager, internal duty, and political obligation) and the group prevented drug use, sexual abuse, gambling, or fighting amongst themselves (Amorim 1993, 66, 77). The revolutionaries were not, however, the only inmate organization at the time. In fact, four other prison gangs that included anywhere from a dozen to twenty men already existed within each of the other cell blocks. These organizations, referred to as *Falanges* (Phalanxes) by the media, were called *Sul* (South), *Coreia* (Korea), *Jacaré* (Alligator), and the *Neutros* (Neutrals). Each had their own unwritten rules, norms, and means of identification but their key characteristic was the abuse and predation of weaker members within the cells (pp. 54–56).

Sometime in 1974, a group of common prisoners in Cell Block B eventually decided that they would form their own organization to end the predation, abuse, and terror that characterized much of prisoner life. In the beginning, their focus was on protecting prisoners from abuse but, as the group grew, it would eventually make demands on the prison administration. Initially referred to as the *Falange LSN* (LSN Phalanx) after the National Security Law, the *Falange Vermelha* (Red Phalanx) for their alleged connection with leftist movements, or just *O Coletivo* (The Collective), they demanded an end to beatings by the guards, freedom to circulate in the common areas (cells were always locked before this), better treatment for visitors, including an end to invasive searches and the ability for visitors to spend the night on the island (Amorim 1993, 83–84).[99] They also founded a soccer team, created the *Clube Cultural e Recreativo dos Internos* (Cultural and Recreational Club of Inmates), which funded different activities for prisoners, and built a library (Amorim 1993, 97–98; Misse 1999, 364). They even created a slogan for their movement, "*Paz, Justiça e Liberdade!*" (Peace, Justice, and Freedom!).

By 1979, the political prisoners had already been transferred off the island as part of the *Lei de Anistia* (Amnesty Law) and Falange Vermelha had incorporated most of the prisoners in Cell Block B. The group that would later become CV gained at least some respect among prisoners of the other areas for their policy of ending abuse and violence between prisoners but increasing tensions with the Falange Jacaré eventually led CV to issue an ultimatum: submit

---

[98] There were, in fact, several different revolutionary groups present: *Movimento Revolucionário 8 de Outubro* (Revolutionary Movement of the 8th of October), *Aliança Libertadora Nacional* (National Liberation Alliance), *Vanguarda Popular Revolucionário* (People's Revolutionary Vanguard), and the *Vanguarda Armada Revolucionária Palmares* (Armed Revolutionary Vanguard of Palmares) (Amorim 1993, 68).

[99] The name Comando Vermelho was first used by Major Nelson Bastos Salmon, the Director of Cândido Mendes Prison in 1979, and was picked up by the media (Lima 1991, 68). The first mention of CV in the *Jornal do Brasil* is 10/21/1980 and in *O Globo* 4/4/1981.

to their authority or be killed (Amorim 1993, 99). Jacaré members refused to disband. In the early morning hours of September 17, 1979, dozens of CV members invaded Cell Block C where the leaders of Jacaré had sequestered themselves in a cell with thirty of their most trusted members. CV members, armed with knives, sharpened spoons, pieces of wood, and pipes, broke open the cell and confronted the Jacarés, eventually killing all the major leaders of the group and injuring many others. The rest of the Jacaré members decided to give themselves up or were later killed as all the other prison gangs immediately submitted to CV's authority (pp. 101–2).

Many of the original CV leaders were quickly transferred to other prisons where they spread the organization further. Although it remained a tightly knit group inside Cândido Mendes, this expansion would irrevocably change the organization. CV would never regain the hierarchical structure and cohesive leadership it had initially. In the first phase of expansion from the prisons (1979–86), the original leaders escaped or were released and returned to the favelas from which they came. At first, this group organized kidnappings and bank robberies to fund the organization and support its members and their families. They also formed strategic alliances with local gangs by loaning guns and personnel to those who sought to take over new territory (Misse 1999, 315, 321). To become part of CV, local gangs had to agree to an alliance against enemies as well as promise to respect, support, and protect residents and friends of the organization. CV's initial concern with normative behavior like preventing abuse of prisoners and respect for women, children, and the elderly in favela communities – values that some gangs had already developed independently – quickly gave way to a focus on profit as they realized the enormous moneymaking potential of their organization (Dowdney 2003, 29; Leeds 1996, 54; Misse 1999, 367).

During the second period of expansion (1986–94), CV spread rapidly to most of the favelas in the city. CV gangs engaged in increasingly violent competition with preexisting local groups for control of the drug trade. Many of the original leaders of CV were killed and a new leadership emerged. These men were younger, more ambitious, and, overall, had less respect for favela communities (Misse 1999, 315). Gang behavior in Rio's favelas became more coercive in the second phase of CV's evolution, especially because CV gangs faced increasing challenges to their dominance by a rival faction.

The origins and evolution of TC are still disputed. Misse (1999, 319, 322) points to another group of prisoners that organized within a different prison (Frei Caneca Penitentiary) in the 1970s with the name Falange Jacaré, which later became known as TC. Amorim (1993, 55) argues that Falange Jacaré from Cândido Mendes was destroyed but that two of the other Falanges (Sul and Coréia) would later unify in a different prison to form TC. According to the autobiography of William da Silva Lima (1991, 63), one of the founders of CV, several members of Jacaré would also be transferred to Ary Franco Prison after the massacre, where they started TC. According to *O Globo* reports from the 1980s, TC either broke from Falange Jacaré or Falange Vermelha inside Cândido Mendes but the two remained entirely separate organizations that controlled different prisons during the 1980s.[100] Perhaps the best evidence regarding the origins of TC comes from the *Jornal do Brasil*, which documented the rise of a rival to CV inside Cândido Mendes in the early 1980s.[101] The group was originally just called *Terceira Galeria* (Third Gallery), a reference to the part of the prison where they were housed, and was first formed in response to the increasingly brutal and violent treatment by CV after the original leaders had been transferred, escaped, or killed. By 1983, Terceira Galeria was also allegedly present in two other prisons in Rio (Lemos de Brito and Helio Gomes).[102] In that same year, 104 prisoners from the Terceira Galeria in Cândido Mendes were transferred to Ary Franco Prison, where CV and Falange Jacaré were also present. As late as 1991, *O Globo* reported that the three factions (CV, Terceira Galeria now referred to as TC, and Jacaré) were still fighting for control of Ary Franco Prison, where TC and Jacaré would allegedly form an alliance against CV.[103] After this, Falange Jacaré seems to have disappeared entirely.[104] Perhaps it dissolved or was fully incorporated into TC. Either way, from the early 1990s on, TC would be the sole competitor to CV for control of the prisons and favelas throughout the city.

Then, in 1994, the CV faction split, the result of ongoing disputes between the older and newer generations of the organization and a series of events that occurred in Complexo do Alemão, a group of a dozen favelas sprinkled over several hills in the Zona Norte of the city, just a short distance from Maré. In July of that year, Orlando Jogador, the Dono of Morro do Alemão (German Hill), and one of the most respected CV gang leaders in the city, was murdered by Ernaldo Pinto de Medeiros, nicknamed Uê, the Dono of Morro do Adeus (Goodbye Hill), a nearby favela also within the Complexo do Alemão. Uê's motivations were likely multiple. He was allegedly an incredibly ambitious young man and wanted control of Complexo do Alemão for himself but also desired revenge on Orlando Jogador for shooting and paralyzing his brother several years earlier. Whatever his motivations, Uê and his men pretended that he had been kidnapped by the police and asked Jogador to help pay the ransom. Jogador agreed and quickly gathered R$60,000 but when he met Uê's men to hand over the money, they immediately killed him and his entire entourage. The killing of a CV Dono without the authorization of the leadership of the faction was explicitly against the rules of the organization and the younger members of CV, many of whom idolized Jogador, demanded vengeance.[105]

---

[100] *O Globo* 4/4/1985; 4/13/1985.
[101] *Jornal do Brasil* 5/15/1983a.
[102] *Jornal do Brasil* 5/15/1983b.
[103] *O Globo* 10/29/1991.
[104] The last mention of the Falange Jacaré in the archives of *O Globo* is 11/11/1994.
[105] For a detailed description of this series of events, see Barcellos (2003, 282–86).

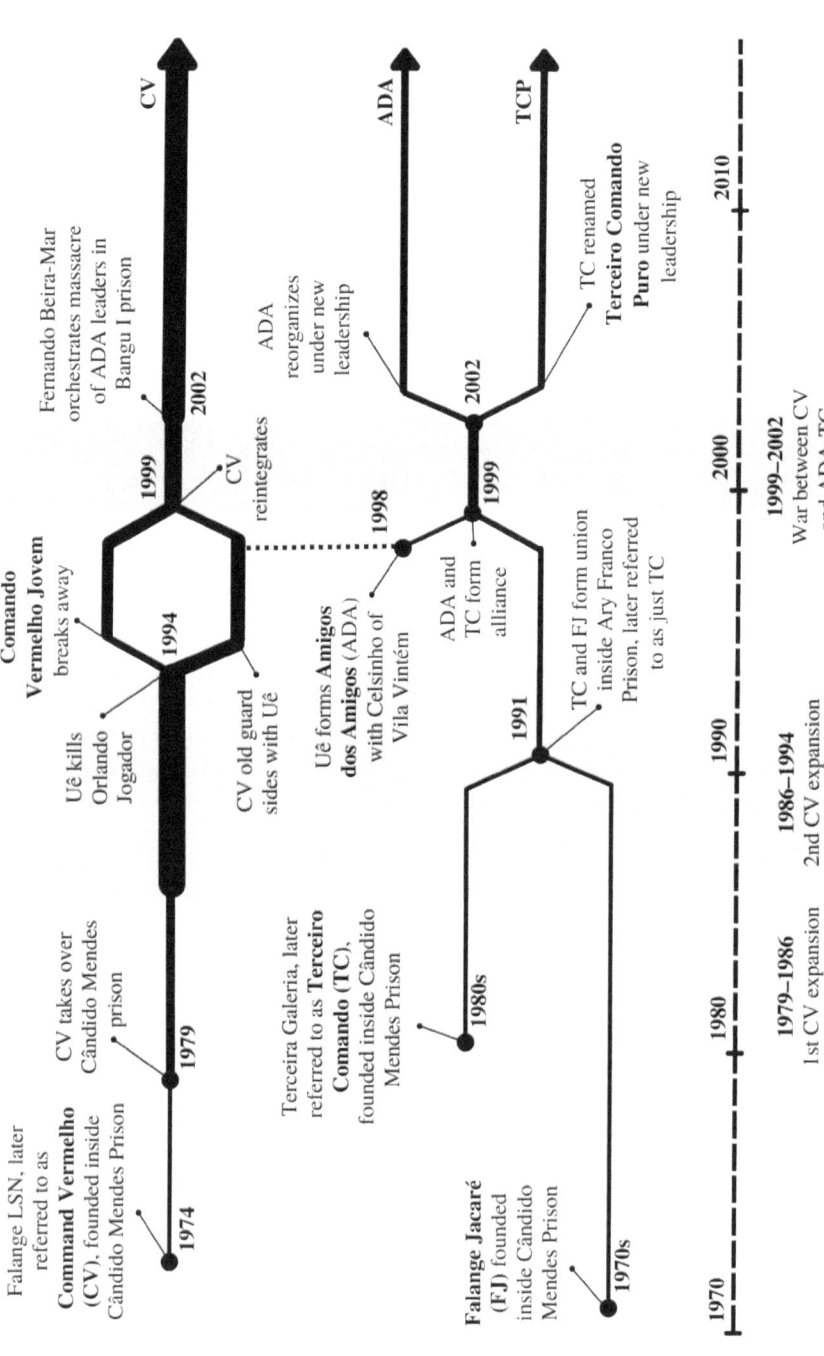

FIGURE 4.5 History of Rio de Janeiro's prison-based factions

Visualization by author. The width of the factions' lines represents their relative size (i.e., the number of favelas they each controlled throughout the city). N.B. The origins of TC and the demise of Falange Jacaré are still disputed.

Some of the old guard of CV maintained close connections to Uê, however, and refused to punish or expel him from the faction. The disagreement fractured the organization. The younger leaders christened themselves *Comando Vermelho Jovem* (Young Red Command, hereon CVJ). For the next several years, the CV and CVJ engaged in a series of assassinations and battles for control of favelas in the city.[106]

Then, in 1998, Uê left CV to create his own faction, *Amigos dos Amigos* (Friends of Friends, hereon ADA), with Celso of Vila Vintém. ADA quickly formed a strategic alliance with TC in 1999 to better compete with the more dominant CV factions, which precipitated the reintegration of CV.[107] It would take several years to fully reincorporate the more than 120 separate gangs that comprised CV and CVJ but by the end of 2002, CVJ no longer existed.[108] In fact, the most powerful leaders of CV from this point on (especially Fernandinho Beira-Mar and Marcinho VP) would be former members of the breakaway CVJ faction.[109] Regardless of the name, the changing of the guard within CV was finally complete. Meanwhile, the alliance between ADA and TC ended on September 11, 2002, when Uê and several other leaders of ADA and TC were brutally murdered in Bangu I, Rio's maximum security prison, by Beira-Mar and the new leaders of CV. The massacre would precipitate the creation of a new faction, *Terceiro Comando Puro* (Third Pure Command) or TCP, as I further detail in Chapter 7. From this point on, every gang throughout the city would at least be nominally connected to one of the three remaining factions: CV, TCP, or ADA (see Figure 4.5).

THE INTEGRATION OF MARÉ'S GANGS INTO THE FACTIONS

In the early 1990s, each of Maré's gangs integrated into one of the two existing factions. The Nova Holanda and Parque União gangs became CV and the Morro do Timbau gang allied with TC. Integration would irrevocably change these organizations and their relationship to Maré's communities. First, instead of just neighborhood gangs with mostly local ambitions, they would increasingly seek to expand their organizations and the control of the drug trade. They quickly began to violently compete for control of Maré. Second, when Maré's gangs integrated, they each had a few dozen members, mostly young men in their late teens and early twenties. Their structure was simple, dominated by the Dono (see Figure 4.6) who was assisted by a *braço*

---

[106] According to one source, the old guard of CV maintained control of 91 favelas and CVJ 35 favelas at the turn of the millennium (*UOL* 1/26/2002).
[107] *O Globo* 9/12/2002.
[108] *UOL* 1/26/2002.
[109] *O Globo* 9/12/2002.

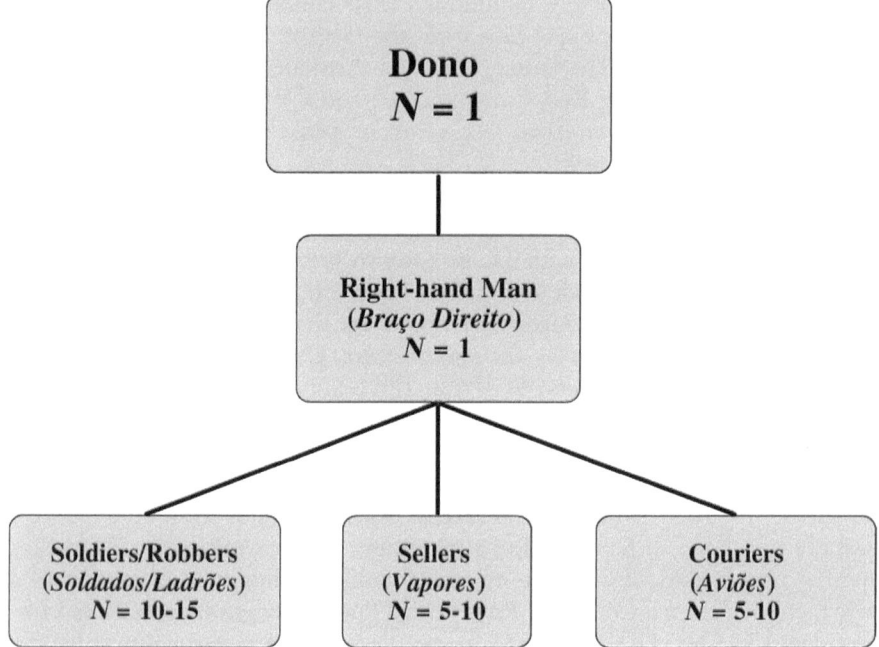

FIGURE 4.6 Organizational structure of Maré's gangs prior to faction integration
Visualization by author. N is the estimated number of gang members for each role.

direito (right-hand man). The roles of the vapor and avião or aviãozinho had already been clearly established but the rest of organization did not have a lot of structure.[110] Most members would take on various roles, including security, participate in robberies outside the favela, or assist with some other aspect of the drug trade.[111] Integration meant increasing access to cocaine through the faction's international suppliers. The number of bocas de fumo in each gang's territory multiplied and became stationary.[112] The gang's structure would also become more elaborate as the roles diversified. Overall, the size of Maré's gangs would increase from just a couple dozen members to three to four times that by the end of the decade.

The integration into the prison factions would change the size, capacity, and resources available to Maré's gangs and shape their governance in myriad ways. Most importantly, the factions would encourage the expansionary behavior of local gangs by providing weapons and men to conquer rival

---

[110] Reinaldo 10/28/2013.
[111] This matches with Zaluar's description of the gangs in Cidade de Deus during the 1980s (1994, 151–52).
[112] Artur 3/18/2014. For his part, Breno was surprised to hear the bocas were ever mobile, "You don't see the McDonalds moving around, do you?" (4/4/2017).

territories, thus incentivizing the more coercive aspects of these organizations. However, the factions would simultaneously control and manage most conflict within the faction, thus creating stable alliances and networks of mutual support. In addition, when there was the need or desire to remove a gang leader, it could only be done with the explicit approval of the faction's leaders in prison.[113] In this way, the factions would also help stabilize gang organizations throughout the city.

Despite the significance of Rio's prison-based factions in the forms of criminalized governance implemented across the city, the favela-based gangs would largely retain their local orientation and autonomy. As mentioned in previous chapters, Rio's factions are better understood as loose and horizontal networks of neighborhood-level gangs than vertically integrated and hierarchical organizations. All decisions regarding governance and the treatment of residents are determined by the local gang and are not dictated by the faction from inside the prisons. Thus, there remains significant variation in governance across even similarly affiliated gangs due largely, I argue, to the very different security environments in which these organizations find themselves.

CONCLUSION

This chapter has traced the emergence of the three gangs that would come to dominate Complexo da Maré. In doing so, it has made a series of contributions to our understanding of criminalized governance. First, the three cases demonstrate how gangs emerged and began to govern at very different times that depended heavily on local context. In the case of Nova Holanda, gangs emerged earlier as the breakdown in previous governance arrangements occurred quickly after the construction of the community. As violence and criminality increased, multiple gangs emerged and quickly began to compete for control of turf, which eventually precipitated more intensive and coercive forms of governance. The Nova Holanda gang that eventually emerged victorious against its rivals would monopolize violence and provide significant benefits to residents early on.

The other two gangs that emerged, in Parque União and Morro do Timbau, would only begin to govern in a similar manner more than a decade later as they remained weak and, at least initially, faced little competition for territorial control. Competition between gangs is fundamental to the move to govern as gangs will seek to control their territory more intensively while also developing organizations capable of providing more benefits. In this way, coercion and benefits are intimately intertwined. That said, the two weaker gangs that emerged in Parque União and Morro do Timbau did

---

[113] There are, however, circumstances where such protocol is not followed, as the case of Uê demonstrates. See also Chapter 5.

provide some limited benefits, especially the control of crime and dispute resolution, even before they began to compete with rivals as they needed the support of residents to avoid police enforcement. Overall, these dual threats have shaped governance from the very beginning of each of these gangs' organizational lives.

The second contribution of this chapter is that resident demands for goods and services are essential to understanding how gangs began to engage in governance. Residents of favelas have always demanded governance: crime fighting, dispute resolution, and some forms of welfare. Before gangs, other favela actors provided these services to varying degrees. In many cases, it was the AM president that maintained contacts with the police (or military) that provided some form of order within these communities. As favelas became further marginalized during the military dictatorship and existing connections with public security institutions weakened, gangs would eventually subsume these governance tasks. Many residents also sought out gang leaders to deal with a variety of local issues: crime, violence, order, and even welfare. By doing so, gang leaders legitimized their authority among residents and were offered the community's silence and even support to evade enforcement. Thus, the relationship between gangs and communities in these early days of criminalized governance should not be understood as a purely coercive one but as more symbiotic and reciprocal as well.

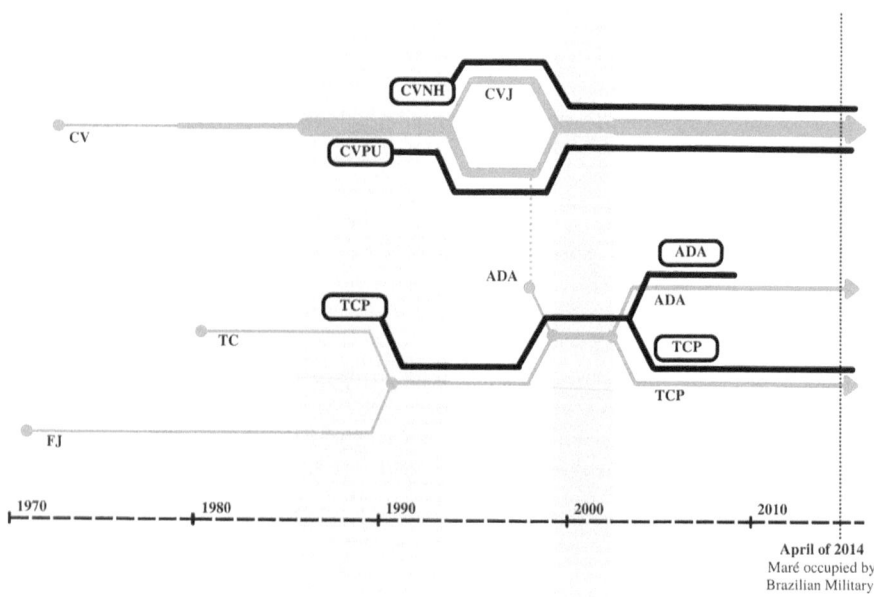

FIGURE 4.7 Maré gang case studies
Visualization by author.

In Chapters 5, 6, and 7, I focus on how each of these gangs and their governance activities evolved over the subsequent two decades, from their integration into the factions until the Brazilian military occupied Maré in April 2014 (see Figure 4.7). Throughout each, I use multiple types of data, including eighteen months of participant observation, 206 in-depth interviews with current and former gang members, NGO workers, AM representatives, and long-time residents in each of the gang territories, more than 400 newspaper and community-based journalistic accounts, and microlevel quantitative data in the form of anonymous denunciations. Together, these cases offer an unprecedented view inside these communities and organizations, showing how and why criminalized governance has evolved over time.

5

Comando Vermelho of Nova Holanda

Para estar na Nova,	To be in Nova Holanda,
tem que estar ligado	you have to be aware
para não pisar em lugar errado.	not to take a wrong step.
Até então bagulho aqui tem divisão,	Because there's the border,
nós aqui tudo Vermelho	here we're all Red Command,
no outro lado os alemão.	on the other side is the enemy.

—Lyrics from a baile funk song, circa 2013, MC Rodson

INTRODUCTION

In this chapter, I trace the evolution of the Nova Holanda gang's governance practices since its integration into the CV faction in the early 1990s until the occupation of Maré by the Brazilian Military in April 2014. The CVNH governance regime evolved significantly over that period. I argue throughout that these changes in governance track closely with the shifting security environment in which the gang has found itself.

Following integration into the CV faction in 1994, the Nova Holanda gang continued many of the same governance practices it had maintained for much of the previous decade. Despite growing levels of intergang violence and threat in other parts of Maré, CVNH maintained a benevolent dictator regime until 1999, when their TC rival began invading Nova Holanda in an attempt to monopolize drug trafficking throughout Maré. Over the next five years, TC mounted dozens of massive invasion attempts, and the two gangs engaged in hundreds of shootouts. These were the most violent years in Maré's history, during which CVNH engaged in extreme levels of coercion. They tortured and executed anyone found disobeying their rules, eventually closed the border with their rival entirely, and assiduously monitored the behavior of residents. The gang also ended its responsive governance practices, forgetting about the community amid the disorder of their turf war.

TABLE 5.1 *Evolution of CVNH governance regime*

Provision	Coercion		
of benefits	Extreme	High	Low
Responsive		Benevolent dictator	Social bandit
	Disorder	1994–99	2004–2009
	1999–2004	2009–14	
Unresponsive		Tyrant	Laissez-Faire

The eventual weakening of their rival and the installation of the 22nd Military Police Battalion within the borders of Nova Holanda changed the security environment for CVNH irrevocably. By 2004, the gang no longer faced the threat of rival invasions while enforcement became active and frequent. The gang implemented a social bandit regime for the next five years by relaxing their coercive activities and providing significant and responsive benefits to the community. Finally, in 2009, TCP conquered the housing projects to their south, defeating their ADA rival. Since then, aside from a short period of warfare and disorder in 2011, the TCP gang has presented a mostly latent threat to CVNH as the possibility of warfare remained always on the horizon. These simmering tensions persisted amid increasing and continuous enforcement efforts by the police against CVNH, especially by a BOPE force that moved their headquarters to Maré in August 2011. I argue that, for this period, CVNH can be considered a benevolent dictator gang, employing high though not extreme levels of coercion while still offering significant and responsive benefits to the community. Table 5.1 summarizes the evolution of CVNH. In the rest of this chapter, I first offer a detailed description of the CVNH territory, then chronologically trace CVNH's governance practices amid these shifting security dynamics.

THE TERRITORY

It is extremely difficult, if not impossible, to understand the nature of criminalized governance without delving into the specifics of the neighborhoods and spaces where gangs and other criminalized groups operate. When and where do they sell drugs and engage in other illicit activities? Where do they maintain security positions and lookouts? Where does intergang violence take place? And where do police operations occur? These dynamics are essential to understanding the relationship that the gang maintains with the community because their governance regime is constituted through countless encounters between gang members and residents within these spaces. Therefore, to offer the reader a ground-level perspective of criminalized governance, I will first describe the built environment of CVNH's territory.

CVNH controls three distinct but contiguous neighborhoods: Parque Maré, Parque Rubens Vaz, and Nova Holanda (see Figure 5.1). As described in Chapter 4, each of these favelas emerged from different settlement processes. Beginning in the early 1950s, Parque Maré was settled haphazardly by migrants that gradually built their own shacks and, later, palafitas. This settlement pattern translated into a neighborhood characterized by narrow and sinuous roads and alleyways that also correspond to nonstandard housing plots and construction. Although its origins are also informal, Parque Rubens Vaz has a more organized layout with just three straight and wide streets radiating from Avenida Brasil and mostly uniform housing plots and construction. In between these two communities lies Nova Holanda, a provisional housing project built by the public authority, which has a more formal checkerboard layout.

These three neighborhoods represent a relatively diverse spatial environment in which CVNH controls territory and engages in the sale of retail drugs. By the time I lived in Maré, the gang operated ten bocas de fumo, maintained several security positions near the border with their rival, and had installed more than a dozen lookout positions at all the entrances to their territory. CVNH members could often be found congregating around the bocas or riding their motorcycles up and down the major thoroughfares of their territory. The numerous alleyways and narrow side streets intersecting the few large thoroughfares offered them easy escape routes and hiding places when police operations occurred and from which to defend and repel their rival during invasions. Unlike much of the rest of Rio de Janeiro, there are no hills or even any perceptible changes in altitude in these three neighborhoods as each is the product of the filling in of a giant floodplain. The entire area sits just a few feet above sea level. Despite their very different origins, these three neighborhoods have integrated to a significant degree over time. It is often difficult, even for residents, to know exactly which streets and houses are part of which neighborhood. In fact, residents generally refer to the entire area as Nova Holanda, a practice I adopt, for simplicity's sake, throughout the rest of this chapter.

Nova Holanda has an incredibly high population density. According to a 2019 census, an estimated 33,185 inhabitants from these three neighborhoods live in just 0.2 square miles (Redes da Maré 2019a). Most of the houses, once made of wood, have all been converted to brick and mortar with multiple stories, as families have built new levels to provide space for their growing families or to rent out.[1] Some houses have as many as five floors. Over the last couple of decades, residents have used every available space for further construction, either by expanding existing homes and businesses or by building shacks and homes in any unused spaces. Nova Holanda also has one of the principal shopping districts in Maré. Teixeira Ribeiro Street has multiple large

---

[1] I lived in one such family home that had gradually been converted to rental units.

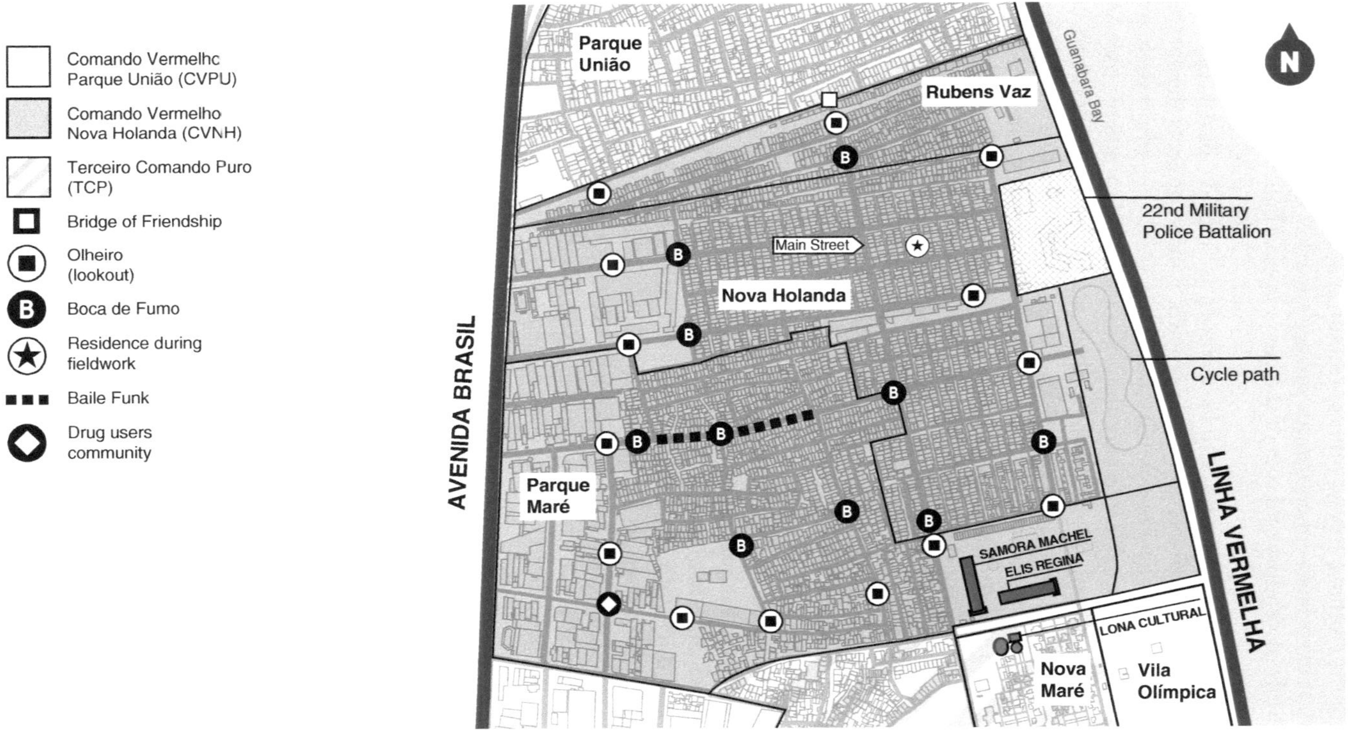

FIGURE 5.1 Map of CVNH territory during fieldwork. Visualization by Bruna Montuori.

grocery chains, clothing stores, offices, restaurants, and small shops of nearly every kind. It even hosts an enormous farmer's market on Saturday mornings with hundreds of vendors and one of the city's largest baile funks on Saturday evenings.

On the western border of CVNH's territory is Avenida Brasil, the busiest and most important highway in Rio de Janeiro, which connects the surrounding suburbs (the Baixada Fluminense) and Zona Oeste neighborhoods to the city center. This is the exclusive way that Nova Holanda residents exit Maré. Everyday, thousands of residents make their way to Avenida Brasil to catch buses that connect to every area of the city. Police patrol cars can often be found parked near these entrances though they never enter Nova Holanda unless part of an organized police operation. Numerous warehouses and manufacturing businesses can be found along the streets immediately surrounding Avenida Brasil as well. Although some of these buildings have been abandoned as Rio's manufacturing sector has been in steady decline for decades, some remain in use. This area along Avenida Brasil has been mostly integrated into the formal grid of the city and the gang is less present in these areas. As Figure 5.1 shows, the gang's presence begins a hundred or so yards from Avenida Brasil.

The northern border of CVNH's territory is constituted by a large drainage canal along which Parque Rubens Vaz was constructed. The canal is roughly fifty feet across and, historically, entirely separated Rubens Vaz from Parque União. It was only with the construction of a bridge in the early 2000s that residents began to move back and forth between these two neighborhoods. The canal also demarcates the border between the CVNH and CVPU gang territories. Other than their common faction affiliation, these two gangs do not overlap. They do not share members nor do they engage in the drug trade or other activities jointly.

Guanabara Bay lies along Nova Holanda's eastern border. Through the considerable landfilling that has occurred in this area, the waters of the Bay have been pushed back nearly 500 yards from where they once reached. Linha Vermelha, another massive highway, was constructed in 1992 and runs the entire length of Maré, nearly 1.5 miles, along Guanabara Bay. The 22nd Military Police Battalion is also located on this eastern edge of Nova Holanda. Inaugurated in July 2003, the Battalion appears more like a military installation than a police precinct. The Battalion is surrounded by a fifteen-foot cement wall, topped with razor wire, and two lookout towers facing the community. One set of enormous metal doors opens directly onto the streets of Nova Holanda through which militarized vehicles pass when police conduct operations. For residents of Nova Holanda, this eastern border offers no entry or exit points for vehicles or pedestrians.

Finally, to the south lies another set of favelas controlled by CVNH's rival, TCP. A single street (Evanildo Alves) separates the two territories. For much of the length of the border, the distance between the two gangs' territories is no wider than twenty feet but as Evanildo Alves approaches Linha Vermelha, a large drainage canal expands the distance considerably. Next to the drainage canal, on the Nova Holanda side of the border, are two of Maré's forty-nine public schools, Samora Machel and Elis Regina. Finally, the Vila Olímpica (Olympic Village), comprising a cycle path, a running track, several soccer fields, two gymnasiums, four tennis courts, and a large swimming pool lies in the far southeast corner of Nova Holanda. Gang members will seldom be observed in this area as it offers few hiding places or escape routes.

THE EVOLUTION OF CVNH GOVERNANCE

Benevolent Dictator (1994–99)

After Jorge Negão's death at the hands of Federal Police in 1992, a man nicknamed Gigante took over the leadership of the gang.[2] Gigante had been Jorge Negão's braço direito and, like his predecessor, tried to maintain his independence vis-à-vis the two prison factions (CV and TC).[3] Apparently, the Nova Holanda gang had even been paying a fee to the CV leadership for protection and to prevent their complete integration for several years.[4] By 1994, both the Parque União and Morro do Timbau gangs had already been integrated into the CV and TC factions, respectively, and were engaging in increasingly aggressive behavior (see Chapters 6 and 7). Gigante managed to delay his own gang's incorporation into the faction for a couple of years but was eventually made an offer he could not refuse.

As described in Chapter 4, a schism within the CV faction set off violent competition between the old guard of CV and the younger breakaway faction of CVJ. In 1994, a large group of the CVJ leaders came to Nova Holanda and demanded that Gigante join their faction or they would invade and take over the area themselves.[5] Faced with the prospect of integration or likely death, Gigante made the obvious choice. Integration also had its advantages. CVNH gained access to high-quality cocaine and heavy weaponry through the faction's *atacadistas* (wholesalers) and matutos. The gang also gained the assistance and support of numerous CV affiliated gangs throughout the city should they need it. By the end of 1994, residents remembered CV tags and graffiti appearing on walls all around Nova Holanda (Mattos 2016).[6]

---

[2] *O Globo* 7/2/1992b.
[3] Josie 7/10/2018.
[4] *O Globo* 7/18/1992. Following his death, Jorge Negão's sister, who had inherited some of the gang's bocas, threatened to end such payments because she thought CV had failed to prevent her brother's death at the hands of Federal Police. In response, Uê, still part of the CV leadership at the time (before he killed Orlando Jogador in 1994), even threatened to take over Nova Holanda himself if the payments did not continue.
[5] Josie 7/10/2018.
[6] CVRL is the most common tag seen in CV areas, referring to CV and Rogério Lemgruber, one of the founding members of CV in charge of the internal order of the group in Cândido

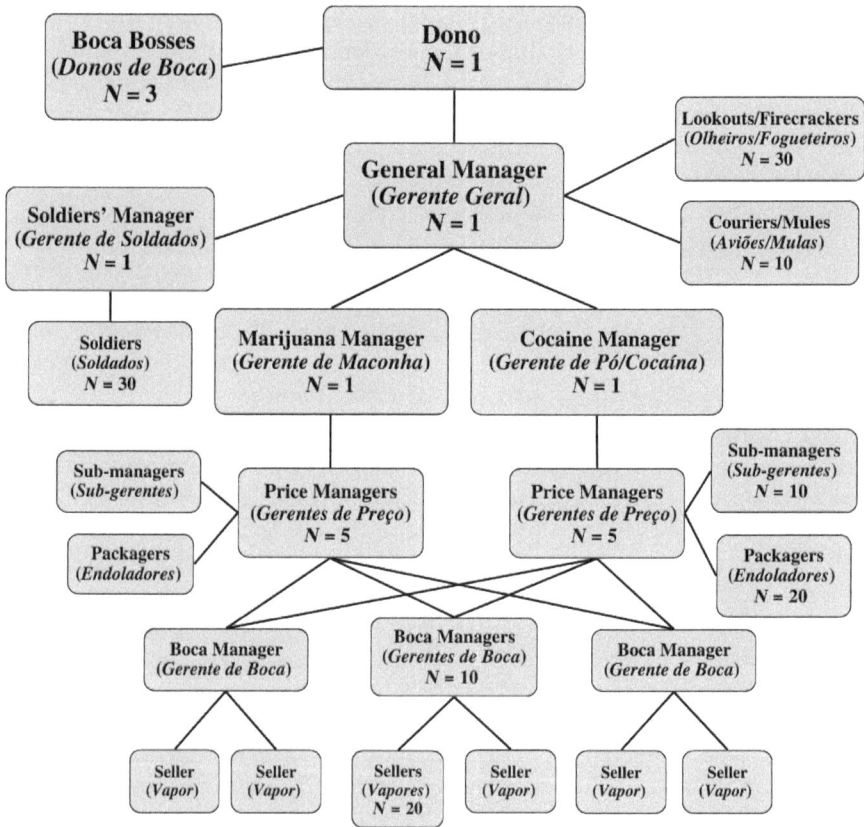

FIGURE 5.2 Organizational structure of CVNH
Visualization by author. N is the estimated number of gang members for each role.

Integration led CVNH to expand its membership considerably. The structure of the organization shifted from being dominated by the Dono with perhaps just a few specified functions beneath him to one with a variety of delineated roles and responsibilities (see Figure 5.2). The Dono's *braço direito* became the *gerente geral* (general manager), below which there was a *gerente de cocaína* (cocaine manager) and *gerente de maconha* (marijuana manager), followed by *gerentes de preço* (price managers) that organized the packaging – for which they hired *endoladores* (packagers) – and the distribution of different quantities of each

Mendes prison (Amorim 1993, 89). RL was commonly added to the CV tag following the schism within CV in which the internal order of the faction had broken down. PJL, for *Paz, Justiça e Liberdade!* (Peace, Justice, and Freedom!), is another common tag in CV areas and was especially popular in the 1990s (Mattos 2016).

drug to the bocas.[7] Several new bocas were added – and became stationary – as *gerentes de boca* (boca managers) were assigned to each and became responsible for the day-to-day functioning.[8] Two, sometimes three vapores exchanged drugs for money at each of the bocas in rotating day and night shifts.

The CVNH gang also became increasingly militarized. The organization's security became more elaborate. Whereas before it was the Dono or his braço direito who personally took charge of the gang's security, a *gerente de soldados* (soldiers' manager) became responsible for organizing the gang's defenses and keeping track of the growing arsenal of weapons and ammunition. Some soldiers were assigned to specific bocas while others were eventually stationed in strategic areas of the territory. Later, the most capable soldiers would eventually serve as personal security for the Dono. Olheiros and *fogueteiros* (firecrackers, i.e., those that set off firecrackers when police entered the area) became permanently stationed at all entrances to the community. These numerous organizational changes were not made immediately upon the gang's integration, nor were they dictated by the faction leadership. Rather, the organizational evolution of CVNH occurred gradually over the course of the 1990s as CVNH would adapt the organizational structure from other CV gangs to meet their local needs.[9]

Like most other CV gangs of this era, CVNH also expanded its criminal activities considerably after integration. The gang began to further promote and incentivize members to engage in armed robberies outside of its territory. Reinaldo described how he and a group of more than a dozen *assaltantes* (robbers) participated in numerous stickups and armed robberies of banks, shops, and trucks during his years of involvement in the 1990s.[10] As a result, the availability of stolen goods, including cars, motorcycles, and jewelry within Nova Holanda increased considerably over these years (Mattos 2016, 5).

The gang also began to arm individuals outside of their turf that were willing to take over new drug-selling territories. Over the course of the 1980s, a group of housing projects were built just to the south of Morro do Timbau that would become the focus of not only CVNH efforts to expand their territorial

---

[7] In the late 2000s, a gerente de crack and several more price managers would be added to the gang.

[8] According to one police report, by 1994, out of 344 bocas in the entire city of Rio, Nova Holanda had two of the fifteen most lucrative (Misse 1999, 312). By 2000, the gang was making an estimated R$24,000 ($12,000 at the time) in drug revenues per week. This number would expand significantly over the subsequent years as the value of the same quantity of drugs multiplied. For instance, in the late 1990s, the gang sold quantities of R$3, R$5, and R$10 of cocaine and marijuana but, by the time I lived in Maré, they were selling R$5, R$10, R$20, R$30, and R$50 packets of each drug.

[9] Nearly every CV gang throughout the city followed a similar organizational template, which was built on the structure of the jogo do bicho, and closely resembles the structure of a firm or military organization.

[10] Reinaldo 10/28/2013.

reach but also the Parque União and Morro do Timbau gangs as well (see Chapters 6 and 7). These new housing projects were all built on land that had previously been in the middle of Guanabara Bay. In a massive landfilling project involving both federal and state governments, by the end of the 1980s, an estimated 5,000 apartments and domiciles were built for residents that had been removed from Maré's palafitas and other precariously housed families in the Zona Norte. Many of the existing familial and social networks from the palafitas in Nova Holanda remained intact, through which CVNH had connections to a gang led by a man named Omar.[11] Prior to integration, Gigante had refused to aid Omar in taking over these new communities because he did not want to jeopardize his stable relations with Kito, the Dono in Morro do Timbau, who had already taken control of Vila do Pinheiro, one of the housing projects in that area.[12] Integration into the CV faction forced Gigante's hand and CVNH began to send arms and men to support Omar in his bid to consolidate control over the area. Omar and Kito's gangs would engage in an all-out war for territorial control of the housing projects for the next several years (see Chapter 7).[13]

At first, Gigante was only providing weapons and men to support Omar. CVNH and TC had not yet begun to compete directly. Conflict, however, was on the horizon. One sign that the two gangs could not coexist peacefully for much longer was observed at the baile funk parties at this time. Throughout the 1980s and early 1990s, it was common for youth and gang members from each of these territories to frequent parties in each other's turf. However, after integration, due to the different faction affiliations, and the growing violence between the gangs in the housing projects to their south, gang members in Nova Holanda and Morro do Timbau stopped crossing over the border entirely. Simmering tensions between unaffiliated youth from these two gang territories even began to erupt into all-out brawls at these bailes. Bruno, who entered CVNH around this time, recalled:

> There used to be dance brawls (*bailes de briga*) where we fought with our fists and really beat the shit out of each other. We would almost try to kill one another. We were just kids at the time and none of us were involved yet... but once some of the kids we fought with turned into TC, we joined CV.[14]

While tensions were increasing over this period, no one from Nova Holanda could remember any gang shootouts or invasions between Gigante's CVNH and Kito's TC until the very end of the decade. Instead, for this initial post-integration period, from 1994 to 1999, the TC threat to CVNH's territorial control was latent, and Gigante and his gang remained vigilant. Especially

[11] *O Globo* 12/15/1995.
[12] Josie 7/10/2018.
[13] *O Globo* 9/28/1992; 3/14/1995; 12/26/1995; 3/20/1996.
[14] Bruno 10/6/2014.

after the installation of new bocas and the expansion of the organization, the gang maintained a heavier presence on the streets than ever before and began monitoring residents more assiduously. They did not refrain from using violence to punish residents for disobedience, especially as it related to the drug trade. One episode, described at the beginning of Chapter 2, bordered into the more extreme use of coercion when Gigante ordered several high-profile and public executions, including the president of the local Samba school, *Mataram o Meu Gato* (They Killed my Cat), that he suspected of wanting to take over the drug trade in Nova Holanda.[15] This type of grisly punishment is clearly connected to the possibility of a rival (internal, in this case) wanting to take over the local drug trade.

The highly public nature of these killings was more obviously a response to a rival threat than the gang's use of punishments to combat low-level crime and provide order for the community, which residents seemed to welcome. Especially during an era when crime and violence were expanding rapidly across the city, a gang that provided order and fought crime was likely viewed as a huge benefit for local residents, even if some young men were killed or severely punished for transgressions. In this way, some of the violent punishments that Gigante and his gang used during this period, like Jorge Negão before him, can perhaps even be considered a responsive benefit the gang provided, again showing how the two dimensions of governance, coercion and benefits, can overlap in certain respects. In fact, according to residents of the era, they did not see Gigante's gang as a particularly coercive one, especially as compared to what would come next. For the most part, Gigante's gang did not restrict movement and circulation within or outside the community, and allowed residents to go about their daily lives without extreme forms of monitoring (Mattos 2016).[16]

On the other hand, CVNH continued to provide significant benefits to the local community. Like his predecessor, Gigante understood the importance of maintaining the support of the residents. He organized enormous holiday parties on Christmas, Easter, Mother's, Father's, and Children's Day, as well as religious holidays, celebrating patron saints such as Cosmas, Damian, and George. At these parties, the gang provided free food and drink, entertainment (music, a clown, fireworks, etc.), handed out small gifts and party favors to children, as well as some consumer goods for the adults.[17] The gang also provided hundreds of monthly food baskets and medicine to families in need.[18] Gigante also continued and expanded the gang's weekly baile funk parties. They began to be held in a local schoolyard where the gang organized music and DJs.[19] The incredible expansion of the Nova Holanda gang, its

[15] *O Globo* 9/28/1993.
[16] Bruno 10/6/2014; Lino 11/3/2014.
[17] *O Globo* 9/28/1993.
[18] *O Globo* 12/15/1995.
[19] Josie 7/10/2018.

increasing drug revenues, and the greater availability of stolen and illicit goods also stimulated the local economy. More and more members of the community, through their familial networks or social relations, would benefit from the economic activities of the gang.

CVNH was also responsive to resident demands. For instance, Breno told me that when he was a young boy in the 1990s, someone had stolen his family's car. His mother, who had avoided interactions with gang members her entire life, had little choice but to approach Gigante to see if he could retrieve the vehicle. He did so. In addition, during a particularly difficult economic period, Breno admitted that his mother had asked and received financial assistance from Gigante. Although these good deeds did not entirely redeem the gang and its members in his mother's eyes, it went a long way toward legitimizing their presence and meant she would *"manter uma boca fechada"* (keep her mouth shut) if anything ever happened.[20] Other residents had similar stories of receiving some benefit or favor from the gang and many described the relationship between the community and the gang as very close during this initial period following integration.[21] Such responsive and beneficial forms of governance meant that CVNH could rely on the local population's silence and support in the face of increasing attention from the public security apparatus. In fact, according to a local police commander at the time, "I consider it almost impossible to apprehend Gigante inside Maré. He is very protected by the population."[22]

Even before integration, Rio's police were already engaging in some operations in Nova Holanda. Although they had deactivated and removed the police post, the Military Police began to engage in periodic *cercos* (occupations or sieges) of Nova Holanda.[23] For instance, on February 22nd, 1996, thirty-five police *camburões* (wagons) accompanied by seventy police occupied Nova Holanda in the early afternoon.[24] They spent the next three hours going block by block to find and capture gang members. This siege only resulted in two arrests – a couple of gang members that had recently stolen a car and unluckily returned to Nova Holanda during the operation – but such short-term occupations were a semi-regular occurrence during these years.[25] I found no evidence of organized confrontations between the CVNH gang and the police during this period.

While most police operations were intended to arrest gang members, others had more nefarious objectives such as kidnapping gang members for

[20] Breno 3/26/2014.
[21] Josie 7/10/2017; Naldo 12/17/2014.
[22] *Folha de São Paulo* 8/15/1997.
[23] Once the police left, local youth immediately vandalized and destroyed the building (Artur 3/17/2014; Eduardo 10/11/2013).
[24] *O Globo* 2/23/1996.
[25] *O Globo* 7/12/1981; 7/2/1992b; 2/23/1996.

ransom (Mattos 2016). For instance, before his eventual imprisonment in 1997, Gigante was kidnapped by police and only released when the gang paid R$300,000 ($100,000 at the time) for his release.[26] Thus, even though Gigante and his gang did not collaborate with the police or maintain durable bribery schemes, police nonetheless found ways to extract resources from the gang.[27] These kidnapping and ransoming practices would continue for the next several decades even as the police actively enforced against CVNH. For instance, Bruno recalled being arrested by the police with R$30,000 in cash and some drugs in a backpack.[28] The police took the money for themselves then demanded another R$10,000 to pretend the backpack was not his. By all accounts, although the gang paid these periodic bribes and ransoms, it would never develop a more collaborative relationship with the police like some other gangs in Maré (see Chapter 7).[29]

Disorder (1999–2004)

In 1997, Gigante was arrested and imprisoned. Although he technically remained the Dono, Gigante put his teenage nephew, Valtim, in charge of the day-to-day operations of the gang. Like many other gangs throughout the city, the imprisonment or death of a respected leader had significant destabilizing effects on CVNH. In fact, much of the violence occurring across the city at this time was due to similar dynamics of conflict and competition between and within gangs as younger, more ambitious, and less restrained members assumed leadership positions within gangs (Misse 1999, 315). In Nova Holanda, Valtim's inexperience immediately led to internal dissent and a weakening of the organization, which would encourage TC to try to take over the area, precipitating several years of warfare and disorder.[30] According to Bruno,

Valtim wasn't ready to handle the responsibility of being Dono so Gigante had Gian, who was born and raised in Nova Holanda and a bit older, take over for him. But he and Valtim had some sort of disagreement over a woman so Gian ended up kidnapping and killing Valtim. Gian made it look like the police had done it but he was found out. Dancer [another nephew of Gigante] and his men killed most of Gian's crew, but he escaped and joined the other side [TC]. Gian became the right-hand man of Espadão

---

[26] *Folha de São Paulo* 8/15/1997.
[27] Misse (1999) refers to these implicit negotiations over the threat and use of force by the police against gangs as *mercadorias políticas* (political merchandise).
[28] Bruno 10/27/2014.
[29] Some gang members did report that the gang paid semi-regular bribes of R$35,000 so that police would not disturb their baile funk parties in the years preceding occupation (Flávio 11/14/2013; Inácio 4/24/2014).
[30] The death of another older gang member, Peruano, who served as an informal mediator between the two gangs, was another factor that contributed to the initiation of conflict (Mattos 2016, 5).

[TC general manager] and helped them invade the area because he knew everything about Nova Holanda. It rained bullets for several years.[31]

The war between CVNH and TC officially began on February 5th, 1999, when the TC gang invaded Nova Holanda for the first time (Mattos 2016).[32] Without a strong leader and with infighting keeping CVNH disorganized and weak, TC was the primary aggressor in the first several years of the conflict. Unlike the war between Candinho's gang and the Irmãos Metralha fifteen years earlier, however, these confrontations were not merely fought with pistols and knives but between highly militarized units. Both CVNH and TC had dozens of sol-dados, access to large-caliber rifles, and even some grenades.[33] The resulting shootouts and invasions share more in common with urban insurgency bat-tles than gangland rivalries in much of the world. Dozens of heavily armed TC members would stream into Nova Holanda using stolen cars and trucks to move into their enemy's territory quickly. TC also had detailed maps and radios to coordinate their attacks and, as Bruno mentioned, they also had sev-eral former CVNH members with intimate knowledge of the territory.[34] The possibility that CVNH would lose their territory was very real.

Then, in December 2000, Gigante was killed in prison, stabbed to death by a fellow inmate.[35] He was thirty-eight years old. Stores and shops in Nova Holanda closed for three days while TC celebrated. "They [TC] played loud music, set off fireworks, and shot their guns in the air to commemorate the death of Gigante," one resident recalled.[36] The lack of a strong, well-respected Dono, even one in prison, would only incentivize further TC attempts to take over the area. "We knew Gigante from when he was a little kid and we really liked him. Now, who's going to look after us? Everyone is going to invade the favela and our lives are going to become hell," one resident concluded.[37] These fears were not misplaced. Frequent invasions continued for the next couple of years (see Figure 5.3). When TC captured CVNH members, they would immediately execute them, sometimes burning the corpses or mutilating the bodies in other ways.[38] The gerente geral of the TC gang at the time, a man nicknamed Espadão (Big Sword), was renowned for his use of extra-lethal violence, his nickname deriving from this predilection.[39]

In response to this existential threat, CVNH engaged in extreme lev-els of coercion. Quickly after the war started, the gang installed a series of

---

[31] Bruno 10/27/2014.
[32] *O Globo* 3/12/1999.
[33] *O Globo* 3/12/1999; 5/26/2000a.
[34] *O Globo* 5/26/2000a; 2/5/2000; 2/12/2000b.
[35] *O Globo* 12/29/2000.
[36] *O Globo* 12/29/2000.
[37] *O Globo* 12/29/2000.
[38] *O Globo* 2/5/2000.
[39] *O Globo* 12/13/2003.

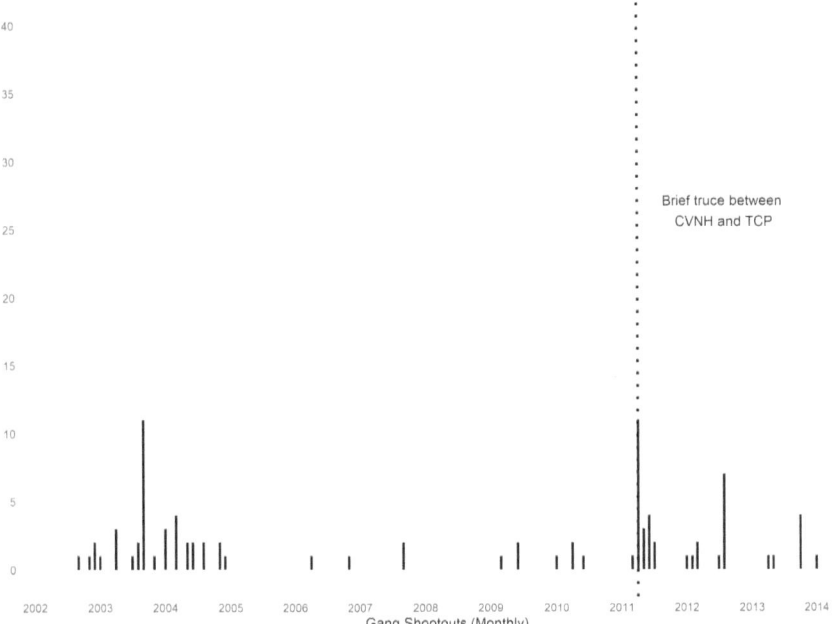

FIGURE 5.3 Gang shootouts in CVNH territory (monthly)
Data from *Disque-Denúncia*. Visualization by Pranjal Drall.

permanent security positions, monitoring the border for any sign of their enemy. Eventually, they closed the border entirely, stopping and threatening women and children trying to cross over, and shooting at cars or pedestrians if they had any suspicions.[40] One fifteen-year-old reported that he had been caught by gang members when he tried to cross over. They tied him up and threw him in the drainage canal along the border. "Before leaving me there, they threatened to kill me if I ever returned," he said.[41] CVNH no longer allowed children from TC's territory to attend school in Nova Holanda nor children from their own area to participate in sports classes at the Vila Olímpica just across the border on the TC side. Residents that wanted to visit family members were forced to meet outside of Maré. "Walking, it would take only five minutes to arrive at my dad's house. But to see him, I have to get a bus to the city center where he works. ...We have to obey these rules to not be killed," one resident said.[42]

Gang members also began to threaten and use violence not just against residents crossing over the border but for anyone they distrusted or did not think belonged in the community. Mattos (2016) describes the behavior of CVNH

---

[40] *O Globo* 5/18/2003.
[41] *O Globo* 8/31/2001.
[42] *O Globo* 5/18/2003.

gang members during this period as "*neurose*" (neurosis), a mix of adrenaline, excitement, fear, anxiety, and alertness that bordered on frenzy because of the frequency of violent confrontations with their rival. In many cases, it was the newest and youngest members that behaved particularly erratically. Severino described how these younger members behaved during warfare: "The younger guys would spend all their ammunition at once. They don't have any experience and their minds aren't fully developed yet so they go in shooting and don't stop until they're out. It's pure adrenaline." Moreover, these young men seldom differentiated between rivals and residents in their shootouts and confrontations. As a result, numerous members of the community were injured, kidnapped, or even killed by stray bullets during gang shootouts.[43] Most Nova Holanda residents described this period of warfare as the most difficult of their lives.

Prior to the war with TC, Gigante had refused to allow adolescents into the gang. After the war began, however, the gang needed a never-ending supply of bodies to defend their territory. They began recruiting younger and younger members, eventually allowing children as young as ten into the gang. Even during the war, CVNH did not struggle to recruit new members. I asked Natan why he thought young men and boys continued to join the gang even with the possibility of being killed. "With two to three thousand reais [$1000] they could wear what they want, eat what they want, and fuck who they want. They could even sustain their families. They gained respect," he said.[44] Many of these young recruits did not last long, however.[45] They had no training to speak of and were often immediately put on the front lines, in the most vulnerable areas. In fact, young recruits are often referred to as "*bucha de canhão*" (cannon fodder) even by gang members themselves.

The members of the community that suffered the brunt of this violence were often young men suspected of collaborating with rivals or of disobeying the rules of the gang. Extreme punishments for young men became so commonplace that residents came to regard them as quasi-natural. Eliana Sousa Silva (2012) writes of the banality of this form of violence when she describes local gang members pushing a cart on which a young boy was bound and gagged, being led through the community before his eventual execution in the early 2000s (p. 82). The frequency of these executions increased radically during the war years, serving as a constant reminder to residents to not disobey gang rules. According to Eduarda, a longtime resident, "The gang did crazy things to try to exercise control of resident life," proceeding to describe some of the horrific scenes she had observed: Victims (mostly young men) were often tied

---

[43] *O Globo* 3/12/1999; 2/12/2000a; 5/26/2000b; 5/18/2003.
[44] Natan 8/8/2013.
[45] One study of gang members in Rio found that young illiterate, black men from poorer families were much more likely to join a gang (12–37 percent higher) and that 20 percent of these new recruits were dead within two years (Carvalho and Soares 2016). Amid an ongoing war, the mortality rate of new members was probably much higher.

up, beaten, had their genitals or other body parts cut off, and then were shot and left to die in the middle of the street.[46] Josie shook her head when she talked about this period of Nova Holanda's history, "It was mostly just poor young black men killing other poor young black men," she said.[47]

CVNH was also extremely concerned about the loyalty of their own members during this period. There were two other *golpe do estado* (coup) attempts early in the war – Clodoaldo tried to take over the gang in 1999 and Valmir, the former Dono Candinho's brother, made a failed takeover bid in 2000.[48] Several other CVNH members eventually defected to their rival and, as Bruno mentioned earlier, used their knowledge of the area to help TC invade.[49] These betrayals incentivized the gang to root out anyone they thought unreliable.[50] The CVNH gang began forcing recruits to demonstrate their commitment to the gang through acts of violence. Osvaldo described how one adolescent was ordered to kill his own brother because they thought he might be involved with their rival.[51] When he refused, they killed them both. This paranoid mentality permeated the organization during the war years when the lack of commitment represented a particularly dangerous threat to the gang. The former girlfriends and family of rival gang members were also forced to move out of Nova Holanda because of a high degree of suspicion and the possibility of violent punishment.[52]

Much of this coercive behavior was promoted or at least not controlled by the leadership of the gang, which remained fractured and weak. When Dancer took over as Dono after Valtim's murder, he was described by some as an *"traficante acelerada"* (accelerated trafficker), meaning that he enjoyed violent confrontations.[53] He was killed by police only a few months later. Alec, another relative of Gigante, then took over and, by all accounts, was a "crazy" Dono and "did a lot of bad stuff" like using drugs and disrespecting residents.[54] André Moral, Alec's brother, allegedly murdered him and took over the gang for himself though he was not native to Nova Holanda nor did he spend very much time there (Mattos 2016). He would not be in charge long either as he was killed by police in Chatuba, another favela in Rio, in 2004.[55]

---

[46] Eduarda 9/19/2013. Such forms of extra-lethal violence resemble Fujii's (2021) "violent displays" in which the violence is intended not just to deter would-be traitors or criminals within the community but also to shape how the entire community thinks and feels about the gang.
[47] Josie 7/17/2018.
[48] *O Globo* 2/12/2000b.
[49] Bruno 10/27/2014.
[50] Gang members frequently used such politico-military language to describe these events. Zaluar also notes on this tendency (1994, 11).
[51] Osvaldo 1/7/2015.
[52] Breno 3/26/2014.
[53] Bruno 10/27/2014; Lino 11/3/2014.
[54] Bruno 10/27/2014.
[55] *Folha de São Paulo* 11/29/2004.

Over the span of five years, amid the war with their TC rival, the CVNH gang had five different Donos. Such rapid turnover in leadership also helped deteriorate the responsive and beneficial relationship the gang had maintained with the community for much of the last two decades. The gang no longer responded to community demands for dispute resolution, and often resorted to threats and violence to resolve any conflicts (Mattos 2016). They provided fewer forms of financial assistance as all available resources were diverted to buying weapons or acquiring new members. The large-scale holiday parties were significantly curtailed as well due to constant violence and the difficulty in organizing parties with a gang that was singularly focused on defending their territory. According to Severino, "The gang forgot about the community during the war because we were worried about invasion."[56] Similarly, Bruno said, "We always had to be ready to drop everything and run to the border to help repel the alemão."

The conflict between CVNH and TC often spilled onto the surrounding highways, bringing the Zona Norte of Rio to a standstill.[57] Both gangs were known to shoot in and amongst the traffic and would sometimes order the occupants of city buses to deboard before they lit the buses on fire.[58] Such tactics should not be understood as psychotic gang behavior but as a consequence of these all-out battles for supremacy and survival. During hours-long shootouts, gang members would do almost anything to preserve their territorial control. Lighting fire to buses was described by several gang members of the era as a last-ditch strategy to encourage police to mount an operation to prevent them from losing their territory to their rival.[59]

For their part, police seldom sought to intervene directly in these encounters. Instead, police operations and occupations often happened hours, days, or even weeks later.[60] During the first two years of Maré's gang war, Luiz Eduardo Soares, an anthropologist, was appointed by then-Governor Anthony Garotinho as Rio's Public Security Secretary, part of a so-called "*inflexão civilizatória*" (civilizing turn) in policing (Garotinho and Soares 1998). For 500 days, Soares engaged in a short-lived campaign to reform the police and reduce

---

[56] Severino 10/2/2013.
[57] *O Globo* 10/18/2002; 3/6/2003; 3/8/2003; 4/22/2003; 5/7/2003; 10/5/2003; 1/22/2004.
[58] *O Globo* 10/2/2000; 12/18/2002.
[59] Severino 10/2/2013; Bruno 10/27/2014. According to some newspaper reporting, residents participated in bus burnings as well. Allegedly, they did so to protest police behavior though it is curious that residents would protest police behavior amid shootouts between the gangs. Witnesses also reported seeing several of the residents armed which seems to suggest it was the gangs leading such behavior. According to the Commander of the local Military Police Battalion, "The traffickers are manipulating these residents... The protests are being driven by criminals" (*O Globo* 10/2/2000). This is not to dispute the real grievances residents had with Rio's police – other more peaceful protests did occur (*O Globo* 7/4/2001; 9/1/2001) – but such violent tactics seem unlikely to have been produced by local social movements.
[60] *O Globo* 3/12/1999.

their violence and abuse before being sacked by Garotinho amid continuing violence and increasing complaints from the police themselves (Soares 2000). Some of the most violent encounters between Maré's gangs occurred during this period.[61] Perhaps the lack of police operations to stop the violence was due to these efforts to prevent police violence. Even after Soares was removed, however, and the public security apparatus shifted to a set of less restrained tactics, confrontations between Maré's gangs continued for several years.

By 2003, the disruption to the city's commerce and order was more than the political elites could take. On June 30th, 2003, the public security apparatus installed the 22nd Military Police Battalion in CVNH's territory.[62] The inauguration ceremony had all of the pomp and circumstance of a military parade and included the participation of an honor guard, more than 600 police, and Anthony Garotinho, the former Governor and then-Public Security Secretary.[63] Residents watched from their rooftops as helicopters flew overheard and dropped 60,000 pamphlets on the communities below, asking for residents' cooperation in finding gang members, drugs, and weapons. The pamphlets listed the number for DD, the anonymous hotline, before announcing, "Peace is arriving! A new life for Maré!"

The proximity of the 22nd Battalion did not, however, put an immediate end to the violent confrontations between CVNH and TC. Shootouts between the gangs in Nova Holanda's territory persisted through 2003 and 2004, nearly a year and a half after the installation of the Battalion (see Figure 5.3).[64] That said, the proximity of the police to the confrontations in Maré alongside the increasing capabilities of the Military Police, which now had armored vehicles as well as helicopters at their disposal, meant that police were able mobilize more quickly to prevent gang confrontations from escalating and spilling out onto the surrounding highways.[65] No longer would Maré's gangs stop traffic and burn city buses.

The end of the war between TC and CVNH happened only after the weakening of TC, which occurred gradually over the course of several years. First, the TC gang fragmented in late 2002, the result of increasing tensions brought on by years of war and the reconfiguration of alliances between the factions at the city level (see Chapter 4). The schism left one gang connected to the newly minted TCP faction in Morro do Timbau and its surrounding neighborhoods and another gang connected to the ADA faction in the housing projects south of Linha Amarela (see Chapter 7), significantly weakening their ability to

---

[61] *O Globo* 3/12/1999; 2/5/2000; 5/26/2000a; 5/26/2000b; 10/2/2000.
[62] It is unclear why the Battalion was placed in CVNH's territory especially considering the focus of police operations were more squarely on the TC gang in the years preceding its installation (see Chapter 7).
[63] *O Globo* 7/1/2003.
[64] Although no reliable data from DD exists for the first few years of the war, it is likely that shootouts were even more frequent for this period.
[65] Rio's public security apparatus acquired its first four helicopters in 2003 (*O Globo* 5/3/2003). The Military Police first began to use *caveirões* (armored vehicles) in 2002 (*Piauí* 4/19/2008).

invade CVNH's territory. Even after the split, however, violence between TCP and CVNH continued. In December 2003, TCP's Dono, Espadão, and his general manager, Bração (Big Biceps), were arrested and imprisoned. The violence continued into 2004 but there were no longer massive invasions involving multiple vehicles and dozens of heavily armed gang members as in previous years. By the end of 2004, after nearly five years of almost constant warfare, active competition finally came to an end. Dozens of residents and hundreds of gang members, many of whom were little more than children, had lost their lives in the intervening years. Neither gang had won or lost any territory.

Social Bandit (2004–2009)

For the preceding five years, CVNH gang members had devoted all their attention and energy to defending their turf from an aggressive and belligerent rival. The end of the war would bring an end to the most coercive period of CVNH governance. The threat from TCP would be absent for the next several years as the gang in Morro do Timbau remained weak and without capable leadership. The CV gang used this opportunity to go on the offensive, mounting several large invasions in the attempt to conquer the TCP area for themselves. In addition, following the installation of the 22nd Battalion within their territory and in the face of more sustained enforcement efforts, CVNH returned to providing more responsive benefits to the community. The gang needed resident support and silence if they were to evade the frequent militarized police operations.

With André Moral's death in 2004, the CVNH leadership passed to Flávio, one of the gang's more experienced managers. Flávio was the first Dono since Jorge Negão not related by blood to Gigante and, by all accounts, was a more serious and less violent leader.[66] Shortly after becoming Dono, a close friend recalled him saying, "I don't want any more blood spilled within the community."[67] True to his word, the gang became much less coercive. Although they remained heavily armed, CVNH quickly relaxed their restrictions on resident movement and behavior. They opened the border and no longer monitored residents as relentlessly. The public punishments and executions that characterized the war years also came to an end.[68] Instead of torturing and executing, Flávio instead preferred to expel members of the gang that shirked their duties.[69] According to Francisco, instead of immediately killing someone for stealing, the first time someone stole they were given a warning, the second time they shot them through the hand, if they got caught again only then would they kill them.[70] Flávio also encouraged his managers to not allow rank

---

[66] Lino 11/3/2014; Eduardo 10/11/2013; Fernanda 11/12/2014.
[67] Lino 11/3/2014.
[68] Fernanda 11/12/2014; Lino 11/3/2014; Bruno 10/27/2014.
[69] Lino 11/3/2014; Bruno 10/6/2014; Everton 4/17/2014.
[70] Francisco 7/17/2013.

and file to shoot off their weapons or mistreat residents.[71] The general manager, a man nicknamed Coroa, was a famously violent man but Flávio never let him kill without his direct approval.[72]

In this regard, Flávio benefitted from the weakening of TCP. For the duration of his tenure, CVNH would face almost no threat from their rival. Containing the violent impulses of his gang would have been difficult, if not impossible, during war. A Dono needs his gang to be hypervigilant and even perhaps a bit overzealous in their use of violence when a rival threat is active. Absent such threat, however, the Dono will likely try to contain these behaviors, especially if enforcement is forthcoming, so as not to anger residents. Another way of interpreting the end of the most coercive CVNH practices would be that Flávio was just a nonviolent gang leader. It was *his* pacifist leadership, not the changing security environment, that ended the gang's more violent practices. However, when I proposed this explanation for the change in the gang's behavior to Fausto, who had maintained a close relationship with the gang for many years, he shook his head and said, "the Donos are very powerful but they're prisoners too. He is forced into doing things because he is very constrained by the organization. A Dono cannot be seen as weak or vulnerable. He must be strong or he will lose his power very quickly."[73] In this regard, numerous gang members and other residents described how CVNH, under Flávio's leadership, had reduced their use of coercion but also became more aggressive, mounting a series of incursions into TCP's territory in 2007 and 2008.

In one mega-invasion, early in the morning of January 12th, 2008, 60 CVNH members alongside gang members from several other CV-affiliated gangs (Mangueira, Santa Marta, Prazeres, and Providência) invaded TCP's territory in twenty stolen vehicles.[74] The invasion was highly coordinated. They cut power to the area by destroying a transformer then divided their forces, entering the TCP territory from three different sides: along their shared border, from the west along Linha Vermelha, and from the south along Linha Amarela. According to reports, the gang planned the invasion for early Saturday morning, when few residents would be on the streets, to avoid casualties. CVNH members were armed with high-caliber assault rifles, as well as homemade bombs. After two TCP members were killed and eight others injured, the rest of the TCP gang fled or went into hiding.

Several of the CVNH members I interviewed participated in this invasion. I asked them why they had decided to invade. "Because the other side was weak," Francisco told me. "How did you know they were weak?" I asked. "People talk. There's always an informant from the other side. They'll say,

---

[71] Francisco 8/20/2013.
[72] Lino 11/3/2014; Bruno 10/6/2014; Everton 4/17/2014.
[73] Fausto 6/16/2014.
[74] *O Globo* 1/14/2008.

'Shit, it's really weak here, you should invade,'" he replied. "How do you know they're not lying or that they're just repeating gossip?" I asked. "Well, you go in a little and take a look around. If you don't see anyone, then you keep going...″[75] Indeed, according to newspaper reports, eleven TCP members had been arrested several days prior to the invasion, leaving them undermanned and vulnerable, another example of successful enforcement efforts precipitating the activation of rival competition.[76]

After taking control of TCP's territory, CVNH members immediately found the tallest building on the Morro and raised a giant flag of the *Torcida Jovem do Flamengo* (Flamengo Youth Fans), the fan association of the adopted football team of the CV faction.[77] Many of the CVNH members I interviewed spoke with a great amount of pride over seeing their flag flying above their enemy's territory, especially after suffering many years of invasions and the loss of numerous friends and colleagues at the hands of their rival. "We couldn't stay though," Francisco said. "It's really hard to hold onto territory that's not yours. You don't know anything, you don't know the residents, or how they're [the enemy] gonna come for you...″[78] Even though these territories border one another, CVNH had little familiarity with their rival's terrain. During the height of the war years, CVNH had cleansed their organization of any members that they suspected of having any allegiance or connection to TCP, including those with family or friends from that area. "If you have cria, it's easier. With kids from the area, you know the residents. You know everything," Francisco told me. He went on to describe how police from the 22nd Battalion arrived quickly after they had taken the territory and proceeded to harass and pursue them for the next several days. "Five of our kids died," he concluded. Without strong connections to the community that would have helped them hide and avoid enforcement, CVNH was quickly forced to retreat back across their border.

Even though they were unable to consolidate control of their rival's territory, CVNH became dramatically less coercive during this period as they were unafraid of losing their territory to a rival. As described earlier, their presence and monitoring along the border diminished significantly and the gang no longer relied on threats or punishments to ensure the obedience and allegiance of the local population. The gang's physical presence would remain high, however, as their access to weapons and the size of the gang would remain elevated, perhaps owing to the dramatic expansion of the organization during the war years.

In addition to a much less coercive set of behaviors, CVNH returned to a responsive and beneficial form of governance during this period. According to

---

[75] Francisco 8/20/2013.
[76] *O Globo* 1/14/2008.
[77] Severino 10/2/2013; Inácio 3/26/2014.
[78] Francisco 8/20/2013.

a close friend of Flávio's, the former Dono once told him, "I don't want people to respect me out of fear but because of the respect I have for them."[79] While a friend of the former Dono may not be an entirely reliable source, according to many residents, the gang did return to resolving disputes in a responsive fashion and many residents that had kept their distance from the gang during the war years again began to avail themselves of the gang's services. According to Josie, the gang was not "resolving" disputes so much as "mediating" them.[80]

> If someone sold someone bad meat, the Dono used to go deal with the problem by making the seller give the money back and then punish them so that it didn't happen again. Then the gang began mediating conflicts, not resolving them. So instead they'd say that the seller needed to give them something in exchange for the bad meat but that didn't prevent the seller from doing it again. It became much less about using punishment or violence to resolve problems. …the gang started accepting a lot of behaviors that they never used to.

Josie's perspective reflects how, in certain cases, the residents themselves may even desire a more violent or coercive approach to governance. While CVNH's mediation services did not always resolve the underlying conflict or prevent the same issue from reemerging, the gang was nonetheless dealing with a huge variety of resident complaints and conflicts.

Flávio and CVNH also maintained good relations with the increasing number of NGOs within their territory. Early in the new millennium, several NGOs were founded in Nova Holanda and began to engage in a variety of education programs and social projects. In part, they located themselves in Nova Holanda because of the preexisting activist networks there – the same ones that had mobilized to end the war between the two gangs in the early 1980s – but also because CVNH allowed them significant autonomy to engage in their projects.[81] Over time, the gang and these NGOs developed a stable form of coexistence. The gang agreed not to sell drugs near their buildings while the NGOs often informed the gang about any events or projects which brought in significant numbers of outsiders or may attract the attention of the police.[82]

Coexistence, however, had its limits. NGO leaders knew that they would not be allowed to stay within the community if they took a more confrontational approach to the gang.[83] For instance, they could not give interviews to local newspapers or publicize any of the illicit or violent activities of the gang (Savell 2015). Despite the significant influence of Nova Holanda's NGOs – they are some of the most prominent and vocal favela-based NGOs in the

[79] Lino 11/3/2014.
[80] Josie 7/10/2018.
[81] Francisco 7/17/2013; 8/20/2013; Eduarda 9/19/2013; Lino 11/3/2014.
[82] See Savell (2015) for a description of some of the ways these activist organizations coexist with gangs in Maré.
[83] Eduarda 9/19/2013; Artur 1/11/2017.

entire city – they were unable to directly shape gang behavior through mobilization and collective demands. This is largely because CVNH had expanded its influence and authority within these neighborhoods over time. Instead of just twenty young men with mostly pistols and a small amount of resources, by the mid-2000s, CVNH was a significant organization with more than 100 members, connected to numerous aspects of resident life, generating millions in annual revenue.

In fact, during this period, CVNH involved itself even further in the financial life of the community even though many residents no longer required the gang's handouts as desperately as they once did. The Brazilian economy was growing at an incredible clip for the duration of the 2000s, and the economic circumstances of many favela residents improved significantly over this decade. By the mid-2000s, many families could afford shoes and school uniforms for their children for the first time and increasingly bought household appliances such as televisions and washing machines, as well as a variety of other luxury goods – jewelry, watches, cell phones. Conditional cash transfer programs such as *Bolsa Família* also provided resources to the most impoverished families. And yet, the CVNH gang was still able to insert itself into the economic lives of these communities by expanding its illicit activities beyond drug trafficking.

For instance, Flávio moved the baile funk from the school playground to Teixeira Ribeiro Street which could fit many thousands of attendees instead of just a few hundred. He allowed dozens of residents to set up small tents to sell drinks and food to partygoers.[84] Flávio also began operating vans, informal transportation services, that ran from Maré to several other areas of the city.[85] He allegedly made R$350 per day from each of the vans while numerous drivers made their living and hundreds if not thousands of residents used these vans to save money on transportation.[86] The gang also began providing cable tv services and, later, internet. Most of these activities not only increased and diversified the gang's revenue streams but also served to create financial relationships with residents. For the CVNH gang, these activities would come to increasingly replace the more direct financial assistance and welfare of the past.

Despite his various efforts to generate even more revenue from his territory, Flávio was known as a "poor Dono" because of his willingness to spend resources on the community rather than accumulating a fortune for himself.[87] On numerous occasions, he offered apartments to families that were unable

---

[84] Josie 7/10/2018.
[85] Inácio 4/24/2014.
[86] I frequently used these vans at the beginning of my fieldwork. The city cracked down on these informal transportation services during my time in Rio and, by the end of fieldwork in 2015, there were very few vans operating in Maré and the rest of the city.
[87] Fernanda 11/12/2014; Lino 11/3/2014.

to provide for their own.[88] He gave unused municipal land to a local church so they could build a soup kitchen.[89] Fausto remembered Flávio giving him money to buy blankets for addicts living on the street during a cold spell one winter.[90] He frequently bought gas, food, and medicine for residents and even organized a Christmas supper.[91] "There were probably a lot of people crying when he was finally arrested," Fernanda told me.[92]

Although Flávio was, according to many, an exemplary Dono, he also developed an addiction to crack.[93] According to DD data, CVNH was the first of Maré's gangs to produce and sell crack beginning in late-2005.[94] The Parque União gang would join them a few of years later in 2009. Flávio began to use crack quickly after the gang introduced it but, according to interviews, he only used when he was at home and never acted erratically because of it.[95] A Dono with an addiction, however, is a serious liability for any gang organization. Gang members known to abuse drugs, especially crack, will often be killed or expelled from the organization because they are so untrustworthy.[96] Perhaps luckily for Flávio, he was arrested in March 2009, and spent ten months in prison during which time he found his faith, got clean, and decided to leave the gang life.[97] Upon his release, he asked the leadership of the CV faction permission to leave so that he could take care of his daughter.[98] The leaders granted his request and Flávio returned to his home state of Paraíba in the Northeast of Brazil, where he allegedly opened an ice cream shop and eventually checked himself into a rehabilitation clinic to treat his addiction.[99]

[88] Lino 11/3/2014.
[89] Maria 12/1/2014.
[90] Fausto 6/16/2014.
[91] Lino 11/3/2014.
[92] Fernanda 11/12/2014.
[93] Inácio 4/24/2014.
[94] Crack arrived to the US market in the 1980s, spreading quickly through a number of East Coast cities, before being seen in São Paulo in the 1990s. It was first reported in Rio de Janeiro in 2003 (*O Globo* 6/8/2017). Crack is made by "cooking" cocaine, sodium bicarbonate (baking soda), and water. A solid substance or "rocks" are produced which can then be smoked. For the user, dopamine floods the brain within a matter of seconds. The feeling is described as euphoric and one of infinite possibility and wonder. The high lasts for about ten minutes. According to CVNH members, the drug is highly lucrative because it is so cheap to make, and users need to buy it frequently to feed their habit. Although there are far fewer users of crack than marijuana or cocaine, the gang allegedly sold between R$1,000 and 2,000 per day when I was in the field. Julio described it as a "*mina de ouro*" (gold mine) for the gang (8/17/2017).
[95] Lino 11/3/2014; Severino 5/15/2014.
[96] There is also a significant stigma regarding the use of crack. Addicts are often referred to as *zumbis* (zombies) and treated as less than human.
[97] Lino 11/3/2014. Gang members have access to some pastoral services within the prisons as several NGOs and religious organizations have a presence within carceral institutions.
[98] Donos usually require the consent of the faction's leadership, referred to as the "*cúpula*" (summit) or the "*quartel geral*" (general headquarters), to leave the organization.
[99] In 2013, Flávio returned to Nova Holanda and rejoined the gang, becoming its crack manager before eventually being arrested again and sent to federal prison in May 2014.

Following Flávio's exit, the leadership of the gang passed to three men that would share the Dono's responsibilities.[100] Coroa, Flávio's general manager, was given the revenue from one boca de fumo, while two of Flávio's other managers, Ninho and BB, shared the profits from six other bocas. Another three bocas have remained the property of relatives of Jorge Negão since his death in 1992 (see Figure 5.2). All subsequent Donos have respected this arrangement though these relatives allegedly play only a small role in the operation of the drug trade.[101] The CVNH Donos take a cut from these bocas to pay for security and personnel. It is incredibly rare for Rio's gangs to divide leadership between more than one Dono and for good reason. It often creates competition between these men and can lead to violence within the gang. Sure enough, Coroa was allegedly displeased with this arrangement, having been given only one boca even though he was the most senior gang member. As reported earlier, Coroa also had some violent tendencies, which was perhaps why the leadership did not pass to him directly. According to gang members familiar with this period, Ninho and BB decided they wanted to get rid of Coroa because they thought he was a liability, so they went to the leadership of the CV faction and asked permission to remove him.[102] The CV leaders acquiesced and Coroa was quietly killed.[103]

Benevolent Dictator (2009–14)

In 2009, the security environment for the CVNH again shifted. In April of that year, the imprisoned leader of TCP, Espadão, was given a work release permit from prison. He walked out but did not return.[104] A little more than a month later, he and his TCP gang from Morro do Timbau invaded the housing projects to their south controlled by an ADA gang at the time (see Chapter 7). Over the course of a very violent couple of months, Espadão and his gang managed to eventually conquer the area and expel their ADA rival. TCP was now in possession of an area with an estimated population of 68,000, and, over the next couple of years, proceeded to consolidate their control over the area. They opened more than a dozen new bocas, increasing

---

[100] Francisco 7/17/2013. In other interviews with former Donos from around the city, similar arrangements where bocas were distributed to different high-ranking members of a gang were not uncommon (Davi 9/9/2013; Lucas 10/31/2013).

[101] Josie 7/10/2018; Lino 11/3/2014; Inácio 4/24/2014.

[102] Bruno 10/6/2014; Francisco 7/17/2013; Lino 11/3/2014. One of the most important ways that the CV faction shapes the behavior of their affiliated gangs is by managing the selection of successors. If a Dono is replaced without the leadership's approval, they may decide to remove them and install a Dono of their own choosing, sometimes someone from outside of the community (Lucas 7/17/2013). In this way, the faction leadership tries to prevent infighting and conflicts within affiliated gangs.

[103] Bruno 10/6/2014; Lino 11/3/2014.

[104] *O Globo* 6/1/2009.

their revenues to an estimated R$3 million per week, not only through the sale of retail drugs but also by becoming a central node in the distribution of drugs for the entire TCP faction. With these resources, TCP expanded the capacity of their organization, recruiting more than 100 new members, acquiring an enormous arsenal of high-powered weapons, while also maintaining a highly collaborative relationship with the police (see Chapter 7). TCP became the dominant gang in Maré and once again presented a latent existential threat to CVNH control.

For the next couple of years, there were no attempts to invade each other's territory but with TCP's enlarged territorial holdings, their expanded ranks, and the history of violence between the two groups, they constituted a significant concern for CVNH. So, in April 2011, when TCP offered a truce, the CVNH Donos were willing to accept if it meant avoiding another period of war. According to multiple sources, the gerente geral of TCP, Bração, walked to the two gangs' border with thirty of his men. He found a CVNH gang member with a radio and told him to inform Ninho, the CVNH Dono, that he wanted to talk.[105] Ninho was dubious about such a meeting with so many armed enemies, so he initially refused. Bração then promised to bring only two of his men with him but cautioned that his gang would shoot up the whole neighborhood if anything happened to him.[106] Allegedly, Ninho and Bração talked for several minutes before agreeing to end their rivalry.[107] For the next several days, hundreds of residents and gang members congregated along the shared border as the two gangs threw several joint parties to commemorate the occasion.[108] "You wouldn't believe it! Everyone was at the border. There were more motorcycles than you've ever seen. We partied for three days!" Bernardo recalled.[109]

Then, just four days after the gang leaders had agreed to end the conflict, TCP invaded CVNH *en masse*. Apparently, during the several days of peace, a couple of CVNH members had been convinced to join the TCP side. These men gave TCP insider information about the CVNH territory and organization. In the early morning hours of April 14th, dozens of TCP members streamed across the border as a surprised CVNH gang struggled to mount a defense. Panicked residents called into DD. "Traffickers from [Morro do Timbau] are making an incursion into Nova Holanda… The traffickers from TCP are constantly exchanging gunfire with CV and can be seen heavily armed even with police in the area. There was a peace agreement between the groups, but it was broken!"[110]

---

[105] Bruno 10/6/2014; Tiaguinho 12/8/2014; Fausto 7/27/2013.
[106] Tiaguinho 12/8/2014.
[107] Bruno 10/6/2014; Tiaguinho 12/8/2014.
[108] DD 4/10/2011; 4/11/2011.
[109] Bernardo 1/16/2017.
[110] DD 4/14/2011b.

"It's chaos in Nova Holanda!" one resident reported, "Dozens of heavily armed traffickers allied with TCP invaded in vans... There's going to be a change in criminal power!"[111] CVNH was outmatched and unprepared. Their members were forced to retreat across the bridge into Parque União, where TCP's offensive stopped. Upon taking control of the entirety of Nova Holanda, TCP scoured the area for any remaining CVNH members. They found several that had been trapped in their homes during the invasion. TCP members allegedly dragged them into the street and executed them.[112] Osvaldo recalled that TCP members kept telling residents that they were "bringing peace" to Nova Holanda.[113]

Like CVNH's attempted conquest of TCP's territory in 2008, TCP only managed to stay in Nova Holanda for a few days. I heard two different explanations for why TCP was eventually forced to leave. The first is that the leadership of the CV faction communicated to Espadão and Bração that if they did not leave Nova Holanda, CV gangs from around the city would mount an all-out invasion of their territories in Maré.[114] It's unclear to what extent the TCP leaders thought this was a credible threat but, given the size of the CV faction – it is, by far, the largest of the three factions – and the importance of maintaining a foothold in these highly lucrative set of neighborhoods, it is plausible. Another explanation was that eventually the police invaded and several TCP members were killed in ensuing confrontations.[115] Given TCP's ongoing bribery schemes and collaborative relationship with the police (see Chapter 7), this seems unlikely but there are various different segments of the Military Police and it is possible that BOPE or some other unit was eventually called in to combat TCP. If enforcement was forthcoming, TCP members were likely unable to easily avoid the police because they had not yet had time to consolidate their control of the area and gain the support of the community. After years of warfare, Nova Holanda residents were particularly wary of TCP and were unlikely to provide them support to evade police enforcement. Whatever the reason, TCP was forced to retreat after only a few days and CVNH quickly reestablished their control of the area.

Although CVNH was weakened by the invasion and their brief loss of territory, they quickly ramped up their coercion. First, they sought to punish any individuals within their ranks that had betrayed them. One of their members who had joined TCP, a young man nicknamed Mimi, had, years prior, killed a ten-year-old and shot an elderly woman during an invasion in the TCP territory. A relative of the elderly woman recognized and confronted him at a party after he had joined TCP. According to Tiaguinho, Mimi began to cry because

[111] DD 4/14/2011a.
[112] DD 4/14/2011c.
[113] Osvaldo 1/7/2015.
[114] Severino 10/2/2013.
[115] Fulton 7/3/2014; Bruno 10/6/2014.

he knew that everyone in TCP's territory wanted him dead.[116] When CVNH offered to take him back, Mimi readily accepted but his old gang killed him immediately and cut his body into pieces. Residents remember gang members driving around on motorcycles, carrying or dragging one of Mimi's legs or arms, showing the community what happened to anyone that betrayed them to their enemy.[117] The gang even put videos of his mutilated body on the internet as a way to further disseminate the lesson.[118] Such horrific acts of torture and mutilation are almost exclusively reserved for those who betray a gang to an active rival.

Although shootouts continued for several months following TCP's failed takeover, the two gangs would only engage in sporadic bursts of violent conflict for the next several years. These shifts between latent and active rival threat translated into a period of more coercive governance though not as extreme as observed during the 1999–2004 war between the gangs. In Chapter 3, I documented the dynamics of coercion during this period as CVNH would relax their monitoring of the border after long periods without violence, then quickly increase the number of gang members stationed along the border when violence broke out again. The gang also quickly ramped up their monitoring of residents and did not refrain from using threats and even violence against anyone they suspected of not belonging during periods of more heightened tension.[119]

Second, the gang maintained a heavy physical presence throughout their territory. Most CVNH members carried semiautomatic rifles as well as handguns tucked into their shorts. Even in the areas farthest removed from the border where there was little chance of violent outbursts, CVNH members were always heavily armed. Much more than the other gangs in Maré, CVNH members were frequently seen riding their motorcycles up and down the main streets, conspicuously carrying their weapons, which served as a constant reminder to residents that the gang was in charge and controlled the streets. I would regularly see Ninho on the streets surrounded by a large security detail of roughly ten heavily armed men all on motorcycles. He never went anywhere without this retinue.[120]

Finally, CVNH also began to allow a huge number of foreign gang members into its territory. In fact, from late 2013 until its occupation by the military in April 2014, Nova Holanda became the central distribution point of the CV faction. The Donos of at least ten other CV gangs would eventually locate

---

[116] Tiaguinho 12/8/2014.
[117] Tiaguinho 12/8/2014; Fabiene 1/14/2017.
[118] Osvaldo 1/7/2015.
[119] Marcos 11/3/2014; Bruno 10/27/2014.
[120] By the time I arrived in Nova Holanda in the middle of 2013, BB was in prison and Ninho had taken over the daily administration of the gang. Although BB would remain Dono, because he was in prison, he was little involved in the daily decision-making of the gang.

themselves in Nova Holanda.[121] This influx caused significant governance issues for CVNH as foreign gang members were more likely to resort to threats and violence. Allowing so many foreign gang members into his territory was a controversial move by Ninho and CVNH members differed in their opinion of this decision. Some said the Dono had little choice in the matter. The leaders of the CV faction had ordered him to open his territory to them as they needed an area in which to receive, package, and distribute drugs after the installation of UPPs in their home favelas.[122] Especially if some of these CV leaders had been instrumental in helping defend the area in the past or by helping to force TCP out in 2011, this may have been a way for Ninho to pay them back or ensure he could continue to rely on them in the future. Other CVNH members, however, suggested that Ninho was being selfish and was more interested in making money than the well-being of the community. Ninho was making significant revenue during this period because the foreign Donos all gave him a share of their profits for the use of his territory. According to Bruno, he did not care that he was *"bagunçando a comunidade"* (messing up the community).[123] Severino agreed, "He says he was ordered but that's just an excuse. He can do what he wants with his territory."[124]

And yet, despite the high levels of coercion and sometimes tense relations with residents, the gang continued to provide significant benefits to the community by resolving disputes, stimulating the local economy, and providing forms of recreation. Due to the frequent and active enforcement efforts by BOPE and other police units, the gang needed residents' silence and support to help them avoid being caught by the police. Especially after BOPE moved its headquarters to an abandoned military base on the outskirts of Maré in August 2011, police engaged in frequent operations in CVNH's territory until the arrival of the military in April 2014 (see Figure 5.4). In this context of active enforcement, CVNH members knew the consequences for angering residents or not responding to their demands. They could not forget about the community or they would pay the price.

As described in Chapter 3, CVNH was highly responsive to community demands for dispute resolution, intimately involving themselves in the personal lives of residents.[125] Nearly all the members I interviewed reported that they frequently resolved domestic disputes and small conflicts that arose between lovers, neighbors, friends, and even sometimes between businesses and customers.[126] The organizational structure of the gang also shifted to better deal with these issues. In previous eras, the structure of the gang had not been divvied up

---

[121] Artur 1/9/2017; 1/11/2017; Breno 3/6/2014; Severino 10/2/2013.
[122] Inácio 4/24/2014.
[123] Bruno 10/27/2014.
[124] Severino 5/15/2014.
[125] Eduarda 9/19/2013.
[126] Marcos 11/3/2014; Severino 10/2/2013; Everton 4/17/2014.

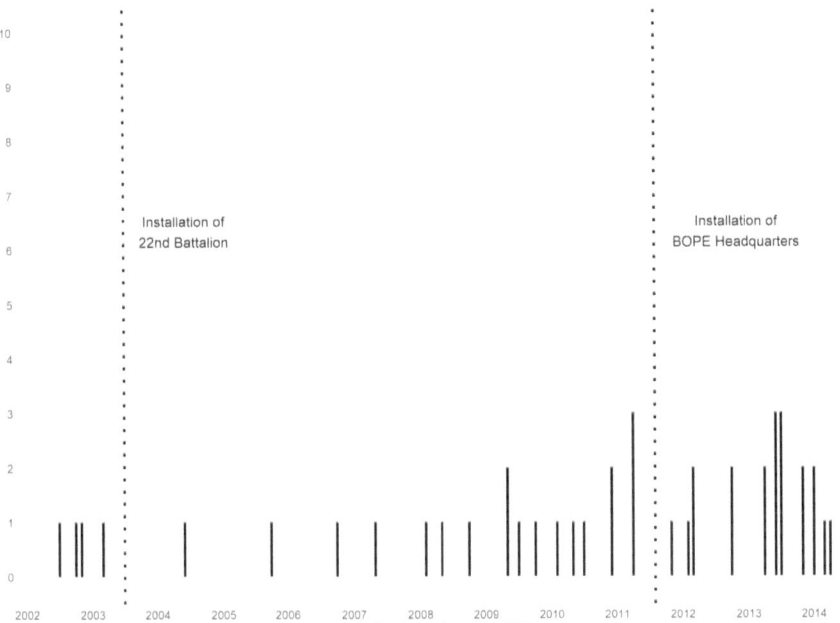

FIGURE 5.4 Police operations in CVNH territory (monthly)
Data from *Disque-Denúncia*. Visualization by Pranjal Drall.

geographically. However, the two Donos began to deal with issues in the areas in which they resided. For instance, Ninho and his primary manager, who lived in the Parque Maré neighborhood (see Figure 5.1), often dealt with problems arising in this part of the territory. Before his arrest in 2013, BB lived in Parque Rubens Vaz and he often dealt with issues in this area.[127] Finally, the gerente geral of the gang, a man nicknamed Radinho (Little Radio), would emerge during this period to deal with governance for much of the Nova Holanda area, not including Parque Maré or Parque Rubens Vaz.[128] This further territorialization of the gang's structure mapped onto their efforts to develop closer relations with residents living in each and every corner of their turf and is yet another example of how the gang sought to further embed itself within the population.

In addition, CVNH expanded their governance by collaborating with or allowing a variety of other actors to engage in some governance activities within Nova Holanda. For instance, in 2013, a community of homeless drug users, pejoratively referred to as a *cracolândia* (crackland), developed just outside the CVNH turf (see Figure 5.1). Between 60 and 100 users eventually migrated to

---

[127] Ramón 1/17/2017.
[128] Inácio 4/24/2014; Fabiene 1/14/2017; Wagner 1/2/2017.

this area, where they could easily enter Nova Holanda to buy drugs. Although the gang did not allow them to spend time in their territory other than to purchase drugs, their presence quickly began to cause problems. Local business owners and residents complained about trash accumulating in the area and how some users were engaging in petty crimes such as theft and prostitution.[129] CVNH began to work with one of the local AMs to manage the user community and resolve disputes. The AM appointed an informal leader of the user community – a user herself – who would report to them if she could not effectively deal with a problem. If the AM also could not handle it, the gang would then step in. According to the local AM representative, this system of governance effectively managed the user community and resident complaints reduced dramatically.[130]

Over time, several of the more influential NGOs also began to expand their governance activities within Nova Holanda, providing occasional dispute resolution and financial assistance to residents in times of need. For issues pertaining to violence, crime, abuse, or the use of space within the community, however, the gang remained the only real option.[131] For instance, in one event I attended at a local NGO, workers discussed what they would do if they received a call from a parent whose child was being threatened with violence by the gang. They went around the room, one by one saying they would go and ask one of the directors of the NGO. Finally, one of the directors spoke up,

It's not a problem we can solve. I would tell them to go to João [one of several residents that could sometimes help mediate such problems] or the Pastor and ask them to intervene on his behalf. I remember a boy once came to me to ask for help because he owed R$20,000 to the gang. I told him to flee and never come back.[132]

No one said anything for a moment then the director continued, "The institution [NGO] cannot take a position in relation to the traffickers because it's a slippery slope. In these situations, only religion or feminine pleas, from the boy's mother or grandmother, could help."

Several other NGO workers then described similar stories of residents or neighbors coming to them for help in the last few years. One said that she had hidden a young man in the trunk of her car to sneak him out of the community. Another recounted how their cousin had dated one of the Dono's girlfriends without knowing it and been forced to flee the community forever. One NGO worker said that someone had been beaten by gang members and she had taken them to the hospital only to have gang members visit her house several

---

[129] Julio 8/17/2015. The prejudice against crack users also likely contributed to many residents, even those not directly impacted by their presence, to complain.
[130] Julio 8/17/2015.
[131] Eduarda 9/19/2013; Doroteia 4/1/2014; Dudu 6/11/2014; Veronica 12/11/2014.
[132] Field notes 12/1/2014.

months later to say – "very calmly," she noted – that she should not testify in the case. Especially for gangs that maintain such a highly coercive posture, such occurrences are not rare. The final decision regarding punishments by a gang is made on a case-by-case basis and, ultimately, depends a great deal on the specific transgression, the person accused, their family, and the social networks in which they are embedded. Overall, the more the gang feels it needs to make examples out of rule breakers, the less willing they will be to commute a sentence. In this respect, the NGOs and other social institutions in the community had limited influence over the gangs.

Thus, despite the NGOs' growing influence, they were unable to shape gang behavior more directly. No longer could they encourage the gangs to lay down their arms or end their physically armed presence as they had with Candinho's gang and the Irmãos Metralha in the 1980s. Instead, several of the more active NGOs adopted more indirect paths toward shaping gang authority and behavior, mostly through empowering residents to take a more active role within the community and to constrain the violent and abusive behavior of the police. One project brought multiple NGOs and all Maré's AMs together for monthly meetings in which they would strategize ways to address issues pertaining to infrastructure, education, social justice, and public security. I attended these monthly meetings for the duration of my time in Maré. In the first few meetings, representatives from the different gang territories were hesitant to collaborate too closely and the gangs were never mentioned. Over time, however, the participants slowly began to create further space for their activities and take more proactive stances regarding public security. Eventually, in the months leading up to Maré's occupation by the military, these meetings even began to include public security officials.

The meetings were held regularly for the next two years, during which NGO directors, AM representatives, and other residents were given the opportunity to hear directly from public security representatives (see Chapter 8).[133] For their part, the police always stressed how much they needed the help of the community – mostly by providing information through DD – if they were to be effective. Community representatives, on the other hand, mostly criticized the violent manner in which police went about their job and continued to demand a change in their approach to policing.

CVNH did nothing to prevent these meetings from occurring. Many of the meetings were even held within CVNH's territory at a local NGO building. The difference between how a gang responds to groups and individuals working or interacting with the police and with a rival is stark. The reaction to any such interactions with a rival would have been swift and brutal. That said, CVNH was likely aware of the details of these meetings through their connections to the AMs and other residents that attended some of the meetings. They were

---

[133] Such meetings or any direct communication between community members and the public security apparatus are incredibly rare in favela territories.

careful, however, not use violence or threats against these actors or during the meetings, especially when they were already the focus of intense enforcement efforts. Instead of reducing the threat of the police, such acts of coercion would likely only deteriorate their security environment further as residents could easily denounce such behavior through the anonymous hotlines. That said, the gang did proscribe certain activities by residents when it came to policing. For example, before its occupation by the military, one of the supermarkets in Nova Holanda installed an ATM and organized to have an armored truck with security enter the neighborhood to replenish the machine. While the armored truck and armed security was on the streets, the gang was forced to pause their drug sales. They eventually demanded that the ATM be removed, and the supermarket complied.

In addition to providing responsive forms of dispute resolution and allowing local organizations significant leeway, CVNH also continued to stimulate the local economy and provide some welfare. Gang members frequently spoke of the help they got from providing handouts to residents.[134] At the same time, many noted on how this dynamic had diminished over the years due to the improving economic conditions of residents. Many no longer needed the gang as they once had though the gang continued to provide the poorest families with a monthly food basket, gas canisters, medicine, or even temporary housing.[135]

CVNH increasingly stimulated the local economy by further expanding their revenue streams beyond the drug trade, what some referred to as *"terceirização"* (outsourcing).[136] For instance, the gang continued to provide numerous residents access to sidewalks and areas of the street to sell food, snacks, and other goods. The gang authorized nearly any unused space within the community, sometimes allowing the construction of a shack or stall right in front of an existing business or home. Some streets became so full of vendors that it became difficult for cars and pedestrians to pass by. CVNH also increasingly began to engage in real estate speculation, buying up existing properties or constructing new ones throughout their territory, which they either used themselves, gave to family or friends, or rented out. This simple form of money laundering also provides some residents with an infusion of cash. For instance, one resident reported that the gang had bought her previous apartment for twice what she thought it was worth, in cash.[137] She used the windfall to buy another apartment on a quieter street, open a small business, and take a vacation to the Northeast of Brazil. The gang has also developed numerous properties and apartments throughout their territory, which they then rent to residents, thus creating an even longer-term financial relationship.

---

[134] Bruno 10/27/2014; Naldo 12/17/2014.
[135] Severino 10/2/2013; Inácio 4/3/2014.
[136] Josie 7/10/2018.
[137] Isabel 4/24/2014.

The demand for the gang's internet services, which started in the late-2000s, only increased over time as more and more residents purchased laptops, smart TVs, or other internet capable devices.[138] Finally, the gang also expanded their activities to include the sale of illegal beverages.[139] Several local shops and bars were known to sell stolen alcoholic drinks and cigarettes or to sell products without the necessary license to do so. The gang directly authorized many of these activities.

Beyond these more direct financial arrangements, CVNH gang members and their friends and family also frequented bars, restaurants, shops, and salons that they did not own or receive any direct benefit from. Many shops and restaurants welcomed gang members as they would any other customer. On numerous occasions, I ate at restaurants where gang members would lean their rifles against a wall, leave their handguns, money, or drugs on a table, and enter the line of patrons to fill their plate from the lunch buffet. While these relationships are not essential to the benefits gangs provide, they are an important element of governance in that the gang is spending their money and resources within the community and are sharing space with residents.

In this regard, one anecdote further demonstrates the more responsive nature of CVNH's governing regime. During my first nine months in the field, I would occasionally eat lunch at a local diner across the street from one of Nova Holanda's busier bocas. There were always two if not three gang members manning the boca: one vapor that exchanged drugs for cash and kept track of the sales in a notepad, and one or two soldados providing security. One particularly warm afternoon, I arrived to find that the boca had moved across the street, directly under the awning of the diner. The gang members had taken over one of the tables to display their wares in the cool of the shade. I pretended to be unaware of the change, ordered my usual, and looked for an empty table, hoping to get a front row seat for the goings on at the boca. The restaurant was full, however, and the woman who took my order, seeing that I could not immediately find a place to sit, came out from behind the counter and demanded that the gang members, both armed, give up their table. Horrified, I told her that I could wait. "These tables are for customers only," she told the two adolescents, who reluctantly began collecting their things and carried them across the street where they sat down in the heat of the midday sun. The woman wiped off the table, pulled out the chair, and motioned for me to sit. I thanked her and told her she hadn't needed to do that. "They know they shouldn't be there," she said. "I can ask them to leave whenever I want." Such a scene was emblematic of the governing relationship the gang maintained with the community. Despite CVNH's heavily armed presence, close monitoring of the border, and use of threats and violence against people

[138] Breno reported that many residents were grateful that the gang had unblocked the pornographic channels later in the evenings (4/4/2017).
[139] Josie 7/10/2017.

who disobeyed them or their rules at the time, gang members were also highly responsive to resident demands. They did not use threats or violence indiscriminately and knew the lines they could and could not cross. Residents, in turn, had certain rights and privileges when it came to the gang, and many were not shy demanding gang members respect the existing norms and rules.

Finally, CVNH also provided numerous opportunities for recreation during the period in which I lived in Maré. The baile in Nova Holanda was one of the biggest in the city during this period. At its height, in late 2013 and early 2014, upwards of 5,000 youth packed a long section of Teixeira Ribeiro Street every Saturday night. The gang spent significant resources on DJs, sound equipment, a small stage, and three giant walls of speakers surrounded by lights.

Like some of the gang's other beneficial activities, bailes are not purely motivated by benevolence. They are as much about generating revenue as they are about gaining the support and adulation of local youth. According to gang members, the gang sold all the drugs to which they had access at the bailes: cocaine, marijuana, crack, ecstasy, and an inhalant, referred to as *loló* or *lança perfume*. The gang reportedly made between half and two-thirds of their weekly revenue from their baile on Saturday night.[140] The importance of the bailes in gaining the allegiance and respect of local youth should not be underestimated. The euphoria and enjoyment on display at some of these parties were palpable, helping attendees make it through the drudgery of their day-to-day lives, attending schools they do not enjoy, working poorly paid and tedious service industry jobs, or perhaps in dealing with other experiences of marginalization, poverty, and neglect.

In addition, the governing philosophy of the gang was made explicit at these parties. The chorus to a particularly famous song from this era, written and performed by MC Rodson, spells it out:

> Bring the weed and bring the inhalant, but pay attention
> Use them far from the kids to avoid complications
> The shit is monitored, what happens will be heard on the radio
> The shit is monitored, what happens will be heard on the radio
>
> Pá pá pá pá pá, we're here and we're not stupid
> Defending the favela, the kids are safe
> Pá pá pá pá pá, if you stray it will get complicated
> Do you get it? We're all from here.

The lyrics describe the type of order that the gang implemented, reminding attendees that the gang has put important limits on some behaviors related to the drug trade, namely, that they do not allow drugs to be used around small children. The song then repeats "this shit is monitored, what happens will be heard on the radio," which refers to the radios the gang used to communicate.

---

[140] Josie 7/10/2017; Márcio 4/17/2014; Everton 4/17/2014; Francisco 7/17/2017.

The second stanza refers to the gang as the defender of the favela and keeping children safe but again warning the listener, "if you stray it will get complicated." The chorus ends by reminding baile attendees that the gang is comprised of members that are native to the favela. Even in these two short stanzas, we can see various ways that the gang both attempts to legitimize itself by respecting and defending residents while simultaneously reminding them that they will be punished if they disobey their rules, a perfect encapsulation of CVNH governing regime during this period. While baile funk lyrics are not always accurate representations of gang behavior and are better understood as propaganda, it is interesting to note that this song corresponded closely with how CVNH thought about their governing regime, coercive yet responsive, a benevolent dictator. Perhaps the song became so famous and well-liked precisely because it mapped onto existing ways of thinking about the local gang.

Another incident at one of the baile funks also offers insight into the responsiveness of the CVNH regime. In the lead-up to occupation, there were several shots fired into the air at one of the baile funks, perhaps done to add emphasis to the lyrics of a song. Some of the partygoers, mistaking the shots for the beginning of a violent confrontation, attempted to flee, producing a brief stampede, which destroyed several of the vendors' tents and their wares. The following night, I watched a couple dozen aggrieved vendors surround two individuals, a man and a woman in their fifties, who organized the vendors for the gang. The vendors were agitated. "They smashed our tent! We lost our grill and they stole our chairs! They robbed us!" one woman shouted. The woman organizer shouted over the din of the crowd, "Everyone will be heard! This is a democracy. Everyone will have their turn to speak. We will try to resolve the problems as best we can. Please, speak clearly into the camera and describe your complaints. We will take them to the person who will decide how to compensate you."

The man took out a video recorder and began filming the crowd. One woman stepped in front of the camera and began listing her complaints and losses. For the next fifteen minutes, each vendor took their turn in front of the camera. Given the considerable list of damages, it was going to be a large sum of money. By the end, the crowd had dissipated. The vendors seemed content that their grievances had been heard and would be dealt with. I never found out how these problems had been resolved but the act of documenting the grievances in this way demonstrates once again how the gang and their affiliates are responsive or at least perform responsiveness to resident demands.

CONCLUSION

In this chapter, I have traced CVNH's governance practices over roughly two decades, over which time they have shifted considerably. After integrating into the CV faction, the CVNH governance regime can best be understood as a benevolent dictatorship from 1994–99 as police continued their active enforcement while the rivalry with TC remained latent. The all-out war the gang fought with their TC rival was a defining period in the history of these communities as the coercive behavior of the gang increased incredibly and disorder pervaded from 1999–2004. The end of the war and the weakening of TCP led to the stabilization of the security environment a renewed social bandit regime from 2004–09. Active police enforcement from the recently installed 22nd Battalion increased the gang's need to maintain the support of the community through a variety of beneficial activities, including resolution of disputes, economic stimulation, and forms of recreation.

In 2009, CVNH's security environment shifted when TCP successfully conquered new territories and became the most powerful gang in Maré. Owing to this renewed latent threat and several moments of active competition during this period, CVNH developed a benevolent dictator regime. Although they would mostly avoid the excessively public and violent punishments of previous periods, the gang closely monitored the movement and behavior of residents, more frequently threatened residents suspected of not belonging, and maintained a highly militarized presence within their territory. Enforcement against CVNH increased even further during this period after BOPE installed their headquarters just outside of Maré in 2011. In response, CVNH continued their beneficial relations with residents by providing dispute resolution services, even more forms of economic stimulation, and multiple opportunities for recreation. Overall, the theory of criminalized governance developed in Chapter 3 is supported by the historical arc of CVNH, capturing many of the complex and dynamic interactions between residents and gang members in these neighborhoods over this period.

6

Comando Vermelho of Parque União

I have a mouth, but I don't speak. I have eyes, but I don't see. I have ears, but I don't listen. I taught my children to live by the same rules.
—Angela, a longtime resident of Parque União and mother of three

INTRODUCTION

In this chapter, I focus on the governance practices of the CV gang that has controlled Complexo da Maré's most populous favela, Parque União, for more than three decades. Like their CVNH allies, CVPU has been part of the CV faction for this entire period. And yet, their governance styles have diverged considerably. While CVNH has shifted back and forth across three different governance regimes, CVPU evinces a less chaotic evolution (see Table 6.1). They have remained, aside from several years at the turn of the millennium, a social bandit regime. Overall, the absence of an active rival threat has produced a gang that employs far lower levels of coercion than their counterparts. CVPU has seldom engaged in serious threats and punishments aimed at residents, maintained a less ostentatious presence on the streets, and taken a more relaxed approach to surveilling the local population. CVPU has also provided significant benefits throughout their history. They have dealt with resident issues and resolved disputes in ways that are attentive to resident demands while also providing some forms of economic stimulation and opportunities for recreation. I tie this more benevolent aspect of the gang to the need for community support to avoid police enforcement, which has been a consistent aspect of gang life in Parque União since the 1990s. This chapter traces the evolution of these dynamics through a combination of interviews and oral histories with residents and gang members, analysis of newspaper archives and anonymous denunciations, as well as participant observation during my time living in Maré.

TABLE 6.1 *Evolution of CVPU governance regime*

		Coercion	
Provision of benefits	*Extreme*	*High*	*Low*
Responsive		Benevolent dictator	Social bandit
	Disorder	1999–2003	1991–99
			2003–2014
Unresponsive		Tyrant	Laissez-Faire

THE TERRITORY

Parque União was officially established in 1961 on the northern edge of the massive tidal plain that was already home to Maré's five preexisting favelas.[1] Parque União was the last favela in Maré to be built entirely by residents though its construction would differ slightly from the other favelas in the area. In a massive land invasion, hundreds of migrants, organized and led by Margarino Torres, a leftist lawyer, invaded a large sandy area near a drainage canal that bordered Parque Rubens Vaz. In its first years of existence, Torres would be the undisputed leader of Parque União. He organized the community, planned the layout, and ensured the permanence of the fledgling community. Subsequent leaders of the community would continue to control migration to the area and Parque União developed in a more regular and uniform pattern, with straighter streets and intersections consisting mostly of right angles. As a result, it is a far easier space to navigate than some of the other favelas in Maré (Parque Maré, Baixa do Sapateiro, and Morro do Timbau, in particular), which were constructed in a piecemeal and haphazard fashion, resulting in sinuous streets, narrow alleyways, and irregular housing patterns. Moreover, Parque União, like much of the rest of Maré, is incredibly flat with few perceptible changes in altitude throughout the entire neighborhood. That said, the streets are narrower than Nova Holanda and Maré's other housing projects and alleyways crisscross the neighborhood, offering gang members numerous ways to defend their space and escape police operations.

Parque União has also grown considerably over the years. As of 2019, the community contains an estimated 20,567 inhabitants, comprising roughly 15 percent of the total population of Maré. The density of Parque União's population is a staggering 220,000 per square mile, making it nearly twice as dense as the CVNH territory. Beginning in the 1990s, most of the houses in Parque União, once wooden shacks, became single-story brick homes and have grown vertically since then. Most buildings are now three or more stories, which has allowed for the swelling of the population within a limited space. Moreover, in

---

[1] These favelas were Morro do Timbau, Baixa do Sapateiro, Parque Maré, Praia de Inhaúma, and Parque Rubens Vaz.

the late 1990s, the local gang helped residents invade an enormous industrial property on the margins of Avenida Brasil (see Figure 6.1). The factory buildings were divided into lots where individuals were allowed to build new homes. This area, referred to as *Sem Terra* (Landless), is home to an estimated 9,000 residents.

Parque União only borders one other favela, Parque Rubens Vaz, to its south. For the first forty years of its existence, this border was impassable as a large drainage canal entirely separated Parque União from the rest of Maré. However, in the early 2000s, the Bridge of Friendship was constructed to allow residents and vehicles to cross over (de Souza 2007). Until then, anyone who wanted to enter Parque União was forced to walk along Avenida Brasil and past the PPC (see Figure 6.1), which was installed in the 1970s and remains in the same location to this day. Just a little further along Avenida Brasil is the Praça do Parque União (Parque União Square), a small plaza with a stage that is surrounded by numerous restaurants, bars, outdoor food stands, and small vendors. Live music shows (mostly *forro*, *pagode*, and *sertanejo*)[2] as well as other community events fill the square in the evenings and outdoor markets can be found there on the weekends. Gang members will almost never be seen in or near the square as its proximity to the PPC and Avenida Brasil make it too vulnerable an area for them to spend very much time. Moving further north along this border, Avenida Trompowski breaks off Avenida Brasil as it heads toward Ilha do Fundão (Foundation Island), which is home to the Federal University of Rio de Janeiro, Petrobras Headquarters, and several other technological firms. There are multiple entrances to Parque União for pedestrians and vehicles along this stretch of road. Together, the several streets emanating from Avenida Brasil and Avenida Trompowski constitute the exclusive means by which residents enter and exit Parque União.

On the farthest northern edge of the community lies the São Cristovão Football and Regatta Club and CIEP 326 Professor César Pernetta, a middle school.[3] A large wall separates the club from the school and the rest of the favela. There are no entry points for vehicles or pedestrians in this area. Finally, Linha Vermelha constitutes the eastern border of Parque União, where a large wall also separates the favela from the highway. Underneath the highway, a small section of Guanabara Bay is accessible, where a community of fisherman dock their boats. Again, there are no pedestrian or vehicle access points here. Overall, the combination of an extremely dense population, narrow streets, numerous alleyways, and relatively concentrated access points means that Parque União is an easily defensible space and perhaps explains, in part, why there has never been a significant invasion of the territory by a rival.

---

[2] These styles of music are especially popular with migrants from the Northeast region of Brazil, which comprise over 44 percent of Parque União's population, the highest proportion of any of Maré's favelas (Redes da Maré 2019a).

[3] Ronaldo Luís Nazário de Lima (Ronaldo Fenômeno) played for São Cristovão as a teenager.

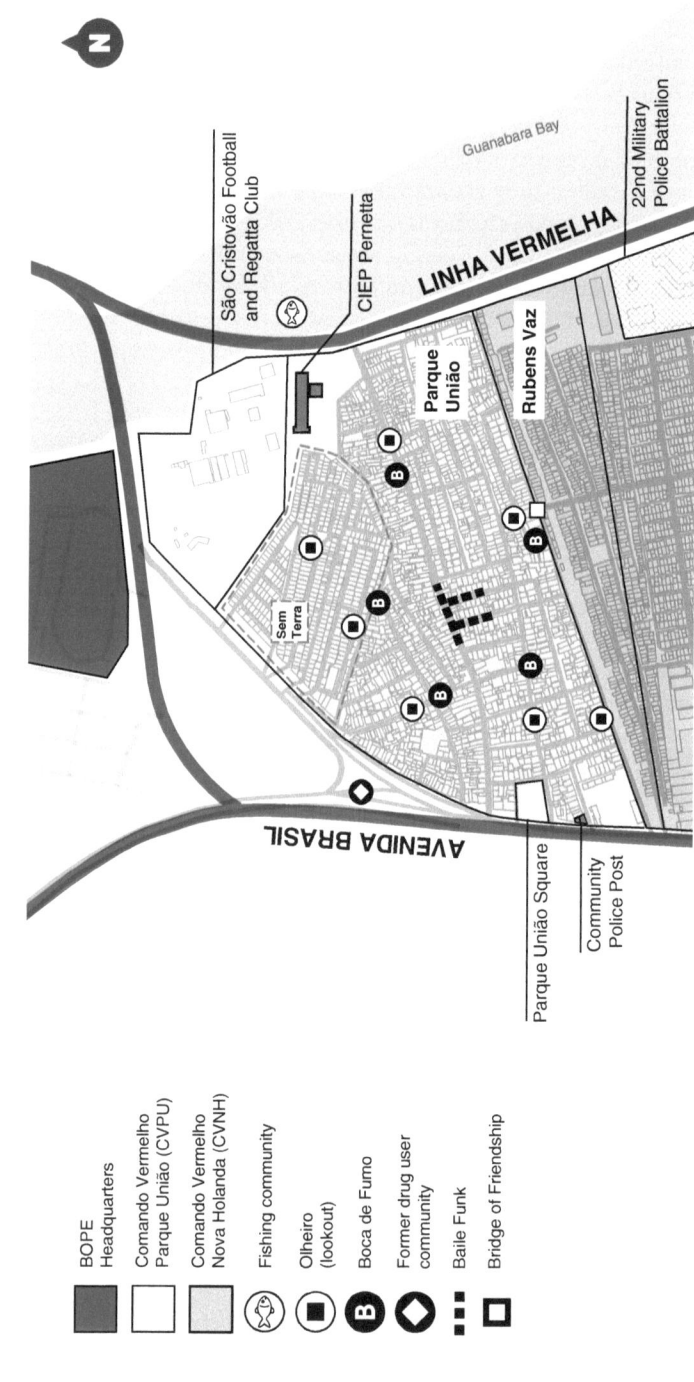

FIGURE 6.1 Map of CVPU territory during fieldwork
Visualization by Bruna Montuori.

I visited Parque União hundreds of times over the course of my fieldwork as the bridge separating the two CV territories was only a three-minute walk from my apartment. Moreover, unlike the border between CVNH and TCP, there was no possibility of violence erupting between these two gangs as they have been part of the same faction since they integrated into CV in the 1990s. The bridge connecting the two territories was always bustling with activity. Various street vendors, local shops, bars, and restaurants populated each side of the bridge. Unlike the border between CVNH and TCP, each gang maintained a boca close to the bridge. The constant pedestrian and vehicle traffic throughout the day and night offered no shortage of possible customers. Moreover, neither of the gangs maintained a highly militarized presence in this area nor were they intent on closely monitoring those coming in or out. In the hundreds of times I crossed the bridge, I never felt like I was being closely watched or monitored by gang members, unlike the border between the two rivals.

Inside Parque União, CVPU located several other bocas along the major thoroughfares, which were all accessible from Avenida Brasil or Avenida Trompowski. Like Nova Holanda, Parque União is an easy place for someone from the outside to enter, make a drug purchase, then quickly exit onto a highway heading in any direction. In total, CVPU had just five bocas compared to the ten which CVNH maintained. Gang members were also less physically present on the streets and far less ostentatious in how they presented themselves and their weaponry. Numerous residents and gang members all commented that Parque União was a *"menos pesado"* (less heavy) area. That said, CVPU still placed olheiros at each of the entrances to their territory to watch for police operations and placed steel beams at each of the entrance points to slow any impromptu police operations and give gang members time to hide. Finally, during the period I lived in Maré, the Parque União gang held two weekly baile funks on Fridays and Sundays, for which they closed several of the primary streets in the heart of the neighborhood. Each baile drew thousands of youth from Maré and beyond. Based on my estimations of the crowd sizes, these two bailes combined attracted as many attendees as the single Nova Holanda baile.

THE EVOLUTION OF CVPU GOVERNANCE

Social Bandit (1991–99)

When we last left the Parque União gang in Chapter 4, Leandro, a teenager had inherited the gang from his uncle, Joãozinho, who had been killed by police in the late 1980s.[4] Leandro was, by all accounts, not prepared to be the gang leader. He disrespected residents, threatened them, offered little in the way of services, and was not viewed kindly by anyone I spoke with in Parque União.

---

[4] *O Globo* 4/10/1988.

It is perhaps unsurprising, then, that Leandro did not last long as Dono. The next gang leader, however, would forever change the nature of the local gang by integrating it within the expanding CV networks emanating from Rio de Janeiro's prisons.

José Evaristo Resende was born in 1957 and migrated to Rio with his family from Ceará, a state in the Northeast region of Brazil.[5] As a young man, José became a *pedreiro* (brickworker) and worked with Danilson, who was about the same age. According to Danilson, the two young men were close but "José was abused by some bandidos then turned into a bandido himself."[6] By the mid-1980s, José was in his late twenties and had become known as Zé Gordo (Fat Joe). He and Joãozinho robbed banks and armored cars together during Lulu's tenure as Dono in the 1980s but by the end of the decade, Joãozinho was dead, Leandro was the new Dono, and Zé Gordo was in prison.[7] Zé Gordo was first sent to Milton Dias Moreira Prison in Frei Caneca, on the outskirts of Rio, where he immediately became a member of the CV faction. According to multiple sources, he had no affiliation before he went to prison and perhaps was just randomly placed in a cell with other CV members.[8] Less than two years later, however, Zé Gordo was one of the leaders within the prison. In 1989, he escaped from Milton Dias Moreira by hiding under the hood of a Volkswagon Beetle and with the help of prison guards.[9] He remained a fugitive for two years, spending some of that time in Parque União but mostly moving around to other CV-controlled favelas to avoid being captured.[10] He counted on the help of numerous CV leaders, including Ernaldo Pinto de Medeiros, the infamous Uê who would later found the Amigos dos Amigos faction, and Wellington Martins da Silva (Zé Penetra) and his brother Gilberto Martins (Mineiro).[11] In January 1991, Zé Gordo was finally recaptured and immediately transferred by helicopter to Bangu I, Brazil's first maximum security prison, where most of the leaders of CV were being housed at the time.[12] He quickly became an integral part of the leadership of the CV faction.[13]

---

[5] An estimated 4,000 of Parque União's residents are migrants from Ceará (Redes da Maré 2019a, 39).
[6] Danilson 7/3/2018.
[7] *O Globo* 6/11/1986; 4/15/1993.
[8] Evaristo 12/23/2013; Vinícius 11/9/2014; Eusebio 11/1/2013.
[9] Vinícius 11/9/2014; *O Globo* 11/23/1989.
[10] *O Globo* 12/9/1989; 9/22/1990.
[11] *O Globo* 9/22/1990.
[12] Zé Gordo was imprisoned with some of the most powerful CV leaders of the day, including Willian da Silva Lima (The Professor), José Carlos dos Reis Encina (Escadinha), Denis Leandro da Silva (Denis of Rocinha), Celso Luiz Rodriguez (Celsinho of Vila Vintém), Darcy da Silva Filho (Cy of Acari), and Francisco Paula Testas Monteiro (Tuchinha) among others (*O Globo* 4/15/1993).
[13] In one particularly notable event in September 1992, Zé Gordo gained access to a cluster grenade (allegedly given to him by his lawyer) and used it to kidnap the director of the prison,

With these powerful connections and upon hearing about the problematic behavior of Leandro on the streets of his home neighborhood, Zé Gordo's decision to assume the leadership of the Parque União gang was likely not a particularly difficult one. He ordered the execution of Leandro, which a man nicknamed Macarrão (Noodles) allegedly carried out in 1991.[14] Upon Leandro's death, Zé Gordo officially became the Dono of Parque União, fully integrating the local gang within the CV faction.[15] The Parque União gang would undergo a radical transformation after integrating into the CV faction, eventually expanding from a couple dozen members to nearly a hundred and gaining access to more weapons and drugs through the faction's suppliers. The gang also became more elaborate and specialized. New gerente positions and a couple more bocas were added. Overall, the CVPU organizational structure closely mirrored that of CVNH (see Figure 5.3) and the dozens of other CV gangs across the city. Unlike CVNH, however, the prospect of war and inter-gang violence did not necessitate the use of younger gang members. The infantilization of CVPU would not happen until more than a decade later.

Despite spending much of the rest of his life in prison, Zé Gordo, through his close contacts within the powerful CV network, would be the undisputed leader of the Parque União gang until his death in 2004. Lawyers and family members allowed him to communicate frequently with the gerentes that he put in charge of the community in his absence.[16] These men would be responsible for the daily operations of the gang and deal with all governance activities though Zé Gordo would frequently be consulted about the most serious issues. Ze Gordo's first gerente geral was a man referred to as Paulo Brasil, who came from Baixa do Sapateiro, where he was involved in drug trafficking before being forced to out by Kito (see Chapter 4).[17] Paulo Brasil was, allegedly, not a very good manager – perhaps because he was not native to Parque União and did not have the connections and social networks of someone that grew up in the neighborhood. He eventually tried to take over CVPU for himself and was killed by his gangmates in the mid-1990s.[18] A man nicknamed Doda took over as Ze Gordo's gerente geral.

Overall, Zé Gordo's tenure as Dono would be characterized by a more mature – he was in his early thirties when he became gang leader – and reasoned

---

Major Francisco Spárgoli Rocha, in an attempt to trade for the release of a trafficker from Morro do Mineiro (Amorim 1993, 262–63).

[14] Vinícius 11/9/2014.
[15] Vinícius 11/9/2014.
[16] Communication with the outside was not difficult in the 1990s. Prison rules were still lenient. Zé Gordo even got married and had a small party inside Gallery A of Bangu I, where Cosminho do Leme, Ratinho, Pivete, Canan, Tuchinha da Mangueira, Isaías do Borel, Robocop, Preá, Pega-Eu, Zé Penetra and Mau-Mau and several family members were all in attendance (*O Globo* 5/7/1995).
[17] Bruno 10/27/2014.
[18] Vinícius 11/9/2014.

approach to governance. In fact, it was only under Zé Gordo's leadership that the gang can be considered to have consolidated the local monopoly of violence. As described in Chapter 4, many other independent bandits and criminals used Parque União as a home base throughout the 1980s. By the 1990s, however, all violent and illegal activities were being consolidated by CVPU as the gang absorbed many of these unaffiliated individuals or forced them to leave the neighborhood.[19] This local monopoly of violence extended not only to other criminals but throughout the community. Evaristo's grandfather (see Chapter 4), for instance, who had kept a shotgun in his bar for decades, was no longer allowed to have a firearm by the 1990s.[20] Moreover, the police, which had been able to frequent bars and restaurants in the community in the 1980s, were also no longer able to do so. After the gang became part of the faction, police only entered the neighborhood as part of militarized operations.

Although these changes did not happen all at once, the 1990s was the first time the local gang had consolidated their dominance over the community in such a comprehensive way. Unlike Nova Holanda, where intense conflict between Jorge Negão and the Irmãos Metralha incentivized the consolidation of gang territorial control and dominance almost a decade before, the Parque União gang only did so after being inserted within the CV faction. Also, unlike Nova Holanda, where the police post was eventually removed, the PPC located on the border of Parque União was never decommissioned. Instead, relations between the gang, police, and residents deteriorated more slowly. In the 1980s, some residents still went to the police to deal with their problems or report crimes occurring within the neighborhood. Until then, the gang was seldom involved in resolving disputes between residents but as it consolidated control and relations with the police became more antagonistic, the gang disallowed any collaboration with the police. Residents, in turn, sought out the gang to solve their interpersonal problems.[21] The gang needed to provide this service if they wanted to prevent police attention and maintain good relations with the community, which they did, because the police began making more concerted efforts to enforce against the gang.

Nearly all the residents I interviewed recalled that police operations became much more common in Parque União in the 1990s. Gustavo said that the police started "making a mess" of things and the community stopped working with them.[22] Evaristo remembered there being a lot of police

---

[19] By the 1990s, the gang was engaging in various forms of crime, including robbery, theft, and kidnapping outside of the neighborhood, and drug trafficking inside the neighborhood (*O Globo* 9/22/1990; 1/19/1991; 7/21/1991; 4/21/1992; 5/1/1992; 9/28/1992; 12/10/1992; 4/2/1993; 4/15/1993; 5/7/1995; 5/4/1996; 8/16/1997; 6/30/1999; 9/22/1999).

[20] Evaristo 12/23/2014.

[21] Gustavo 11/19/2014.

[22] Gustavo 11/19/2014.

operations when he was a kid.[23] Similarly, Antônio recalled, "After the faction arrived, my parents wouldn't let me play on the street at night anymore for fear of police operations."[24] Finally, Eusebio, a former gang member, recollected that the police began entering the favela in militarized operations looking to find and kill gang members around the time he joined in the early 1990s.[25]

Despite frequent and militarized police operations, CVPU maintained its noncoercive approach to governance. They allowed residents to move about freely without monitoring the local population and seldom if ever threatened residents even when faced with the possibility of arrest or death at the hands of the police. According to Evaristo:

The relationship with the traffickers was very good. They were always around and everyone knew them. I remember one time when a gerente was running from the police, he entered an abandoned area behind our house. My father shouted at him, 'Leave here now!' and the guy left immediately. At that time, it was common for gang members to be *cobrado* (disciplined) for endangering residents.[26]

Evaristo's memory of this era matches with how most residents spoke about the gang during the 1990s. Zé Gordo was viewed as an ideal Dono. He brought no conflicts with other gangs to his community and his gang did not needlessly confront the police. He did not allow graffiti and he implemented strict rules for the treatment of residents. "Zé Gordo disciplined his men and never let them stray," was how Vinícius put it.[27]

Moreover, CVPU provided significant benefits to the community during the 1990s. In addition to dispute resolution, they were also known to provide various forms of welfare and recreation. The gang held parties on numerous holidays (Mother's, Father's, and Children's Days, Easter, and Christmas, among others), provided monthly food baskets to the poorest residents, and paid for medicine, transportation, and cooking gas.[28] It was not just Zé Gordo that became famous for his social banditry. After the death of Paulo Brasil, the gang's new gerente geral, Doda, was seen by many residents as a Robin Hood figure. "He would give out money on the street and distribute small toys to children," Bernardo recalled.[29] When he was accidentally killed while cleaning his gun several years later, they laid his body out in the AM so that everyone could pay their respects. "I never saw gang members cry before. ...When they took him to the cemetery, there were hundreds of cars and trucks in the procession," Bernardo said.[30]

---

[23] Evaristo 12/23/2014.
[24] Antônio 12/17/2017.
[25] Eusebio 11/1/2013.
[26] Evaristo 12/23/2014.
[27] Vinícius 11/9/2014.
[28] Bernardo 1/16/2017; Eusebio 11/1/2013; Vinícius 11/9/2014.
[29] Bernardo 1/16/2017.
[30] Bernardo 1/16/2017.

In 1997, the local gang expanded their provision of benefits even further. Zé Gordo authorized the invasion and occupation of an adjacent territory that was owned by Tekno, an industrial firm. With Zé Gordo's blessing, the AM proceeded to distribute plots to residents. The gang also provided building materials to help some of the residents construct their first homes.[31] Danilson was the president of the AM at the time. When I interviewed him, he had recently been elected for his fourth, nonconsecutive term as AM president. He showed me a giant map of the neighborhood in his office, pointing to the areas they had taken over, while explaining how they did it.

Here we invaded their football field first. We fit 3000 people in that area. Then we took over the buildings here and here when the factory finally closed down. We fit another 3000 in there. We separated each of the areas into lots and gave them away to people who were renting then sold some of them to people that could afford it. Zé Gordo told me I could do it. I was arrested but they let me go because they couldn't prove I had stolen anything.[32]

Sem Terra, as the area came to be called, encompasses more than six acres, almost a third of Parque União's total territory. Thousands of families would eventually receive property that they otherwise never would have had access to. Angela was one such resident. We spoke on the third floor of the house she and her family had built there.

My family and I came from Bahia [a state in the Northeast of Brazil]. We rented a place on Roberto Silveira [one of PU's main streets] for fifteen years before we were given property in the Sem Terra. ...There were a bunch of us. Maybe twenty in our group, more or less. We invaded at night and camped out for three weeks. The AM finally registered us through some legal process... We divided it up with the other people we were with. My husband and I got space for two houses. We live in this one but rent out the other house now. ...If anyone comes and wants to take this house away from me, I'll tell them Zé Gordo gave it to me.[33]

Angela's experience was echoed across much of the Sem Terra community. Even many residents who did not receive property in Sem Terra often referenced the goodwill that Zé Gordo and the local gang received from providing housing to thousands. Eduarda, for instance, said that "Sem Terra is the primary reason why so many people still support the gang in Parque União."[34]

Despite increasing police operations over the course of the 1990s, intergang competition was completely absent in Parque União until the very end of the decade. That said, perhaps due to Zé Gordo's insertion into the leadership of the CV faction and his connections to various other Donos throughout the city, he supported violent takeover attempts of other areas of Maré, including

---

[31] *O Globo* 8/16/1997.
[32] Danilson 7/3/2017.
[33] Angela 8/3/2015.
[34] Eduarda 2/21/2014.

Morro do Timbau and Vila do João. At first, the gang in Nova Holanda, led by Gigante, did not support these efforts as they attempted to remain neutral and still maintained more amicable relations with Kito, who controlled Morro do Timbau and Baixa do Sapateiro.[35] Zé Gordo had no such friendly relations with Kito and was not on particularly good terms with Jorge Negão or Gigante as he had once been close to the Irmãos Metralha, which had eventually lost the war for Nova Holanda.[36] Moreover, Zé Gordo was part of the old guard of CV as he had been imprisoned with many of the founders of the faction. Meanwhile, CVNH had been integrated into the CVJ wing of the faction. Although there was never any violence between them, CVNH–CVPU relations were not as harmonious as the CV moniker would tend to signify. In this regard, it was perhaps lucky that the two communities were not as integrated as many other areas of Maré because the canal prevented easy movement across the border.[37]

Nonetheless, the two CV gangs would eventually work together against their TC rival in Maré, foreshadowing how the larger CV faction would come together when TC and ADA formed an alliance against them. Zé Gordo first began supporting a man named Omar, also connected to CV at this time, and his efforts to consolidate territorial control of Vila do João and the rest of the newly built housing projects in the southernmost area of Maré (see Chapter 7).[38] Zé Gordo offered weapons and men to help conquer these neighborhoods.[39] It was only when the Nova Holanda gang finally became part of the CV faction in the mid-1990s that the two gangs began working together against Kito, who had allied with CV's main rival, TC. By the late 1990s, increasing violence characterized the relationship between the two CV gangs and TC though most of this violence was confined to the housing projects (see Chapter 7). The ascendance of TC at the end of the decade and their yearslong campaign to conquer Nova Holanda would change the nature of governance not only for CVNH but CVPU as well.

Benevolent Dictator (1999–2003)

As noted in Chapter 5, by 1999, TC had consolidated its control of the housing projects in the south of Maré and began to make incursions into CVNH territory. The levels of violence and dislocation caused by the activation of the conflict far outweighed anything that Maré had yet experienced. Although the brunt of the violence occurred in Nova Holanda, CVPU nonetheless felt its impact. On several occasions, TC allegedly made it all the way to the Parque

[35] *O Globo* 12/15/1995.
[36] Josie 7/10/2018.
[37] Evaristo 12/23/2014.
[38] Josie 7/10/2018.
[39] *O Globo* 9/28/1992.

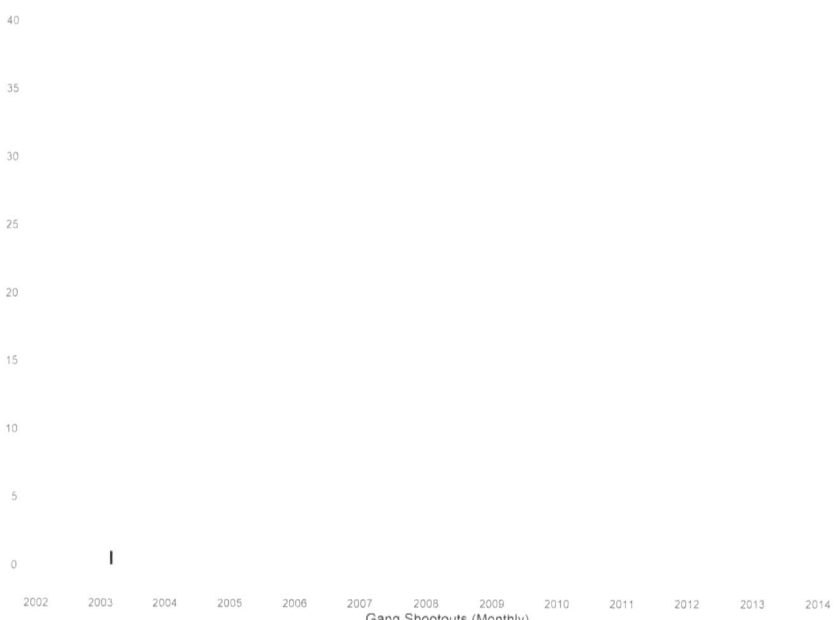

FIGURE 6.2 Gang shootouts in CVPU territory (monthly)
Data from *Disque-Denúncia*. Visualization by Pranjal Drall.

União border and engaged in shootouts with CVPU from across the canal.
Eusebio, a gang member from that era, recalled that TC had tried to invade on
three occasions during that period though the DD database only contains one
reported shootout in March 2003 (see Figure 6.2).[40] The summary of the call
includes the following description: "There was an intense shootout last night
that left residents desperate and unable to sleep. In the morning, many heavily
armed gang members and lookouts are still on the streets and spread throughout the community. Many of them are not from the area."[41]

These foreign gang members were likely from Nova Holanda as the gang
had been forced to retreat into their ally's territory. According to interviews
with gang members, this was the most unstable period in Parque União's history and the likelihood of TC defeating CVNH was a very real possibility.[42] If
that happened, the security environment in Parque União would have immediately become untenable as all-out warfare with TC would have been unavoid-
able. Aside from these brief invasion attempts, CVPU mostly experienced this
period as a latent threat from their rival.

[40] Eusebio 11/1/2013.
[41] DD 3/29/2003.
[42] Eusebio 11/1/2013; Inácio 3/26/2014; Bruno 10/6/2014.

To prevent a TC takeover of Nova Holanda, Zé Gordo, who had escaped from prison again in September 1999, frequently provided reinforcements (both weapons and soldados) to CVNH to help defend their territory.[43] And yet, despite the significant assistance CVPU provided to CVNH, the relations between the two CV gangs remained strained. First, the two CV gangs struggled to coordinate their efforts, perhaps due to the weak leadership of CVNH during this period.[44] Eventually, the leaders of the two CV gangs were called to a meeting with the CV faction's leadership in Complexo do Alemão in an effort to resolve their differences because the deteriorating relationship was threatening their ability to defend the area.[45] The problems were allegedly resolved but the relationship between the two gangs would continue to be described by residents and gang members of each territory as one of *convivência* (coexistence) more than *amizade* (friendship).

Overall, the increase in rival threat from absent to latent with several brief moments of active competition produced a more coercive CVPU than had previously existed. Many residents recounted the more violent behavior of the gang within the community. For example, Evaristo said that when someone broke the rules during this period, "They were lucky if they just shot them in the hand or expelled them from the neighborhood. Many were executed."[46] He recalled one such incident in which "a guy messed up. They dragged him through the streets, allowing the children to join in beating him. It was like he was a Judas. He was bleeding a lot," he recalled.[47] Similarly, Beto remembered watching gang members beat an adolescent to death for stealing a bicycle around this time. "They would have accused me of being a vacilão and punished me too if I had helped him. I was crying I was so scared," he said, still visibly upset from the memory of it. Bernardo, who was a young boy at the time, agreed that the gang became more violent during this period. "They broke bones and killed a lot of people within the favela. They used to take them to the edge of the community to execute them."[48] Sergio recalled,

When I was 14–15 years old [2000–2001], the gang used the area near our house for executions. I became very anxious and had a breakdown once. I was crying and shaking because I heard a guy dying outside of our house. He was moaning and crying through the entire night. These types of executions went on for about two years.[49]

Vinícius, close friends with several gang members during this period, summed up the approach of the gang at this time as one that focused on implementing a

---

[43] Gilson 11/19/2014.
[44] Evaristo 12/23/2014.
[45] Bruno 10/6/2014.
[46] Evaristo 12/23/2014.
[47] Evaristo 12/23/2014.
[48] Bernardo 1/16/2017.
[49] Sergio 12/17/2014.

strict form of order and putting a premium on obedience.[50] This period was also characterized by a greater willingness of the gang to transgress the rules pertaining to the treatment of residents, more generally. Evaristo, for instance, remembered that gang members wanted to enter their family house to access their roof sometime in the year 2000. When his father locked the door to the staircase to make sure they could not, the gang members just broke the door down. "Before, the Dono would have punished them for doing something like that," he said.[51]

These years also corresponded to more violent dynamics within the gang itself. In the early 2000s, there was an apparent coup attempt by Doda's successor, a man nicknamed Bahia. A rumor began circulating within the community that Bahia was speaking with "the other side" (TC) and was interested in taking over the gang for himself.[52] Zé Gordo's two grown sons, Gordo Jr. and Adriano, took it upon themselves to remove the would-be traitor. Bahia was quickly killed, and Gordo Jr. took over as gerente geral.[53] It is unknown whether these rumors were true but the paranoia and fear created by the generalized warfare occurring across much of Maré likely played a contributing factor.

The more coercive approach to governance, however, was not without consequence for gang–community relations. For example, Sergio described how one of their neighbors in Sem Terra, a very popular man that used to organize barbecues for the whole street, began an affair with a woman who was also dating Doda at the time.

When Doda found out, he beat him with his pistol in the middle of the street then shot and killed him. The man's wife screamed that she was going to call the cops so he killed her too. The street did not accept this but there was little we could do. If they could kill an extremely well-liked and popular guy, what would stop them from killing one of us? Doda threw a party and invited the whole street to try to smooth things over but no one went. After that, the relationship between our street and the gang became *mais seca* (distant). People stopped going to the gang for things and the gang stopped using that area to execute people. They found other areas to kill people.[54]

Although this tragic story could have perhaps occurred at any point in the gang's history – girlfriends are often viewed as the exclusive property of the gang member – it coincided with CVPU's more coercive period. The tendency of the gang to use violence was already heightened and questioning the obedience and respect for the acting gerente geral of the gang by dating *his* woman was not going to be taken lightly. Interestingly, Doda's response – throwing a party to smooth over relations with the rest of the street – suggests he understood how important the support of the community was to the gang, especially

[50] Vinícius 11/9/2014.
[51] Evaristo 12/23/2014.
[52] Evaristo 12/23/2014; Bernardo 1/16/2017; Danilson 7/3/2018.
[53] Bernardo 1/16/2017; Danilson 7/3/2018.
[54] Sergio 12/17/2014.

in an area they used for executions and the disposal of bodies. The fact that the gang ended this practice in this area suggests they were afraid that the community would no longer keep quiet about such activities. While residents may lack effective avenues to shape gang behavior, Sergio's story suggests the community does not always accept the benefits a gang provides and their refusal to support the gang can shape gang behavior, more generally.

Although CVPU became more coercive during this period, they continued to provide more responsive benefits. The parties and welfare never stopped.[55] Even Sergio, who bore witness to some of the most coercive acts of the gang, believed, "The gang continued to respect the community. They still had a lot of contact with the residents. Most of the houses were only two floors and you would run into them often. They were *enraizado* (rooted) in the community."[56] Similarly, Bernardo said the gang continued to try to find just ways of resolving conflicts between residents despite their more coercive behavior. He recounted how he and his mother had moved around a lot, no less than four times, when they first moved to Parque União in the 1990s. His mother could not find full-time employment and they struggled to afford rent. Finally, they ended up living on the first floor of a big house where his mother took care of the landlord, who had a long-term illness, in exchange for rent. The landlord promised that after he died, they could stay there as long as they wanted. After he passed, however, his daughter wanted to evict Bernardo and his mother so that she could rent the space to someone else. She was friends with some of the gang members and tried to use these contacts to force them out of the house.[57] Bernardo recalled several gang members coming to their house when he was about twelve years old (c. 2002) and, initially, telling them they had to leave but once they explained their side of the story, the gang members said that they had every right to live in the house. They told the owner's daughter that she could not evict them. She tried several other times to convince gang members to help her get rid of them, but each time the gang sided with Bernardo and his mother.[58] By all accounts, despite their more violent tendencies during these years, CVPU never strayed from a responsive relationship with the community.

Social Bandit (2003–14)

In late 2002, TC would split in two, the result of an internal disagreement between their leadership, setting off a civil war. The war with CVNH also continued for another couple of years even as the newly coined TCP (Puro

---

[55] Bernardo 1/16/2017; Beto 1/13/2017.
[56] Sergio 12/17/214.
[57] Such strategies are not uncommon in gang-controlled areas where connections with gang members can facilitate all sorts of advantages for residents and businesses (see Arias and Rodrigues 2006).
[58] Bernardo 1/16/2017.

was added to their name) faced an ADA rival to their south. TCP, however, was no longer able to make incursions deep into CVNH territory. As a result, the security environment in Parque União improved soon thereafter. By 2004, TC was so weakened that they were barely able to maintain control of their own territory. Moreover, at the end of June 2003, the 22nd Battalion was inaugurated in Nova Holanda, just a short distance from Parque União. The proximity of the Battalion reduced the prospect of rival gang invasions even further and, perhaps counterintuitively, served to stabilize and consolidate gang control and authority in Parque União and the rest of Maré. Residents remained unable to go to the police for any reason, and police only entered gang territories to engage in militarized operations. Otherwise, any violence, internal disputes between residents, or other matters of governance that police handled in the formal parts of the city were completely left to the gangs. For the next decade, rival threat was almost entirely absent for CVPU. We can observe this lack of intergang violence in the DD data as well. Figure 6.2 shows that aside from one reported shootout in the early 2000s, CVPU territory has experienced none of the intergang violence observed in Nova Holanda. This has translated into a very different type of coercive presence within the community.

First, the violent punishments and executions which had characterized the previous period came to an end. Evaristo, for one, could not remember any executions for many years and Sergio said that the gang no longer killed people in the same way.[59] "There's a lot less violence than there used to be, when they felt like they had to make examples out of people," Bernardo said. Other residents agreed, reporting that although the death penalty still existed in Parque União, it was only used in extreme cases.[60] For instance, Beto recounted the story of a local DJ who played a show in an adjacent area controlled by a milícia. "They ended up killing the kid right on the street. His mother went to the media and the whole family had to leave the community."[61] A newspaper article described how officials had to fish the mutilated body of the young DJ out of Guanabara Bay.[62] Apparently, the gang had cut his head, arms, and legs off. All they found of his body was his torso. This was not a subtle message. Even though CVPU has rarely resorted to such performative coercive acts over the years, the DJ had performed in a milícia-controlled area just across Avenida Brasil from Parque União. Given the fact that a milícia had already infiltrated another area of Maré (Roquette Pinto and Praia de Ramos), such a punishment was likely driven, in part, by the fear that the milícia would eventually attempt to wrest territorial control from the local gang even though no outright violence had occurred between the two organizations. It was only because the

[59] Evaristo 12/23/2014.
[60] Lino 11/3/2014; Josie 7/10/2018.
[61] Beto 1/13/2017.
[62] *O Globo* 3/12/2013.

DJ's performance was advertised on posters that the gang even found out. Allegedly, the gang even warned the DJ not to perform there and his refusal to comply with the order was the immediate cause of his death.[63] Overall, however, such executions were said to be incredibly rare since the early 2000s.

The gang has continued to deal with a variety of other infractions with some violent punishments. Danilson described how the gang still dealt with thieves. "If you steal in Parque União, they shoot your hands," he said, putting his hands together like he was praying then laying them flat on the table. "They shoot both hands together like this. That way, every time they look at their hands, they'll remember."[64] Others said that the gang still used violence to punish rapists or molesters and they've been known to expel individuals for not complying with gang rules.[65] Residents in Parque União, like in Nova Holanda, seemed to even support the use of violence in the community so long as it was intended to keep order and prevent bad behaviors. "They're smart," Danilson said, "They don't want any problems within the community."[66]

In 2004, Zé Gordo, collapsed and died of a heart attack while on the street in Parque União.[67] His son, Gordo Jr., immediately became the new Dono. Such transitions of leadership to younger generations – Gordo Jr. was around twenty years old at the time – can produce instability within gangs, as exemplified by the CVNH case (see Chapter 5). Unlike in Nova Holanda, where Gigante's nephews became Donos during a particularly volatile period, eventually leading to several coup attempts and the breakdown of the CVNH structure, the turnover in CVPU leadership occurred within a much more stable environment. There was no ongoing intergang violence at the time and rival threat was almost completely absent in Parque União. Thus, despite Gordo Jr. not being prepared for or, by all accounts, particularly interested in being the gang leader, his leadership did not produce the centrifugal effects experienced by CVNH.[68]

After just a couple of years as Dono, Gordo Jr. was arrested in 2007.[69] While in prison, he decided the gang life was not for him and entered the church. The leadership of the gang passed to his stepbrother, Adriano, who turned out to be an extremely capable and rigorous Dono. Adriano quickly consolidated his control over the organization and centralized its coercive practices.[70] "When he took over, he started to control violence to a much higher degree," Bernardo said. "He didn't allow people to kill or abuse anyone without his permission. They had to speak with him before."[71] Vinícius agreed, "He likes things done

[63] *O Globo* 9/27/2012.
[64] Danilson 7/3/2018.
[65] Gustavo 11/19/2014.
[66] Danilson 7/3/2018.
[67] Eusebio 11/1/2013.
[68] Evaristo 12/23/2014; Vinícius 11/9/2014.
[69] Dias 8/14/2021.
[70] Artur 1/11/2017.
[71] Bernardo 1/16/2017.

the right way. He doesn't like a mess."[72] Adriano's leadership amidst the lack of any intergang violence has translated into a very different type of coercive profile for the CVPU.

In numerous interviews with residents of Parque União, they often referred to the fact that the gang seldom threatened or made residents uncomfortable, that problems between the local gang and residents were rare, and that the gang mostly kept to themselves and merely engaged in the drug trade.[73] "The gang never abuses anyone who doesn't deserve it. They don't break down anyone's doors. If a trafficker leaves a gun where you don't want it, you can go ask them to remove it. They're just doing their job," Angela said.[74] "The gang doesn't make a mess in the community," José agreed.[75]

Many residents described CVPU behavior in relation to the gang in Nova Holanda. "They're more evolved. They don't have the same type of barbarity. They're *mais arrumadinho* (neater and tidier)," Gilson thought.[76] "They're more serious and not as ostentatious. There are a lot more confusions and aggressions that occur in Nova Holanda," Bernardo concluded.[77] Dagoberto put it a different way, "The difference is that in Nova Holanda, if you pass in front of a gang member instead of behind, you might be disciplined. The guys in Parque União generally don't have a problem with that."[78] He was referring to the fact that many CVNH members feel the need to demonstrate their dominance by demanding obedience and respect from residents whereas CVPU members do not.

Bernardo related a story that brought home the difference between the two gangs. He said his mother, who suffers from bipolar disorder, regularly visited the health post in Parque Rubens Vaz within CVNH territory because Parque União does not have one. One afternoon, his mother began screaming at the employees of the health post because they refused to attend to her.[79] CVNH members were called and, once they learned she was from Parque União, delivered her to their CVPU colleagues. A CVPU gerente came, listened to the story, then took Bernardo aside. "Make sure she doesn't do this kind of thing in Nova Holanda again because, next time, they will probably tie her up and leave her in the sun. That's how they solve problems there but we still control these inclinations," he said.[80]

[72] Vinícius 11/9/2014.
[73] Beto 1/13/2017; Bernardo 1/16/2017; Vinícius 11/9/2014; Artur 1/11/2017; Gustavo 11/19/2014.
[74] Angela 8/3/2015.
[75] José 1/10/2017.
[76] Gilson 11/19/2014.
[77] Bernardo 1/16/2017.
[78] Dagobert 1/18/2017.
[79] It is very common for health posts within favelas to be understaffed and overwhelmed by demand.
[80] Bernardo 1/16/2017.

In addition to the difference in how these two organizations punish such behaviors in their territory, this story suggests an interesting relationship between where residents are from and the authority to punish them. Although the dispute occurred within CVNH territory, because Bernardo's mother was from Parque União, punishing her could have caused problems between the two gangs, especially if she had connections to the local gang, so the CVNH gang members delivered her to CVPU. Because these two gangs are allies, there is a mutual respect for the rights of residents in these contexts. If this same dispute had happened across enemy lines, an entirely different set of considerations would come into play.

Even residents of Nova Holanda also recognized the difference between the two gangs. "They have a more serious and rational approach over there," Lino said. After being threatened by a CVNH gang member, Artur commented, "They would never allow that kind of behavior in Parque União."[81] CVNH's own gang members even described their counterparts as "more organized," "more professional," and as maintaining a "menos pesado" presence. And yet they made a point of criticizing CVPU members for thinking too highly of themselves. "They think they're rich playboys," Márcio said, referring to the fact that CVPU members often wore sneakers and t-shirts while CVNH members could often be found in sandals and shirtless.[82] When I asked him why the CVPU was so different from CVNH, Severino simply said, "They don't have a history of warfare over there."[83]

The differences between the two CV gangs in Maré were manifest. In addition to less violent punishments, CVPU monitored their turf less intensively than CVNH and maintained less than half the number of bocas and security positions than their CVNH counterparts (see Figure 6.1). In addition, CVPU members were more restrained in their display of force. I spent significant time on the streets of Parque União over the course of fieldwork and was able to monitor the types of guns and numbers of gang members at various locations within the community. Many CVPU gang members still carried weapons, even some large-caliber automatic rifles, but they never carried more than one (a common occurrence in Nova Holanda) and were less often seen riding their motorcycles up and down the streets of the community as a constant reminder of their dominance. It was also rare to view large numbers of heavily armed gang members surrounding bocas in Parque União. The difference between these two governing styles is easily felt on the streets of these communities.

Finally, the monitoring and surveillance of residents by CVPU was far less intensive than CVNH. The Parque União gang generally paid little attention to residents coming and going. Only one person I interviewed could

---

[81] Artur 1/11/2017.
[82] Bruno 10/6/2014; Inácio 3/26/2014; Márcio 4/17/2014; Everton 4/17/2014.
[83] Severino 10/2/2013.

recall being stopped and questioned upon entering the community. Even then, Bernardo said that this had surprised him and that it was nothing like what goes on in Nova Holanda or other places in the city where two gangs border each other.[84] By all accounts, CVPU has never placed any restrictions on movement into or out of the community. They seldom even monitor some of the entry points. Instead, the gang is mostly concerned with police operations and have placed steel beams in cement holes on the streets along Avenida Brasil or Avenida Trompowski to prevent caveirões from quickly entering the community. If other gangs or rivals used these access points to invade, the gang's attitude would surely not be so relaxed.

The lack of gang presence along these major thoroughfares has also provided space for significant commerce to develop as motorists, not all of whom are residents of Parque União, stop, park, and eat at one of the many restaurants. This is virtually unheard of in favelas dominated by a gang as powerful as this one. Sitting at these restaurants or in the open-air bars that surround Parque União Square, I never observed a gang presence. There are no automatic weapons nor bocas anywhere in sight. In fact, gang members will not be seen for a hundred yards or so beyond the square. The area feels much less like a favela and more like a middle-class neighborhood. When I asked José, a local business owner, about the relationship with the gang here, he motioned with his arm. "Look around. They don't bother anyone here."[85]

As described in Chapter 5, the incorporation of foreign gang members can also influence a gang's coercive profile. CVPU had far fewer foreign members during the time I lived in Maré. This dynamic was made especially visible in the lead-up to the World Cup and Olympic Games as UPPs quickly expanded to the largest favelas in the Zona Norte of the city. CV gang leaders and personnel were displaced from these territories, some of them finding a safe haven in Nova Holanda. The Dono of CVPU, however, refused to allow foreign CV gangs to enter his territory.[86] I asked Everton how Adriano was allowed to do this. "He can do what he wants because he's the Dono. …If I were Dono, I wouldn't accept other bosses in my territory either because they would make a mess and cause problems," he said.[87]

Adriano's refusal to allow other Dono's into his territory also mirrors his response to the ill-fated peace agreement between TCP and CVNH. According to Bernardo,

TCP walked into Parque União with a big group of guys. The TCP gang leader went to shake Adriano's hand but he just crossed his arms and said, 'I don't know who told you

---

[84] Bernardo 1/16/2017.
[85] José 1/10/2017.
[86] Andrea 3/20/2014; Inácio 3/26/2014; Everton 4/17/2014.
[87] Everton 4/17/2014.

could come here. You made an agreement with Nova Holanda, fine, but take your guys and get out of here now.' After this, Adriano placed bombs on the bridge to blow it up if he needed to. ...After three days of parties on the border, TCP invaded Nova Holanda and Ninho had to ask Adriano for reinforcements. This time, Adriano would only give them guns but refused to send any of his men.[88]

Adriano's vision clearly diverges from his CVNH counterparts. Although some of this difference may be idiosyncratic, the local security environment has undoubtedly shaped the decision-making processes of these gang leaders and the organizations around them. In particular, the lack of long-term inter-gang violence and threat in Parque União has allowed CVPU to avoid the numerous considerations and problems that warfare brings with it. This has translated into a gang that is, overall, more relaxed, secure, and measured in their approach. CVPU has had the luxury of longer time horizons. Intergang violence and threat is not the only security consideration, however.

While the installation of the 22nd Battalion in 2003 allowed the military police to quickly enter Maré and engage in operations, it appears, at least initially, to not have coincided with a huge increase in the number of militarized police operations in Parque União. Much of the Battalion's attention was initially turned toward the most violent areas in the south of Maré where the old TC faction had fragmented into two rival and warring gangs. With the creation and expansion of the Pacification program and the public security apparatus' increasing focus on the CV faction, CVPU began to face much higher levels of police enforcement in the late 2000s. In 2009, shortly after the inauguration of the first of the city's UPPs, BOPE began carrying out more aggressive military-style operations in both Nova Holanda and Parque União. Then, in 2011, BOPE established its new headquarters on the defunct military base on the edge of Maré, just north of Parque União, to prepare the area for its eventual "pacification."[89] For the next several years until the military occupation in April 2014, BOPE patrols and operations became a consistent and regular part of life in Parque União (see Figure 6.3).

BOPE operations in Parque União, like other areas of Maré, always involved militarized vehicles and helicopters. BOPE would often enter quickly to try to catch the gang off guard and provoke confrontations. According to Dagobert, "Some of the BOPE invasions happened really fast. They were instantaneous! They would sometimes even do an operation right at the end of a baile when everyone was trying to go home."[90] While there was at least one occasion in

---

[88] Bernardo 1/16/2017.
[89] I include quotes around this term because it connotes the problematic nature of the terminology which developed around the UPPs – that gangs and favela communities, more generally, were viewed as inherently violent entities and spaces in need of order. This language and securitization process resembles closely other "pacification" efforts during the Vietnam War, European colonial projects, and indigenous policies virtually everywhere (Neocleous 2011).
[90] Dagobert 1/18/2017.

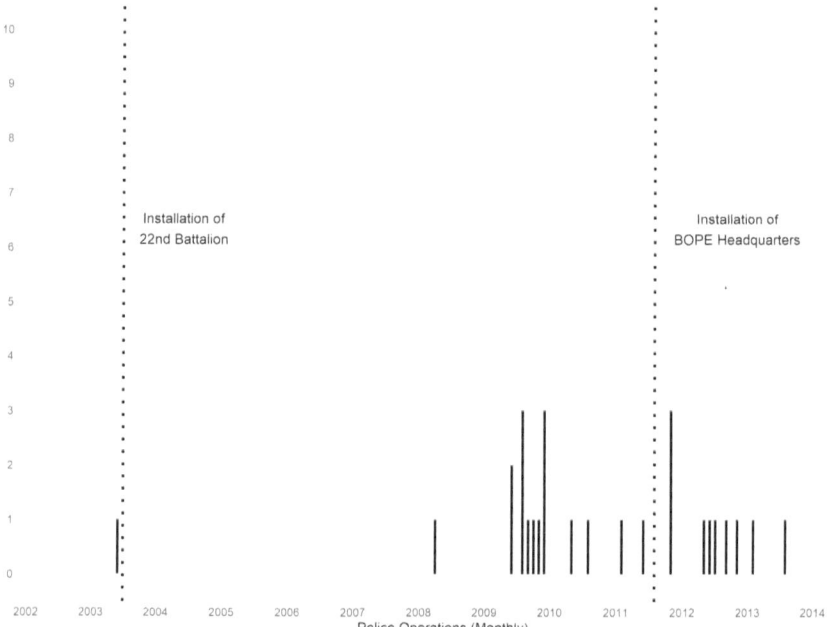

FIGURE 6.3 Police operations in CVPU territory (monthly)
Data from *Disque-Denúncia*. Visualization by Pranjal Drall.

which a police operation led to an intense shootout with CVPU gang members, the majority occurred without confrontation and were short-lived.[91] Once they became aware of the incoming operation (generally through the use of firecrackers), gang members would quickly find places to hide. BOPE then moved through the neighborhood in their vehicles, stopping only to search the homes and businesses where they thought gang members might be hiding. According to Evaristo, "They commonly searched the shops on the street where my mother works. She eventually learned to just close her shop and go home whenever there was an operation."[92]

Bernardo told me that BOPE police had invaded his house when they had smelled marijuana from a joint his mother was smoking.

There was a bunch of them. They were dressed in all black with masks on. They were hopped up on coke or something. They all had huge guns. I tried to be as calm as possible, as rational as possible. I told them they didn't have the right to enter the house. Then they yelled at me and threatened us. I put my mother in the bathroom and started to film them. They suddenly got really scared. The colonel came in and told me he was going to arrest us. I said that my mother is bipolar and that the marijuana helps her. It

[91] *O Globo* 12/20/2008.
[92] Evaristo 12/23/2014.

wasn't true but I wanted to try to explain it. So one of them says, 'Oh, so she's crazy then?' 'No,' I said, 'she's bipolar.' I asked them what their mission was because surely it wasn't to invade a house and arrest a woman. Finally, they said that if I agreed to erase the video that they would leave. I was fine with that because I didn't want them to know that I had a video of them on my phone anyway.[93]

This type of aggressive and indiscriminate behavior by Rio's police does little to encourage residents to help them in their efforts to enforce against the gangs. If anything, it pushes some residents to further support, or at least not denounce, the gangs. That said, many residents do not have this vision and may even blame the gang for the frequent police operations and disruptions to their life. "People don't really reflect on the whole situation," Dagobert began, "They don't understand how the War on Drugs has led to this situation. Operations don't do anything. BOPE is basically walking around hunting children. Those that understand how the system really works are angry but it's not very many," he concluded.[94]

Overall, police enforcement of this intensity and frequency has created a set of incentives and constraints on the governing strategies that CVPU implements. While the gang does not face the possibility of losing its territory, at least in the short term, BOPE and other police units are actively seeking to arrest and even kill gang members. In interviews with current and former gang members, denunciation to the police was a commonly held concern.[95] Extremely high levels of police enforcement between 2009 and 2014 produced an environment in which gang members had to continue to be aware of how residents thought and felt about the gang and their presence within the community. In this context, the gang continued to be more responsive to resident demands by offering certain benefits to the local population.

First, CVPU has been responsive to resident demands for dispute resolution. The gang continued to resolve serious disagreements or fights between family members, neighbors, when someone was unwilling to pay rent, or forms of property damage. Most of the residents I interviewed commented on how frequently residents use these services. "Everyone seeks out the traffickers to resolve problems. Even *I* went the Dono to help me with something," Vinícius admitted, "They're like an NGO. People can use their services freely," he said.[96] According to Gustavo, "Anytime someone gets into a fight or has some other problem, they'll go to the gang. I have more trust in the *meninos* (boys) to resolve a dispute than I ever did in the police."[97] Similarly, Beto reported that he had always had positive interactions with the gang when he asked

---

[93] Bernardo 1/16/2017.
[94] Dagobert 1/18/2017.
[95] Eusebio 11/1/2013; Lidiane 12/15/2014; Dagobert 1/18/2017.
[96] Vinícius 11/9/2014.
[97] Gustavo 11/19/2014.

for their assistance even if he didn't agree with all of their "other" behavior.[98] "They helped resolve a really big fight between my dad and my uncle," Evaristo said, "If they didn't do it, then no one would have because you can't go to the police." Sergio's mother, Angela, said she had gone to the gang when the bar next door put a huge speaker below her window for a birthday party. "They never put it there again," she said with a smile.[99]

Although CVPU has been responsive to community demands along this dimension, they have not inserted themselves into the personal lives of residents to the same degree as CVNH. Instead, they have placed some restrictions on the type and quantity of problems they are willing to deal with. For instance, Bernardo's mother, Theresa, who had used the gang to resolve numerous disputes with her neighbors was eventually cut off.[100] Similarly, Evaristo recalled a neighbor who used to go to the gang with every little problem. "They told him to stop," he recalled.[101] Why CVPU has limited their dispute resolution services is difficult to parse. One plausible explanation is that because CVNH faces much higher levels of insecurity, through a mix of rival threat and police enforcement, it has been incentivized to develop as intimate a relationship with residents as possible, inserting itself into various aspects of their personal lives. These tighter, more intimate relationships can facilitate access to social and familial networks and help the gang feel more secure and embedded within the territory. CVPU, on the other hand, has perhaps put some limitations on their governance services because they do not feel as vulnerable and insecure. This reflects yet another way in which the types of threat can combine or complement one another.

CVPU has also delegated some of these demands for dispute resolution to the AM, a departure from their CVNH allies, which have mostly sidelined the AM in favor of more direct forms of governance. Eusebio, a former gang member, was the president of the Parque União AM when I interviewed him in 2013. He said that the gang often sends him people with problems, "because they know me." He explained that the relationship between the AM and the gang had been weak until the 1990s when the AM realized they could have a lot more influence if they worked with the gang. "They have more power behind their words if they are supported by the gang. But it comes at a cost," he said. When I asked to describe his relationship with the gang, Eusebio thought for a moment, then said: "I'm more of an intermediary than anything else. I deal with any problems that pertain to property, like water damage, trash collection, and construction, but I don't have any power to take sides and rule in favor of one person or another. I send them to someone else if I can't resolve the problem."[102]

---

[98] Beto 1/13/2017.
[99] Angela 8/3/2015.
[100] Bernardo 1/16/2017.
[101] Evaristo 12/23/2014.
[102] Eusebio 11/1/2013.

The close relationship between CVPU and the AM was corroborated by a variety of residents. "The gang supported the new president very heavily in the most recent election," Beto said.[103] "They're all *mandados* (controlled)," Vinícius opined.[104] "The gang is definitely behind the AM here," Angela thought.[105] "The connection with the AM is strong in Parque União," Artur said.[106]

Also, unlike Nova Holanda, Parque União had no notable NGOs.[107] That said, it had a large Catholic Church parish and at least fifteen Evangelical churches, some of which allegedly maintained close connections to the gang. I spoke with several of the Evangelical pastors in the community. Pastor Patrício said that his church had little to do with the gang though they remained open to gang members using the church to leave the life.[108] In my interview with Pastor Ronaldo, he said he still knew a bunch of the guys involved from his life before becoming a Pastor – he was never directly involved with the gang but had thought about joining in his youth – and had even hired a former gang member in his church. He repeatedly reminded me that his connections with the gang were not like what some of the other pastors in Parque União were doing.

I don't bless the wickedness like some. Bad behaviors exist everywhere, even in churches. The pastors that have strong connections with the gang are imbeciles. They are looking to get access to power and money but when they start doing favors for them, they lose their moral compass. …The gang even asked me to give one of their members last rights when he was dying. I went and gave the sign of the cross and said, "In the name of God" but I wasn't going to intervene more than that.[109]

Like for the AM, it seems that the gang had not forced these relations on the churches but, instead, it was the strategic efforts of some pastors that had produced this type of collaboration. This dynamic resembles little how these types of relations have been described and theorized by previous scholarship.[110]

Another example of the responsiveness of CVPU concerns the sale of crack, which began in 2009, several years after CVNH started to sell.[111] By 2011, an entire community of users were living along Avenida Brasil, just outside of Parque União (see Figure 6.1). This eventually led to problems with petty theft and drug use in the community.[112] The user community even became

---

[103] Beto 1/13/2017.
[104] Vinícius 11/9/2014.
[105] Angela 8/3/2015.
[106] Artur 3/18/2014.
[107] Eusebio 11/1/2013.
[108] Patrício 6/27/2014.
[109] Ronaldo 7/31/2018.
[110] See Arias (2006a), McCann (2014), and Gay (1999).
[111] In the DD dataset, the first mention of crack being sold or consumed in Parque União is from May 2009.
[112] Evaristo 12/23/2014; Gustavo 11/19/2014. The DD dataset also contains dozens of complaints about this community of users.

so conspicuous that the local media began to pay attention.[113] Eventually, the situation became untenable and, despite being extremely lucrative, Adriano decided to stop selling crack. The gang put up a large banner at one of the entrances to the favela that read: *"Não vende mais crack aqui"* (Crack is no longer sold here).[114] The user community quickly moved to an area just outside of Nova Holanda, where CVNH continued to sell crack despite the problems it caused for them (see Chapter 5). A couple of years later, CVPU began to sell crack again though they have limited the ability of users to enter and move around the community.[115]

CVPU has also continued to provide welfare and stimulate the local economy. According to Eusebio, this social aspect of the gang is one of the primary reasons why they maintain some level of "respect" within the community.[116] These sorts of services, however, have become less widespread than they once were likely because Parque União, perhaps more than any other community in Maré, has developed considerably over the last twenty years. Many of the nicest shops, restaurants, and bars in Maré are located in Parque União. Residents commonly refer to it as the "Zona Sul" of Maré, referring to the region of the city with the famous beaches and wealthiest neighborhoods. With such economic development, many residents of Parque União no longer need the gang handouts.[117] As Sergio put it, "residents need the gang less today. They are more easily able to make money, raise a family, and solve their problems through legitimate means, which has decreased their proximity to the gang."[118] Eusebio said that the purchasing power of the residents had increased incredibly since he was involved with the gang. He referred to the "chic" restaurants in Parque União where a lot of people from the community take their families for meals. "But there are still people who need the gang," he said, "so they get close to them and ask them for handouts. Others that don't need them so much will keep their distance."[119] Fausto, similarly, suggested that the key difference between the Nova Holanda and Parque União gangs was due to how the community needed them. "The relationship in Nova Holanda is closer, more intimate, because it's poorer. They need the gang more. …It's also blacker."[120]

The difference between Nova Holanda and Parque União when it comes to race is stark. According to a recent census conducted by a local NGO, only 5% of Parque União identifies as black while nearly 20% of Nova Holanda does so (Redes da Maré 2019a). Nova Holanda's residents arrived to Maré after being

---

[113] *O Globo* 11/12/2012; 10/18/2012.
[114] Inácio 3/26/2014.
[115] Vinícius 11/9/2014.
[116] Eusebio 11/1/2013.
[117] This does not mean that poverty is not still an issue in Parque União only that it is less widespread than in other parts of Maré.
[118] Sergio 12/17/2014.
[119] Eusebio 1/11/2013.
[120] Fausto 7/30/2018.

removed from older favelas in the center of the city that were overwhelmingly comprised of former slave populations. By contrast, Parque União's inhabitants descend mostly from rural farmers and the urban poor from the Northeast of Brazil and are much more likely to identify as white. Accordingly, over 42% of Parque União compared to just 29% of Nova Holanda identifies as white. This racial profile may partly explain the difference in policing practices dating back to the early years of these communities. It may also partly explain why Nova Holanda has remained poorer and blacker over time as residents with the financial resources to move away from Nova Holanda, especially the border between the rival gangs, have done so while the most marginalized and impoverished – largely though not exclusively black and brown – have remained and been forced to endure the extreme levels of violence witnessed in Nova Holanda. Such structural forces are not deterministic but the fact that Nova Holanda is blacker *and* poorer than Parque União should not come as a surprise to anyone familiar with the dynamics of race and racism in Brazil. Once heralded as a "racial democracy" – in which race and racism was less formalized in state law as it was in the US and South Africa, for instance – Brazil is better understood as a "pigmentocracy" (Telles 2014) as race and skin color underpins nearly every social and economic interaction, shaping access to education, living situations, social mobility, and exposure to violence.[121] While the subject of race has consumed little of the explicit focus of this book, it underlies the very the existence of these communities, the public security policies developed to address them, and the socioeconomic realities on the ground. In these ways it may even contribute to the variation in criminalized governance practices; the difference between Parque União and Nova Holanda is only the most prominent example.

In response to the improving economic conditions and the diminishing need for gang welfare in Parque União, CVPU has found ways to continue to distribute some economic benefits to the community. For one, the gang has moved to offer fewer but larger items to residents on holidays. Over the last decade or so, instead of just food, drinks, and small gifts, the gang holds a raffle a couple of times a year (on Children's and Mother's Day) in which the winners receive televisions, refrigerators, stoves, and bicycles.[122] Danilson, the president of the AM, showed me numerous photographs of these elaborate parties replete with massive cakes, baskets of toys, and the electronics and appliances that they give away. He was not shy about how he worked with the gang to organize and fund these parties. "We also still give away some food baskets as well, but only 25–30 each month," he said.

For Dagobert, these economic activities "are just small forms of support. The gang doesn't really engage in community development. They could absolutely

---

[121] For instance, 70 percent of the Brazil's wealthiest are white while 75 percent of the poorest identify as black (Informação Demográfica e Socioeconômica 2022).
[122] José 1/10/2017; Beto 1/13/2017; Bernardo 1/16/2017.

do more, but they don't have that vision."[123] This is precisely the point. The gang does not want to end the community's reliance on them. They just want to stay on their good side. It is a fundamentally conservative, not a progressive, political project that the gangs are engaged in. In this vein, like many other gangs around the city, CVPU has expanded its economic activities to include property development and the monopolization of certain markets like cooking gas and informal transportation. During the period I lived in Maré, a local commercial building was abandoned. Eusebio, the president of the AM at the time, started to use the space for a boxing academy.[124] Several years later, on one of my return trips to Maré, I heard that the gang had decided to take over the building for themselves, forcing Eusebio and his gym out, so that they could convert the space into numerous *kitchenettes* (studio apartments) that they subsequently rented out.[125] Aside from the access to alternative revenue streams, such economic practices strengthen the gang's position of authority within the community as residents rely on them not just to resolve problems and gain access to some basic welfare (for the poorest residents) but also for housing and income.

Some have argued that the reason gangs diversified their revenue streams was because profits from the drug trade have shrunk over time.[126] I found no evidence of this. Eusebio, for instance, said that the gang and its members had made far less money when he was involved in the 1990s.[127] The gang's two weekly baile funks each brought in an estimated R$300,000–400,000 with about the same amount in weekly sales at the bocas.[128] These estimates suggest CVPU makes as much as their Nova Holanda counterparts with only two thirds of the labor costs.[129] Moreover, because of Parque União's location along two heavily trafficked highways and because the area was known to be less violent, "there were always a lot of outsiders coming here to purchase," Bernardo said. "I bet 80–90% of the drugs they sell is to outsiders," he concluded. This may help explain why Parque União had only half the number of bocas as Nova Holanda, all but one of which was located near the highways running past the community (see Figure 6.1).

Despite the efforts of the gang to avoid enforcement, the constant operations by BOPE and other police units in the years prior to occupation did have consequences for CVPU. Due to the high number of arrests, the gang was

---

[123] Dagobert 1/18/2017.
[124] Breno 3/6/2014.
[125] Apparently, this had caused some disagreement between the gang and Eusebio and he had eventually been forced to leave the community (Danilson 7/3/2018).
[126] á12/20/2008.
[127] Eusebio 1/11/2013.
[128] Márcio 4/17/2014; Everton 4/17/2014.
[129] The Parque União gang had an estimated 100 members while Nova Holanda had 150 during fieldwork.

forced to slightly modify its organizational structure. For one, the Dono implemented a *rodizio* (rotation)-style structure. According to Bernardo,

Before, you would have a bunch of gerentes and they would have some vapores working under them. Adriano changed this so each guy would spend a week in charge of the boca before switching positions. This way, they spread the profits throughout the organization. This also helps if one is arrested then another can easily step into his place.[130]

This evolution perhaps explains why more of the CVPU members can afford expensive sneakers and clothes, something that is mostly lacking for many of the lower-level CVNH members.[131] Adriano has also further centralized his authority by removing some of the gerentes of varying ranks or prices, thus streamlining the organization (see Figure 6.4). That said, frequent arrests and killings by the police would eventually lead the gang to enlist younger members. "There used to be a lot of older guys involved. Now there's a lot more kids," Sergio said.[132] Bernardo thought that this was an ingenious if negative development for the local gang. "It's a highly flexible organization. They put youth in charge on the street and at the bocas de fumo. This means that when they are captured by police, they aren't sent to prison but to juvenile detention and are often released a short time later. This has been a huge adaptation and a very sad one."[133]

The final governance activity of CVPU has been to provide recreational opportunities for residents. Since the mid-2000s, the Parque União bailes on Friday and Sunday nights have been some of the largest and best organized in the city.[134] During the period I resided in Maré, the gang constructed eight to ten walls of speakers that they placed strategically along four intersecting streets in the center of the community. They put up huge tents to provide shelter for attendees and to cover the sound equipment in case of rain. Several thousand local youth danced, drank, and ate until the next morning for these parties. The purpose of the bailes was not merely to make money but also to remind attendees of the gang's legitimacy. Like in Nova Holanda, DJs play songs with lyrics that are, equal parts, sexually explicit and intended to extol the virtues of CVPU, characterizing them as a benevolent presence within the community. For example, one of the most famous funk songs from Parque União begins, "*O Parque Uniao é 100 por cento CV/ Quem tá de frente é os cria*" (Parque União is 100 percent Comando Vermelho/Who is in charge are those from here). The lyrics speak to the pedigree of the local gang that has

---

[130] Bernardo 1/16/2017.
[131] Elsewhere, Levitt and Venkatesh (2000) have described this highly unequal pay structure as a tournament model, in which lower ranking members discount current pay and risk for the possibility of rising up through the hierarchy to eventually make much more.
[132] Sergio 12/17/2014.
[133] Bernardo 1/16/2017.
[134] Bernardo 1/16/2017.

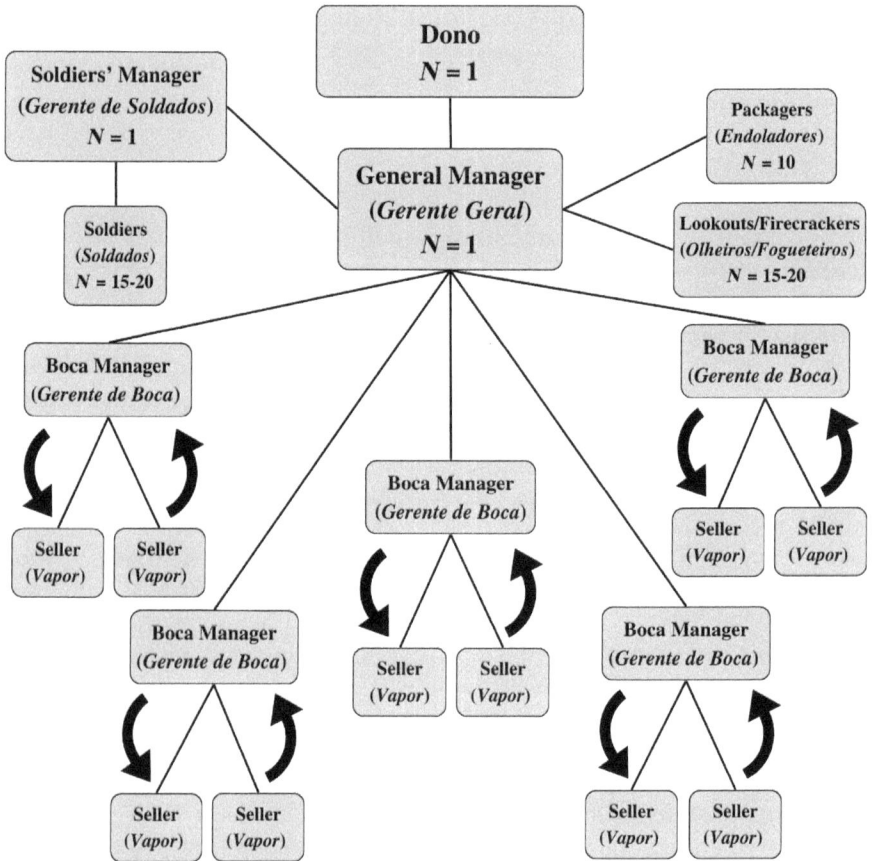

FIGURE 6.4 Organizational structure of CVPU
Visualization by author. N is the estimated number of gang members for each role.

been part of CV for more than three decades and that retains strong connections to the community through members that are born and raised there.

The gang also used the bailes as an opportunity to engage in ritualistic
behavior that heightens the feelings of solidarity among their own members
as well with local youth. For instance, every time a song, *Bonde do Zé Gordo*
(Zé Gordo's Entourage), mentioned the former gang leader, it was customary
for gang members to shoot their weapons into the air. Beto always reminded
his daughters, who frequently attended bailes, to leave the party when they
heard that song because gang members were known to shoot off their guns for
several minutes.[135] At one Parque União baile I attended, the DJ stopped the
music and asked the crowd for one minute of silence in remembrance of a gang

member who had recently been killed by police. Thousands of youth packed the streets, shoulder to shoulder, and stood in complete silence. After a minute, the DJ thanked the crowd and the deep bass track started up again. The crowd erupted, cheering the DJ on, quickly easing back into the rhythm of the funk. Such moments of ceremony and ritual, although seemingly less important than other forms of governance is fundamental to shaping how the local community thinks and feels about the gang.

CVPU also facilitated the use of space within the community although not to the same degree as the Nova Holanda gang. The Parque União gang did not authorize nearly as many barracas though the wider streets of Nova Holanda helped facilitate this phenomenon. If, however, anyone wanted to use public space in Parque União for an event, they often sought the approval of the gang. For instance, when one local group wanted to show a children's film in one of the public squares and wanted to make sure that there were no guns or drugs around so parents felt comfortable bringing their children, they informed the gang and asked if they could refrain from being present during the event. The gang complied.[136] Dagobert, who ran a hip-hop collective, said the gang had often helped him put on concerts. "They've let us use their sound equipment. We just have to tell them when we'll be having an event and they're always supportive. Sometimes we even have cameras and record everything!"[137] CVPU was clearly willing to make exceptions to their rules to support local events. In sum, the Parque União gang should be understood to provide responsive and significant benefits to residents, part of their social bandit strategy to avoid enforcement by gaining the support of the community.

CONCLUSION

The case of CVPU demonstrates, above all, that governance varies dramatically even within the factions. Over the course of its three decades in control of Parque União, CVPU has faced little existential threat from rival gangs and has implemented a far less coercive governing regime than their CVNH counterparts. Aside from several years in the early 2000s when intergang violence peaked in Maré, the CVPU has limited their use of threats and violence, maintained a less heavy presence, and seldom restricted or monitored the movement and behavior of residents. Moreover, while the leadership of CVNH would change hands numerous times, a single family has maintained seamless control of the CVPU organization for the past thirty years. Numerous residents, when describing the dynamics of CVPU referred to it as a *"lança de família"* (family business).[138]

---

[136] Beto 1/13/2017.
[137] Dagobert 1/18/2017. The use of cameras within gang territories is usually prohibited for fear that gang members and activities will be recorded.
[138] Bruno 10/6/2014; Artur 1/11/2017.

Despite the less coercive and violent approach of the gang, they have none-theless faced significant police enforcement over the years. A police post has existed on the border to the community since the 1970s, then the 22nd Military Police Battalion was constructed in 2003, and finally, the BOPE headquarters were built in 2011. Parque União has remained the focus of police enforcement for the duration and, as a result, has provided a responsive form of governance to the local community throughout. Residents could not remember a period in which the gang forgot about the community and although the gang does not maintain as intimate or direct a governance style as CVNH, residents none-theless described them as an important source of benefits and order within the community. CVPU has also provided significant forms of welfare over its his-tory, in particular, the provision of housing for thousands of residents during the 1990s, though the better socioeconomic conditions in Parque União have limited the demand for these services in recent years. Finally, the gang offered numerous recreational opportunities in the form of holiday parties and baile funks, that have served to supplement their legitimacy in the eyes of many residents. Overall, the historical trajectory of CVPU's criminalized governance practices substantiates the theoretical framework developed in Chapter 3.

7

Terceiro Comando (Puro) of Complexo da Maré

Guerra é um inferno.

War is hell.

—Valdemir, a longtime resident of Vila do João

INTRODUCTION

The TCP case differs from Maré's CV gangs in important ways. First, TCP controls a much larger territory, encompassing ten contiguous neighborhoods with an estimated population of 68,000 residents, more than twice that of either of the CV-connected gangs. These neighborhoods are constituted by both the oldest favelas in the Complexo (Morro do Timbau and Baixa do Sapateiro) as well as the newest housing projects (Nova Maré and Salsa e Merengue). Such a diverse spatial landscape and urban design offers an opportunity to analyze how one organization governs very different types of communities. In addition, TCP's turf has changed significantly over time as the gang has lost and won territory through violent battles with several rivals. Even more than CVNH case, TCP's trajectory demonstrates the horrifying consequences of gang warfare for both gang members and residents. Third, the TCP case shows how gangs can shift the nature of their relationship to the police over time. While both CV gangs have maintained a more antagonistic relationship with the police for the duration, TCP developed highly collaborative relations with the police especially after 2009, and, as a result, faced lower levels of enforcement.

I will begin the chapter by focusing on the integration of Kito's gang into the TC faction and the increasing levels of violence between TC and a CV-connected gang in the newly built housing projects in the south of Maré in the early 1990s. The disorder brought about by this war would only end when TC finally managed to defeat their rival and consolidate their exclusive control over the entire

TABLE 7.1 *Evolution of TC(P) governance regime*

Provision of benefits	Coercion		
	Extreme	*High*	*Low*
Responsive	Disorder 1992–96 2002–2005	Benevolent dictator	Social bandit 1996–2002
Unresponsive		Tyrant 2005–2009	Laissez-Faire 2009–14

southern half of Maré. I then outline how TC implemented a social bandit regime for the duration of the 1990s and into the 2000s. In 2002, TC split in two, the result of simmering tensions between its leaders and dynamics occurring within Rio's prisons. One of the resulting gangs helped found the TCP faction while the other allied with ADA. The ensuing war between these two gangs and ongoing violence with CVNH brought even higher levels of violence and disorder to these neighborhoods. By 2005, the war had ended, leaving both TCP and ADA severely weakened but with neither being able to defeat the other. For the next several years, each of these gangs can be considered tyrants as they provided little in terms of benefits to the local population while relying on threats and violence to retain control of their respective turfs.

In 2009, following their leader's escape from prison and with the assistance of local police, TCP invaded and conquered the housing projects, expelling the remnants of the ADA gang from Maré. TCP consolidated their control over these neighborhoods and provided responsive benefits to win over the local population. This conquest and consolidation of new territory dramatically changed the security dynamics for TCP. The subsequent period before occupation by the military, 2009–14, can be characterized as a laissez-faire regime as TCP faced little rival threat and maintained a collaborative relationship with the police though I note on some differences in how TCP governed their historic territories versus the housing projects. Throughout this chapter, I weave multiple types of data, including eighteen months participant observation of TCP governance practices, dozens of semi-structured interviews with current and former gang members and residents, as well as journalistic accounts and anonymous denunciations from the DD hotline. Together, these microlevel data allow me to trace how the local security environment has shaped TCP's governance practices over time (Table 7.1).

THE TERRITORY

The Historic Territories

TCP's historic territories are constituted by Morro do Timbau, Baixa do Sapateiro, Nova Maré, and Bento Ribeiro Dantas (see Figure 7.1). The Morro and Baixa (how residents refer to them) are Maré's oldest favelas though, as described in Chapter 4, their early years were quite different in that the Morro was controlled by the military until the 1980s (see Chapter 4). In addition, as the name implies, the Morro is the only area of Maré that is not flat. Although it rises only a couple of hundred feet above the rest of Maré, it dominates the surrounding landscape. The Morro is less densely populated (6,709 residents) than many other areas of Maré because the military limited migration to the area, though its meandering streets, numerous alleyways, and elevation make it a difficult area for police and rival gangs to try to invade. Baixa do Sapateiro has a similarly irregular design and, like the CVNH and CVPU territories, a larger and denser population (9,329 residents). The narrow streets and alleyways of this neighborhood also make it an ideal area for gang members to avoid police enforcement and to defend their territory against a rival.

With the completion of Project Rio, a massive federal infrastructure project, in the 1980s and the massive landfilling that occurred in the surrounding areas, Bento Ribeiro Dantas (1992) and Nova Maré (1996) were eventually built on two other adjacent and unused pieces of land. Both housing projects were part of the *Morar Sem Risco* (Living Without Risk) program, designed to provide housing for residents of favelas from other areas of the city susceptible to flooding and landslides. Both communities were built in a post-modernist style, with numerous houses of exposed brick and concrete. Residents often refer to these areas as *"as casinhas"* (the cottages). With wide streets and a regular layout of conjoined houses surrounded by large courtyards, these housing projects are more difficult areas for the gangs to defend. They were also built to prevent additions and improvements being made so these neighborhoods have retained much of their original character while Maré's other housing projects, such as Nova Holanda, have come to resemble the surrounding favelas. Nevertheless, quickly after their construction, TC quickly integrated these two communities into their turf, bringing the total population in this territory to an estimated 22,806 (Redes da Maré 2019a).

The combination of the Morro's verticality and irregular layout with the two housing projects' more formal design, makes this gang's territory the most varied of any in Maré. While the two housing projects are more difficult areas to control, the Morro and Baixa are easily defensible spaces and help explain why the gang has maintained their control over these neighborhoods despite repeated attempts to conquer them by several rival gangs. When I lived in Maré and spent significant time in this area, TCP maintained eight bocas de fumo, the majority of which were in the Morro and Baixa. Each of the housing projects only had one boca. The gang also maintained lookout and security positions throughout their territory, though they manned these less diligently than the CVNH gang described in Chapter 5. Although TCP was more visible along the border with their rival when violence increased, the gang maintained a more relaxed presence throughout the rest of these neighborhoods. TCP members were not as heavily armed and did not ride their motorcycles up and down the streets to the

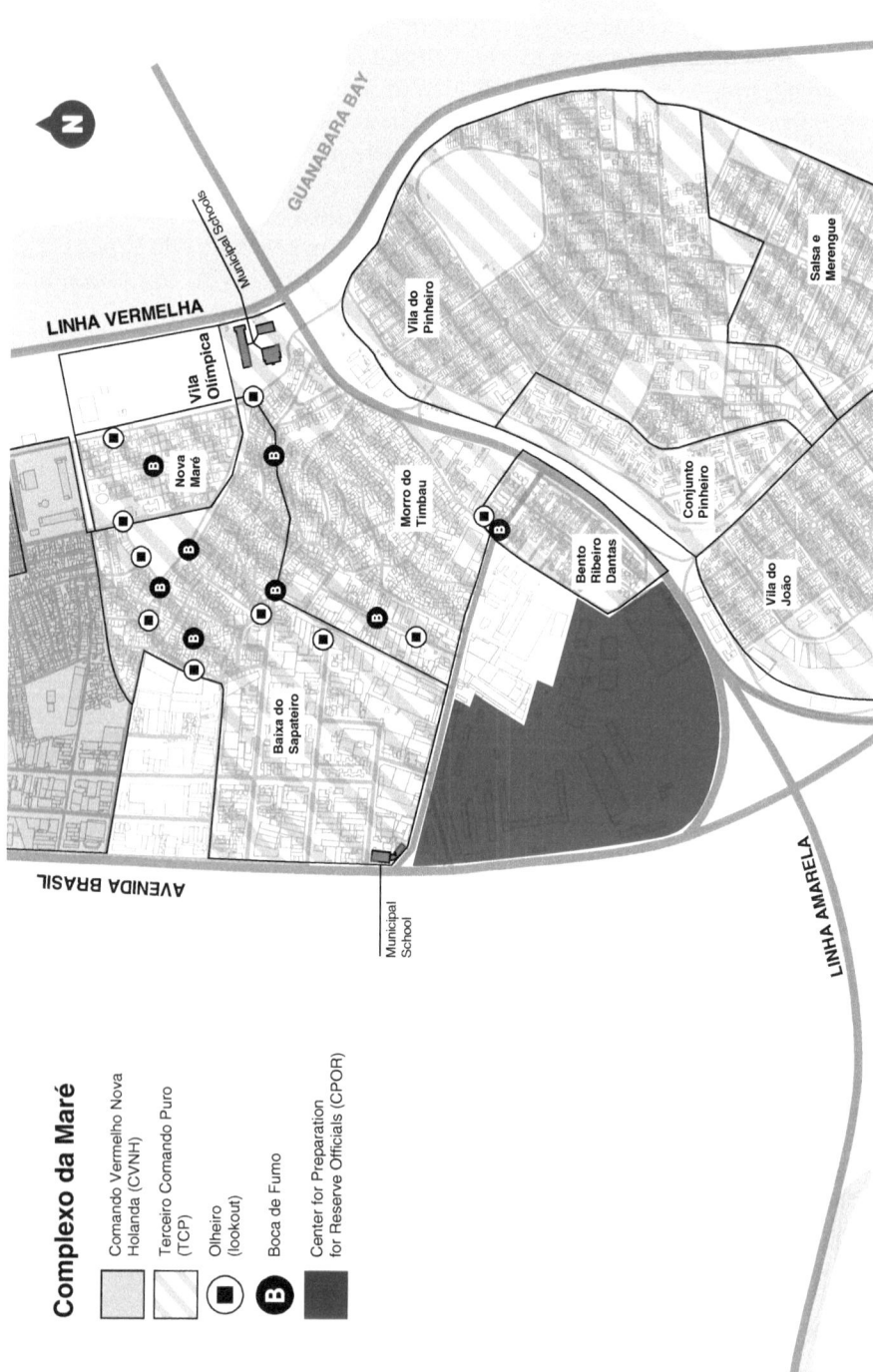

FIGURE 7.1 Map of TCP historic territory during fieldwork Visualization by Bruna Montuori.

same degree as CVNH. I would only rarely spot a large group of gang members surrounding one of the bocas. That said, this set of neighborhoods is far less commercial than either of the CV territories. There are fewer shops and restaurants, and the number of carts and stalls along the streets and sidewalks pales in comparison to Nova Holanda. The gang had historically organized bailes in one of these plazas but they were no longer happening when I lived in Maré.

TCP's historic territory can be accessed from all sides. Along their northern border, which they share with CVNH, there are numerous side streets and alleyways, which make this a difficult border to defend. The gang is more present in this area with several lookout positions and bocas. Avenida Brazil and the *Centro de Preparação de Oficiais da Reserva* (Reserve Officials Preparation Center) or CPOR, the military base which has been located on those same grounds since the 1940s, constitute the eastern border of these territories. Despite technically being located within the border of Baixa do Sapateiro, the gang was seldom present in the streets closest to Avenida Brasil. These areas have become more formalized and received access to all the infrastructure and services of the city. Numerous churches, office buildings, and high-rise apartments have been built there. The gang's turf began a couple hundred yards from the highway, where the more informal parts of the favela started.

The southern border of this territory is constituted by the Linha Amarela, a highway running east to west, which eventually ends in Barra da Tijuca, a sprawling and heavily populated middle and upper-class neighborhood. Like Linha Vermelha and Avenida Brasil, Linha Amarela is a heavily trafficked highway at all hours of the day and night. Bento Ribeiro Dantas is situated along this highway and there are several entrances to the TCP territory for vehicles and pedestrians here. The gang is little present within this neighborhood with only one boca located at the far end, closest to the Morro. Many residents use this area to exit Maré as they catch buses to other areas of the city at several stops along the Linha Amarela. Finally, Linha Vermelha constitutes the western border of the TCP turf where there is only a single entrance point for vehicles. There are no bus stops along this highway and the area is little used by pedestrians. Finally, three municipal schools are located on opposite ends of the community, one close to Avenida Brasil and two others at the intersection of the Linhas Vermelha and Amarela.

The Housing Projects

Beginning in the early 1980s, Maré was the subject of intense public scrutiny and attention. The tens of thousands of palafitas had created a public health disaster and an urban planning nightmare. The federal government eventually invested hundreds of millions in a total renovation and urbanization of the area. Two major highways were built (Linha Amarela and Linha Vermelha) and more than half a square mile – roughly 250 football fields – of Guanabara Bay were filled in by the massive housing development and upgrading initiative called Project Rio.[1] Four new housing projects, Vila do João (John's Village, inaugurated in 1982), Conjunto Esperança (Project Hope, 1982), Vila do Pinheiro (Pine Village, 1983), and Conjunto Pinheiro (Pine Project, 1989), were eventually built on land that had previously not existed (see Figure 7.2). Many of the residents of these communities would come from Maré itself. Most of Vila do João and Vila do Pinheiro, for instance, were initially inhabited by former residents of Baixa do Sapateiro and Parque Maré that had lived on palafitas. A fifth community, Salsa e Merengue (1997) would be built more than a decade later, on an adjacent piece of land.[2] Overall, these housing projects are home to an estimated 44,821 residents and constitute roughly a third (32.3 percent) of Maré's overall population (Redes da Maré 2019a).

Although each of these housing projects has a slightly different design and construction, they all have wide streets, checkerboard layouts, and are either comprised of large apartment buildings or conjoined multistory family houses. Some of the larger thoroughfares in these neighborhoods are full of shops and restaurants with Rua Principal (Main Street) in Vila do João constituting one of the major commercial districts in Maré. Moving through these neighborhoods, they have a very different feel than the favela neighborhoods described earlier or in the previous chapters. In Maré's favelas, there's an inescapable feeling of claustrophobia. Every inch of livable space is taken up by tightly packed houses, restricting one's view to just a short distance. In these housing projects, there's much more open space. You can often see for long distances and there are numerous empty fields and uninhabited spaces though, over time, shacks and informally built housing have slowly begun to fill in those interstitial spaces. Moreover, the bottleneck entrances of some Maré's favelas do not exist here. Pedestrians and vehicles can enter at numerous different points, some of which are expansive open fields or large boulevards. For these reasons, the entire area is a much more difficult space for a gang to defend, and helps explain why the territory has changed hands several times over its history.

The northern border of this area is constituted by Linha Amarela. There are several entry points for both vehicles and pedestrians along this stretch of highway. Vehicles can enter at five points though I never saw gang members checking the vehicles anywhere close to these entrances. Pedestrians use sidewalks (nonexistent in most of the rest of Maré), dirt paths, and shortcuts across open fields and undeveloped lots to enter these neighborhoods. Again, no gang members ever seemed to be checking these areas. Instead, the gang's presence was set back a street or two in Conjunto Pinheiro or even four or five in Vila do Pinheiro.

---

[1] For a description of Project Rio and its impact on Complexo da Maré, see *Rio on Watch* (7/16/2017; 9/5/2017; 9/20/2017).

[2] Construction for Salsa e Merengue, officially named Conjunto Novo Pinheiro, began in 1996 but was delayed by the discovery of numerous cadavers and remains that had been buried on the site by the gangs (*O Globo* 10/2/1996). It took more than a year for the housing project to finally be inaugurated (*O Globo* 12/4/1997).

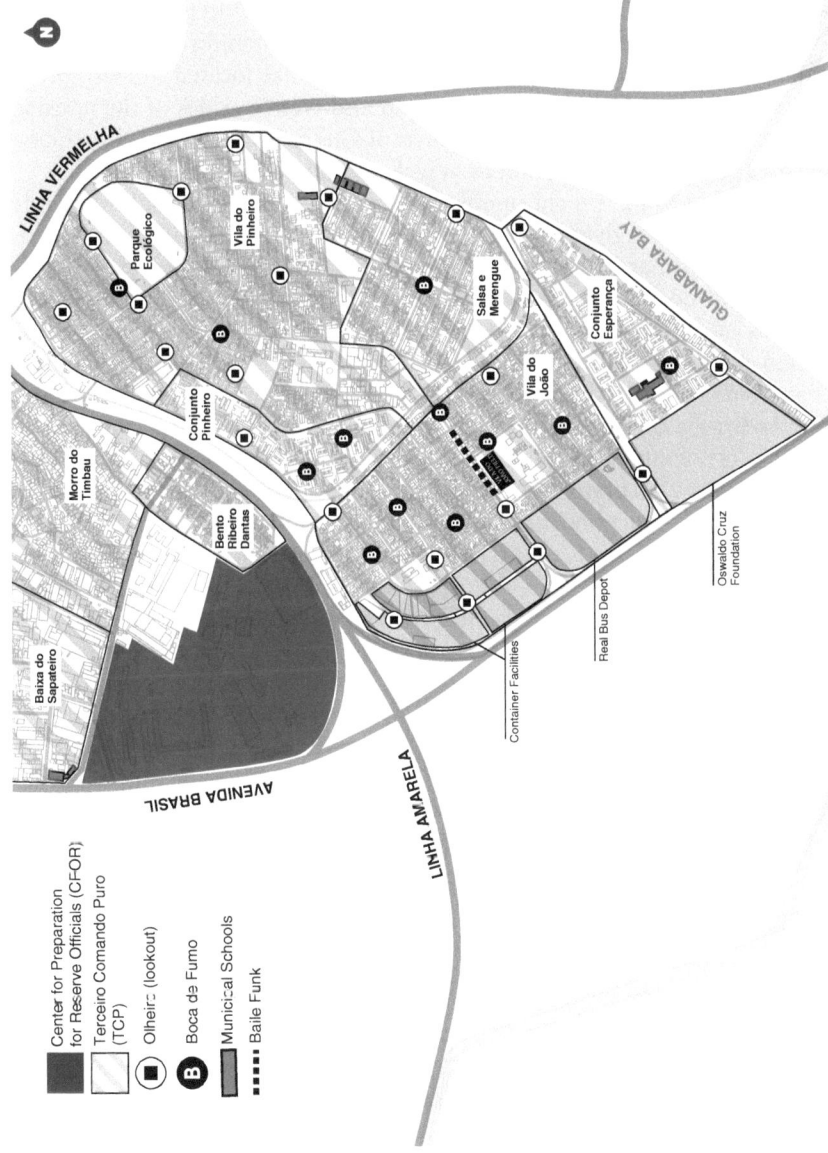

FIGURE 7.2 Map of TCP housing projects during fieldwork Visualization by Bruna Montuori.

The eastern border of this part of TCP's territory is constituted by Avenida Brasil. Two huge industrial firms – a container facility and a bus company – as well as the Oswaldo Cruz Foundation, a walled-off research center, sit directly along Avenida Brasil, which funnels pedestrians and vehicles into one of several primary entrances. Together, these are the busiest entrances to this area of Maré as thousands of buses stop here each day. The gang monitors all these entry points diligently because their most lucrative bocas are located in close proximity of Avenida Brasil. Finally, the southern and western sides of the housing projects are bordered by the remaining parts of Guanabara Bay as well as Linha Vermelha. There are no pedestrian or vehicle entrances along these sides.

When I lived in Maré, I spent significant time in this area as well. I frequently biked or walked through these neighborhoods as I visited NGOs, AMs, cultural events, gyms, bars, or restaurants. As I did so, I always paid close attention where and how the gang was present. TCP maintained roughly fifteen bocas sprinkled throughout these neighborhoods. Vila do João had many more bocas than any of the other communities perhaps because it was the primary way that residents entered the community and, like other areas of Maré close to Avenida Brasil, outsiders could quickly enter, purchase drugs, then leave. While numerous gang lookouts and security positions were located near these main entrances, TCP's presence was less pervasive and more subdued throughout the rest of these neighborhoods. Heavy armaments were only visible at a couple of locations along the main thoroughfares, and I never witnessed gang members carrying multiple rifles as I often did in CVNH's territory. That said, TCP members did frequently use motorcycles to move through space; the area is so large it requires a vehicle to move back and forth across these neighborhoods. The gang's more subdued presence was also due, in part, to the urban layout of these neighborhoods; with wider streets, more open spaces, and buildings constructed further apart, the gang's presence never felt oppressive in the same way as CVNH. The gang also organized a large baile funk party on Saturdays though they were not nearly so well attended or promoted as the CV ones, at least during the period in which I lived in Maré. Overall, TCP maintained a slightly heavier presence in these neighborhoods than in their historic neighborhoods, but it could not be described as ostentatious.

THE EVOLUTION OF TC(P) GOVERNANCE

Disorder (1992–96)

In the early 1990s, Kito's gang integrated into the TC faction, which had emerged as the only competitor to CV dominance of the city's favelas (see Chapter 4). The exact source of the connection with TC is unclear as Kito had yet to be imprisoned but it is likely that his desire to expand his turf to a newly built set of housing projects just to the south of Morro do Timbau incentivized him to ally with one of the factions. He needed weapons, manpower, and access to more retail drugs if he was going to successfully expand his territory to an area where there were several smaller gangs already operating.[3] A connection with one of the factions was the primary means through which to achieve these territorial ambitions. In this way, the rapid expansion of the factions into Rio's favelas was not solely the result of gang members being imprisoned, as in Parque União, or the threat of conquest, as in Nova Holanda, but was also due to ambitious gang leaders who wanted access to the resources of the factions.

As described in the previous chapters, the organizational structure of Rio's gangs in this initial period after integration (irrespective of faction) was relatively uniform with gerentes, vapores, soldados, endoladores, and olheiros running and protecting the drug trade in any favela territory. The number of bocas in Kito's territory began to increase from just one or two to a handful as the number of full-time members also expanded. Some of the gang's new members were young men with little experience in violence and crime while others were bank robbers or stickup artists who already lived in the Morro or Baixa but previously had no connection to the gang. Like in Parque União and Nova Holanda, these men would be integrated into the TC organization or forced to leave the neighborhood.[4]

Sporadic violence in Vila do Pinheiro and Vila do João began in the early 1990s and by 1992 an all-out war between Kito's TC gang and a CV-affiliated gang led by Omar enveloped these neighborhoods. In 1992 and 1993, TC was documented invading the housing projects on numerous occasions often with several dozen men armed with AR-15 rifles, machine guns, and shotguns.[5] They would eventually manage to consolidate their control over one of these neighborhoods, Vila do Pinheiro, even as Omar and his gang – heavily supported by Zé Gordo and other CV gangs – controlled Vila do João.[6] The fighting, however, was not reserved to the housing projects as Omar and his CV allies took the fight to Kito and his turf. In one such invasion in April 1992, Omar led a group of fifty men in an assault on Morro do Timbau.[7]

As these violent battles for territorial control were occurring, TC expanded its turf when Bento Ribeiro Dantas and Nova Maré were built next to the Morro and Baixa (see Figure 7.1). Mateo, who moved to Bento Ribeiro Dantas with his family when he was 11 years old in 1992, remembered that immediately after they had moved into the housing project, "the gang [TC] came

---

[3] For the first ten years of existence, there were a bunch of small-time criminals and fledgling gangs that tried to control these housing projects but they did not wield much power. Some of the most prominent individuals from this era were Xangu, Muscatin, Beto Negão, and Doge. Alinho was the first gang leader to really consolidate control of the area. After he was arrested, Omar took over in Vila do João (Valdemir 1/9/2015).

[4] Valdemir 1/9/2015.

[5] *O Globo* 4/21/1992; 11/14/1993.

[6] *O Globo* 5/1/1992; 12/15/1995.

[7] *O Globo* 9/28/1992.

down the hill with a bunch of arms and made clear that they were in control of the area."[8] Several years later, Henrique similarly recalled moving to Nova Maré from the palafitas in Roquete Pinto, an area of Maré controlled at the time by another gang connected to the TC faction. "The first night was really tense. The city brought us there in trucks and just left us without any instructions. It was dark because they hadn't put in any street lights yet. The gang from the Morro [TC] came in the dark. They told us we could stay and everyone relaxed a bit."[9] These two housing projects would add another 6,700 residents to TC's territory.

In 1993, Omar was imprisoned and Kito and his men would spend the next year attacking Vila do João, eventually taking it over for a short period.[10] In March 1995, Omar escaped from prison and orchestrated one of the largest invasion attempts in the history of Rio when he led more than one hundred men connected to twenty-one different CV gangs from around the city to retake his old turf.[11] The CV coalition used more than two dozen cars, three vans, and a large truck to invade the area and would eventually kill and decapitate eight TC members.[12] They would not stay in control for long, however, because less than a year later, in early 1996, TC went on the offensive and eventually took over the entire set of housing projects, expelling Omar and the remnants of his gang.[13]

The coercive practices of TC – as well as the CV gang which controlled these neighborhoods during this period – were extreme. Before the war, few residents could remember any of the gangs using very much violence against residents. As intergang violence increased, however, residents were caught in the middle of these warring parties. Any existing governance arrangements broke down and disorder reined. Valdemir, a longtime resident, described how three gang members broke into his family's house and held them hostage for three days in the midst of this war.

They needed a place to hide out and wait for an invasion that was supposed to happen. They kept us there. My parents couldn't go to work, I couldn't go to school. They didn't have any money either. We had to give them water and food. When the invasion finally happened, they just left. I don't know what happened to them.[14]

The gangs often shot at anyone they found suspicious or cars that they did not recognize. In one of the many tragedies during these years, a car with

---

[8] Mateo 1/13/2015.
[9] Henrique 12/8/2014.
[10] *O Globo* 11/14/1993.
[11] *O Globo* 3/14/1995.
[12] The invasion was later immortalized in a funk song, "Rap do Omar," which describes in detail the events of that day and all the various CV gang leaders which participated in the invasion (*O Globo* 12/26/1995).
[13] *O Globo* 1/15/1996.
[14] Valdemir 1/9/2015.

four waiters was surrounded and shot at by gang members, injuring three and killing one, when gang members did not recognize the car when it entered the community.[15] In another notorious case, TC members shot up a van full of eleven Santos (a famous São Paulo football club) fans that had taken a wrong turn into their territory during a confrontation with Omar's CV gang.[16] According to the gang members allegedly responsible for the death of one of the Santos fans, they had thought the van was full of police.[17] There are numerous other similar reports of gangs confronting police in the midst of intergang confrontations during these years.[18]

The monitoring and surveillance of the local population also ramped up during this period. Before the war, residents in Maré moved freely between the different gang territories as many had relatives, friends, worked, or went to school across these boundaries. The borders between the rival gangs were closed entirely. Both the TC and CV gangs restricted movement in and among the housing projects by stopping and questioning residents who tried to cross over and using violence against those they suspected of collaboration with their rivals. Osvaldo recalled gang members frequently threatening residents and causing a lot of problems for people who lived near these borders.[19]

In interviews with residents, they described numerous scenes of spectacular brutality and extra-lethal violence during this period of warfare and disorder. Mateo remembered that when TC finally conquered the rest of the housing projects, they captured Omar's braço direito, decapitated him, played soccer with his head, and left his headless body in the goal.[20] Thiago told a similar story. He and his family moved to Vila do João when he was a young boy. When Omar came back with the huge invasion, "They killed a bunch of people that day and put their heads on display," Thiago recalled.[21] Such extreme forms of violence are not only a reaction to the anxiety and fear that gang members feel in the midst of war but also serves a coercive function; it sends a clear message to the community that they are in power and capable of punishing their enemies. In this way, extreme forms of coercion are intended to shape the behavior of residents and deter any would-be rival.

When the gangs won territory, they tried to cleanse the area of any residents known to have close relations with the former gang. They did so to prevent any information from reaching their rivals and any future attempts to retake the area. Thiago described the cleansing that follows conquest as "a natural process. They expel a bunch of people and hire the local boys to become a part of

---

[15] *O Globo* 9/28/1992.
[16] *O Globo* 12/19/1995; 12/16/1995a; 12/16/1995b.
[17] *O Globo* 12/19/1995.
[18] *O Globo* 10/30/1993; 1/15/1996; 6/9/1995; 10/22/1995; 2/5/2000; 5/21/2002.
[19] Osvaldo 1/7/2015.
[20] Mateo 1/13/2015.
[21] Thiago 1/9/2015.

the gang. They need information and help. After a while the community begins
to accept them even if they're not from there because a lot of the boys are from
the community."[22] I asked him what it was like during the war between TC
and CV in Vila do João. "After CV returned with Omar's invasion, they killed
several residents who had cooperated with TC. The *chaveiro* (keymaker), the
barbeiro (barber), and *um rico* (a rich guy) were all killed from our street. CV
killed a lot when they were here because they were surrounded by TC. They
were always afraid of losing their territory."[23]

I asked him how CV knew about these connections. "They heard about
these people by becoming friends with some of the locals and employing some
of the young men. Eventually, they found out everything," he said. Thiago's
father had even guarded TC's guns and smoked their marijuana when they
were in control of the area. "That's why CV came after us," Thiago's mother,
Rosalyn, told me.

We weren't home the first time they came. We were in Pinheiro at my mother's house
at the time. Someone came and told me that CV was looking for my husband because
they had heard he was involved. When I got back, all the windows were busted and
there was glass all over the floor. I swept it out and put my mattress in the doorway
so they would see me when they came back. I was so mad. I wanted to ask them why
they did that. When they came back at 3 am I told them we didn't have anything to do
with trafficking but they didn't care. They said my husband could never come back to
the community after that. Then they went to our neighbors' house and killed the man
in front of his wife and then raped her. We were lucky my husband was in Caxias
[a neighboring city] for work. He's never been back to Maré since.[24]

Such stories are not rare in areas rife with intergang violence. It is quite common for anyone connected to the old gang to flee their homes with only what
they can carry when a rival gang takes over.

TC engaged in some of the same types of threats and executions in their historic territories as well. They wanted to ensure that residents were not providing information to their enemy. For instance, some of the families that arrived
in Bento Ribeiro Dantas in 1992 were from Manguinhos, a community controlled by a CV gang. Mateo remembered that after the violence between the
gangs started, TC members would come down from the Morro at night and,
in the morning, they would find the body of someone who had connections to
CV. I asked him how they knew who was involved. "It must have been someone inside the community," he began, "Most of the people that were executed
did, in fact, have connections. More than a dozen people were killed in that
way," he said.[25]

[22] Thiago 1/9/2015.
[23] Thiago 1/9/2015.
[24] Rosalyn 1/9/2015.
[25] Mateo 1/13/2015.

The use of extreme forms of punishment was not reserved to those who had connections to their rival. Residents also began to see more drug addicts and other *marginais* (outcasts) becoming victims of the gang. They would often throw their bodies in the *valão* (sewage ditch). Henrique recalled that his grandfather used to take him and his siblings to see the corpses anytime one showed up. Pointing to the corpse, he would explain to the children, "'that is what happens to people who use drugs.' We saw a lot of dead bodies over the years," Henrique said.[26]

The coercive behavior of TC also focused inward. Valdemir remembered a friend of his, Silvio, joined the gang in the 1990s. "On his first day, the manager gave him a gun and told him to shoot two of the other gang members. They were begging for their lives and told him to put the gun down. He didn't do anything, so they killed him for it," Valdemir said.[27] Such tests of mettle were not uncommon for new recruits. Those that demonstrated a willingness to kill were quickly integrated and moved up the chain of command while those who were not were removed. In this way, the more violent members of gang organizations often come to the fore when the gang is at war, increasing even further their coercive tendencies. According to Valdemir, "Omar was the most cowardly of all. He used to send kids to do the fighting and he wouldn't put himself on the front line. He used to kill his managers if he thought they were getting too powerful. He'd go looking for reasons to kill them."[28] This perhaps explains why Omar was never able to fully gain control of the area despite being assisted by numerous CV gangs throughout the city: He had systematically removed his most capable managers to make sure that he never faced competition for the leadership of the gang. While this may seem like an obvious mistake, the pressures of war on a gang leader can be considerable. They must walk a tightrope of maintaining the allegiance of their members while simultaneously encouraging them to take incredible risks and possibly die for the cause.

Finally, in the early months of 1996, Omar was pursued tirelessly by the police and finally arrested in São João de Meriti, a suburb of Rio de Janeiro, where he had gone into hiding after being expelled from his former turf by Kito and his men.[29] TC fully consolidated its control of the housing projects in Maré and CV would never again threaten or even try to invade these territories.[30] Kito was arrested a short time later, leaving two men in charge of his respective territories. In the gang's historic territories, Espadão became the *gerente geral* while the housing projects to the south were managed by Paulo César da Silva Santos, better known as Linho. In the ensuing years, these two

---

[26] Henrique 12/8/2014.
[27] Valdemir 1/9/2015.
[28] Valdemir 1/9/2015.
[29] *O Globo* 12/26/1995; 2/23/1996; 3/20/1996.
[30] *O Globo* 3/20/1996; 3/26/1996.

men would eventually usurp Kito's authority and become two of the most powerful Donos in the city.

Social Bandit (1996–2002)

After consolidating control over the housing projects, TC began to reap the benefits of a more stable environment in which to sell drugs. In particular, Linho developed a thriving retail drug business in the housing projects over the next few years. Fundamental to this growth were his connections to the TC faction, which formed an alliance with ADA in 1999 (see Chapter 4).[31] For the next several years, TC and ADA became, for all intents and purposes, one faction, allowing Linho to expand his connections to a new set of drug-trafficking contacts.[32] A very entrepreneurial and savvy businessman, Linho made international connections to arms and drug traffickers in Paraguay and other foreign countries.[33] He then expanded his retail business in Rio by lending arms to gangs willing to take over new areas, demanding that they pay him 40 percent of the profits and only buy drugs from him.[34] By the end of the decade, he was allegedly moving a ton of marijuana and 120 kilos of pure cocaine per month, half of which was being sold in Maré, totaling more than R$1.3 million in monthly revenue.

More than any other gang leader at that time, Linho began to diversify his revenue streams. In addition to the drug trade, he organized and masterminded assaults, robberies, kidnappings, extortion, and engaged in various other illicit markets, including gas, transportation, and housing speculation.[35] He even hired an accountant, a man merely referred to as *O Ministro* (The Minister), to keep track of his various business interests. He also built more than a dozen underground bunkers and hideouts in Maré, replete with armories, office equipment, and fully furnished living quarters.[36]

By the late 1990s, the TC gang in Maré was one of the most powerful and well-financed in the city. Linho and Espadão then turned their attention to the CVNH gang to their north. Over the course of the next couple of years, they would mount numerous large-scale invasions of Nova Holanda as they attempted to monopolize drug trafficking throughout Maré.[37] In one particularly audacious attempt, Linho paid prison guards R$200,000 to help nine incarcerated police-turned-mercenaries escape so that they could lead an invasion into Nova Holanda.[38] And yet, even as TC was aggressively waging war against the Nova

---

[31] *O Globo* 9/12/2002.
[32] *O Globo* 9/20/2002; 9/22/2002.
[33] *O Globo* 9/22/2002.
[34] *O Globo* 5/9/2002.
[35] *O Globo* 5/9/2002; 9/20/2002.
[36] *O Globo* 5/9/2002.
[37] *O Globo* 3/12/1999; 2/5/2000; 2/12/2000a; 5/26/2000a; 5/26/2000b.
[38] *O Globo* 2/12/2000b.

Holanda gang, their own territories felt less of the impact of this violence, at least initially. For the first several years of the war, CVNH was barely able to defend their territory much less mount any serious invasions into TC territory. As a result, TC remained more relaxed when it came to controlling their own neighborhoods, especially the housing projects. Residents could freely move around, avoided the gruesome punishments of the war years, and were largely left unmonitored by the gang. TC was so strong and well-financed during this era that they had little fear of rivals invading and trying to take over their territory. In fact, residents of these neighborhoods seldom remembered much about the violence or coercive practices of this era perhaps because it was sandwiched between two periods of horrific and difficult-to-forget violence.

Residents did recall that TC was responsive to community demands throughout this period. Such a governance style was incentivized by the sustained enforcement activities of the public security apparatus. In fact, even more than CVNH and CVPU, TC was the focus of significant public security attention throughout this period. The archives of *O Globo* newspaper contain dozens of articles on the various police operations and enforcement strategies used to try to combat TC throughout the 1990s and early 2000s. At the time, it was considered the most confrontational gang in Maré. For instance, according to the Commander of the 22nd Battalion (located outside of Maré at the time), "Gigante [from CVNH] is a more moderate criminal. He doesn't have the profile of those that live to challenge the police. Instead, he tries to avoid confrontations."[39] In fact, TC appears to have directly confronted the police on numerous occasions.

For instance, a small police post, named the *Centro Comunitário do Combate a Criminalidade* (Community Center for Combatting Criminality), or the CCCC was installed in Morro do Timbau in 1993. After a particularly aggressive police operation, the gang surrounded the CCCC and opened fire, killing one officer and injuring several others.[40] TC members were also known to terrorize and rob city buses,[41] kidnap businessmen,[42] and even detained then expelled Eduardo Paes, the Deputy Mayor of Barra da Tijuca and future Mayor of Rio de Janeiro, along with several dozen families when they came to see the houses they had been promised in the then-new housing project, Nova Maré.[43] In response to such a confrontational gang organization, the public security apparatus even developed new tactics which included surprise raids and an "*asfixia*" (asphyxia) approach in which BOPE and other newly created militarized units took total control of TC's territory for several hours to conduct

[39] *O Globo* 2/24/1996.
[40] *O Globo* 10/30/1993.
[41] *O Globo* 3/18/1994.
[42] *O Globo* 3/30/1995.
[43] *O Globo* 2/23/1996.

house-to-house searches and seizures.[44] Over time, such tactics would become standard policing practice throughout the city and, eventually, TC and the city's other gangs would learn to avoid direct confrontations with the police.[45]

Even while the gang engaged in sporadic confrontations with police, they simultaneously sought high levels of support from residents by providing responsive goods and services. They continued to understand that the support of the community was essential if they were to avoid police enforcement. First, the gang resolved numerous disputes within their territory. Longtime residents recalled that for the duration of the 1990s and into the 2000s, the gang leaders used to sit in one of the community's plazas and long lines of residents would wait their turn to speak with them to resolve problems.[46] Gang members of this era remembered how gerentes would also frequently encourage residents to speak with them to deal with their problems. Luiz, for one, recalled that one gerente would host a barbecue every weekend and residents would often take the opportunity to ask him favors. "Tell them to come talk to me," Luiz remembered him often saying when he heard of a resident having problems.[47] Even rank and file gang members were encouraged to be responsive to community demands. "Everything was a conversation. You had to listen to both sides of the story," Daniel, who had first joined the gang in the 1990s, told me.[48] He tied this directly to the possibility of residents becoming dissatisfied with the gang and the ramifications this had for the gang. "We helped residents because residents would help us. They would give us food and water while we were working or help us when a police operation was coming."[49] Josué, similarly, said that they had to resolve these problems to avoid "*bagunçando a comunidade*" (messing up the community), which meant not allowing conflicts to go unresolved which could become problematic for the gang if they led to denunciations or police attention.[50] "We had to be attentive to these things 24 hours a day. We were always on," Daniel recalled.[51]

By the mid-1990s, the gangs already knew about DD, the anonymous hotline, and foresaw the problems it would create for them. In one police operation, six telephones were found in a gang member's hideout.[52] They had been removed from houses that gang members thought were responsible for denunciations against them. The gang also began removing pay phones from their territories so that residents could not use them to denounce their activities.

---

[44] *O Globo* 5/1/1995.
[45] According to Misse et al. (2011), Rio's police militarized for the first time in the 1990s as they added more powerful weapons, armored vehicles, and, later, helicopters to their operations.
[46] Nanda 2/12/2013; Osvaldo 1/7/2015; Carlitos 10/2/2013.
[47] Luiz 7/30/2014.
[48] Daniel 8/21/2014.
[49] Daniel 8/21/2014.
[50] Josué 7/15/2014.
[51] Daniel 8/21/2014.
[52] *O Globo* 1/15/1996.

From this point forward, the police would consistently encourage residents to call DD to report any activities occurring with the gangs.[53]

TC also provided significant welfare and economic stimulation to residents living in their territories during this period. Many families found the gang to be a stable source of assistance. Luiz told me that the Dono and the gerentes used to frequently help the poorest families by paying for medicine, gas, food, transportation, or other costs. He estimated that, over time, somewhere around 60 percent of people in the community had received some sort of benefit from the gang.[54] One particularly important way that the gang helped families was by distributing food baskets through a local samba school. Luiz remembered gang members handing out tickets and the long lines that formed as families waited to get their monthly basket.[55] Similarly, Osvaldo recalled, rather nostalgically, the Robin Hood aspect of the gang as they used to distribute gifts and loot following big heists or robberies.[56] Such forms of assistance were not, however, purely generous but involved an implicit *quid pro quo* in which the gang expected help from the community. "They [gang members] would pay for something and the residents would have to help them hide weapons or they would ask for one of their kids to keep watch," Henrique said.[57]

Older gang members and residents also recalled that the gang used to throw large bailes near one of the schools located within the TC territory, to which residents from all over Maré would come. Thiaguinho, for one, said he went to many TC bailes in his youth and that he and many of his friends attended almost every week.[58] These parties were a very effective recruiting tool as they put the gang's access to women, drugs, and money on full display. These events also helped the gang maintain their popularity and support among local youth even if they did not become involved. Naldo, for one, believed they were one of the primary ways that the gang legitimized itself within their territories.[59] In addition, TC also used to organize large parties on Mother's, Father's, and Children's Day, handing out toys and candy to the children and offering free food and drink for the adults.

Disorder (2002–2005)

The rising power and influence of Linho would eventually strain his relationship with Espadão. In the early 2000s, TC continued to mount numerous invasions into Nova Holanda. Because most of the violence was occurring near TC's

[53] *O Globo* 12/17/1995.
[54] Luiz 7/31/2014.
[55] Luiz 7/30/2014.
[56] Osvaldo 1/7/2015.
[57] Henrique 12/8/2014.
[58] Thiaguinho 12/8/2014.
[59] Naldo 12/17/2014.

historic territories, Espadão's revenue from the drug trade dwindled (as the violence kept customers away) even as Linho was expanding his profits and becoming one of the richest traffickers in the city.[60] In interviews with TC members of the era, they told me that in addition to these "business disagreements," Espadão had also killed Linho's cousin who had attempted to use his territory to invade Nova Holanda without his approval. They also suspected that a dispute over a woman may have also contributed to the final break between the two men.[61]

At the same time, the alliance between TC and ADA was falling apart at the highest levels. On September 11, 2002, Fernandinho Beira-Mar, one of the leaders of the CV faction, with the assistance of several prison guards, gained entry to ADA's prison block in Bangu I (Rio's maximum security prison), where he and his accomplices proceeded to execute (by burning alive) Uê and several other ADA leaders in their prison cells.[62] After hearing of the death of their faction's leadership and the possible betrayal by one of their own, Celsinho of Vila Vintém, who had miraculously survived the attack unscathed, Espadão decided to form a new splinter faction with another Dono, a man nicknamed Matemático from Senador Camará, another neighborhood in the Zona Oeste of the city. They resolved not to make any pacts with any other factions – hence, they added the word *Puro* ("Pure") to the name to create Terceiro Comando Puro.[63] For his part, Linho, upon hearing of the massacre of his former accomplices, allegedly sent a wreath to lay on Uê's grave which read: "*Saudades, do amigo fiel, Linho*" (I miss you, from your faithful friend, Linho).[64] He switched factions, immediately becoming ADA's most powerful Dono and inheriting several of Uê's former territories.[65]

Thus, TC in Maré split in two. Former allies became enemies as violence exploded between the newly converted TCP, which retained control of the historic territories, and ADA, which controlled the housing projects. TCP began invading the housing projects even as shootouts and violence continued with their CVNH rival to the north. ADA responded by mounting invasions into TCP territory. Kito, the former TC Dono, who had spent the intervening years in prison, was released around this time but both Espadão and Linho refused to give him back his territories. Kito eventually joined Linho's ADA as a gerente and would spend the last several years of his life planning and executing invasions of his former turf.[66] The violence became so intense that there were

---

[60] *CrimeNews* 3/19/2015.
[61] Luiz 7/31/14; Josué 7/22/2014.
[62] *O Globo* 9/12/2002.
[63] Bruno 10/27/2014; Mateo 1/13/2015.
[64] *O Globo* 9/20/2002.
[65] *O Globo* 9/12/2002.
[66] Luiz 7/29/2014; Josué 7/15/2014; Bruno 10/6/2014; *O Globo* 10/10/2007.

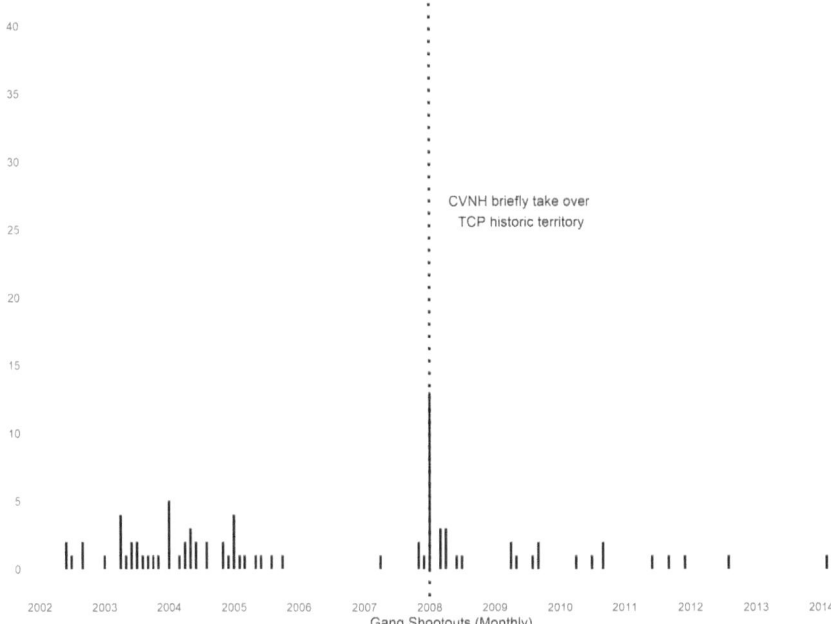

FIGURE 7.3 Gang shootouts in TCP historic territory (monthly)
Data from *Disque-Denúncia*. Visualization by Pranjal Drall.

even allegations (unsubstantiated) that Linho solicited the help of Angolan refugees and former rebels to train his members in insurgency tactics.[67]

Shootouts became a daily occurrence in both the housing projects and the favela neighborhoods. The DD dataset documents much of this violence as the two territories exhibit frequent shootouts from the end of 2002 until the middle of 2005 (see Figures 7.3 and 7.4). In the housing projects, ADA's territory, violence peaked in March 2003 with forty shootouts reported just that month, the highest reported levels in all Maré for the entire period of 2002–14 (see Figure 7.5). According to residents and gang members alike, it was common for TCP to climb onto the rooftops on the Morro and shoot down into the housing projects below, not bothered by whether the bullets hit gang members or residents. In response, ADA would shoot back from the roofs of apartment buildings in Conjunto Pinheiro. Bento Ribeiro Dantas, caught between the two gangs firing at each other, even became known by the nickname *"fogo cruzado"* (crossfire) because bullets were so frequently passing over the community from each side.

In fact, TCP vacated its presence within Bento Ribeiro Dantas almost entirely during this period because it was too vulnerable an area to control.

---

[67] *O Globo* 4/4/2004.

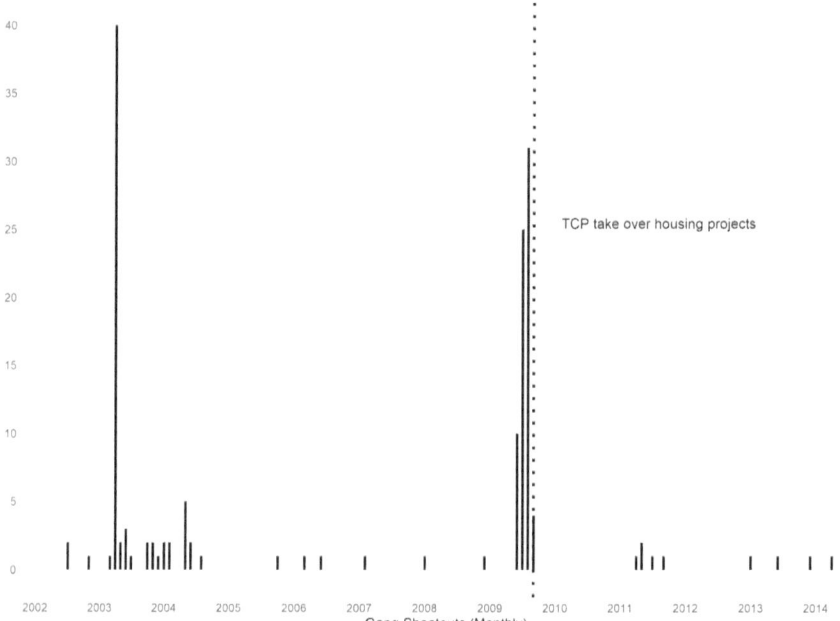

FIGURE 7.4 Gang shootouts in TCP housing projects (monthly)
Data from *Disque-Denúncia*. Visualization by Pranjal Drall.

According to Mateo, the gang tried to install a boca and security check-points in the community after the conflict with ADA started but there was nowhere for the gang members to escape if their rivals invaded or if the police mounted an operation. The gang tried several times to maintain a stronger presence there but each time lost personnel and significant amounts of drugs. In the end, they decided to leave the community. This example demonstrates both the strategic logic of the gang and the importance of geography in how gangs govern their territories. Although TCP surely wanted to maintain the drug trade in Bento Ribeiro Dantas, they found it too costly, at least for a while.[68]

Espadão and his primary gerente, Bração, would be arrested at the end of 2003 and the security environment would become even worse for the remnants of TCP.[69] In interviews with gang members who joined or were already members during this period, they recalled the extremely high levels of violence they were subject to. For instance, Fulton described becoming a gang member in 2000. "At first, I started out as a lookout, then became a seller, then a soldado

---

[68] By the time I lived in Maré, they had reinstalled a small boca at the far end of the community, as far away from Linha Amarela and as close to the Morro as possible (see Figure 7.1).
[69] *O Globo* 12/13/2003.

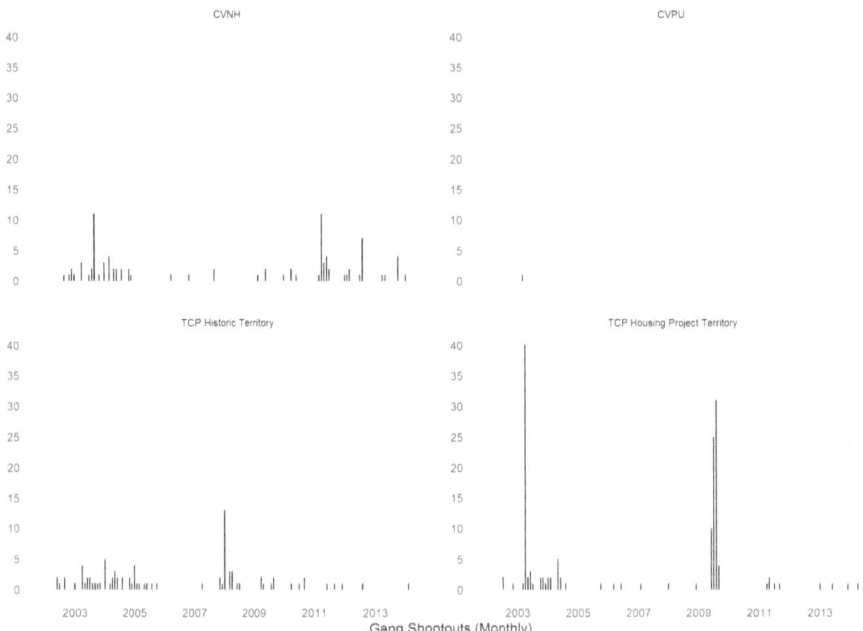

FIGURE 7.5 Shootouts in Maré's gang territories (monthly)
Data from *Disque-Denúncia*. Visualization by Pranjal Drall.

and even a gerente for a while but I didn't like it because you have to manage your friends. So I decided to stay a soldado." I asked if being a soldado was a lot more dangerous especially when they were fighting a war. "No," he said, "because when the enemy comes in, they'll kill you whether you have a gun in your hand or not. I lost a lot of friends and comrades during those years. It was a tough time. We could never relax," he said.[70]

Eventually, ADA would weaken. By 2005, Linho had disappeared. For several years, he had been Rio's most wanted man and was forced to be permanently on the run. He frequently moved around to his different territories in Rio and to São Paulo, where he allegedly had many contacts.[71] It is still unknown what happened to Linho. Some I interviewed said that he got plastic surgery and lives a life of luxury abroad.[72] Others heard that he owns a gas station somewhere and lives a normal life.[73] Either way, since the early 2000s, Linho had not spent much time in Maré and provided little leadership to the local gang. Instead, a man nicknamed Samson, Linho's gerente geral, was left in charge. In November 2005, he too was arrested after

[70] Fulton 7/3/2014; Josué 7/15/2014; Luiz 7/31/2014.
[71] *O Globo* 9/22/2002.
[72] Thiago 1/9/2015.
[73] Mateo 1/13/2015.

organizing years of invasions and shootouts in TCP's territory. He had been hiding in one of Linho's subterranean bunkers for several years, only emerging at night to lead invasions and defend his territory. He allegedly offered police R$1 million to let him go when they finally captured him.[74]

Residents of both the TCP and ADA territories suffered much during these years. Stray bullets killed at least a dozen residents who were not involved in the drug trade.[75] One resident of Vila do João at the time said, "My four daughters and I lay on the floor many nights praying for fear of the shootouts. I want to sell my house, but no one would even pay a dollar to live here."[76] The violence became so constant that dozens of families living in TCP's territory eventually fled the area, preferring to live in abandoned warehouses and factories without running water or electricity outside of Maré than subject themselves to living in a warzone.[77]

The two gangs once again restricted the movement of residents. Mateo, who lived in Bento Ribeiro Dantas, told me, "It was really difficult because most of us had family or girlfriends or boyfriends in Pinheiro or Vila do João. The gangs prohibited anyone from crossing over. Only older people could do so and generally only during the day. ADA killed or beat people when they caught them."[78] Naldo, who lived in Baixa do Sapateiro, recalled being stopped and asked to open his backpack by TCP members he was friends with. He told me they were being dominated by their rivals at the time and had become so paranoid they even searched people they knew.[79]

In interviews with longtime TCP members, they described how the gang also became especially sadistic during this period. Thiago and Luiz recalled that they were "surrounded by enemies," and were always afraid of losing their territory which, they thought, explained why they killed and punished a lot more.[80] Even women, normally spared the most brutal forms of violence, were not exempt. In one episode, TC executed three women because of a connection they had to their CVNH rival. These murders were, supposedly, in revenge for the deaths of five of TCP's members.[81] In the cruelest incident, a thirteen-year-old girl was tortured and killed by TCP members for dating a rival ADA member. According to interviews and media reports, TCP members took her from her home, gang raped her, then made her walk naked through the streets before tying her up and beating her to death.[82]

---

[74] *O Globo* 11/5/2005.
[75] *O Globo* 3/6/2003; 5/7/2003; 7/9/2003; 1/23/2004; 8/16/2004; 11/4/2004.
[76] *O Globo* 1/23/2004.
[77] *O Globo* 1/31/2005.
[78] Mateo 1/13/2015.
[79] Naldo 12/17/2014.
[80] Luiz 7/30/2014; Thiago 1/9/2015.
[81] *O Globo* 3/25/2000.
[82] Osvaldo 1/7/2015; Mateo 1/13/2015; *O Globo* 12/17/2003.

Even the most powerful and well-connected residents became targets. For instance, in late 2004, at the height of intergang violence, TCP members murdered the president of the Association of AMs in Maré (UNIMAR) because he was involved in the distribution of food baskets in communities that were controlled by CV.[83] The TCP gang, struggling to gather the resources necessary to arm themselves and defend their territory even began to extract payments from local institutions, including health posts.[84] In 2003, Espadão demanded a weekly "protection" payment of R$30,000 from the Vila Olímpica, a state-sponsored athletic facility where an estimated 12,000 children practiced a variety of sports. The Director of the Vila Olímpica refused to pay and the facility was forced to shut its doors for a period.[85] Such outright extortion, which was far outside the bounds of the existing social contract between the gang and the community, demonstrates once again how the governance arrangement had thoroughly broken down during this period. It should perhaps come as no surprise that Espadão was arrested less than a week after the Vila Olímpica was shuttered, the result of a series of denunciations by residents to DD.[86]

Following the split between TCP and ADA, police operations became even more militarized and intense. During three months in mid-2003, confrontations between gangs and police were so frequent that two police were killed and thirty-eight injured.[87] In other cases, police responded by taking control of areas of Maré for several days or even a week or more, carrying out numerous search-and-seizure operations in an attempt to put an end to the violence.[88] Then, in June 2003, the 22nd Military Police Battalion was installed in CVNH's territory. In the year preceding the installation, the major avenues bordering Maré had been shut due to gang violence no less than forty-one times, causing huge problems for travelers and businesses throughout the city.[89] The Battalion did not, however, immediately reduce violence and improve public security in Maré. In its first year, the violence persisted and nightly shootouts between TCP, ADA, and CVNH continued.[90] In just the first two months of the Battalion's existence, there were sixty-six violent deaths in Maré.[91] The public security apparatus intensified their enforcement efforts even further by increasing the number of police permanently stationed in Maré from 100 to 240 in 2004.[92]

[83] *O Globo* 2/11/2005.
[84] *O Globo* 2/11/2005.
[85] Artur 3/17/2014; *O Globo* 12/9/2003.
[86] *O Globo* 12/13/2003.
[87] *O Globo* 4/4/2004.
[88] *O Globo* 5/18/2003; 7/26/2003; 10/12/2003; 4/4/2004.
[89] *O Globo* 7/1/2003.
[90] *O Globo* 10/12/2003; 1/23/2004; 8/16/2004; 11/29/2004.
[91] *O Globo* 10/12/2003.
[92] *O Globo* 1/22/2004.

Tyrant (2005–2009)

Eventually, the cumulative effects of increased policing efforts and several years of intergang violence led to a weakening of TCP. "At one point, we only had one *fuzil* (rifle) and there were just a small number of men still involved," Josué said.[93] According to Naldo, a longtime resident of TCP's territory, during these years, "There wasn't anyone in the community who was known to be in charge, and nobody had any leadership skills."[94] TCP's territory would remain insecure for much of this period as ADA and CVNH would continue to make sporadic invasions, looking to take over the area and kill the remaining TCP members. In 2007, for example, Kito led a group of two dozen ADA members in an invasion of the Morro. They took a family hostage in an attempt to use their house as a base for further attacks but the plan was quickly discovered and they were eventually surrounded and arrested by police.[95] In 2008, CVNH even managed to conquer TCP's entire territory and raise their flag on top of the Morro as described in Chapter 5.

That said, the threat from ADA and CVNH was not consistently active for this period like it had been during the years of warfare (2002–2005). Although the gang refrained from the most extreme forms of coercion, they continued to focus what few resources they had on defending their territory (monitoring borders, punishing anyone suspected of disobedience, etc.), largely forgetting about the well-being of the community and providing few benefits to residents.[96]

Another reason why TCP failed to provide responsive benefits was that they began to develop a more collaborative relationship with the police. TC had once maintained the most antagonistic relationship of any of Maré's gangs with the police and, as a result, had been the focus of active enforcement efforts for many years. However, Linho had laid the foundation for more collusive relations with some police, counting on them for protection and support even as his gang engaged in confrontations with other segments of the public security apparatus.[97] TCP would eventually develop highly collaborative arrangements with police. In fact, perhaps one of the only reasons TCP was not conquered during this period was due to the willingness of police in the 22nd Battalion to engage in constant operations when one of TCP's rivals tried to take over their territory. For example, in two large-scale invasions in 2007 by ADA and in 2008 by CVNH, it was the police that had eventually ended those invasions and prevented the takeover. The relationship between TCP and the police would only deepen over time.

---

[93] Josué 7/22/2014.
[94] Naldo 12/17/2014.
[95] *O Globo* 10/10/2007.
[96] Osvaldo 1/7/2015; Breno 10/2/2013.
[97] *O Globo* 6/22/2003.

In 2007, Bração, TCP's gerente geral, was offered an "extramural benefit" during his prison sentence. He walked out and never returned.[98] At the time, TCP was still very weak but Bração slowly began to organize the group. According to Naldo, Bração came into the store where he worked one day in 2008. "I couldn't believe it. He was right there in front of me! He wanted to throw a big party for Carnaval and asked if he could rent some equipment. He started to throw some parties and the gang began making more money and buying more weapons."[99] Unlike most members, who join gangs in their early adolescence and have little formal education, Bração completed high school and even had some further training from a short stint in the military.[100] In addition to organizing parties, he began to instruct his gang how to use some of the tactics he had learned.[101] Daniel and Fulton both remembered doing workouts (pushups and running) as well as some tactical exercises on the football fields. "Bração is very intelligent. He knew military tactics. Whenever we had shootouts, he always knew the right strategy," Daniel said.[102]

In early 2009, TCP went on the offensive against ADA. "We started by attacking different areas of Vila do Pinheiro. They weren't full invasions. We were just probing their defenses, trying to figure out how to weaken them," Fulton said.[103] Then, in April of that year, Espadão was also released from prison on a work permit and immediately fled. Together with Matemático of Senador Camará, with whom he had founded the TCP faction, and Bração's newly trained gang, they planned an all-out invasion of ADA's territory for the end of May.[104] "They got a bunch of people together," Naldo recalled. "They even enlisted guys not normally involved, who worked as *mototaxi* (motorcycle taxis) or *kombi* (van) drivers. They were all promised a lot of money if they helped them take it over. They all went down to Pinheiro together."[105] TCP also paid police at the Battalion R$130,000 to drive them into ADA's territory in their armored trucks.[106]

On May 30th, the gang commenced their invasion and managed to gain a foothold in Vila do Pinheiro, killing two of the ADA gerentes in the process.[107] Block-to-block fighting continued over the next two weeks as TCP pushed ADA back into Vila do João and Conjunto Esperança. More than fifteen were

---

[98] *O Globo* 4/27/2013.
[99] Naldo 12/17/2014.
[100] *O Globo* 4/27/2013. The involvement of former military personnel in drug-trafficking gangs in Rio is not rare (Varsori 2021).
[101] *O Globo* 12/13/2003.
[102] Daniel 8/21/2014.
[103] Fulton 7/3/2014.
[104] *O Globo* 6/1/2009.
[105] Naldo 12/17/2014.
[106] *O Globo* 6/12/2009.
[107] Bruno 10/27/14.

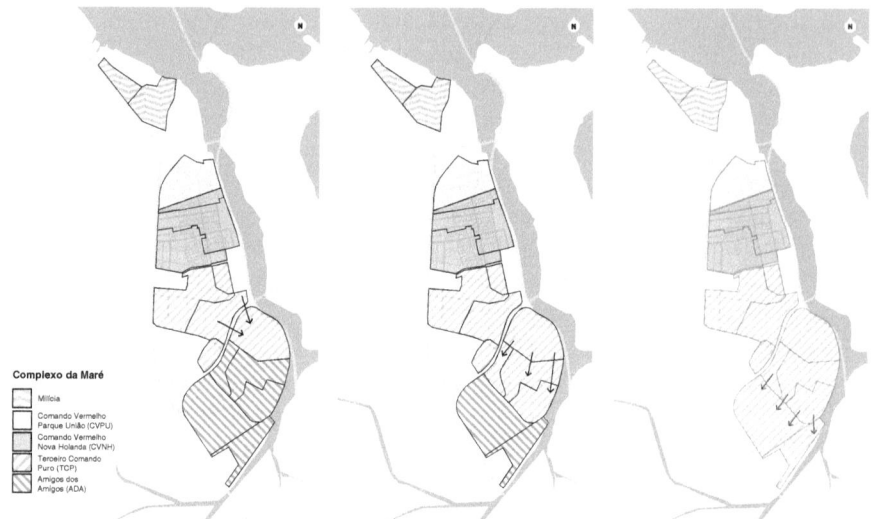

FIGURE 7.6 TCP conquest of housing projects, 2009
Visualization by Bruna Montuori.

killed in the confrontations, including several residents and police.[108] Over
the course of the next several months, TCP and ADA continued to engage
in shootouts and invasions. Finally, in September, TCP forced the remaining
members of ADA out of the area entirely, killing Kito, the former TC Dono, in
the process (see Figure 7.6).[109] TCP had finally defeated their rival, more than
tripling the area they controlled, and increasing the population they governed
by some 45,000 residents, once again dramatically changing their security
environment and criminalized governance practices.

Laissez-Faire (2009–14)

Like previous territorial conquests, TCP first sought to cleanse the area of anyone who may have provided information and support to ADA.[110] Lucas said
that residents with connections to the former gang have to suffer consequences
because otherwise they will provide information to their enemy.[111] Both Josué
and Luiz said that the gang killed roughly thirty residents suspected of such
connections over the next couple of years. "We killed the men but if it was a
woman, it depended on what they said."[112] I asked how they knew who had

---

[108] *O Globo* 6/1/2009; 6/2/2009; 6/12/2009; 6/13/2009.
[109] *O Globo* 9/17/2009; *O Dia* 9/17/2009.
[110] Valdemir 1/9/2015.
[111] Lucas 9/20/2013.
[112] Josué 7/22/2014.

these connections. "The other residents in the community denounced them," Luiz said.[113] Davi described the process in this way:

The people who were involved [with the former gang] were already gone. They had left on their own. That's why you often see families leaving with all their clothes and furniture when a new group takes over... The rest stay quiet until they know you're going to stick around. So we start selling and get some of the local kids involved. Then the families that are suffering will give you information if you give them some handouts and resolve problems for them. But sometimes a resident who doesn't like their neighbor will say they were involved with your enemy... You have to analyze these claims carefully. You have to keep your head... You don't just show up and kill someone because they are fighting with their neighbor. They could be using you.[114]

In this way, residents can exploit the new gang to punish other residents or try to manipulate them for their own benefit. A gang that does not restrain itself may end up alienating the local population or creating a set of perverse dynamics. Either way, whom a gang targets relies almost entirely on information provided by residents, once again demonstrating how criminalized governance (both benefits as well as certain forms of coercion) is coproduced by gangs and residents.

Despite their efforts to cleanse their territory of would-be enemies, TCP members also felt there was not a lot of allegiance to the former gang and that it was not difficult to win over the local population. Josué thought that residents were dissatisfied with their treatment by ADA.[115] According to Fulton, "ADA had lost the respect of the residents. When we took the area, a bunch of people seemed really happy. They invited us into their houses. One woman cooked us dinner and told us to never leave."[116] Valdemir, a longtime resident of Vila do João, felt similarly, "By the end, ADA was really weak. Something had broken their internal structure."[117]

While there seemed to be relatively little resident support for the former ADA gang, TCP needed to establish networks of information and support that they could rely on. Most importantly, they needed a huge number of new recruits to consolidate control of these territories and expand the drug trade. Some of the younger ADA members chose to stay behind and asked to be integrated into TCP.[118] Incorporating members of a rival gang is a risky strategy but given TCP's demand for labor and the desire to make a rapid and smooth transition – they needed personnel with intimate knowledge of these communities – some of these young men were allowed to join.[119] I asked

[113] Luiz 7/30/2014.
[114] Davi 9/9/2013.
[115] Josué 7/22/2014.
[116] Fulton 7/3/2014.
[117] Valdemir 1/9/2015.
[118] Thiago 1/9/2015.
[119] Thiago 1/9/2015; Valdemir 1/9/2015.

Fulton how the gang incorporated these new members into the organization. "It's the same as a firm or a corporation. We hired new people and if they proved themselves and were loyal, we gave them more responsibility," he replied.[120]

In the end, the number of gang members in the TCP organization grew to more than 200. TCP installed more than a dozen new bocas in the housing projects (see Figure 7.2), which quickly led to significant drug sales. Eventually, the gang's weekly revenue ballooned to an estimated R$3 million.[121] With the expansion of their territory, the TCP gang also shifted its structure. Instead of being organized solely according to the drug trade (see Figure 5.2, for example), TCP shifted to a more geographic structure (see Figure 7.7). Each neighborhood had its own *gerente de comunidade* (community manager) that answered directly to the gerente geral. Drugs were still packaged by each of the drug and gerentes de preço but then were distributed to each gerente de comunidade by the gerente geral instead of directly to the bocas.[122] Fulton described how it worked: "He [gerente geral] gives them [gerentes de comunidade] the packages and tells them how much they owe. The gerente de comunidade then distributes the *cargas* (bags of drugs) to the various gerentes de boca and vapores in their area."[123] He and other gang members reported that there were seven such gerentes de comunidade across TCP's territory, two in their historic territories and five in the housing projects.[124] "They have frequent meetings with the gerente geral about the vision of the gang and the management of business," Fulton said.

The remnants of ADA would find refuge in Caju, a set of favelas just to the south of Maré, controlled by another ADA gang. They would try to retake this area of Maré a couple of times over the next five years but, according to Josué, the manager of the soldiers at the time, "There was no way they could come back. We had too many rifles."[125] Despite this periodically active threat from ADA, TCP did not seem particularly concerned about invasions when I visited these communities during fieldwork. Overall, as described earlier, their presence was more discrete and relaxed than their

---

[120] Fulton 7/3/2014.
[121] Josué 7/22/2015. This estimate is likely high but according to reports, a similarly sized favela, Rocinha, allegedly sold R$10 million worth of drugs per month, so the estimate is plausible (*Extra* 11/20/2013).
[122] Fulton 7/3/2014.
[123] According to TCP members, weekly earnings for each of the positions were estimated to be: gerente de comunidade R$3,000–12,000 depending on the community, gerente de preço R$1,500–2,000, gerente de boca R$1,000–1,500 depending on how much they sold, vapor R$500–700 also depending on how much they sold (those stationed at busy bocas allegedly made upwards of R$1,500), soldados R$500–700, olheiros R$200–300, and endoladores R$150.
[124] Fulton 7/3/2014; Josué 7/22/2014; Luiz 7/31/2014.
[125] Josué 7/22/2014.

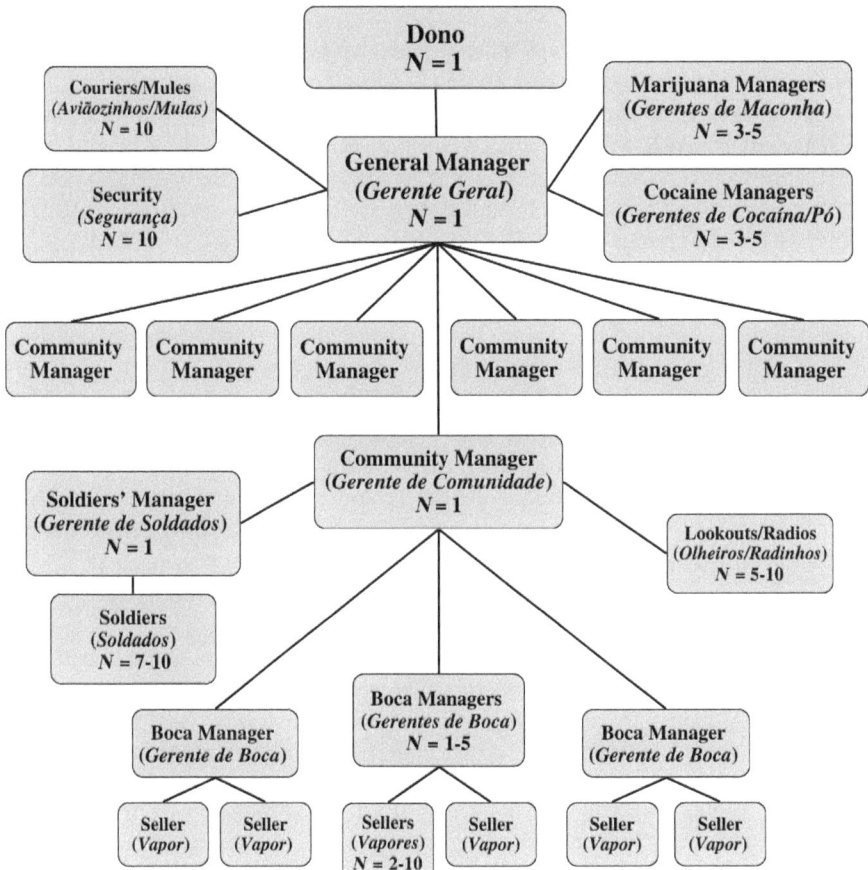

FIGURE 7.7 Organizational structure of TCP after conquest of housing projects
Visualization by author. N is the estimated number of gang members for each role.

CVNH counterparts.[126] They continued to monitor the entrances to their territory but I never heard of the gang questioning or threatening anyone. Some heavily armed TCP gang members could regularly be seen along one of the major roads in Vila do João, where they would often congregate around one of the main bocas. They could also be seen moving through their territory on motorcycles, but this area was not nearly as ostentatious as Nova Holanda.

The conquest and consolidation of territorial control in the housing projects would also change the nature of criminalized governance in TCP's historic territories. First, confrontations along the border with CVNH quickly ceased as CVNH learned not to provoke a larger, better-funded, and police-supported gang. Luiz described this as being all about "*dissuasão*" (deterrence). "We

---

[126] Thiago 1/9/2014.

increased our empire and CVNH knew this. It's the logic of war (*lógica bélica*)," he said.[127] TCP would face decreasing levels of rival threat as invasions into their territory stopped almost completely after 2009. The denunciation data clearly demonstrates the massive reduction in the violent encounters between TCP and their rivals following 2009 though there continued to be the occasional shootout reported, roughly one or two per year (see Figure 7.3). Overall, these are the lowest levels of inter-gang violence in these neighborhoods for the twelve years (2002–14) collected.

Even in the areas bordering Nova Holanda, the coercive tendencies of TCP diminished considerably. In the time I spent in this area, there were few gang members located at security checkpoints along this border. According to Luiz, a longtime TCP member, the visibility of weapons and gang personnel on the street had historically served as a reminder to residents that any "vacilação" would be dealt with harshly but that these tendencies had diminished considerably after their expansion.[128] Only once in my time living in Maré did I hear of TCP stopping someone and asking where they were from.[129] TCP members were also less often seen riding their motorcycles up and down the streets of their historic neighborhoods and it was rare to view large groups of heavily armed gang members surrounding their bocas.

In addition, the use of the most violent forms of punishment had been curtailed. Residents and gang members could recall few instances of extremely violent punishments in recent years. Nearly all the noteworthy examples of punishment that they told me about occurred during past periods of instability and violent intergang competition. Finally, movement between the different areas became much easier. For one, the border between TCP and ADA disappeared entirely. In addition, crossing over the border between TCP and CVNH became possible again. As a result, many families were reconnected, businesses had access to new customers, and people of all ages could visit friends and experience culture they had been prohibited from enjoying. After their short-lived peace agreement and TCP's attempt to invade and conquer Nova Holanda, CVNH had become more vigilant in their monitoring of the border while TCP continued to maintain a more relaxed approach. For the next several years, until the occupation of the Maré by the military, TCP was the primary aggressor as it attempted several invasions of Nova Holanda. CVNH was mostly on the defensive during these years.

As the city of Rio prepared to host the World Cup (2014) and the Olympic Games (2016), the entire public security apparatus began to focus heavily on the CV faction. Maré was no exception. The DD data on police operations in

---

[127] Luiz 7/29/2014.
[128] Luiz 7/31/2014.
[129] It occurred immediately following the violent encounter I witnessed in October 2013 (Breno 10/23/2013).

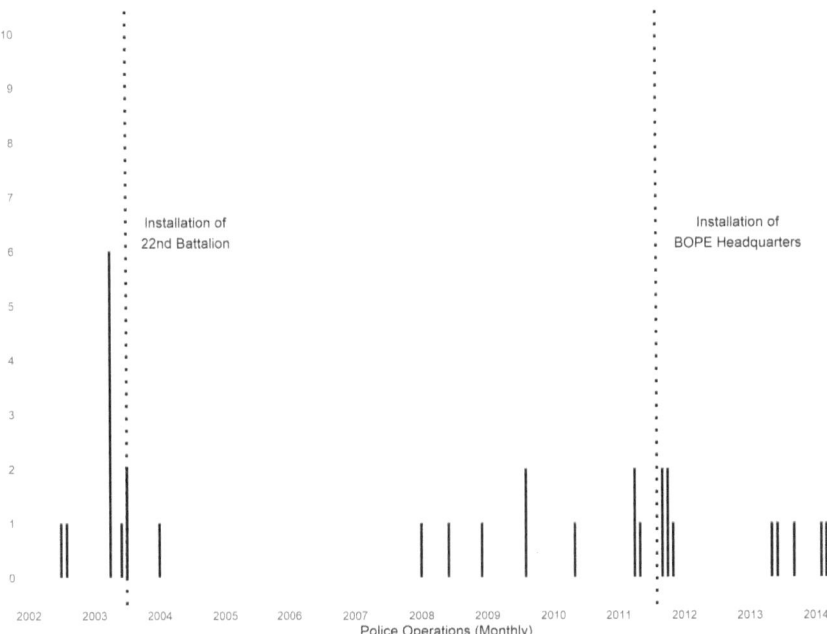

FIGURE 7.8   Police operations in TCP historic territory (monthly)
Data from *Disque-Denúncia*. Visualization by Pranjal Drall.

both TCP's territories show a different trajectory as compared to the two CV gangs (see Figure 7.10). First, there are far more operations in the first few years of the series likely owing to the police's attempts, especially following the installation of the 22nd Battalion in 2003, to prevent TCP-ADA confrontations from spilling out onto the surrounding highways (see Figures 7.8 and 7.9). Second, while there are still several operations reported later in the series, especially after the installation of BOPE's headquarters in 2011, many of these denunciations by residents mention that the operations are *"simulada"* (simulated) or *"uma farsa"* (a hoax), that the police had already informed TCP that there would be an operation, or that gang members could even be seen "inside the caveirão talking and laughing with police."[130] Thus, the police operations reported in TCP's territory seldom resulted in enforcement. Such collaborative police-gang interactions were not reported in either of the CV territories.

Qualitative evidence further supports the DD data. TCP members described how they made regular payments to the 22nd Battalion. "We paid each *viatura* (patrol car). Some received R$500, others got R$1000. There were fifteen cars that we had to pay every week," Fulton said.[131] According to Josué, "The

---

[130] DD 12/8/2008; 10/13/2011; 9/6/2012; 5/14/2013; 2/26/2014.
[131] Fulton 7/3/2014.

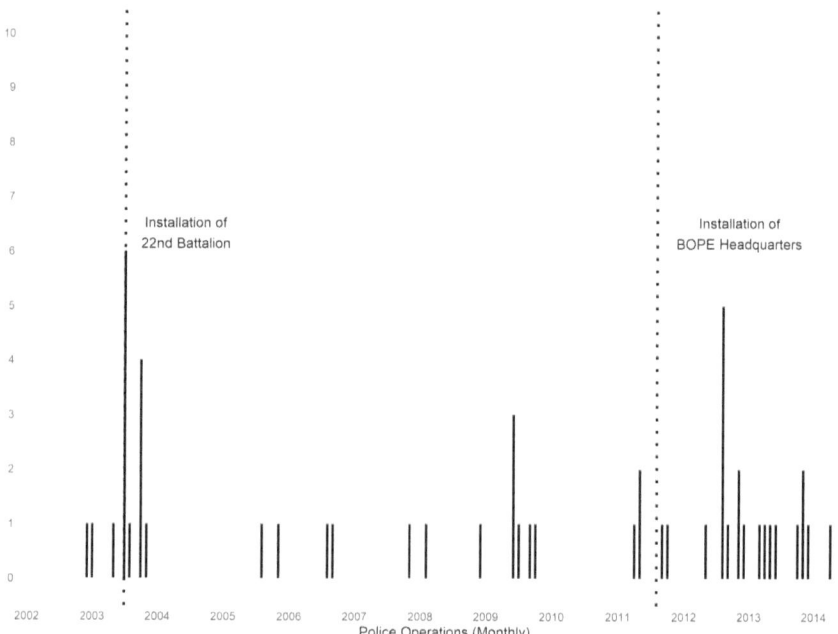

FIGURE 7.9 Police operations in TCP housing projects (monthly)
Data from *Disque-Denúncia*. Visualization by Pranjal Drall.

arrego (bribe) was usually paid under the Linha Amarela bridge. Their car
would pull up and a mototaxi would make the drop-off."[132] In exchange,
police operations would only occur between Monday and Thursday and the
gang received notice of when and where such operations would take place.[133]
When I asked if they ever did not pay, TCP members uniformly said they
always paid because they knew what would happen if they did not.

Gang members estimated the payments were, initially, between
R$30,000 and 60,000 per month before 2009.[134] These payments reached
the very highest levels within the Battalion as the Commander took a cut
and then distributed the rest throughout the Battalion.[135] According to
an investigation of these claims, TCP paid regular bribes to at least ten
police inside the 22nd Battalion.[136] The bribe amounts increased dramatically after TCP expanded their territory in 2009. According to Josué, the

---

[132] Josué 7/22/2014.
[133] Daniel 8/21/2014.
[134] Fulton 7/3/2014; Josué 7/22/2014.
[135] Artur 3/17/2104.
[136] *O Globo* 6/12/2009.

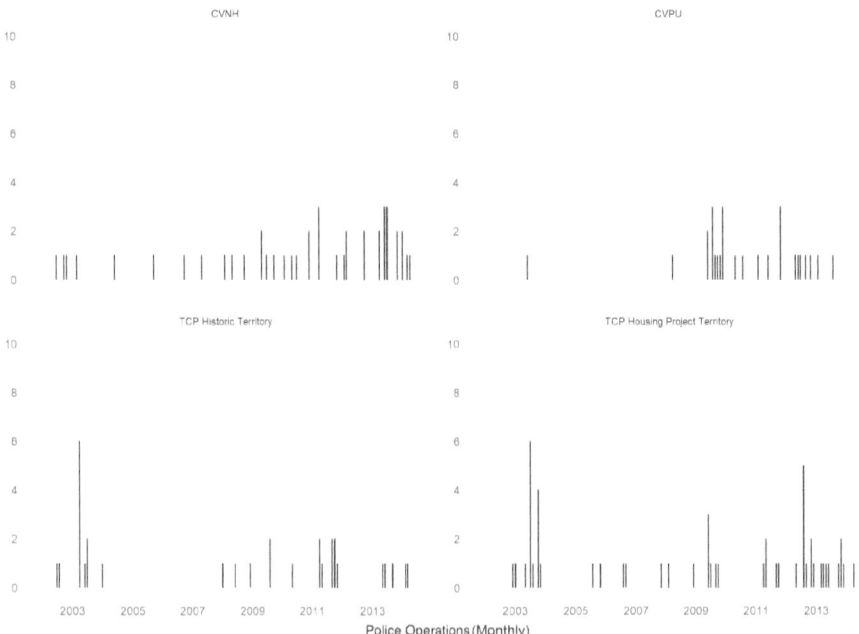

FIGURE 7.10 Police operations in Maré's gang territories (monthly)
Data from *Disque-Denúncia*. Visualization by Pranjal Drall.

gang paid an estimated 20 percent of their total weekly revenue after 2009, an estimated R$600,000.[137]

Even more surprising are the collaborative relations that TCP developed with BOPE. According to a series of internal investigations, BOPE maintained lucrative bribery schemes with gangs from all three factions.[138] In Maré, however, they only developed such collusive relations with TCP. One BOPE sergeant was documented providing information to TCP about upcoming operations, training gang members how to use various weapons, and even bringing a TCP member to a police outfitting center in 2012 where they purchased uniforms, camouflage, and other tactical gear to which only BOPE had access.[139] Although some BOPE operations would continue, enforcement against TCP can be considered largely absent for this period. The provision of benefits was irrevocably shaped by these dynamics.

Initially after taking over the housing projects, the TCP gang provided more responsive goods and services. Valdemir remembered gang members promising benefits to residents even before they had taken control of the area.

---

[137] Josué 7/22/2014.
[138] *O Globo* 6/12/2009; *Veja* 12/15/2015.
[139] *Veja* 7/6/2015; *O Dia* 7/7/2015.

"When they started invading, they promised to pay for more and that they would protect the favela. This always seemed strange to me because they were the ones invading and causing instability but there were a lot of residents that believed them."[140]

At least initially, the gang seems to have followed through on these promises. Josué said they made concerted efforts to help resolve problems for residents, organized bailes for the young people, and bought things that people needed. "I even said '*bom dia*' (good morning) to people as they passed me on the street," he recalled, chuckling.[141] Fulton also reported that the gang initially paid for a lot of cooking gas, food baskets, and medicine for families.[142] Thiago told me the gang would even give people a place to live when they first took back the territory.[143]

The gang also began organizing large baile funks in their new territories. They understood that gaining the confidence of youth in the area was essential to their rule there as these groups represented their recruitment base and were an important source of information and support within the community. In the couple of years following their conquest, TCP's baile funks in the housing projects became so popular that some famous football players even attended.[144] Bração also moved his family to this area of Maré, an important signal to residents that the gang was investing resources and better able to attend to local issues, thus, increasing his popularity and the gang's legitimacy within the area.[145] TCP also began hosting Mother's, Father's, and Children's Day festivities again with the help of local AM, offering food and drink to attendees as well as toys, candy, electronics and even laptops to residents.[146]

In fact, several of the AMs in this area sought out close connections with TCP after they took over. One of the AM presidents had even reportedly gotten 70 percent of the residents in their area to pay membership fees (an unprecedented rate) because they had such strong connections to the gang.[147] Another of the presidents kicked everyone out of the AM building when ADA made a surprise invasion in 2012, because they thought ADA members would probably come for them given their close relationship to the gang.[148] Like in

---

[140] Valdemir 1/9/2015.
[141] Josué 7/10/2014.
[142] Fulton 7/3/2014.
[143] Thiago 1/9/2015.
[144] *O Globo* 4/27/2013. One professional football player that attended one of these bailes was found flirting with one of Bração's girlfriends. He and his friend were kidnapped and tortured with electric shocks before being released. For her part, the girlfriend was shot five times in the leg. Bração allegedly apologized to his girlfriend – not to the footballer – for what he claimed was a "fit of jealousy" (*O Globo* 4/27/2013).
[145] Daniel 8/21/2014.
[146] Carlitos 10/2/2013.
[147] Vicente 11/6/2013.
[148] Breno 12/16/2014.

the other territories of Maré, these relations between the gang and the AM seem to be driven as much by the desire of the presidents to have the power of the gangs behind them than they are the gangs trying to gain access to the political and social capital of the AMs.

The period of more responsive services in this territory would quickly fade, however, and after less than a year, the gang had scaled back many of these services. According to Josué, it only took six months to really gain the confidence and support of the communities after which they did not need to focus as much on providing benefits.[149] The difference in the governance approach between the gang's two areas diminished as TCP's control of the housing projects became consolidated. First, the TCP became largely unresponsive to demands for dealing with interpersonal conflicts during this period. Carlitos commented on the fact that the gang had stopped resolving a lot of people's problems. "They got tired of doing this and now it's the AM that deals with most conflicts."[150] Breno agreed with this assessment, saying that it had been a while since the Dono sat in the plaza and resolved problems for people.[151] Lúcio, one of the AM presidents in TCP's territory admitted that he had taken over dispute resolution in the area. He described dealing with all sorts of problems, including issues with sewage, asphalt, water damage, and, in recent years, disputes between families and neighbors.[152] "I'm on call 24 hours a day!" he complained.

For their part, TCP members said that they no longer dealt with problems between men and women or between family members.[153] Even when they spoke of problems that they had resolved in recent years, they only spoke of the types of punishments they occasionally doled out. Henrique told me that the gang continued to shave the heads of women that got into fights.[154] Josué said that he had "*deu uma surra*" (given a beating) on a couple of occasions to deter "marginais" from engaging in smaller crimes.[155] Luiz described two problems he had been asked to resolve recently, one of which was a man that had sexually abused a child and the other was a girl who had stolen someone's camera. In each case, he had used violence to resolve the issue but wouldn't be more specific.[156] While other gangs in Maré will also engage in the violent punishment of individuals, they also deal with a much larger range of issues. Moreover, unlike the two CV gangs, TCP members did not describe the listening and adjudicating they had to engage in to make sure all parties were not angered by the result.

---

[149] Josué 7/10/2014.
[150] Carlitos 10/2/2013.
[151] Breno 10/2/2013.
[152] Lúcio 11/6/2013.
[153] Josué 7/22/2014; Daniel 8/21/2014.
[154] Henrique 12/8/2014.
[155] Josué 7/10/2014.
[156] Luiz 7/30/2014.

Despite their significant resources, the gang also provided less welfare and economic stimulation to the community. Osvaldo, for instance, said that the beneficial relationship that once existed with TC had been lost. "They used to offer help and assistance to the community, but I don't see much of this anymore. The gang doesn't care much for the residents anymore."[157] Like Maré's other gangs, there has been a general decline in the welfare provided by TCP due to the improving financial circumstances of many of the residents. Many no longer relied on the gang to make ends meet.[158] Despite similar trends in both the CV gang territories, each of those gangs found ways to provide welfare and services to residents by other means. TCP, meanwhile, significantly scaled back their welfare services within their territories and did not seek to provide the same kind of economic stimulation.

Many thought that TCP seemed less interested in using their resources to gain the allegiance and support of residents than they did in making money. For instance, Luiz reported that the Dono often took a cut from any major transactions occurring within these territories, such as when an investment came in for a construction project. "If it's going to cost R$50,000, he takes R$10,000," Luiz said.[159] Thiago, reflecting on the cause of this decline in gang welfare, argued it had everything to do with TCP's relationship to the police. He said that if the gang had a more antagonistic relationship with the police, like CV, they would have to pay out more welfare because residents could denounce them. "TCP is more interested in the game and making money than they are in confronting cops. They have even outlawed stealing outside the community to not bring attention to themselves. But they also don't provide assistance anymore," he told me.[160]

TCP also limited the forms of recreation that they offered to residents during this period. The weakening of TCP during the mid-2000s and the lack of the organizational capacity meant that bailes stopped entirely. When Bração was released from prison, he organized parties for a period of eight months or so. Naldo said this was more of an attempt to make money so that the gang could buy weapons to invade the ADA territory than it was to cultivate the support of the local population.[161] Although the gang threw bailes in the housing projects after their conquest, they no longer happened in their historic territories. Moreover, holiday parties also ceased in this area of their turf, demonstrating once again how little the gang felt it needed the support of residents.[162] Mateo contrasted TCP's more

---

[157] Osvaldo 1/7/2015.
[158] And yet, TCP has some of the poorest neighborhoods in Maré within their territory. Salsa e Merengue, Nova Maré, and Bento Ribeiro Dantas have the lowest development levels according to the most recent census (Redes da Maré 2019a, 22–23).
[159] Luiz 7/30/2014.
[160] Thiago 1/9/2015.
[161] Naldo 12/17/2014.
[162] Carlitos 10/2/2013.

distant and unresponsive governance style to that of the CV gang from Manguinhos, where his family had previously lived and where he was still a social worker. "In Manguinhos, they throw lots of parties for families and children and gave money to the community. They do everything for the community. They're still considered heroes there," he said. Unlike TCP, the CV gang in Manguinhos wanted to be the primary source of recreation, benefits, and financial assistance in the community.[163] Overall, TCP's unresponsive benefits and low levels of coercion during this period are indicative of a laissez-faire governance regime.

CONCLUSION

The TCP case further demonstrates how gangs strategically engage in governance in areas under their control. Specifically, the evolution of the TCP gang provides strong evidence regarding the causal relationship between rival threat, police enforcement, and criminalized governance. First, TCP's territorial control expanded and shrunk several times over the course of these two decades, resulting in dramatic shifts in their security environment and, consequently, their governance practices. On one hand, the fragmentation of the TC gang and the activation of rival threat had disastrous consequences on criminalized governance. It encouraged the use of extreme forms of violence not just against each other but also directed at residents and often at the police as well. The disorder created during these gangland wars should not be underestimated as violence pervaded these organizations and territories, sometimes spilling over into surrounding neighborhoods. Conversely, the conquest and consolidation of territorial control by a single gang had stabilizing effects as borders vanished and the possibility of an active rival threat receded. Although TCP continued to use violence and threats to cleanse their territories of ADA loyalists following the conquest of the housing projects, overall, the gang became much less coercive.

TCP's evolution also shows how gangs can shift their relationship to the police over time. The TC-turned-TCP gang directly confronted the police on numerous occasions (mostly amid wars with their rivals) for more than a decade. If anything, these tactics only called greater attention to the gang and its activities which then required even higher levels of support from the local population. An alternative response to active enforcement is to seek more collaborative relations with the police, curtailing enforcement at its source. This appears to have been a particularly successful strategy for TCP as it not only reduced the possibility of confiscation of illicit goods and the arrest or death of their members but helped the gang retain territorial control and even expand it. Once again, this case demonstrates how rival threat and enforcement are not mutually exclusive phenomena but can shape one another in myriad ways.

[163] Mateo 1/13/2015.

Finally, the conquest of the housing projects in 2009 demonstrates the highly strategic nature of criminalized governance. Even though they faced little possibility of enforcement because of their collaborative relations with the police, TCP nonetheless became more responsive in their newly conquered territories as they sought to gain the support of the community and expand their organization. They simultaneously used high levels of coercion and violence to eradicate any former allegiances to ADA despite the relative absence of a rival threat. This period, however, was short-lived. As TCP consolidated control of its new territories, the gang's governance activities became less coercive and responsive, settling into the patterns incentivized by their security environment.

8

Criminalized Governance during Military Occupation

Crack, maconha, pó! Crack, maconha, pó! Crack, maconha, pó!
Crack, marijuana, powder! Crack, marijuana, powder! Crack, marijuana, powder!
—Gang vapores shouting to advertise their product
during Maré's military occupation

INTRODUCTION

The night before the tanks rolled in, a bar in Nova Holanda stayed open late. A mixture of NGO workers, journalists, and residents filled the small establishment, spilling out into the street. The mood wasn't exactly festive, but people were drinking, eating, and chatting about what the future might hold. Just before dawn, I walked across the street and sat down on a cement bench. I was exhausted. Three adolescents came and sat on the curb near me. I recognized them as olheiros for the CVNH gang. These boys spent most of their days and nights watching the entrances to the gang's territory for police operations and rival invasions. They were the gang's eyes and ears and its first line of defense. As the first rays of sunlight hit the tops of the houses, they came over and shook my hand. Each of them. One by one. They were no older than twelve or thirteen. I was seated so our eyes met. "*Boa sorte!*" (Good luck!), one of them said and smiled. Then they went over to the other bar patrons and shook their hands as well. There was something funny about the formality of it, but we all understood what was happening. Along with a few dozen other boys of around the same age, these three were all that remained of the CV gang in Nova Holanda.[1] They were the last representatives of a form of order and an

---

[1] The more senior members of CVNH had already left, driven into exile by intensive police operations and the impending military occupation. In the preceding weeks, BOPE and a variety of

alternative rule of law that was coming to an end, at least for a while. The gang members knew that what came next was going to be a difficult period for them, but they seemed ready for it. I was not so sure if I was.

At 6 am, the military invaded. We heard the tanks before we saw them. They entered Maré from Avenida Brasil, their diesel engines rumbling as they came, accompanied by several companies of camouflaged soldiers on foot. Behind the tanks and the soldiers, followed another army of journalists who all wore helmets and bulletproof vests with *IMPRENSA* (PRESS) written in large block letters. The soldiers immediately spread out across Maré. Several journalists followed each squad, taking thousands of pictures and speaking with any residents they could find. I trailed one group at a distance as they moved through the deserted streets. A couple of soldiers always had their rifles aimed at the surrounding rooftops. The leader of the group frequently consulted his notebook, which presumably contained information on the locations of suspected gang members or their hiding places for guns and drugs.[2] Over the course of an hour or two, they searched several buildings each time exiting with nothing to show for it.

Late in the morning, I sat down on a curb as they searched a home at the end of an alley. An elderly man was sweeping his front stoop nearby. He pushed several cans and wrappers into a small pile before walking over to where I was sitting. We exchanged greetings and watched the troops for a moment. "How's it going be with the military here?" I asked. "I've heard they're abusive," he said, looking at the soldiers pointing their rifles at the surrounding rooftops. "I don't need the military on the street, I need someone to clean up the trash in front of my house," he muttered before returning to his sweeping.

The occupation of Maré by 2,500 army and marine soldiers was the culmination of Rio's UPPs, intended to recapture the state's ostensive control of hundreds of the city's favelas by imposing their physical force, repairing community–police relations, and integrating these neighborhoods further within the infrastructure and services of the city. The military's intervention in Maré occurred just two months before the start of the 2014 World Cup. The four community policing units that were supposed to be installed by the end of July would never materialize. Instead, the military occupied Maré for the next fifteen months, during which time they conducted frequent searches and seizures, around-the-clock patrols, and installed fixed and mobile checkpoints combined with "hearts-and-minds"-style counterinsurgency tactics. For this entire period, Maré's drug-trafficking gangs lost their territorial

---

other specialized police units had invaded homes, hid out on rooftops and in schools, eventually arresting 162 individuals suspected of involvement with the gangs (*UOL* 3/30/2014; 4/4/2014).

[2] In a subsequent meeting, Mariano Beltrame, the Public Security Secretary, described how warrants had been issued for "micro-regions" or 3–4 houses because they were unable to identify the exact houses of gang members (Meeting #9).

control, the ability to operate their open-air drug markets, and many of the forms of governance they had engaged in for most of the last three decades. And yet, when the military's tanks finally left, each of Maré's gangs reestablished their territorial control and resumed their routine drug-trafficking operations within a matter of hours. This chapter seeks to understand how Maré's gangs survived fifteen months of military occupation and the intensive efforts to weaken and dismantle them. What were the challenges that occupation presented for the gangs? How did they adapt to this new reality? And what can we learn from this period regarding criminalized governance?

By the time the military arrived, I had already been living in Maré for nine months. I would continue to live in Maré for another nine months, documenting the various strategies the military employed to combat the gangs and gain the support of the local population as well as how the gangs and residents responded to this dramatic shift in governance. I found that Maré's three gang organizations reacted in divergent ways to military occupation. TCP quickly remilitarized, attempted to maintain a significant presence on the streets of their territory, and even engaged in direct confrontations with the military. The governance regime in these territories during this period can be best described as disorder. CVNH, on the other hand, remained demilitarized throughout occupation though the gang would maintain a significant presence within their territory. The leaders of this gang returned to the community shortly after occupation and began engaging in some of the governance activities though without the monopoly of violence. This gang's regime approximates that of a social bandit. Finally, CVPU remained demilitarized and maintained a limited presence within their territory throughout the occupation period, most closely resembling a laissez-faire governance regime. Overall, I argue that these divergent gang responses were due to the distinct security threats which these organizations faced during occupation.

The chapter is organized as follows: I begin by describing the confluence of factors that led to the Brazilian military's intervention in Maré, then trace the process of occupation and the new form of order they implemented. Next, I analyze how each of Maré's gangs responded to the challenges of occupation, arguing throughout that the military lacked the capacity to fully expel or dismantle the gangs though their presence shifted the dynamics of rival competition and threat, producing the divergent gang responses observed. I conclude the chapter by evaluating the possibilities and limitations of military interventions to combat gangs and other OCGs.

AN EVOLVING STATE SECURITY APPARATUS

Following more than two decades of military dictatorship (1964–85), Brazil's 1988 constitution officially returned the Armed Forces to civilian control. At the same time, article 142 of the constitution, referred to as the *Garantia de Lei e Ordem* (Guarantee of Law and Order, hereon GLO), offered a path for the military to intervene in domestic affairs but only at the request of the President. In subsequent years, a series of laws refined the GLO framework to apply "after having exhausted the instruments for the preservation of public order" and only when the Military Police are "unavailable, inexistent or insufficient to the regular performance of their constitutional mission."[3] Despite this still rather vague criteria, the GLO clause has been invoked more than a dozen times over the years, including to provide security for mega-events, elections, visits by foreign dignitaries, and workers' strikes (Samset 2014). Several other GLO operations have targeted what were initially referred to as "opponent forces" but was later revised to "public order disturbance agents" (p. 8). In every case, this meant drug-trafficking gangs.

With the inauguration of the UPP program, the role of the military in domestic policing expanded even further. The Pacification methodology had four stages, the first two of which involved military personnel. In the first "tactical intervention" stage, elite police units (BOPE et al.) conducted massive assaults on gang-held favelas, which often involved the use of military tanks, helicopters, and soldiers. During the "stabilization" stage, soldiers and police then occupied the community and conducted weeks or, in some cases, months of sweeps and operations to find any remaining drugs, weapons, and gang members. The third and fourth stages of Pacification did not include military cooperation but involved the installation of new proximity policing units and the provision of social welfare, development projects, and infrastructure upgrading. The fourth stage, monitoring and evaluation, was never fully implemented in any of the UPPs.

Between 2008 and 2014, the city installed 38 separate UPPs that impacted more than 250 favelas with an estimated population of one million.[4] In the first couple of years, the UPPs were mostly installed in the favelas of the Zona Sul and city center but as the Pacification project moved further into the sprawling favelas of the Zona Norte, the military took on a more active role. For example, in late 2010, 800 army and marine soldiers occupied Complexo do Alemão, a set of a dozen favelas considered the CV headquarters outside of the prisons. *Operação Arcanjo* (Operation Archangel), as it was termed, was intended to be brief but ended up lasting for eighteen months during which time 8,764 Army soldiers rotated through service, conducting 63,489 patrols by foot, 48,142 by vehicle, as well as installing more than 4,000 roadblocks and checkpoints (Harig 2015b). Although Operation Archangel did not produce transformative improvements in the lives of Alemão's residents, the military's occupation was considered, by most accounts, successful. Both gang and police violence decreased precipitously and many residents preferred the

---

[3] *Ministério da Defesa* 1/31/2014, p. 18, 25.
[4] The Pacification program and methodology did not officially exist until 2011 but earlier favela takeovers by the police, such as Santa Marta, were integrated into the program.

presence of the military to that of the police (Savell 2014). The success of Operation Archangel set the stage for an even larger and more ambitious occupation of Complexo da Maré several years later.

Maré's occupation cannot be fully understood without also delving into the evolution of the Brazilian military. In 2004, then-President Luiz Inácio Lula da Silva, seeking to expand Brazil's profile internationally, sent several thousand troops to lead the new United Nations Stabilisation Mission in Haiti (MINUSTAH). The connections between this foreign military operation and domestic interventions are manifold. First, many of the troops stationed in Haiti would later be involved in Rio's Pacification program and, eventually, in the occupations of Alemão and Maré. In addition, the military's strategies to combat Haiti's gangs borrowed from and refined tactics the military had employed in previous GLO operations to combat Rio's gangs (Harig 2015b; Hoelscher and Norheim-Martinsen 2014). In particular, the *"pontos fortes"* (strongholds) approach to retaking gang territories by establishing footholds within these areas was a strategy developed in Rio then further refined in counter-gang operations in Port-au-Prince, later becoming the heart of the Pacification methodology (Harig 2015b, 144–45).

From a broader perspective, these tactics have been built on an emerging set of methodologies in counterinsurgency contexts – from Iraq and Afghanistan, in particular, as well as other UN "stabilization" missions – in which militaries combine the use of force with development and infrastructure projects to alleviate poverty (Muggah 2014). Such tactics and strategies have sometimes been referred to as post-COIN or as "softer" approaches to policing in violent urban contexts but others have argued that the rhetoric of governance and development merely masks the use of force and delays the implementation of more significant and transformative development policies (Müller and Steinke 2018; Siman and Santos 2018).

On March 31st, 2014, Defense Minister Celso Amorim, in the name of President Dilma Rousseff, transferred the authority over Complexo da Maré to the Brazilian Armed Forces beginning at midnight on April 4th. Once the intervention began, Rio's public security apparatus would no longer have jurisdiction over this area of the city. That is, the command passed to the General of the Armed Forces tasked with the occupation. Nonetheless, Maré's occupation proceeded with the intimate involvement of police personnel. More than 200 Military Police were even integrated into the military's force and numerous senior police officials accompanied the occupation.

After several years of planning, 2,050 soldiers from the Army's Airborne Infantry Brigade, 450 Marines, 200 Military Police, and an advanced tactical police squad from Rio's 21st Military Police Battalion, invaded and occupied Maré in the early morning of April 5th, 2014. Even before the actual occupation of the territory, the military set up a large base camp on the military grounds of the CPOR, the same military base from which officials had controlled and extorted the residents of Morro do Timbau for nearly four decades

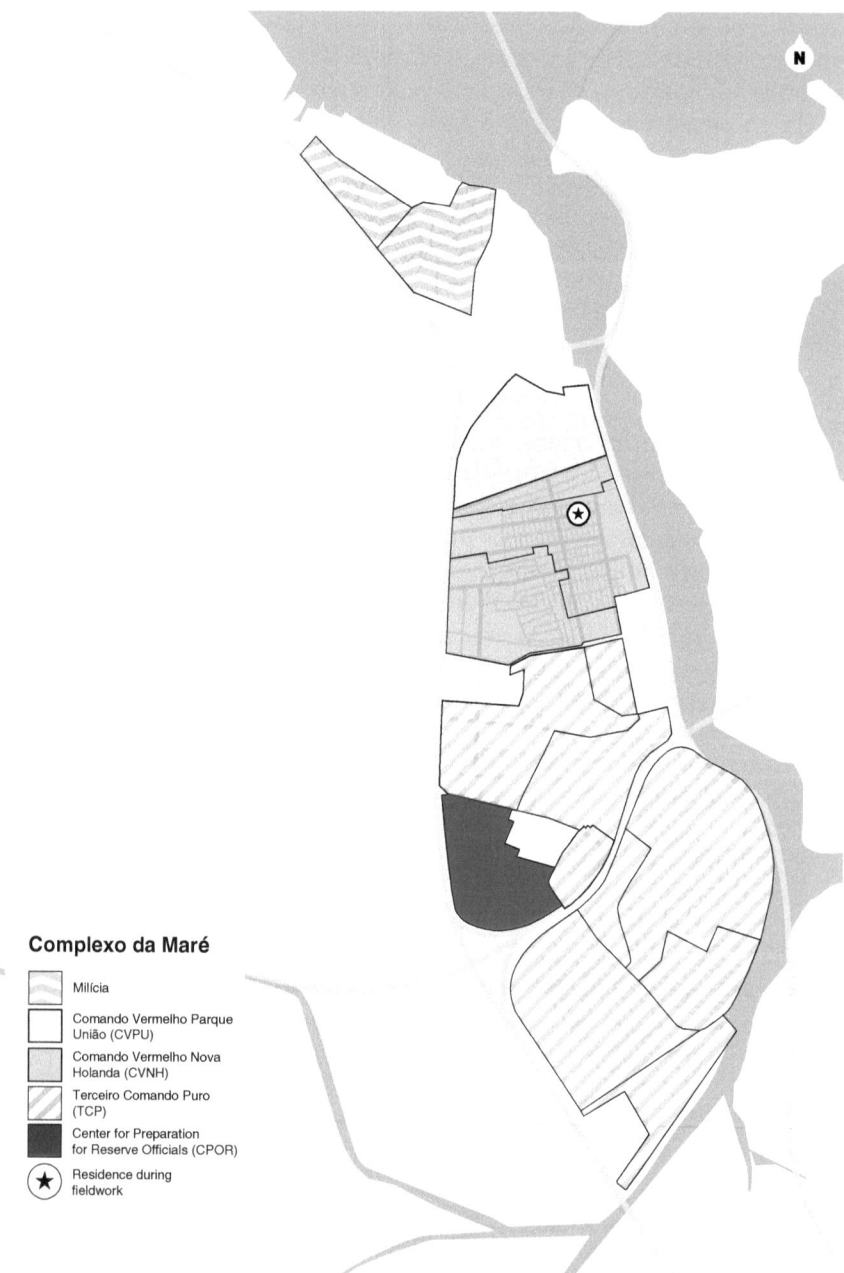

Complexo da Maré

☐ Milícia

☐ Comando Vermelho Parque
    União (CVPU)

☐ Comando Vermelho Nova
    Holanda (CVNH)

☐ Terceiro Comando Puro
    (TCP)

■ Center for Preparation
   for Reserve Officials (CPOR)

★ Residence during
   fieldwork

FIGURE 8.1 Map of Complexo da Maré during military occupation
Visualization by Bruna Montuori.

(see Chapter 4). They constructed dozens of rows of tents and barracks for the troops, who had undergone several weeks of training in GLO practices leading up to their deployment (Figure 8.1).

A NEW FORM OF ORDER

The military quickly imposed a new and very different form of order in Maré. Of the 2,500 soldiers permanently stationed there, 800 were "on duty" at any given time.[5] Some of these soldiers would be involved in support duties, such as cooking, cleaning, and the administration of the troop barracks at the CPOR. Meanwhile, 400–500 soldiers were assigned to mobile patrol units in which up to a dozen soldiers would ride in the back of jeeps and flatbed trucks, monitoring the main thoroughfares of each of the gang territories (see Figure 8.2). During the day, these mobile units also conducted on-foot patrols in many of the narrow streets and alleyways through which the vehicles could not pass (see Figure 8.3). At night, the jeeps and trucks were replaced with tanks and more heavily armored vehicles, which stayed exclusively on the main thoroughfares and were accompanied by roughly a dozen soldiers on foot (see Figure 8.4). According to the Commanding General Roberto Escoto, this "*saturação de operação de patrulhamento*" (saturation patrolling) strategy, in which units were moving through Maré's streets twenty-four hours a day, was necessary to avoid patrols becoming "static" and allowing the gangs to operate in areas where the military was not.[6]

Another hundred or so soldiers manned permanent checkpoints around Maré, many of which were strategically placed at entrance points, on major streets, and along the border between the TCP and CVNH territories. These spatialized tactics were intended to prevent gang members from moving freely within Maré and from engaging in any intergang violence. At the checkpoints, soldiers stopped and searched all cars, motorcycles, and persons for weapons and drugs. These searches were highly targeted and racialized. Darker-skinned adolescents and young men were disproportionately stopped and searched, a strategy the military assured residents was necessary because these young men were the most likely to "disturb public order."[7]

Over the course of nine months, I witnessed hundreds of these searches. The soldiers would select young men, ask them to put their hands on a wall or against a vehicle, and proceed to search their entire person and belongings. They would then inspect their bicycle, motorcycle, or car, while the young men waited. Some of my interlocutors were searched dozens if not hundreds of times during occupation. While many of these encounters were not antagonistic, the

---

[5] Meeting #21.
[6] *O Globo* 4/6/2014.
[7] Meeting #24.

FIGURE 8.2 Photograph of daytime military patrol during World Cup game
Photograph by Antonello Veneri.

FIGURE 8.3 Photograph of daytime military foot patrol
Photograph by Antonello Veneri.

FIGURE 8.4 Photograph of nighttime military patrol
Photograph by Antonello Veneri.

searches were a daily source of frustration for them.[8] "They [the soldiers] can treat us like that cause they're wearing the fatigues, but you take them off and you're just another guy like me from a poor family," Fulton told me.[9] Women and children, on the other hand, were less commonly searched. As for me, the military only stopped and searched me twice even though I passed through their checkpoints every day.

In addition to the imposition of force and the monopolization of violence in Maré, the military implemented a series of measures to gather intelligence. Building on similar tactics used by the American military in Iraq and Afghanistan, they organized a company of roughly 140 soldiers to gather intelligence about Maré's gangs and the local population.[10] The military encouraged residents to denounce gang activities to a hotline they created, *Disque Pacificação*, the number for which was emblazoned on the side of every military vehicle. According to officials, the hotline received 1,495 calls in the first seven months of occupation, though the number of denunciations had reportedly dropped to just a few dozen per month by July.[11]

---

[8] Fulton 7/3/2014; Breno 7/15/2014.
[9] Fulton 7/15/2014.
[10] *Driss Ghali* 8/11/2017.
[11] Meeting #26; *Montedo.com* 11/7/2014.

The military also immediately began to implement what can be termed a "hearts-and-minds" approach to governance. They engaged in a variety of initiatives to build relationships with local institutions and organizations, holding dozens of meetings with NGOs and representatives of Maré's sixteen AMs (see Figure 8.5). Some of these meetings included state representatives to help facilitate public services (roads, sewage, trash, education, health, etc.) while others were more social in their orientation. For instance, one afternoon, the highest-ranking military officers, including the Commanding General of the occupation forces, invited all the AM presidents to the CPOR for a barbecue with a roasted pig, caipirinhas, and a full buffet of food.[12] The military also engaged with some of the numerous Evangelical churches present in Maré, organizing several *cultos* (worship services) for the soldiers and with local congregations.[13]

Military officials also engaged with the broader public through a series of open meetings in which they described their presence and activities in Maré. At one of these meetings, the Commanding General explained how most of his soldiers and officers had been involved with Brazil's MUNISTAH force in Haiti and that although this experience would help them in Maré, there were important differences between the two contexts.[14] Unlike Haiti, Brazil was a functioning democracy, and the levels of development and state capacity were quite distinct. That said, he reminded the audience that "the task of the force is similar in preventing violence" and that the presence of the military should be "*aproveitada*" (taken advantage of) by the local population. He described the "*centro de gravidade*" (center of gravity) of their operation as being the population itself and how he wanted to avoid, at all costs, seeing residents or even local gang members as an enemy.

The General went on to say that the Civil and Military Police could continue to carry out operations in Maré but they had to have his direct authorization to do so. "Apprehending criminals is not the job of the military but we are capable of doing so if we see a crime happening," he said. He then reminded those present that less than 1 percent of the population were involved in drug trafficking, roughly 500 boys and men, and that 99 percent of the population was on the "*lado do bem*" (side of good).[15] At the end of the meeting, the General described how all of the troops, including himself would change every two months to avoid any corruption that became more likely with extended deployments. Subsequent troops would not have the same experience in Haiti, but

---

[12] Luana 7/1/2014.
[13] Patrício 6/28/2014.
[14] Meeting #21.
[15] This good-versus-evil rhetoric is extremely common among police and military officials as they attempt to neatly separate the criminal elements from the rest of the community, implicitly suggesting that those involved with gangs are irredeemably "*mal*" (evil) and in need of removal or destruction.

FIGURE 8.5 Photograph of military meeting with community organizations
Photograph by Antonello Veneri.

they would do their best to communicate their experiences to the next group so that there was as much continuity as possible. In practice, there would be little continuity between the deployments as each new set of troops brought a different set of tactics and policies determined by the new Commanding General. Moreover, building long-term trust between members of the community and the troops was an impossibility with such short deployments.

Nonetheless, the military also organized a series of *ações sociais* (social actions) to try to win over residents. Perhaps most importantly, they allowed for significant upgrades to local infrastructure (roads, electricity, and sewage) as well as the construction of eighteen brand new schools.[16] They held a series of events focused on maternal health at local health posts, including one on *anti-concepção* (contraception) and another on *mamaço* (breastfeeding).[17] They held weekly painting, music, and *Luta Livre* (Jiu-jitsu) classes and gave presentations at several of the middle schools to teach youth about appropriate volume levels for parties and music. They aided the Electoral Campaigns Commission to remove several thousand unauthorized campaign posters and materials.[18] The military also hired Naldo Benny, a popular DJ and musician, to play a sparsely

[16] *O Globo* 4/14/2015.
[17] Meeting #30.
[18] *O Globo* 8/28/2014.

attended concert at the soccer stadium in Vila Olímpica, where they organized food and nonalcoholic drink vendors.[19] Finally, the military organized a document fair, where more than 5,000 residents received birth certificates, *carteiras assinadas* (worker's cards), or other government documents and forms.[20]

To say that military occupation transformed life in Maré is an understatement. Some of Maré's residents' lives improved dramatically as they and their families were no longer subject to the security and health concerns that corresponded to gang territorial control and the retail drug trade. The violent confrontations between TCP and CVNH ended immediately and the frequent BOPE operations that characterized the several years leading up to occupation also came to an end. Gone also were the numerous bocas de fumo, the baile funk parties, and the hundreds of heavily armed gang members hanging out on street corners and riding their stolen motorcycles up and down the streets. As a result, many residents commented on the greater calm and reduced noise that came along with military occupation.[21]

The benefits of military occupation, however, were not felt evenly across Maré's population. As referenced earlier, the freedom and movement of young men and adolescents, even within their own neighborhoods, was significantly curtailed during occupation. Moreover, forms of recreation and entertainment diminished significantly during occupation. Impromptu parties and family events that had customarily been held in the middle of streets were no longer possible because the military made the bureaucratic process for organizing them so difficult. As a result, many residents spoke nostalgically of gang control. "There was a lot more freedom before. There were a lot of motos and parties. I miss it," one young mother told me.[22]

Some residents also lost access to forms of economic assistance and governance upon which they had previously relied. Many informal and illicit forms of economy vanished or significantly reduced. Streets once lined with numerous shacks and carts selling all manner of food and household items were now empty. The money that hundreds of families had made at the weekly baile funks was also gone. The military also imposed a more regularized building code under which many residents bristled. The military even bulldozed dozens of informal huts and shacks on the margins of these neighborhoods or in areas of new development. Hundreds of families lost their homes.[23]

While the military presence did perhaps provide a more regular form of order, when it came to resolving interpersonal disputes and lower-level crimes, they were far less effective than the gangs. As reported in other "Pacified" favelas, incidences of theft, domestic and sexual abuse, and interpersonal violence

[19] Meeting #30.
[20] Vitor 8/22/2015.
[21] Meeting #24.
[22] Luiza 10/2/2014.
[23] Breno 7/22/2014.

increased (Cano et al. 2012; Savell 2014). Several gang members told me that a lot of boys and adolescents used the opportunity of occupation to steal and break laws because they thought that the gang was not in control anymore.[24] One former member said that during the first couple of months of occupation, when he was in hiding and almost never left his house, residents had sought him out to deal with several cases of robbery and rape. It was not just gang members that reported the rise of crimes and low-level violence within the community. In the first few months of occupation, NGO workers and a variety of residents also noted the increase in theft and petty crime.[25] A local pastor reported that he had received several complaints about sexual violence, which was something he was not accustomed to dealing with.[26]

GANG ADAPTATION TO MILITARY OCCUPATION

Most full-time gang members chose to flee Maré in the days and weeks preceding the arrival of the military. Many of them found refuge in other faction-affiliated favelas or in the urban sprawl beyond the borders of the city. As a result, for the first month of occupation, all but the youngest gang members (twelve to fourteen-year-olds) were almost entirely absent from each of Maré's gang territories. And yet, the gangs were able to quickly adapt to this new reality.

First, all three gangs shifted their drug-selling techniques. Instead of stationary bocas de fumo located near all the entrances and many of the major thoroughfares, the retail drug trade moved deeper within Maré and became mobile. I immediately observed young gang members carrying backpacks and placing themselves at the entrances to alleyways along the busy streets. Initially, they were careful to not call attention to themselves but, eventually, they more openly advertised their product by shouting: "Crack, maconha, pó!" The gang members with backpacks were always accompanied by several other unarmed youth that served as olheiros, watching for any sign of the soldiers on the surrounding streets. When a military truck or foot patrol came by, the boys would scatter, quickly ducking into a side street or turning down one of the many alleys that crisscross Maré's neighborhoods. In most cases, these mobile bocas went unnoticed by the troops but, on several occasions, I watched soldiers pursue the adolescents. When this happened, the boys would throw their backpacks onto awnings or rooftops after turning a corner so that, even if they were caught, the soldiers would find no contraband.[27]

---

[24] Severino 5/15/2014.
[25] Marcos 11/3/2014; Sergio 12/17/2014; Naldo 12/17/2014.
[26] Patrício 6/27/2014.
[27] From residents, I heard of several such pursuits in which the soldiers had shot live or rubber bullets at the adolescents (Meeting #33; Breno 7/22/2014).

Nonetheless, the mobile bocas became a permanent aspect of the occupation period of each gang territory.

This method of drug sales allowed the gangs to maintain at least some of their revenue but the loss of their open-air drug markets and baile funk parties cost them significantly. According to CVNH members, drug revenues decreased by roughly 75 percent, from between R\$1.2 and R\$1.6 million each week to just a few hundred thousand, while TCP reported that their revenues were just one-tenth of what they were before occupation.[28] While the mobile bocas served Maré's internal demand, the gangs lost almost all the income from selling to those living outside of Maré. That said, the cost of maintaining the gang also diminished. The salaries of a huge number of gang members that formerly provided security, served as olheiros, or made money in the drug trade (either through sales, transportation, or production) were no longer paid or significantly reduced. According to gang members, many of these members were left to fend for themselves.[29] Some found formal or informal work while others attempted to leave the gang life entirely (more on this later). Senior gang members continued to earn reduced amounts from the drug trade or from salaries paid by the gang leader.[30] Moreover, TCP's costly bribery schemes were gone as police, for the most part, were no longer present in the area and, at least initially, the gangs did not need to supply their members with the same quantity of weapons and ammunition as before.

In addition, each of the gangs understood that although the military did not constitute an existential threat to their organizations, the constant presence of military soldiers in their turf was a significant cause for concern. Resident cooperation with the military was their primary preoccupation. As a result, gang members initially used some low levels of coercion to try to prevent resident collaboration with the military. Just before occupation, one high-ranking gang member told me that he had heard someone say that trafficking was done in Maré when the military arrived. "That sort of talk won't be tolerated," he said.[31] I asked what would happen if it did. He motioned across his neck with his thumb.

In the first several weeks of occupation, the gangs sanctioned any residents that publicly shared their support for the military presence. Several residents had given television or newspaper interviews praising the military immediately following the occupation. They were each approached by gang members. One older resident had publicly stated that he was "in heaven" after the military arrived. The traffickers went to his house and threatened to send him to hell.[32] A middle-aged woman that had participated in a ceremony commemorating

---

[28] Inácio 3/26/2014; Márcio 4/17/2014; Everton 4/17/2014; Josué 7/22/2014.
[29] Inácio 3/26/2014.
[30] Josué 7/23/2014; Luiz 7/31/2014; Bruno 10/27/2014; Severino 5/15/2014.
[31] Inácio 3/26/2014.
[32] Sofia 4/1/2014.

the arrival of the military was also questioned by gang members.[33] Another elderly resident told me about her neighbor's son, a gang member, who had threatened her to not say anything to the military when she saw him enter his house.[34] As a result of these incidents, residents became wary of speaking with soldiers or journalists. Many avoided having any direct contact with soldiers. I myself avoided all interactions with soldiers on the street and would only speak with them when they held private meetings. Several journalists I spoke with even complained that they were having a difficult time finding any residents willing to speak about what was happening in Maré.[35]

As occupation progressed, however, these more coercive behaviors in response to the presence of the military quickly faded. The gangs became less concerned that the military's presence was a significant threat to their activities. Interestingly, in interviews with residents, many even viewed these incidents of gang coercion for cooperating with the military as primarily the fault of the residents themselves. Referring to a woman who had been given a "*corretivo*" (corrective or beating) after she had been seen speaking with police, one longtime resident said, "She should have known better. Everyone knows you don't give interviews and you don't talk to police."[36] Another male resident accurately summed up the perspective of most Maré residents in an interview to a local newspaper: "The favela is only bad for those who don't know how to live. You can't involve yourself in other peoples' lives. I always said, 'I know nothing, I saw nothing.' I have always lived like this. This is a bad place for people who see and talk about everything."[37]

While all three of Maré's drug-trafficking gangs lost ostensive control of their territories and each implemented the mobile boca strategy of retail drug sales, it quickly became apparent that the dynamics of occupation were diverging in each of the gang territories. As occupation progressed, I increasingly observed how each gang shifted their structures and activities accordingly. In turn, the military responded to these gang strategies by also adapting their methods and tactics.

Terceiro Comando Puro

Although most TCP members initially went into hiding, within a couple of weeks, it was clear that they had decided to take a different approach. Visiting these neighborhoods each day, I noticed multiple TCP members were openly carrying pistols and providing armed security for the mobile bocas. Their armed presence was noticeably different from both the CV territories where

[33] Sofia 4/1/2014.
[34] Valéria 4/1/2014.
[35] Field notes 4/6/2014; 4/9/2014.
[36] Doroteia 4/11/2014.
[37] *O Globo* 4/16/2014.

few if any weapons were observed for the duration of occupation. It was also apparent that TCP was willing to engage military soldiers directly. In the first month of occupation, TCP members were involved in several shootouts and confrontations with soldiers that resulted in the deaths of a couple of innocent bystanders.[38] In a series of public and private meetings one month into occupation, both residents and military officials commented on the volatile situation in the TCP-controlled area.[39]

The primary reason why TCP quickly renewed their physical armed presence was due to the activation of the threat from their rival, ADA.[40] Quickly after occupation, ADA members began infiltrating the area from which they had been expelled in 2009. Many of these ADA members, including one of its leaders, had been born and raised in Maré and, since TCP no longer controlled the streets and could not monitor the numerous entrances to the area, ADA was able to surreptitiously invade their former turf. During a massive public audience in Maré, Rio's Public Security Secretary, Mariano Beltrame, refuted the possibility of territorial contestation between gangs amid military occupation.[41] In a private meeting with NGO officials, however, the Commanding General of the Occupation Forces, Roberto Escoto, admitted that ADA members had, in fact, managed to infiltrate the area.[42] Despite numerous checkpoints being placed at all the entrances, the military could not check the many thousands of residents crossing over these borders every day. According to the General, ADA's presence had already resulted in a series of confrontations between the gangs and soldiers. In further interviews and public meetings, residents corroborated the General's admission, remarking on the presence of gang members they did not recognize and describing confrontations between the rival gangs and also with soldiers.[43] According to Thiago, a resident of one of TCP's neighborhoods, "They [TCP] had to get back on the street. They retook their posts, monitored the entrances that the army didn't, and started carrying guns to defend their community."[44]

The details of these intergang dynamics also became known to me through my involvement with an NGO project designed to rehabilitate gang members.[45] Nearly thirty TCP members would eventually enroll in the program, and, over the course of six months, I accompanied the project while conducting dozens of interviews with these men. Many of them described their

[38] *O Globo* 4/16/2014; 4/21/2014.
[39] Meeting #10; Meeting #13; Meeting #17.
[40] Olívia 9/26/2014; Valdemir 1/9/2015.
[41] *O Globo* 4/3/2014.
[42] Meeting #17.
[43] Valdemir 1/9/2015; Meeting #9; Meeting #13; *O Globo* 4/16/2014; 4/12/2014.
[44] Thiago 1/9/2015.
[45] The program involved a series of interventions, including primary and secondary-level classes and tutoring, individual and group counseling sessions, a monthly stipend, and opportunities for legal employment in the service sector.

frustration that the military was either unwilling or incapable of preventing ADA from making incursions into their territory. They feared their rival would manage to take back the territory, which would mean they and perhaps their families would be expelled or killed even if they were no longer formally involved with the gang. In one memorable interview, Josué described how ADA had been searching for him, "They went to my house and grabbed my wife. They pointed a pistol in her face and asked where I was. They told her they were going to kill me. My kids were there too. Those guys are cowards!"[46] Other former TCP members similarly reported that ADA had been searching for them and that their situations were also becoming insecure.[47] The coordinators of the rehabilitation program told me they were having a difficult time keeping some these men in the program.[48] As confrontations increased in the third and fourth months of the occupation, several men dropped out of the program altogether and rejoined the gang.[49] Subsequently, I saw these men at security positions and carrying weapons in the area. By the end of occupation, nearly half of the TCP members had dropped out or were suspected of rejoining the gang.

Despite the military's efforts to quell the violence, as occupation progressed into its sixth and seventh months, ADA continued making incursions into the area. In September, the two gangs and the military were engaging in daily shootouts.[50] "The situation is horrible!," Olívia, an NGO worker, decried, "The streets are totally empty after 2PM because everyone knows that ADA is hiding in some of the houses."[51] Local schools, which serve more than 7,000 students, were closed for several weeks.[52] Even after ADA's leader was arrested in late September, invasions, skirmishes, and shootouts between the gangs and with military soldiers continued through the end of the year and into January, sometimes spilling out onto Avenida Brasil and stopping traffic on the city's busiest highway.[53] My time spent in these neighborhoods became restricted to the mornings and early afternoons. Riding my bike through these areas, I saw TCP members congregating in large groups and carrying heavy weaponry, some even carrying two semiautomatic rifles. When an army patrol came near, gang members would quickly disperse, move indoors, and wait for the vehicle to pass before reemerging to monitor the streets.[54] TCP became, by far, the most ostentatious and physically present gang for the duration of military occupation.

[46] Josué 7/15/2014.
[47] Timo 7/15/2014; Fulton 7/15/2014.
[48] Valdemir 12/1/2014; Manoel 9/15/2014.
[49] Valdemir 12/1/2014; Manoel 9/15/2014.
[50] *Estadão* 9/21/2014; *Extra* 9/23/2014.
[51] Olívia 9/26/2014.
[52] *O Globo* 10/1/2014.
[53] *O Globo* 10/1/2014; 5/25/2015.
[54] Field notes 10/6/2014.

It was at the height of this intergang violence that one of the most tragic events of my fieldwork occurred. In the middle of September, a colleague messaged me asking if I had heard the news. She informed me that Carlitos, the president of the Morro do Timbau AM, had been killed. Apparently, a young man arrived at the AM office on a motorbike. He entered the building still wearing his helmet and asked for Carlitos by name. The young man then took out a pistol and shot Carlitos seven times, in the neck, thorax, and abdomen.[55] Carlitos died shortly thereafter. A woman resident who was in the building at the time was also hit by one of the bullets but survived.

Carlitos was a retired Military Police Sergeant, who had grown up in Baixa do Sapateiro, lived in Nova Holanda, and then moved to Morro do Timbau, where he had raised a family. He was in his third term as the president of the AM and had been heavily involved in the meetings with the public security apparatus surrounding the Pacification process. I had interviewed him several times over the course of my fieldwork and interacted with him frequently at NGO and AM meetings. Earlier that week, he had given a TV interview in support of the military occupation and Pacification project. Many of those I spoke with pointed to this interview as the proximate cause of his death but Carlitos had given numerous such interviews over the course of the previous year.[56] Although no one has ever been charged and, thus, no definitive motive revealed, it is unlikely mere coincidence that the assassination of Carlitos coincided with the most violent and prolonged encounters between TCP, ADA, and the military. This would match a pattern of the most coercive behavior corresponding to periods of active rival threat that reaches back several decades.

In response to the growing levels of violence in the TCP territory, the military employed even more aggressive tactics. They closed parts of Avenida Brasil to mount massive operations involving dozens of tanks and militarized vehicles. Hundreds of soldiers went house to house searching for gang members.[57] They broke down doors and entered homes and buildings without warrants. After a number of soldiers were injured and one killed in an encounter with TCP members, the military ramped up their coercive presence even further.[58] They installed permanent bunkers with machine guns at strategic points in the community and placed snipers and lookouts on the roofs of schools and apartment buildings. Finally, in early 2015, TCP scaled back their fighting strategy. According to Valdemir, "the *chefe* (boss) has ordered to stop shooting at soldiers because the army was gaining the upper hand."[59] Confronting the military had taken its toll on TCP but, by then, ADA had ended their takeover attempts as they had also suffered the consequences of months of fighting. The

[55] *O Dia* 9/16/2014.
[56] Luna 9/22/2014; Bruno 10/6/2014; Valdemir 12/1/2014; Ademir 12/4/2014.
[57] Meeting #33; *O Globo* 10/1/2014.
[58] *O Globo* 11/28/2014; 6/29/2015.
[59] Valdemir 1/9/2014.

threat presented by ADA once again reverted to a latent one. For the last several months of military occupation, TCP was able to relax their coercive tactics and presence without the possibility of losing territorial control.

For their part, residents of the TCP area became increasingly frustrated with the behavior of the military and began protesting, which occasionally brought them into direct conflict with the military.[60] Several residents with no known gang involvement were allegedly shot and killed by soldiers.[61] In a public meeting with the press, numerous residents and civil society leaders described dozens of violations and episodes of violence and abuse in this area.[62] According to a survey conducted by a local NGO, residents of the TCP area reported twice as many violations by soldiers and twice the number of bad or terrible evaluations of the military (Silva 2017, 75–79). Some sporadic confrontations between TCP and the military would occur until the very end of occupation on June 30th, 2015, likely the result of these much more aggressive tactics by the military.[63] By the end of occupation, twenty-three soldiers had been injured and one killed in confrontations with gangs, nearly every one of them in TCP territory.[64] Of the twelve civilian deaths that the military was responsible for in Maré, eleven occurred in the TCP territory, eight of which were alleged gang members.[65]

Comando Vermelho of Nova Holanda

The response of CVNH to military occupation was different than that of their TCP rival. Although CVNH can be described as the most heavily militarized and antagonistic toward the police prior to occupation, the gang changed their behavior radically for the duration of occupation. During the nine months I lived in Nova Holanda under military occupation, I only observed CVNH members carrying a pistol once. Local newspapers only reported two incidents involving gunshots in the CVNH area and it is unclear whether CVNH members were even involved in these episodes.[66] CVNH's shift in strategy occurred largely because the active threat from TCP reverted to a latent one for the duration of occupation.

The sporadic confrontations and shootouts between the CVNH and TCP along the border, which had characterized the period leading up to occupation, ended immediately. Neither of the two gangs would attempt to invade or infiltrate their rival's territory during occupation. This was partially because the

---

[60] Meeting #33.
[61] *Bom Dia Brasil* 6/23/2015.
[62] Meeting #33; *O Dia* 11/5/2014; 2/22/2015; *Folha de São Paulo* 11/5/2014.
[63] *Estadão* 6/26/2015; *Bom Dia Brasil* 6/23/2015.
[64] *O Globo* 5/25/2015.
[65] *Pública* 10/31/2018.
[66] *Extra* 7/8/2014; *O Globo* 11/3/2014.

military had strategically placed around-the-clock checkpoints and militarized vehicles at several places along the border where the gangs were accustomed to invading each other's territory. Similar checkpoints, however, had been unable to prevent ADA from infiltrating TCP's territory. More importantly, unlike ADA, neither of these gangs had members who had been born and raised in their rival's territory. Therefore, they were not motivated to "retake" their home turf nor did their members have the intimate knowledge and social connections that would have allowed them to infiltrate these areas undetected. The TCP–CVNH rivalry would remain latent for the duration of occupation.

Immediately following the arrival of the military, CVNH's presence was significantly reduced. The only gang members that remained on the streets in the first month of occupation were the youngest members of the organization. While TCP began carrying pistols quickly after occupation and eventually larger weapons as violence escalated, CVNH would remain demilitarized for the duration of occupation. The lack of active rival threat between CVNH and TCP was most visible along their shared border. Quickly following occupation, numerous shops and stores appeared where none had existed before. Residents were able to move through this area without concern for shootouts or being questioned by gang members though they were often stopped by the military. In a public meeting held in early July 2014, nearly three months into occupation, numerous residents from the CVNH area remarked on the lack of shootouts and greater calm that occupation had brought to their lives.[67]

Nearly twenty CVNH members would also eventually join the gang rehabilitation program mentioned earlier. I accompanied this group as well. The former CVNH members did not describe the same difficulty with occupation like their TCP counterparts. In fact, many of them believed occupation to be an improvement over the previous era of gang control, suggesting that the need to defend their territory against an aggressive rival had caused a lot of problems. In fact, nearly every one of CVNH's members had participated in or been present during at least one shootout between the gangs while several reported being involved in dozens. Such long-term and frequent violence had clearly taken its toll on many of the CVNH members. Severino, for instance, thought "it would be better for everyone if there weren't territories."[68] Inácio, a former senior member, even hoped that the drug trade would eventually become more like the US where "you just call someone and they bring the drugs to your house."[69] Former CVNH members also believed the military to be less violent and aggressive than Rio's Military Police, which, given BOPE's focus on the CV areas in the lead up to occupation, is unsurprising.[70] While many of the CVNH members also complained of a

---

[67] Meeting #20.
[68] Severino 5/15/2014.
[69] Inácio 3/26/2014.
[70] Bruno 10/27/2014; Severino 5/15/2014.

lack of parties and entertainment, they found military occupation a much less stressful atmosphere and, according to the coordinators of the program, the CVNH members did not have the same issue with recidivism, at least during occupation.[71]

Although many of the senior CVNH members initially fled, after less than a month of occupation, I heard reports that they had returned and were hiding out.[72] In the subsequent weeks and months, I occasionally observed these men, unarmed and unaccompanied by the large security details which had surrounded them prior to occupation. They maintained low profiles, only emerging at night. Inácio, a close friend of the gang leader, Ninho, said he had returned to resolve fights or conflicts between residents or within the organization because "he doesn't want to lose his territory, which can happen if you spend too much time outside."[73] Several other CVNH members agreed that it was important for the gang leader to not be absent, especially when occupation ended, and police operations and violence with TCP would likely resume.[74] When I asked Severino if there was something different about the governance that the gang offered during occupation, he said, "It's not as intense. They don't have the same resources and capacity for violence (*poder bélico*) to back up their authority like before."[75]

Although violence and conflict was significantly reduced from preoccupation levels, large numbers of unaffiliated adolescents began to assert their own control over the space within Nova Holanda. They began by stealing skateboards and horses from the TCP side of the border, which eventually led to outright confrontations between these groups of youth. I witnessed one such skirmish in which several dozen boys threw rocks at one another along the border. While the presence of armed TCP members likely prevented these adolescents from engaging in any confrontations with the soldiers in that area, the fact that CVNH was not trying to intensively control space or be as physically present on the streets allowed these young boys and adolescents significant room to operate. They increasingly came into conflict with the military.[76] I personally witnessed several occasions in which soldiers pointed their rifles at local youth and shouted racial slurs and insults at them.[77] The frustrated youth responded by harassing and provoking the soldiers. They would often congregate on the main streets of Nova Holanda late at night, shouting obscenities, and throwing rocks and bottles at the soldiers.[78] Troops used rubber bullets

---

[71] Manoel 9/15/2014; Valdemir 12/1/2014.
[72] Field notes 4/29/2014; Inácio 4/24/2014.
[73] Inácio 4/24/2014.
[74] Inácio 3/26/2014; Severino 5/15/2014; Bruno 10/27/2014.
[75] Severino 6/11/2014.
[76] Meeting #33; *O Dia* 11/5/2014; *Folha de São Paulo* 11/5/2014.
[77] Field notes 7/22/2014; 9/7/2014.
[78] Felícia 7/1/2014; *O Globo* 6/9/2014; *Extra* 7/8/2014.

and tear gas to disperse them.[79] According to CVNH members, these boys and adolescents were not gang members but wannabees and hangers-on.[80] Confrontations between unaffiliated youth and the military continued until the end of occupation. When the military's tanks left the community for the last time, CVNH members quickly reestablished their control over the streets and disbanded these youth groups.

Comando Vermelho of Parque União

Like Maré's other two gangs, the mobile bocas were the only visible aspect of the CVPU immediately following the military's occupation. Despite this similarity, the CVPU response was distinct from either of the other two gangs. I never observed pistols or rifles on the streets and, aside from several mobile bocas, more senior gang members did not return to this neighborhood like in CVNH's territory. Residents even complained that the absence of the Dono and senior gang members made resolving problems within the community very difficult.[81] CVPU's choice to remain outside their territory during military occupation was, I argue, the result of the absence of a rival threat.

Despite spending significant amounts of time and maintaining numerous contacts in this area, I had a difficult time finding CVPU members to interview during occupation. While both CVNH and TCP had many members join the gang rehabilitation program, not a single CVPU member enrolled. Why? First, I noticed that many of the TCP and CVNH members that did enroll were older – the average age was twenty-five – and most had experienced significant violence during their tenures.[82] All but four of the gang members in the program reported that they had lost at least one if not several friends to violence.[83] Many of them were disillusioned with gang life and described the cumulative effects of stress from the fear of victimization and death.[84] Although CVPU had suffered intense and frequent policing operations for the past five years (see Chapter 6), neither residents nor gang members could ever remember shootouts between gangs. In fact, the gang had experienced no rival threat (latent or active) for the past decade largely because CVNH provided them a buffer against their closest rival, TCP. The relationship with CVNH, although not always harmonious, had never involved any violence and the two gangs had remained allies and part of the same overarching faction for more than two decades. This more stable environment meant that CVPU gang members

---

[79] Field notes 7/22/2014; Meeting #29.
[80] Severino 5/15/2014.
[81] Sergio 12/17/2014; Evaristo 12/23/2014.
[82] Data provided by NGO.
[83] Data provided by NGO. Timo 7/15/2014; Fulton 7/15/2014; Josué 7/15/2014.
[84] Josué 7/10/2014; Fulton 7/3/2014; Bruno 10/6/2014; Daniel 8/21/2014.

were less likely to be traumatized by their gang tenure and, therefore, perhaps the draw of rehabilitation and leaving the gang life were less attractive.

Another explanation for the lack of CVPU members in the rehabilitation program is that some of the TCP and CVNH members used the program to stay in their respective communities during occupation, given the higher levels of threat and their possible need to defend their territory. CVPU members, by contrast, could stay away, avoid possible enforcement and harassment by the military, and still be unconcerned that their territory would be there for them when occupation ended. Either way, the lack of territorial competition (prior to and during occupation) likely shaped the unwillingness of CVPU members to join the rehabilitation program.

The antagonisms and confrontations between the military and members of the community I witnessed in Nova Holanda were neither observed personally nor described in interviews with residents in this area. In public meetings, nearly every denunciation and complaint came from other areas of Maré. Part of the reason may be that Parque União had been a less violent area for quite some time and, consequently, more economically secure. As described in Chapter 6, this neighborhood has many of Maré's most expensive shops and restaurants and receives many visitors from outside. This more stable context likely helped contribute to a more pacific occupation. I did hear one resident complain that the groups of adolescents from the CVNH territory would sometimes enter into the CVPU area when the military were cracking down on them in Nova Holanda but residents did not report any of the confrontations between youth and military in this neighborhood.[85] Despite CVPU being little present in their territory for the duration of occupation, when the military finally left Maré, CVPU members quickly returned to the area, reasserted their presence on the streets, and resumed the open-air drug trade.

DISCUSSION AND ALTERNATIVE EXPLANATIONS

The occupation of Maré by the military meant that all three gangs could no longer maintain the same governance regimes they had previously. First, numerous gang members were imprisoned, fled the territory, were forced into hiding, or tried to exit the gang life altogether. As a result, the three gangs were neither able to sustain the same physical presence on the streets nor could they effectively monitor and defend their borders as before. Each gang also lost significant economic resources as the drug trade could no longer operate at the same volume. Without these capabilities and resources, the gangs struggled to resolve disputes, no longer provided economic stimulation or welfare, and could not throw parties. And yet, despite the gangs' inability to govern to the same degree, the presence of the military nonetheless did not constitute an existential threat to these organizations. Each of the gangs

[85] Field notes 7/19/2014.

adapted to this new reality and found ways to maintain their organization. Military occupation did, however, undeniably change the local security environment, which shaped how each of the gangs responded to occupation.

In the case of TCP, ADA used this opportunity to infiltrate their former turf which precipitated TCP's remilitarization and violent contestation between these gangs and eventually included direct confrontations with the military. TCP attempted to exert its physical presence within those territories and even likely targeted one prominent local politician with execution though the ability to threaten and punish residents for other transgressions was likely reduced due to the presence of the military within their territory. TCP's focus remained squarely on defending their territory for the duration of occupation, providing little in terms of benefits to the local population. For their part, residents tried to avoid interactions with gang members as violence could erupt at any moment. This finding corroborates the close connection between active rivalry and disorder in the other empirical chapters.[86]

For Maré's other two gangs, the security environment became more stable. Gone were the violent encounters between TCP and CVNH and neither of the CV gangs suffered from the aggressive and frequent BOPE operations. Most senior CVNH members returned to their territory and maintained a noticeable but low profile for the duration of occupation. Although they could not engage in as intensive a form of governance as before, they resolved some disputes and remained a resource for residents. CVPU, on the other hand, mostly stayed away. This difference is also related to territorial imperatives vis-à-vis rivals. For more than two decades, CVNH had fought an on-again off-again war with TCP. Even if that threat was diminished during occupation, they were not going to quickly forget about their longtime rival. CVNH needed to be prepared for the reactivation of this territorial threat whenever occupation ended.[87] Meanwhile, CVPU's grip on their territory was never in doubt. The gang had been led by members of the same family since the 1990s and had never faced any territorial competition.[88] Returning to the community during occupation was unnecessary and would have only put CVPU members in danger of being discovered and arrested.

There are several plausible alternative explanations which must also be addressed. First, could the violent reaction of TCP to occupation be the result of some other internal gang process? For instance, Bração, TCP's gerente geral, was arrested by Federal Police in a luxury apartment in the Zona Oeste of the city several weeks prior to occupation.[89] Perhaps TCP members became

---

[86] This finding also reinforces existing work on state crackdowns, which find that the weakening of incumbent territorial control drives violent OCG responses to military intervention (Dell 2015; Flores-Macías 2018; Osorio 2015; Rios 2013).

[87] *O Dia* 6/30/2014; *O Globo* 7/29/3014.

[88] Vinícius 11/9/2014; Evaristo 12/23/2014.

[89] *O Globo* 5/27/2014.

violent due to the lack of control of the rank and file or because of internal conflicts rather than the threat from ADA. However, in interviews with TCP members, they all maintained a clear idea of the leadership structure of the gang, never once mentioning any internal fighting or conflicts. It is more likely that the arrest of Bração prior to occupation further reinforced ADA's belief that they could take back their territory.

Another possible explanation is that the various gang responses were the result of the military's different approaches to confronting them. The troops, at least initially, were divided into three bases, which could have varied their tactics to produce the different gang reactions. However, the military's bases did not match up with the borders of the gangs but overlapped them significantly.[90] Moreover, as mentioned earlier, the entire troop contingent, from the Commanding General down to every soldier, was rotated out of service every two months. By the end of occupation, 23,500 troops would eventually participate in the occupation of Maré.[91] While the strategies of the military certainly evolved over time, the differences in gang responses were observed across multiple troop deployments.

Next, following the work of Lessing (2017), perhaps TCP remilitarized and confronted state forces in their effort to return to a corrupt equilibrium, from which they benefitted before occupation. Brazil's military, however, has no history of corruption like Rio's police and, by all accounts, soldiers did not engage in any corrupt behaviors while in Maré. In fact, part of the reason why the military decided to rotate their entire personnel every two months was to prevent the emergence of such corruption schemes. It is unlikely that the TCP would have engaged in a yearlong campaign of violence and confrontation if they had little hope of developing durable corruption schemes.

Finally, Magaloni, Vivanco-Franco, and Melo (2020) argue that we should observe CV-affiliated gangs responding to state intervention more violently than the other factions due to CV's greater organizational capacity (it is the largest of the three factions) as well as its longstanding antagonistic relationship with the state. The outcomes from Maré's occupation were quite the opposite, suggesting that microlevel imperatives outweigh overarching faction affiliations and policies. Magaloni et al. also argue that preexisting governance regimes determined the outcomes of Rio's UPPs (of which Maré's occupation was technically a part though UPPs were never installed). They hypothesize that Pacification interventions should reduce violence and improve security in territories where gangs maintain abusive relations with local populations while deteriorating social order where they cooperate with residents. As the preceding chapters demonstrate, Maré's gang–resident relations preceding occupation are neither wholly abusive nor cooperative but considerably more complex, multifaceted, and variable. That said, in the period leading up to

[90] Meeting #17.
[91] *Estadão* 6/26/2015.

occupation, the most abusive gang–resident relations were found in the CVNH territory due largely to the need for the gang to defend their territory against their rival and the huge number of foreign gang members allowed to reside in the area. For many residents in the CVNH territory, occupation improved the security environment dramatically because they no longer had to deal with abusive foreign gang members nor the violent confrontations between CVNH and TCP. Thus, Magaloni et al.'s predictions seem to be borne out in this case. However, the less abusive relations between CVPU and residents also resulted in a more pacific occupation period. Overall, governance dynamics preceding occupation do not seem to determine the outcome of such interventions. Rather, I would argue that both governance dynamics and gang responses to state intervention are subservient to territorial imperatives vis-à-vis rival groups and intervention forces.

CONCLUSION

By the time the last of the troops left Maré on June 30th, 2015, the Brazilian military had conducted an estimated 83,000 operations, arrested 674 individuals, apprehended 255 minors, and made 1,356 seizures of guns, ammunition, drugs, and stolen vehicles.[92] And yet, within hours of the military's departure, each of the three gangs had reestablished their presence on the streets and dozens of bocas de fumo were open for business. The four UPPs which had been planned for Maré never came to fruition and none of the military's development or security initiatives remained in place. If the goal of military occupation was to permanently weaken the gangs in the area and reestablish the Brazilian state's monopoly of violence for the long-term, it had failed.

That said, according to Rio's Institute of Public Security, the homicide rate in Maré did decrease from 21 to 6 homicides per 100,000 during occupation.[93] From this perspective, it might seem like occupation was a success. And yet, this number obfuscates the frequent confrontations and shootouts between TCP and ADA that shut down schools and major thoroughfares, as well as the numerous human rights abuses by the military.[94] A myopic focus on the homicide rate also ignores the increase in low-level crime and public disorder in some areas of Maré, yet another reminder that social order can actually deteriorate when OCG control and authority are removed (see Arias and Barnes 2017; Magaloni, Franco-Vivanco, and Melo 2020). The falling homicide rate also masks the fact that 2,500 military troops with all the resources of the Brazilian state never threatened the long-term presence and viability of Maré's gangs. Their divergent experiences during occupation further demonstrate the capacity of gangs and other OCGs to adapt to wildly

[92] *O Globo* 6/29/2015.
[93] *Estadão* 6/26/2015.
[94] Meeting #33; *O Dia* 11/5/2014; *Folha de São Paulo* 11/5/2014.

different environments. They do not require a specific organizational form or leadership structure to operate and can effectively reproduce themselves without significant revenue streams for extended periods of time. The absence of violence does not necessarily signify the underlying effectiveness of these operations.

In this regard, perhaps the biggest failure of the military in Maré was its inability to garner resident support in their efforts to combat the gangs. This is not for lack of trying. The Brazilian military had spent several decades developing just such a methodology from existing counterinsurgency policy and stabilization missions (Harig 2015b; Hoelscher and Norheim-Martinsen 2014; Siman and Santos 2018). In fact, an estimated 60–90 percent of the troops eventually stationed in Maré had already been deployed to Haiti, where they used an almost identical set of development tactics and militarized operations (Harig 2015a). In Maré, the military made significant upgrades to the infrastructure, collaborated with local civil society, and engaged in 24,000 social actions, spending an estimated R$350 million in the process.[95] And yet, the military simultaneously implemented increasingly violent and repressive tactics to confront gang violence in TCP's territory. They installed bunkers, placed snipers in schools and on rooftops, entered homes, threatened and abused residents, and even killed several citizens that had no involvement with the gangs. Such tactics contradicted and overwhelmed their more benevolent efforts. By the end of occupation, less than half of 1,000 surveyed Maré residents said the military had had a positive impact (Silva 2017, 87). According to one local NGO leader at a public meeting toward the end of occupation:

The approach (*abordagem*) of the military is little different from the police that came before. The 'Pacification' of Maré was a lie and an abstract term that doesn't reflect the reality. There are twelve dead civilians since the military arrived. We've brought these and other violations to the military itself and they have changed nothing about their practice. They haven't implemented more responsive institutions and although they have sought out civil society to develop relationships, this is more in theory and serves as subterfuge for them to control the space.[96]

In this regard, the occupation of Maré provided the military an opportunity to further apply and refine a methodology and set of tactics that they had been developing over the past two decades both domestically and internationally. While their efforts clearly failed in providing the kind of transformative change that the state had promised leading up to the occupation of Maré, military officials characterized the operation as an unequivocal success.[97] In this way, it served to solidify and expand the role of the military in

---

[95] *Bom Dia Brasil* 6/23/2015; *O Globo* 5/26/2014.
[96] Meeting #33.
[97] *Driss Ghali* 8/11/2017.

policing Rio de Janeiro's favelas. Just two years later, the military would take control of Rio's entire public security apparatus for ten months, employing many of the same tactics and strategies they had refined in Maré, this time without the development rhetoric. Maré's occupation, then, takes on added significance as it represents the beachhead of further military involvement in domestic public security and foreshadowed the even more militarized efforts of the state security apparatus to control Maré and other favela populations and spaces in the subsequent years, a period I turn to in Chapter 9.[98]

---

[98] A version of this chapter was previously published in 2022 in *Comparative Political Studies* 55(5): 789–831.

9

Conclusion

The police believe that residents are the accomplices of the gangs because they know that there is an interdependence which exists between them. And, in truth, that interdependence exists but not because the residents choose to do bad things but because they don't have another choice. It's a coexistence thing.
—Eduarda, an NGO worker from Maré

INTRODUCTION

Over the course of my fieldwork, I attended dozens of meetings with public security personnel. Most were organized by Maré's various NGOs and AMs, working in concert, to demand that the military and police be transparent about their practices and, ideally, accountable to the local population. In early August 2014, several months into military occupation, I attended one such meeting in which Colonel Castanheira of the Military Police and the presumptive Commander of Maré's impending UPPs (this plan had not yet been scrapped), was asked to communicate how police would approach their mandate and the protocols they had in place to protect residents from police abuse. After being introduced by the Commanding General of the occupation forces, Castanheira rose and warmly greeted the few dozen NGO workers, AM representatives, residents, and assorted police and military personnel. A heavyset man with wispy hair, Castanheira was clearly comfortable speaking to a room full of people. I got the feeling he had done this many times before.

Over the next forty-five minutes, Castanheira led us through a presentation outlining the basics of policing in favela communities. He spoke at length about the tension and anxiety that police feel when operating in favelas before moving on to how they learn to identify criminals. Using theories from outdated psychology research, he explained that when people look to the left they are recalling something from memory but anyone who looks to the right, up, or down when answering a question is lying. He described how people who look and behave "*anormal*" (abnormally) usually have something to hide, giving the example of someone wearing a winter coat during the summer.

"Feelings and emotions are transparent if you know how to read them," Castanheira asserted as he displayed a series of photographs of human faces in various emotional states (happy, sad, angry, perplexed, etc.). He explained how police get very good at reading expressions and body language to discern intentions. "Female police are even better at observing these details because they have these natural instincts," he pointed out. I noticed several sideways glances from some of the women in the audience. "Police learn to sense who is guilty and who is not through experience. Anyone who has dark skin can complain about the racist behavior of the police but we have a good idea as to who is guilty and who is not," he said. Several of the NGO workers shifted in their seats and exchanged knowing looks. Castanheira then presented a long list of laws and protocols governing police conduct during stop-and-search encounters: the dignity and physical safety of both the suspect and police must always be guaranteed, police should explain in simple terms why they are conducting the search, and the suspect has rights irrespective of the result of the search, among many others.

Castanheira's presentation ended with a demonstration of a stop and search. A group of six police came forward. One plainclothes officer, who coincidentally (or not) was black, played the role of the suspect alongside five uniformed officers. At the beginning of the demonstration, the suspect was standing on one side of the stage, typing on his cell phone, and carrying a backpack. The five officers approached him with their guns (an assortment of rifles and handguns) already drawn and pointed. One of the officers shouted for him to put his arms up and the suspect immediately hid the cell phone behind his back. The officer again demanded that he raise his arms and then told him to put his hands on the wall and spread his legs, which the suspect did willingly as the officers fanned out and secured the surrounding area. The lead officer then did a quick search of the suspect and, having found no illicit material, said "*tenha um bom dia*" (have a good day) and let him go. According to Castanheira, this was a textbook encounter, respectful and legal in every sense. The second scenario proceeded in the exact same fashion only the suspect was reluctant to be searched. The police officers forced him against the wall and more violently searched his body. Castanheira concluded by saying that the police often must use greater force when a suspect is unwilling to cooperate. The phone was likely stolen, Castanheira pointed out, otherwise, why would the thief hide it behind his back. He then opened the floor for any comments or questions.

Marielle Franco was the first to speak.[1] She pointed out that the young man was not doing anything wrong, and he likely hid the phone because he

---

[1] Franco was born and raised in Maré and continued to participate in local social movements until her assassination in 2018. She attended several of the public security meetings during this period.

was afraid the police would take it from him. "He was not admitting guilt but merely reacting to his own beliefs and understandings of what the police do," she emphasized. Then two residents spoke up. One woman gave her own demonstration of how the police search for guns and drugs inside the school she worked at, pointing her fingers as if she were carrying a rifle. "They're threatening and abusive!" she shouted. A middle-aged man then accused the soldiers of using pepper spray against kids at night even when unprovoked. Before others had a chance to pile on the grievances and accusations, one of the NGO directors took the microphone.

Thank you, Colonel, for the presentation. This is very important information for us to understand. It is not clear to everyone how police are trained or what their protocols are. We have been working for several years to inform residents of their rights in these encounters and we will be disseminating some of what we learned here today to improve their understanding. I share many of the frustrations just expressed. Although antidiscrimination is enshrined into law, in reality, it is young, black men who are overwhelmingly searched and abused. The intimidation by police is omnipresent for these young men and this impacts their view of the police and their interactions with them. Our different perspectives were made obvious to me in your demonstration. Although you may see the first encounter as respectful, it is likely that many in the audience saw it as humiliating and abusive.

Many in the audience nodded their heads in agreement. Castanheira responded:

First, I want to say that bad police behavior needs to be condemned and denounced in all its forms but, in my twenty-two years of police service, I have never heard that the way police treat favela residents is considered disrespectful. For residents, gang members are known to everyone within the community, but the police cannot arrest them without proof. So we end up searching these men many times. We focus on youth and adolescents because this is the population that creates the biggest problems.

The NGO director interjected: "But you're misinterpreting the behavior of the young men, Colonel. When they won't look you in the eye, don't respond to direct questions, or try to hide from you, it's not because they're lying or guilty but because they're afraid of you." Castanheira thought for a moment.

I didn't realize that. Our theories of behavior rely on eye contact and assume individuals who are willing to engage in such a way. ...I also want to remind you that being a police in a favela is not like walking around a children's playground. There are very real threats we face in these environments that people from favelas may not understand.

The conversation went back and forth like this for another thirty minutes before the organizers brought the meeting to a close.

The fact that Castanheira would have likely become the Commander of Maré's UPPs, had they been installed, was disquieting. Even more discouraging is the fact that Castanheira likely represents the more enlightened and progressive element within the public security apparatus, one of those police at least willing to interact and have conversations with favela communities about the policing tactics they implement. Although few in the meeting were surprised by the Colonel's comments, the methods he outlined, or the demonstration at the end, some of the NGO workers and AM representatives I spoke with afterward thought it was a step in the right direction. Having the police present themselves and defend their practices – almost unheard of in favela communities – was an important milestone even if they vehemently disagreed with what was said. And yet, two years of regular meetings did little to convince residents and community leaders that the state security apparatus was any more of a reliable partner than before. Instead, the meetings mostly demonstrated the vast ocean that separated Rio's police from the communities and citizens they were supposed, at least on paper, to serve.

In the rest of this chapter, I ponder the possibilities for meaningful change in Maré and Rio de Janeiro, given the nature of the public security institutions and policies. Before doing so, I first bring the reader up to date by describing the key developments since the end of the primary period of fieldwork in 2015. I then suggest several possibilities for improving outcomes for Maré and its residents, from the most practical, small-scale steps, to the most far-ranging and transformative. In the second half of the chapter, I assess how well the theory developed in this book applies beyond Maré's borders, first to the rest of Rio de Janeiro, then to other cities in Brazil and beyond. I conclude with the implications for research and suggest some questions and dynamics which deserve further consideration by scholars interested in criminalized and other forms of armed governance.

THE MORE THINGS CHANGE...

Most of the fieldwork for this book (2012–15) came during a particularly momentous period for Complexo da Maré, Rio de Janeiro, and even Brazil. The years since have proven to be even more turbulent. First, the optimism that pervaded the city and much of the country when I arrived in Rio in 2012, amid Brazil's rapid economic expansion and the height of the *Partido dos Trabalhadores* (Worker's Party) power, are a distant memory. The very public and legally dubious impeachment of Dilma Rousseff in 2016, the conviction and imprisonment of former President Luiz Inácio Lula da Silva in 2017, and the eventual election and presidential term of Jair Bolsonaro (2019–22), a far-right politician from Rio de Janeiro with suspected links to the city's milícias, completed the country's rapid descent into populist and authoritarian politics.[2]

These seismic shifts in the national political landscape were matched if not surpassed by Rio de Janeiro's decline. By the time I left the field in

---

[2] At the time of publication, it remains to be seen how the reelection of Lula in 2022, followed by Bolsonaro's conviction of abuse of power in 2023, barring him from holding public office until 2030, will shape Brazilian politics moving forward.

February 2015, the initial promise of the Upps had long faded. Already by 2012, the decline in the program was evident when the case of Amarildo de Souza became public, revealing how UPP police in Rocinha, Rio's largest and most iconic favela, had kidnapped, tortured, and disposed of the bricklayer's body then attempted to cover it up. *"Cadê Amarildo?"* (Where's Amarildo?) became a rallying cry for favela communities and social justice movements across the city. Then, in 2013, massive public protests in response to increasing transportation costs and the misuse and misallocation of public funds connected to the upcoming mega-events continued to erode confidence in public institutions (Barnes 2016).

Although the mega-events proceeded as planned, the city teetered on the edge of bankruptcy, unable to pay its public employees, including police. The economic disaster eventually precipitated a massive federal bailout and another military intervention. This time, federal troops took control of Rio de Janeiro's entire public security apparatus from February until December 2018 (Barnes and Savell 2018). Under the direction of the military, 1,534 citizens were killed by public security agents in 2018, a record at the time (ISP-RJ 2023a). Clearly, the "hearts-and-minds" and developmental rhetoric that public security forces had adopted during the era of Pacification – always thought to be just *"maquiagem"* (makeup) by many favela residents – had finally been abandoned, revealing the public security apparatus' violent underlying complexion.

Rio's return to even more violent and repressive policing matches Maré's trajectory as well. One local NGO, *Redes da Maré*, began to systematically document police operations and their consequences in 2016. According to their data, Rio's police engaged in 165 militarized operations from 2016 to 2021, during which they killed 109 residents and forced schools and health posts to close for a combined 210 days (Redes da Maré 2021). I observed some of the scars left by these operations during a return visit to Maré in January 2017. Walking down one of Nova Holanda's main streets, I noticed a series of small holes in the pavement. I knelt to take a closer look. Each hole was several inches long and just an inch or so deep. I asked my colleague what they were. He seemed surprised that I didn't know. "The police are now shooting from the helicopters down into the streets," he said. I stood up and looked for the end of the bullet holes. There were dozens perhaps hundreds of them running down the street.

As argued throughout this book, these violent police tactics have not been successful in threatening the gangs' dominant position within these communities. The borders of Maré's gang territories have not changed since I left Maré in 2015 and CVNH, CVPU, and TCP continue to govern local populations in much the same way as when I lived there. To varying degrees, the three gangs maintain a constant armed presence on the streets, punish disobedience through a mix of threats and violence, and continue to monitor their borders and the behavior of residents. For their part, CVNH and TCP have continued their decades-long conflict, engaging in periodic shootouts and invasions along their shared border, leading to an estimated 114 such confrontations between 2016 and 2021 (Redes da Maré 2021). CVPU, on the other hand, continues to experience no intergang violence even as BOPE and other police units conduct regular militarized operations in Parque União. Maré's lone milícia continues to operate in Roquete Pinto and Praia de Ramos while facing very little police scrutiny, indicative of the very different relationship these groups have with the state (see later).

The drug trade in Maré also continues to operate in much the same fashion. Each gang sells drugs at numerous bocas scattered throughout their territories. In return visits to the field, I noticed the number of bocas had increased even further with several new ones where none had existed before. The existing bocas have also expanded. When I lived in Maré, the largest bocas were just a couple of small plastic tables with a handful of bags filled with different amounts of marijuana, cocaine, and crack. By 2018, these had grown to include multiple large wooden tables with dozens of plastic tubs filled with different quantities of multiple drugs. Alongside their traditional wares, the gangs also sold lôlô or lança perfume, black lança (a different version of this inhalant), *skunk* (a more potent flower form of marijuana), and *craconha* (a mixture of marijuana and crack, also referred to as *desirée* or *criptonita*). The prices have also increased. When I arrived to Maré, the largest bag of cocaine cost R$50. In 2023, the same sack of cocaine cost R$300.

The gangs have also expanded and systematized their revenue generating activities beyond the retail drug trade. According to Severino,

They [CVNH] have about 200 barracas at each of the bailes that can make about R$800 a night selling drinks and things but they have to pay the gang R$80 for the space. The gang even started charging R$20 a week for the barracas that line each of main streets in Nova Holanda. …A lot of the favela is the property of the gang now. If anything belongs to the city, the gang will appropriate it and find a way to make money off it. They've been buying lots of apartments and renting them out too.[3]

I also heard that the gang was increasingly looking to buy property outside of the favela itself and had taken an interest in some of the new apartment buildings that were being built on the other side of Avenida Brasil.[4]

Each of the gangs, to varying degrees, also continues to provide benefits. Some residents still seek out gang members to resolve personal conflicts and disputes though several interlocutors suggested that the gangs have increasingly shifted away from these sorts of services because it is too time-consuming and difficult.[5] Ever since military occupation, more and more of the gang

---

[3] Severino 7/4/2018.
[4] Field notes 3/5/2023.
[5] Josie 7/10/2018; Sergio 7/24/2018.

membership is comprised of youth. "It's all kids now," Severino told me.[6] These younger gang members are less able to resolve disputes because they are not familiar with the local social terrain. As a result, fewer residents will seek them out. More of the members are also not born and raised in these neighborhoods. Vinícius described the importance of gang members being cria in this way: "Guys from outside create problems in the community because no one knows them. I don't know them! It's different when you know someone from infancy. The conversation is different. You ask how their kids are, you talk about family. The community will always seek out the gang members from here to solve their problems."[7]

Instead of dispute resolution, the gangs have increasingly relied on economic stimulation to gain the support of residents. They have diversified their revenue streams both to profit from their territorial control but also to forge more dependent relations with the community. Many hundreds if not thousands of residents in each gang territory rely on the gang for their housing, to make money, or gain access to informal and illicit markets that only the gang can provide. These residents rely if not directly then at least indirectly on the gang for their economic livelihood, thus providing gangs higher levels of security when facing active enforcement by the police.

For their part, the baile funks are even larger and better produced than before, with light shows, multicolored tents, stages, and prominent DJs. Nova Holanda and Parque União each have two bailes a week (Thursday and Saturday in Nova Holanda and Friday and Sunday in Parque União) while TCP produces one of the largest and most popular bailes in the city, the *Baile da Disney*, on Saturday nights in Vila do João. Drug sales at the bailes, once just a large table at the entrance with sacks of drugs haphazardly arranged, have multiplied. Numerous smaller bocas appear the nights of the bailes, surrounding the main party area, while the main boca is even more prominently displayed with spotlights and glass jars for the different flavors of skunk. Although a full analysis of the evolution of criminalized governance since the end of military occupation is not possible here, the dynamics described and theorized in this book appear to be intact nearly a decade after the primary fieldwork was completed.

POSSIBILITIES FOR THE FUTURE

When I first arrived in Rio de Janeiro, I believed, like many during those heady early days of the UPPs, that progress was indeed possible. The UPPs represented the best chance for Rio de Janeiro to exit the cycles of violence from which the city had been suffering for the past three decades. A new

---

[6] Severino 7/4/2018.
[7] Vinícius 11/9/2014.

relationship between police and favela communities could be built from within the existing public security apparatus, by employing new police, training them in human rights, paying them better, and through the implementation of a community policing methodology. By the time I left the field, I was no longer optimistic. Reports of abuse and corruption within UPPs across the city had become commonplace and the old behaviors and tactics of Rio's police were returning. Moreover, during my time in Maré, I witnessed and documented a huge range of abuses and violations by the police: from illegal invasions of homes, destruction of property, verbal threats, physical beatings, kidnappings, bribery schemes, extortion, extralegal executions, and even a "mega" massacre.[8]

These ugly truths about policing in Rio de Janeiro do not absolve the gangs of their equally violent and abusive acts but serve as a reminder that gangs do not exist in a vacuum.[9] Their emergence and evolution are the direct result of how the Brazilian state and the city of Rio de Janeiro have constructed their political and economic institutions, how favela communities emerged and grew, and how the police have been tasked with controlling and repressing these communities. Policymakers and the public security apparatus have used the excuse of the presence of drug-trafficking gangs to both promote and allow violent and illegal policing practices with near absolute impunity. Without a shift in state policy and practice, the future of Maré and Rio de Janeiro's other favelas looks much the same: an unending "War on Drugs," continuing mass incarceration of young black men and women, and the death and injury of thousands each year, all forms of violence which contribute to the ongoing marginalization and criminalization of these communities. Amidst all of this, Rio's gangs will continue to govern, providing some limited benefits in the attempt to stay just on the good side of the community so that they can avoid enforcement and continue to profit from their illicit activities.

Any change to this status quo must begin with Rio's approach to policing. Perhaps the best we can hope for, given the multiple pathologies of the public security apparatus and the lack of political will to fully reform the institution (never done following the end of the dictatorship), is to focus on limiting violence, especially its most lethal forms. To do so, political elites as well as

---

[8] A *chacina* (massacre) is the killing of three or more people at once while a *mega chacina* (mega massacre) is the killing of eight or more people (Hirata et al. 2023).

[9] In another public meeting in Maré, Luiz Eduardo Soares, the eminent anthropologist and former Public Security Secretary came to speak about policing in favelas. He did not avoid the brutality and abuse inflicted on these communities by the public security apparatus but reminded the attendees that police are also the victims of abuse. "I receive tons of denunciations from police on a daily basis. They describe terrible working conditions. They are prohibited from organizing politically and for this reason they turned into milícias. Police feel enslaved and exploited by the state and they pass this victimization onto the favelas. The police are not the enemy, they are workers," he concluded emphatically (Meeting #18).

the larger public must acknowledge, first and foremost, that militarized police operations are not a solution to gang territorial control nor are they effective in reducing violence or crime, more generally. When I began fieldwork for this book, police killings in Rio were at their nadir, with just 416 reported incidents in 2013. Since then, however, police killings have returned to and even surpassed their previous records. In 2019 alone, police killed 1,814 citizens, accounting for almost half (45 percent) of all homicides in Rio de Janeiro, a horrifying statistic for any society much less an ostensibly democratic one (ISP-RJ 2023b). Police operations have also become increasingly indiscriminate as police have been allowed to shoot from helicopters while punishing and abusing residents that are viewed as collaborating with the gangs, practices that were either not allowed or more effectively controlled during the early years of Pacification. In Maré, for instance, a reported 283 rights violations – including illegal home invasions, destruction of property, assault, kidnapping, torture, murder, and sexual violence – were reported in 2022, 92 percent of which occurred during police operations (Redes da Maré 2023b).

Controlling the most violent police operations will also have knock-on benefits for favela residents. As police have become more indiscriminate, some of the incentives for good gang behavior have been lost. First, if gang members are targeted regardless of their behavior, then each individual gang member is less likely to worry about how they treat residents. Second, police operations that also punish or target residents, even those not involved with the gangs, will only further drive these communities toward supporting the gangs, regardless of their behavior. Either way, enforcement most effectively produces more responsive and beneficial behaviors on the part of gangs only if police selectively target gang members, especially those who behave poorly by either abusing residents or refusing to provide them benefits. Unrestrained police behavior means that gangs need to provide even less to gain the support of the community.

It is also worth noting that police operations that successfully target gangs can also produce higher levels of violence. Significant enforcement efforts targeted at one gang can create power imbalances that incentivize rivals to become more aggressive as a weakened opponent offers opportunities for territorial expansion. In this sense, there is a delicate balance between enforcement encouraging better behavior from gangs while not destabilizing the organizations so much that it produces more competitive relations with their rivals. Such a connection between police operations and intergang violence is documented throughout the empirical chapters of this book and has been further demonstrated by subsequent developments in Maré.

Redes da Maré began tracking police operations and their consequences in 2016. They then used these data to petition Rio's government to put an end to nighttime police operations, install cameras and GPS tracking devices on all police vehicles, make ambulances available during operations, and elaborate plans to reduce harm during operations (Redes da Maré 2023a).

The *Ação Civil Pública* (Civil Public Action) that resulted from this mobilization officially began in June 2017, following a decision by Rio's *Tribunal de
Justiça* (Court of Justice). Although the public security apparatus refused to
fully comply with this juridical order, over the next year and a half, the number
of police operations decreased by 61 percent. Simultaneously, armed confrontations between Maré's gangs shrank by 43%, and the number of days with
school and health post closures were reduced by 71% and 76%, respectively
(Hirata et al. 2021, 24). When the ACP was suspended in 2019, police killings
and confrontations between the gangs returned to previous levels (Redes da
Maré 2019b).

To date, the ACP represents the most robust attempt by favela communities to hold the police accountable and reduce their repressive and predatory
tactics within these territories. It also convincingly demonstrates how police
operations often fail to prevent or reduce gang violence, and may, in fact,
stimulate it. The ACP of Maré can also be seen as an indirect attempt by local
social movements and civil society to influence criminalized governance. By
constraining the counterproductive policies of the public security apparatus,
social movements and NGOs are also seeking to reduce the violent impulses
of the gangs and improve the local security environment, more generally. As
exemplified in the quote at the beginning of this chapter, favela communities have limited options regarding gangs. Without a reliable and accountable
public security apparatus, directly resisting and challenging gangs remains
unthinkable in Maré and most other favelas in the city.[10]

In the long run, it is still unknown how reducing police operations and
lethality will impact criminalized governance but a shift in policing to only
use militarized operations to prevent intergang violence or to pursue and
investigate the most violent types of crime, such as homicide, could be one
way to encourage gangs to avoid confrontation, and reduce lethal violence
considerably. At least according to data collected from the Public Ministry,
in 2022, the stated objectives of police operations in Maré were mostly to

---

[10] Other evidence connecting police violence to intergang competition relates to a similar court
order preventing police operations during the COVID-19 pandemic. In May 2020, following an
egregious police killing of an adolescent, João Pedro, in a nearby municipality, then-Governor
of Rio de Janeiro state, Wilson Witzel, briefly suspended police operations in favelas. The sus-
pension was then extended by the Brazilian Supreme Court, which prohibited police operations
other than in extreme circumstances. Lethal violence fell precipitously across the city. Police
killings immediately dropped 60 percent as homicides also fell by 58 percent even as other
forms of crime were unaffected (Trudeau 2022). Perhaps violence levels would have dropped
even further had Rio's Civil and Military Police not refused to comply with the court-ordered
prohibition. After only two months, police operations, many of which were in direct contraven-
tion of the judicial ruling, returned to previous levels (Bianchi 2021; Hirata, Grillo, et al. 2021;
Redes da Maré 2021). Combined, these developments suggest that "pacifying" Rio's police
could produce a more stable, less violent city overall. How that could happen is a more difficult
question. If Brazil's Supreme Court is unable to control the violent tendencies of Rio's police, it
is difficult to see what domestic institution could accomplish this.

recover stolen cars or other items (54%), combat the drug trade (22%), or are unknown (16%) (Redes da Maré 2023b). That year, only one of thirty-seven operations was to investigate a homicide, and none were used to prevent or stop violence between the gangs. I am not suggesting that stolen cars and other crimes are not worthy of police attention, but focusing more on the prevention of violence, especially lethal forms, and encouraging gangs to shift away from confrontation would be an enormous step in the right direction. Amidst less competitive relations, gangs could reduce their coercive profile, allowing for greater freedom of movement, less monitoring, and fewer punishments of residents. Reducing intergang violence could also open space for less repressive and violent public security policies while allowing more positive, longer-term relationships between the public security apparatus and marginalized communities to emerge.

Another mechanism that could also be further developed in addressing violence between Rio's gangs would be negotiations or mediation between these groups. In this regard, several Latin American states have experimented with negotiating directly with gangs and other OCGs to reduce violence.[11] Such policies are not a panacea and face considerable obstacles. For one, such negotiations can serve to strengthen these organizations by institutionalizing their political authority and making the state subservient to their interests (Bunker 2015; Cruz and Durán-Martínez 2016). Moreover, negotiations with OCGs often require a very particular set of circumstances to even be possible: a centralized gang leadership as well as continuity in state-level politicians. That said, negotiations could be a useful tool for public security officials to employ to contain violence within areas of persistent conflict in the city.

In addition to reducing violence, a more robust and practical set of drug policies emphasizing harm reduction and moving away from prohibition and criminalization are sorely needed. The "War on Drugs" and the mass incarceration policies that the US has exported to Brazil and numerous other Latin American countries have failed to contain illicit drug use or prevent its production and retail sale. Instead, prohibition has only served to make these illicit markets even more profitable, as confiscation and enforcement increases their value, further incentivizing suppliers to enter the market. For several decades now, gangs and a variety of other OCGs have been some of the primary actors in the production, transshipment, and retail sales of these substances, allowing them to profit and expand their capacity for violence but also their ability to corrupt and influence state agents.

---

[11] Ecuador even legalized gangs for a period (2008–17) and provided them funding to engage in social projects, which reduced violence incredibly (Brotherton and Gude 2021). Although difficult to envision in the context of Rio de Janeiro, where gangs have already evolved into powerful armed actors, the key lesson is that the further the state represses and marginalizes these individuals, the key lesson is that the further the state represses and marginalizes these individuals, they will become increasingly vulnerable and feel the need to provide for their own security.

Drug criminalization has also contributed to mass incarceration. Brazil has the world's third largest prison population with 750,000 inmates, 29 percent of which are incarcerated for drug offenses.[12] And yet, few mainstream politicians at either end of the political spectrum have taken practical steps to change the status quo despite rhetoric to the contrary.[13] For their part, the UPPs only reinforced this prohibitionist and punitive public policy even if they took a purportedly community policing approach to doing so (Franco 2014). There have been some notable shifts in cannabis legislation across the Americas but there is little political support for doing the same to cocaine, heroin, and methamphetamines. Legalization and decriminalization policies will remain controversial as long as the public is convinced that these substances are dangerous and need to be combatted with imprisonment and violence. Unfortunately, without a more robust political and social movement advocating an end to the global drug prohibition regime, transformational change in this area is unlikely in the short-term.

While a much larger wave of legalization and decriminalization would, no doubt, harm the interests and revenue of Maré's gangs and many other OCGs around the world – as well as law enforcement branches and a variety of private industries that rely on prohibitionist frameworks – it is overly optimistic to imagine that such a shift will also bring an end to repressive public security practices, mass incarceration policies, or the vast social and political inequities that have given rise to criminalized groups and their governance. Moreover, gangs are highly strategic and flexible organizations, capable of responding to any new policy environment by expanding their illicit and violent practices in other directions. In this regard, Maré's gangs have already diversified their economic activities and, if drug profits were to dwindle, they would likely further shift their revenue generating activities toward protection rackets, property speculation, and the monopolization of a variety of other informal and illicit markets. Regardless, given the immense costs of continuing the "War on Drugs," drug legalization remains a promising path forward as it pertains to gang and police violence as well as reform of the criminal justice system.

Finally, it is difficult to separate race and racism from questions surrounding gangs and favelas. Part of the reason why a large portion of society

---

[12] *Departamento Penitenciário Nacional* 2022.
[13] Jair Bolsonaro's term in office produced a mostly abstinence-based approach to drug policy and reinstituted involuntary commitment, in which drug users could be forced in detox programs, some run by Evangelical movements (*Lei N° 13.840*). For his part, Luiz Inácio Lula da Silva promised to end Brazil's "War on Drugs" in his most recent presidential campaign and the Brazilian Supreme Court decriminalized marijuana for personal use in 2024. In Lula's first two presidential terms, however, he showed no signs of combatting drug criminalization or mass incarceration. In fact, his national drug policy law of 2006 was responsible for further criminalization of drugs (*Lei N° 11.343*) with the prison population more than doubling during his tenure (Institute for Crime & Justice Policy Research 2023).

continues to accept and even support police violence of the sort witnessed daily in Rio de Janeiro is precisely because it is used against communities that are still largely perceived as lazy, backward, and criminal in the public imagination. These stereotypes and prejudices have changed very little over time and, given the sheer weight of popular media and news attention which focuses on precisely these more unsavory aspects of favelas, they are unlikely to change anytime soon. This book does little to remedy or address those misconceptions though I want to emphasize that Maré is simultaneously the site of significant artistic and cultural production, collective action, and political mobilization.[14] Moreover, I hope this book contributes to a more complex understanding of gangs as more than just purely violent, psychotic, and antisocial organizations to ones that maintain multifaceted relationships with local communities, simultaneously engaging in more benevolent and prosocial practices even as they traffic drugs and employ violence and coercion.

We must also not forget about the mostly black and brown men and women who make up these organizations. Brazilian society, like the rest of the world, has spent very little time and resources planning and providing meaningful paths away from gangs and violence. For instance, the UPP program included no formal amnesties or demobilization and disarmament programs for gang members to leave these organizations. Instead, the state sought their detention and arrest or expected these individuals to find their own way or to flee the communities which they called home. Without viable alternatives, other than prison or death, it is unrealistic to expect these men and women to pursue other paths. Over the course of my fieldwork, I accompanied several projects which attempted to help gang members leave these organizations. To varying degrees, they offered gang members services and formal employment opportunities. Although their methodologies and success rates varied, they were instrumental in providing opportunities for gang members to find other possibilities in life.

For every gang member that successfully exits the gang life there are dozens more waiting to enter. Until now, the Brazilian state has attempted to control favela youth and adolescents through arrest, detention, and harassment. Such methods of deterrence and repression are counterproductive. They push youth to find security and meaning in gang membership. Instead, favela youth must be engaged, protected, reincorporated into community structures, and offered viable economic and social alternatives. Prevention programs and services targeted at youth vulnerable to joining a gang, especially those that are struggling in school and may grow up in difficult family circumstances, have, until now, mostly been provided by local NGOs and other community organizations. They must be expanded considerably to disrupt the gang pipeline. So long as

---

[14] My desire to combat these monolithic understandings of favelas also directly led to the development of other collaborative projects (Barnes, Poets, and Stephenson 2021).

gangs and other OCGs have such a constant and unending source of expend-able labor, their influence and control will not wane.

GENERALIZABILITY AND IMPLICATIONS

This book has valued depth over breadth. The theory building and empiri-cal testing (if we can call it that) have occurred almost exclusively within the confines of Complexo da Maré, just one set of neighborhoods. And yet, my objective has always been a comparative one. I have compared criminalized governance across time and space within Maré, which offers, I believe, analyt-ical purchase over some of the driving forces behind these behaviors and their consequences. Implicitly, I have also been comparing criminalized governance in Complexo da Maré to other contexts in which gangs and other types of armed groups govern, both across the rest of Rio de Janeiro and beyond. In this section, I make these comparisons more explicit, providing some initial indications that the theory developed herein travels and can be useful in under-standing armed governance in other contexts.

Drug-Trafficking Gangs in Rio de Janeiro

The city of Rio de Janeiro contains more than 1,074 favelas and 406 hous-ing projects within its municipal borders, almost all of which are controlled and governed by drug-trafficking gangs or milícias (Instituto Pereira Passos 2023).[15] What has historically made comparing across these many different contexts difficult or even impossible is that, until recently, there were no reli-able data concerning the location of these groups in the city.[16] Thanks to the *Grupo de Estudos dos Novos Ilegalismos* (Study Group of New Illegalities, or GENI) and several other research initiatives, the location and activities of all illicit actors operating in Rio de Janeiro are now being mapped, analyzed, and made accessible.

A preliminary analysis of the GENI data suggests that, although an out-lier in terms of population, Maré is representative of the larger universe of cases in Rio. For instance, between 2006 and 2021, CV has remained the dominant faction in the city with between 700,000 and 1,100,000 citizens living under CV gang control (Hirata and Couto 2022). By contrast, TCP has controlled territories with a population between 250,000 and 400,000, and ADA between 100,000 and 350,000 residents for that same period.[17]

---

[15] Many of the smallest favelas and housing projects, which often have only a few hundred resi-dents, may not have a fully fledged gang or milícia present.

[16] Rio's newspapers stopped mentioning the names of the gang factions in the early 2000s and the police refuse to make such information publicly available.

[17] Although they do not enumerate the total number of gangs or milícias, GENI provides an inter-active map (https://fogocruz.github.io/mapafc/), which displays all such territories throughout the city and the rest of the state.

Over time, Maré has been home to gangs connected to all three factions and is broadly representative of the population proportions though, since 2009, TCP's territories are more populous (≈68,000) than the two CV gang areas combined (≈54,000).

How representative are the levels of threat that Maré's gangs experience as compared to the rest of the city? One recent study tracked every intergang shootout between 2008 and 2019, finding that Maré's gang territories were not even in the top ten most violent areas of the city (Perpétuo 2021). Morro do Timbau and Baixa do Sapateiro, TCP's historic turf, were eleventh on the list with forty-three shootouts during that period, TCP's housing projects were eighteenth with thirty-seven shootouts, and Nova Holanda twentieth with thirty-three shootouts (p. 24). Even if we combine all three of these territories, it would still be behind Morro do Juramento, which experienced a staggering 129 shootouts over that same period. Thus, although Maré may seem like an especially conflictual case, it is by no means an outlier in terms of rival threat. Moreover, only 30 percent of favelas and housing projects report any shootouts at all (p. 22), suggesting that many of Rio's gangs share more in common with CVPU's security environment, in which there is very little or no rival competition and violence.

As for police enforcement, a similar lack of available data has, until recently, made comparisons across the city impossible. For the long history of gang territorial control and governance in Rio de Janeiro, there has been no systematic accounting of when and where police operations and enforcement practices against gangs and milícias occurred nor the outcomes of such operations. Such a lack of transparency on the part of the public security apparatus is nothing new though the Institute of Public Security has, over time, made significant strides in systematizing and making crime and enforcement statistics accessible. Again, GENI has provided systematic documenting of police operations from 2007–18, finding that Complexo da Maré accounts for roughly 4.8 percent or 400 of the 8,162 police operations conducted in the city over this period (Hirata and Grillo 2019a). This statistic is on par with the other major favela complexes in the city: Alemão (5.5%), Penha (4.5%), Bangu (3.6%), and Costa Barros (3.6%) (p. 10). Although these statistics provide some clue regarding the willingness and ability of the police to pursue and enforce against gangs, they do not include the equally important off-the-record activities that police engage in while conducting operations, including executions, disappearances, kidnapping, and extortion, or, bribes and other more collaborative exchanges. These activities may vary significantly across the city but remain largely obscured from view.

Overall, Maré's cases can be considered to span the full range of security environments found across Rio, yet another reason why the theory developed here should generalize to other gang territories. Nearly every favela within the city contains a similar history of competition, conquest, defeat, enforcement, and governance. Further tests of rival competition leading to coercion and enforcement producing more responsive benefits are needed to confirm or falsify the claims made in this book. With the greater availability of cross-favela data, this is becoming increasingly likely though the exact mechanisms leading to these behaviors will require more qualitative methodologies to corroborate as well.[18]

Milícias in Rio de Janeiro

This book has largely avoided the discussion of milícias. Over the last two decades, these police-connected racketeering organizations have spread and multiplied throughout the city. Their origins can be traced to a group of death squads and vigilante groups operating in the 1970s and 1980s (Huggins 1991). The connections between these groups and the public security apparatus, although perhaps once less collaborative, became stronger over time as off-duty and retired police increasingly began to populate the membership of these groups (Manso 2020). By the 1990s, a more durable and territorial organization formed in Rio das Pedras, a large favela in the Zona Oeste of the city, and began running local protection rackets (Arias 2017; Manso 2020). By the 2000s, dozens of milícias had emerged and, with the help of police stationed in local precincts and battalions, had taken control of areas previously dominated by drug-trafficking gangs (Cano 2008; Manso 2020). For a short period in the late 2000s and early 2010s, at the height of the UPPs, the state sought to uncover and prosecute some of these groups and their leaders.[19] This period did not last long, however, and after the weakening of the Pacification program and a return to more repressive policing practices, the milícias recommenced their expansion (Hirata, Cardoso, et al. 2021). By 2022, milícias controlled more territory with roughly the same number of citizens in the city as all three of Rio's drug-trafficking factions combined (Hirata and Couto 2022).

Two favelas within Complexo da Maré, Roquete Pinto and Praia de Ramos, are even controlled by a milícia, which invaded the area in 2006, expelling a gang connected to TCP. I did not include these territories in the book for several reasons. First, conducting interviews and participant observation in milícia territories is extremely dangerous, much more than gang neighborhoods, because of the higher levels of impunity these organizations enjoy. In addition, although I visited these two neighborhoods dozens of times over the course

---

[18] Perhaps the best place to find evidence of the mechanisms and behaviors I theorize in this book are in the numerous journalistic articles and books, autobiographies, and documentaries concerning Rio's gangs, which offer numerous insights into the dynamics surrounding warfare, enforcement, and governance (see Alvito 2001; Amorim 1993, 2000, 2010; Barcellos 2003; Dancing with the Devil 2009; Notícias de Uma Guerra Particular 1999; Glenny 2016; Lima 1991; Manso 2020; Bill and Athayde 2006; Silva 2012; Soares 2000; Soares, Bill, and Athayde 2005; and Ventura 1994; among others).

[19] *Comissão Parlamentar de Inquérito 8/14/2008.*

of fieldwork and even conducted interviews with some residents of this area, I decided not to pursue interviews with milícia members because I thought doing so could endanger myself or my interlocutors if Maré's gangs found out. Second, although Rio's drug-trafficking gangs and milícias can both be included within the broader category of OCGs, they could not be more different. Like gang members, most *milicianos* also grew up in favelas, though they are usually in their twenties, thirties, or even older when they join these groups. In addition, because they are mostly off-duty or retired public security personnel (military or civil police, firefighters, or even private security), they often have at least a high school education, some professional skills, and training in combat and violence. This differs incredibly from the trajectory of most gang members, who join these groups when they are adolescents or teenagers, have little or no education, no financial resources, no training, and lack the social or political capital of adults when they join.

Moreover, gangs are criminalized by the state and society in ways that milícias are not. Gang members are viewed by a large majority of the public as unredeemable criminals, deserving of imprisonment or death, and although some gangs maintain relations with low-level politicians, they are not considered legitimate political actors. Milícia members, on the other hand, are seldom criminalized to the same degree even if they are known to engage in extremely unsavory acts. Instead, they have largely been left to dominate and control numerous favela territories throughout the city with relatively few efforts to combat them even if their activities are technically illegal. As a result, these organizations have increasingly infiltrated and corrupted the public security apparatus and the political institutions of the city, state, and even federal government. In this regard, the milícias have used their control of favelas and neighborhoods as a political base to win elections with some milicianos even becoming politicians themselves (Hidalgo and Lessing 2014).[20] It is unthinkable for any gang members to be involved in the same sort of political project.

The political economy of milícias also differs from the gangs. As noted previously, although gangs have diversified their economic activities over the last decade, the bulk of their profits still come from the drug trade. For most of their history, milícias refused to engage in the drug trade, at least openly, instead developing an alternative set of revenue generating activities, including charging protection fees from local businesses and monopolizing informal markets (cooking gas, cable television, transportation, and property speculation) within and around the areas they operated (Arias 2013; Manso 2020). Their recent expansion has led some of these groups to be more involved in the drug trade, though they do not yet seem to be engaging in retail sales directly.[21]

---

[20] *Comissão Parlamentar de Inquérito* 8/14/2008.
[21] *UOL* 1/7/2019.

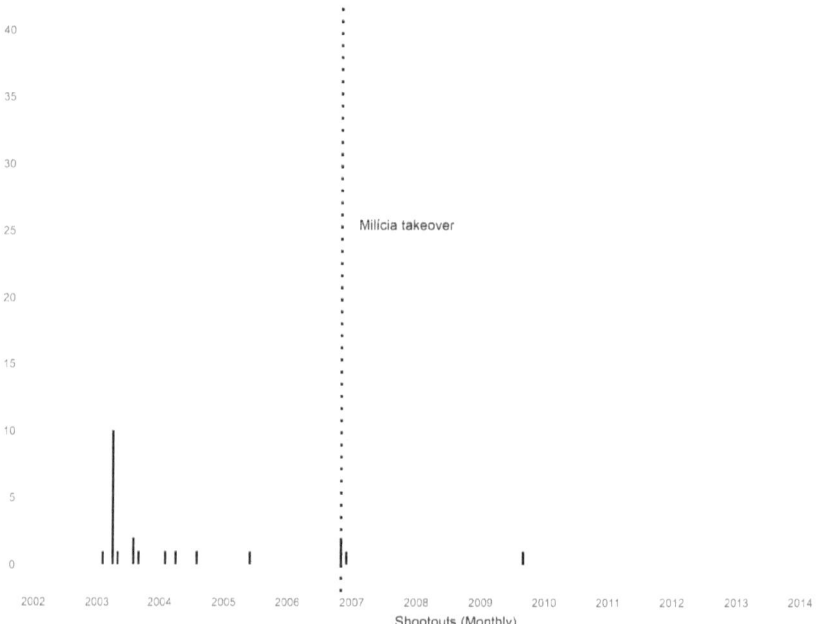

FIGURE 9.1 Shootouts in milícia territory (monthly)
Data from *Disque-Denúncia*. Visualization by Pranjal Drall.

For all these reasons, milícias are extremely different organizations than the gangs my research focused on. Even so, we can see how the theory developed in this book provides some insights into their governance activities. For one, until recently, milícias seldom engaged in violent competition with each other for territorial control. Notice the almost total lack of shootouts in the milícia-held neighborhoods of Maré after their takeover (see Figure 9.1). There are some rare cases of milícias confronting one another and the police but these conflicts more often occur quietly, through assassinations and disappearances rather than military-style takeovers we observe during gang warfare.[22] Due to this relative lack of existential threat, milícias take an even more hands-off approach to surveillance and monitoring than the most laissez-faire gangs. In my numerous visits to the milícia neighborhoods in Maré, I never once saw a milícia member on the streets nor any weapons within the territory. The milícias monitor the behavior of local residents closely through their networks though they seldom do so as overtly or ostentatiously as gangs.

Milícias also employ significant amounts of coercion within their territories by expelling and killing individuals that refuse to comply with their

---

[22] *O Globo* 10/25/2023.

rules, fail to make protection payments on time, or are viewed as undesirable – unregistered workers, persons experiencing homelessness, drug users, and trans or gay individuals, among others. In fact, many milícias are known to be even more violent and coercive than many of the city's gangs. For instance, in Santa Cruz, Campo Grande, Bangu, and Realengo, neighborhoods dominated by milícias in the Zona Oeste of the city with very low levels of armed confrontations between these groups, the number of homicides are nonetheless the highest in the city (Borges 2016, 21). This suggests that milícias' coercive behavior is driven by other, perhaps more political or economic, objectives rather than fear of a violent takeover by a rival.

The dynamics surrounding enforcement and provision of benefits also differ greatly from gangs. For one, the collaborative relationship milícias maintain with the public security apparatus prevents the aggressive enforcement efforts we observe in many gang territories. Police operations, although not unheard of in milícia territories, are much rarer. In Praia de Ramos and Roquete Pinto, there have been extremely few police operations since the milícia took over these neighborhoods in November 2006 (see Figure 9.2). According to one study, only 6.5 percent of the police operations conducted in 2019 were in milícia-dominated neighborhoods (Hirata, Cardoso, et al. 2021). Another study found that between 2016 and 2019, of the roughly 3,000 shootouts

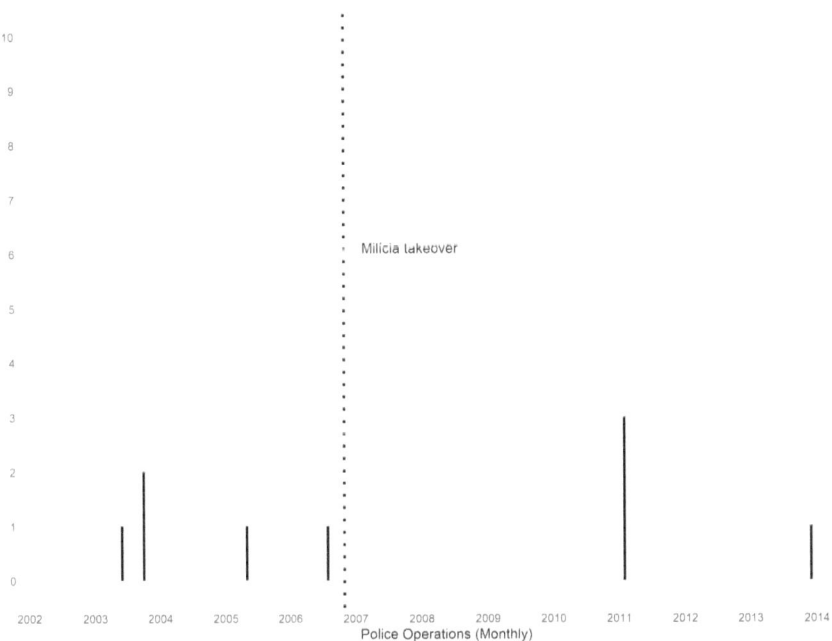

FIGURE 9.2 Police operations in milícia territory (monthly)
Data from *Disque-Denúncia*. Visualization by Pranjal Drall.

involving police across the city, only 88 (2.97 percent) involved milícias.[23] With little chance of enforcement, residents of these territories have even less influence over milícias than gangs.

Nonetheless, milícias still provide some goods and services to residents though they appear to be part of an effort to capitalize on the local monopoly of violence and less about maintaining local support. Through their political connections, the milícias have increasingly engaged in infrastructure and development projects. For instance, the federal housing program, *Minha Casa, Minha Vida* (My House, My Life), built hundreds of housing projects for low-income families, the vast majority ending up in milícia-dominated areas of the city (Hirata, Cardoso, et al. 2021). More generally, the milícias often illegally appropriate land, demand a cut of the sales of all homes and businesses within favelas, and tightly control the real estate market in what some have called *"urbanismo miliciano"* (milícia urbanism) (Benmergui and Gonçalves 2019). These infrastructure and development projects are often welcomed by many residents within these communities and create varying levels of economic dependence. If and when residents are on the receiving end of a bad deal or disagree with milícia initiatives or decisions, however, they are powerless to stop them (Arias 2017, 231–33).

If the public authority in Rio eventually decides to start combatting these organizations more aggressively, it remains to be seen how the threat of enforcement will incentivize a different set of governance strategies and if their criminalization will increase the possibility of inter-milícia violence or even milícia-police confrontations. Overall, although milícias constitute a very different type of OCG than the gangs I focus on in this book, my findings have interesting implications for milícia governance, especially concerning how their local security environment shapes the incentives and constraints to coerce and provide benefits to communities but also how it could impact their economic activities and political behaviors.

Beyond Rio de Janeiro

Moving beyond the borders of Rio, a natural comparison is São Paulo, Brazil's other big industrial city. Like Rio, São Paulo witnessed the exponential expansion of neighborhood gangs, vigilante groups, and police violence in the final decades of the twentieth-century as well as the emergence of a prison-based drug-trafficking faction, the PCC, in the 1990s. Unlike Rio, however, where several different factions formed, setting off competition for control of the lucrative drug-selling favela territories, the PCC quickly monopolized control of the entire penitentiary system within São Paulo (Biondi 2009, 2014; Dias 2013; Feltran 2018). Any preexisting gangs or other criminal groups

[23] *UOL* 1/7/2019.

were eradicated or eventually incorporated into the PCC as it gradually expanded from the prisons throughout the city's favelas and urban periphery (Feltran 2010b). Since then, homicides in the city have plummeted from a rate of 52.6 per 100,000 in 1999, one of the highest in Latin America, to 4.6 in 2022 (Secretaria da Segurança Pública do Estado de São Paulo 2023), what has been termed a *pax monopolista* (Biderman et al. 2019).

As a result, São Paulo has none of the competitive and militarized territorial dynamics observed in Rio de Janeiro. For instance, PCC members need carry no weapons in the neighborhoods where they live. They've even created a "gun library" in which members can check out weapons only when they need them (Denyer Willis 2014). They have also developed a very different type of drug-trafficking operation. Instead of engaging in retail sales directly and selling only within specific territories, the PCC employs a consignment model, in which they offer the drugs on loan to small-scale retailers often not part of the organization itself (Hirata and Grillo 2019b; Lessing and Denyer Willis 2019). Moreover, although PCC members continue to be pursued and imprisoned by the police, aggressive and militarized police operations are much rarer than Rio. A couple of brief episodes of outright confrontation between state security forces and the PCC, most notably in 2006 and 2012, have occurred but these are the exceptions. Once known for its equally brutal and aggressive tactics, São Paulo police have also managed to reduce the scale of their violence and even tacitly collaborated with the PCC in managing and regulating violence across the city (Denyer Willis 2015; Feltran 2010b).

These dynamics are only possible because of a near total lack of rival competition within the city. The absence of rival factions has created a completely different set of PCC governance behaviors. Although they still use some degree of coercion and punishment to ensure rules compliance by their members, payment by their customers, and to prevent and control certain forms of violence in peripheral neighborhoods, they use this tool sparingly. The organization keeps exhaustive records of any misconduct by their members' and their drug-selling clients, what some have referred to as "criminal criminal records," which allows them to punish more systematically and less coercively (Lessing and Denyer Willis 2019). Moreover, coercion is not intended to prevent or punish individuals from cooperating with rivals which do not exist and there seem to be no geographic or territorial components to the use of coercion. Overall, the PCC in São Paulo lacks the coercive dynamics so ubiquitous in Rio de Janeiro.

The PCC has also refrained from governing as intensively or providing the same level of services as some of Rio's gangs. Although the PCC maintains some social policies that peripheral neighborhoods can avail themselves of, including *"debates"* (tribunals) to control and regulate violence in these neighborhoods, they are less involved in the daily lives of residents and have not sought to provide dispute resolution mechanisms broadly, do not offer welfare to hundreds of families in need, nor do they throw massive and elaborate parties. Instead, most of the PCC's governance activities seem to be focused internally, as they provide legal teams, bookkeeping, social assistance, and a raffle for cars and houses exclusively for members (Denyer Willis 2014, 2015). By not tying themselves to particular territories which they must defend and populations they must control and gain the support of, the PCC has avoided a more intensive governance role in these neighborhoods, at least within São Paulo.

Beyond Rio de Janeiro and São Paulo, gangs are a ubiquitous urban phenomenon in Brazil. Most cities have smaller-scale gangs that often operate in *quebradas* (micro-territories), and that little resemble the highly centralized and specialized gangs I have described and theorized in this book. Many of these groups have not consolidated their territorial exclusivity, either because they lack the organizational resources to do so or because competition and violence with other neighboring gangs has not yet led to more significant organizations (Wolff 2015). However, over the last two decades, an increasing number of cities have witnessed the rapid expansion, consolidation, and violent competition between these groups, undergoing much the same process that Rio de Janeiro did several decades ago. This evolution is not inevitable, by any means, but the result of expanding illicit networks and drug markets, the implementation of mass incarceration policies, and the emergence and involvement of prison-based factions. In fact, although Rio de Janeiro may seem to be a particularly violent city, as measured by homicides, it is no longer in even the top fifty most violent Brazilian cities when based on population size (Igarapé Institute 2023). While not all homicides in Brazil can be directly traced to intergang or gang–police violence, one recent study demonstrated that aggregate levels of violence across four Brazilian cities (São Paulo, São Luís, Maceió, and Porto Alegre) are directly tied to the dynamics of conflict between gangs and prison-based factions (Feltran et al. 2022).

In this regard, it is also increasingly difficult to separate the dynamics of Rio de Janeiro and São Paulo from these other contexts. Through the massive expansion of the prison system across the entire territory of Brazil – growing from roughly 400 carceral institutions in 1997 to 1500 in 2020 (Denyer Willis and Loureiro 2023) – both CV and PCC have spread to each and every one of Brazil's twenty-seven states as well as several other Latin American countries, including Bolivia, Paraguay, Uruguay, Argentina, Peru, Colombia, and Venezuela (de Lima et al. 2018; Lessing and Denyer Willis 2019). In doing so, they have connected and incorporated hundreds if not thousands of neighborhood gangs, providing them organizational resources, financing, and access to drugs and weapons, while encouraging their expansionary efforts. This has led other local gangs to form alliances between themselves or with rival prison-based factions to resist these invasive networks (Feltran et al. 2022). Until 2016, CV and PCC maintained a long-running nonaggression pact, but when this alliance broke down, it set off a series of prison riots and massacres across Brazil while further incentivizing competition and violence between neighborhood gangs in the peripheries and favelas of numerous cities.[24] Many of the governance dynamics I have theorized in this book, although perhaps once unique to Rio de Janeiro, are being observed over an increasing swath of Brazilian cities. At least initially, the theory developed here could prove useful to understanding these outcomes.

Finally, the insights of this book are also relevant to a great many urban spaces beyond Brazil, where gangs are engaged in a similar set of governance practices as they compete for territory with rivals and attempt to avoid the enforcement efforts of police. Dozens if not hundreds of cities in the Americas have witnessed a similar set of dynamics, most notably Chicago, Los Angeles, Newark, St. Louis, Ciudad Juarez, San Salvador, San Pedro Sula, Tegucigalpa, Guatemala City, Port-au-Prince, Caracas, and Medellín. In this regard, forty-six of the fifty most violent cities in the world reside in the region (CCSPJ 2021). In addition, other cities around the world, including Karachi, Mumbai, Dhaka, Nairobi, Lagos, Kinshasa, Cape Town, Johannesburg, London, Liverpool, Birmingham, and Glasgow have already or are currently undergoing similar processes of violent gang competition and increasingly militarized enforcement. To be sure, the constellation of gangs and various other OCGs, the specificities of local illicit markets, as well as the composition of the public security apparatus and the nature of political institutions will shape the exact governance practices in which these groups engage, but, in nearly every case, gangs are shaping the local social order and providing some limited benefits to marginalized populations. Making these international connections and further elaborating the primary drivers behind their governance activities will require further work but scholars in this area should be increasingly cognizant of how these patterns are being replicated across most of the world's urban spaces.

The theory and findings of this book likely apply to other types of OCGs, including cartels, mafias, militias, and paramilitaries, among others. Much research has already documented how competition between these groups drives levels of violence.[25] This book builds on these works by developing a more specific set of mechanisms through which violence increases: rival competition between OCGs incentivizes a set of coercive practices targeted at citizens that inhabit their own territories. Many of these groups may look little like gangs – they can be entirely adult organizations, are often less criminalized by the state, are located in rural areas with little or no state presence, and, in some

---

[24] *The Guardian* 1/10/2017. Some scholars have even begun to connect these interfactional disputes to the governance practices of neighborhood gangs (Siqueira, Nascimento, and Moraes 2022).

[25] See Arias (2013, 266), Calderón et al. (2015), Dell (2015), Durán-Martínez (2018), The Economist (2012), Holland and Rios (2017), Magaloni et al. (2020), Sánchez-Jankowski (1991, 164), Skarbek (2014, 82–83), Trejo and Ley (2018, 2020, 2021), and Yashar (2018) among others.

cases, have managed to fully compromise the state and its representatives in the areas they operate. How such organizations attempt to govern local communities might look quite different from the practices I document here. That said, I suspect that their use of coercion and provision of benefits are similarly determined by their security environment and what these organizations need from local communities.

Much of the research in this area has, so far, not differentiated between rival and police threats and how each may shape the behavior of these groups in divergent ways. Although there may be circumstances where the state represents as existential a threat as a rival, it is hard to find examples where an OCG has been eradicated by the state. In fact, some of the only examples of states effectively repressing OCGs in the short-term are when the state fully commits to use all the indiscriminate and coercive power at its disposal, leading to the violation of numerous civil and political rights. Such a set of policies means the state has irrevocably shifted toward authoritarianism, a move we have observed most recently in the case of Nayib Bukele's crackdown on the maras in El Salvador (Blitzer 2022), Rodrigo Duterte's "War on Drugs" in the Philippines (Johnson and Fernquest 2018; Kenny and Holmes 2020), and in the case of Mussolini's campaign against the *Cosa Nostra* in Sicily (Dickie 2007), among others. These efforts have perhaps been successful at repressing criminalized groups in the short term but seldom eradicate them for good and have dramatic negative consequences on citizen populations, more broadly. While the processes of democratization and liberalization in the latter half of the twentieth century led to the exponential increase in OCGs across a great many states in the world, it remains to be seen if a shift back toward authoritarianism can put the genie back in the bottle.

Finally, the theory of criminalized governance developed here has implications for the study of rebel governance. Scholars of this area have shown that relations with civilians during wartime is heavily influenced by strategic considerations regarding territorial control. For instance, Metelits has argued: "When an insurgent group does not face competition over resources, the level of violence against civilians is more likely to be low. In contrast, when an insurgent group faces competition – a threat to control of resources – the level of violence against civilians is likely to rise" (2009, 11).

This argument mirrors Kalyvas' finding that armed groups which face no competition for territory use little selective violence targeted at civilians while contexts of contestation produce much higher levels (2006, 173–208).[26] Nordstrom lends ethnographic details to these theories when she describes how the relatively peaceful communities in the Mozambican civil war were

---

[26] Kalyvas does hypothesize, however, that zones of parity or equal control between two armed groups also leads to low levels of violence (p. 204). This might also be the case when two gangs are equally matched in terms of violent capabilities, neither wanting to disrupt the balance of power to initiate a conflict they are unsure they can win.

places where the rival armed group was not present and the rebels did not need to make examples of residents (1997, 100–107). In the Colombian context, Arjona has also argued that competition between armed groups will likely lead to more coercive and disordered relationships with local communities: "When two or more warring sides compete for territorial control, disorder emerges... The defending group tightens its control over the population and redirects all available resources to defend itself. ...abuse of civilians becomes more common as the group tries to prevent cooperation with the enemy. Preexisting rules regulating combatant behavior towards community members are often violated" (2016, 202).

In addition, Mampilly has also outlined how rebel groups prioritize military objectives over pursuing civilian administrative goals when the intensity of conflict increases, while armed groups focus fewer resources on monopolizing violence and territorial control during periods of relative calm (2011, 81–82). Finally, Kasfir has shown that in the case of the National Resistance Army in Uganda, the military threat from the state caused them to dismantle civilian governance arrangements and end its dedication to civilian participation, implementing a more one-sided and coercive form of order (2005, 291).

In most of these contexts, whether it is a state's military or another rebel or paramilitary group as the belligerent seems to matter little. In this regard, over the last fifteen years, the phenomenon of inter-rebel fighting in the midst of civil war has been increasingly documented and theorized (Bakke, Cunningham, and Seymour 2012; Christia 2012; Cunningham 2018; Fjelde and Nilsson 2012; Pischedda 2020). And yet, whether and how such inter-rebel conflicts impact governance differently from rebel–state ones remains unclear. At least according to most of the existing literature, these groups exist within an anarchic environment in which all threats, be it state, rebel, paramilitary, or other, can be equally existential.[27] I wonder if this, in fact, is the case. Does a state military constitute the same type of threat to a rebel group as a competing non-state armed group? Would a rebel group faced with a belligerent rebel or paramilitary organization respond the same as they would to military forces?

Moreover, with the tendency for states to employ "hearts-and-minds" counterinsurgency tactics – in which they have at least tacitly accepted that they cannot win the war with violence alone and instead attempted to gain the support of local populations by restricting their use of indiscriminate violence, building infrastructure, and through the provision of some goods and services – do we observe the same divergence in governance responses? That is, do rebel groups shift their governance activities further toward

---

[27] Some recent research has looked at rebel governance in contexts with multiple non-state armed groups competing and collaborating with one another in the midst of a larger conflict with the state or occupying army though there are still no conclusive findings regarding how these dynamics shape governance practices (see Berti 2023; Kalyvas 2015b; Revkin 2020).

providing benefits to the local population when the state attempts to combat them through "hearts-and-minds" tactics rather than violence alone? In
areas where the state maintains a limited presence and little or no legitimacy,
do rebels not fear the state's attempts to govern just as Maré's gangs seemed
to little fear the military's attempts to win over residents?[28] These are mostly
idle questions on my part. Whatever the answers, there are multiple ways
in which the dynamics I observed could overlap and resemble rebel governance notwithstanding the multiple differences in the origins, motivations,
and behaviors of these groups.

The final implication of this book for the study of rebel governance concerns
the role of civilians. As pointed out in Chapter 1, an entire subliterature on
wartime civilian agency has emerged, documenting and theorizing how and
why civilians should not be considered unwitting or passive actors in these
conflicts but deeply involved in their dynamics and consequential to the outcomes. A similar literature has attempted to understand how and why citizens
relate to gangs or OCGs, mostly focusing on their strategies of resistance.[29]
Until now, these two literatures have mostly existed in parallel, subtly and
indirectly cross-pollinating one another (Barnes 2023). There is ample room
for greater convergence as the strategies civilians and citizens have at their disposal appear to be quite similar (Arjona 2017).

This book has added to these debates by theorizing two ways that residents
of gang territories can influence governance outcomes: through denunciation
and by making demands. These are just the most obviously consequential
behaviors. There are a variety of other resident responses that may matter for
criminalized governance but which remained beyond the purview of this study,
including how and why residents attempt to avoid gangs while nonetheless
living in their territories, the various ways they can resist these groups, and,
finally, how a large number of residents may collaborate with gangs in subtle
and not-so-subtle ways. Much more research is required in this area because
how residents respond to governance by gangs, OCGs, and a variety of other
armed groups, not to mention state security forces, has enormous social,
political, and economic consequences for these communities, and thereby, our
larger societies.

In the end, I hope that this book can be useful not just to those interested
in the academic study of these topics but to anyone who has lived in such
contexts and is searching for greater understanding of criminalized groups
and their behavior. In this regard, places such as Complexo da Maré are not

---

[28] Research from Medellín recently found that when the state experimentally increased its presence and services sixty-fold across eighty gang (combo)-held territories, there was virtually no
effect on governance, legitimacy, or crime (Blattman et al. 2023). This is also reminiscent of the
failed attempts to win over Maré's population during military occupation.

[29] See Arias (2006a), Arias and Rodrigues (2006), Arjona (2017), Ley, Mattiace, and Trejo
(2019), and Moncada (2019a, 2019b, 2022).

the exception but, increasingly, the rule with an estimated 77 to 101 million citizens of Latin America alone subject to the governance of one kind of OCG or another (Uribe et al. 2024). Many marginalized communities have become contested territories, divided between these groups, as battle lines have been drawn around and through these neighborhoods with disastrous consequences for all involved. For their part, states have failed to contain and mostly exacerbated these developments. A new and different path forward must be charted. I hope this book provides some insights into what that future might be.

10

Epilogue

> We aren't bad people. Others might think they know who we are, but they don't know our hearts.
>
> —Severino, former CVNH member

ONE LAST INTERVIEW

When I last saw Severino in early July 2018, he had been out of the gang for several years, since the military had occupied Maré. Part of his incentive to leave was that his boss, Flávio, the gerente de crack for CVNH at the time, was arrested just one month into the occupation. Severino had worked under Flávio for most of his career and his fortunes within the organization were directly tied to him. This is how upward mobility in the gang worked: If a gerente did well within the organization and worked his way up, from managing a boca to overseeing one of the types of retail drugs to perhaps being in charge of security or even becoming the gerente geral, he brought the men with whom he worked most closely along with him. Once Flávio was arrested, however, Severino was left to fend for himself and suddenly had no concrete position within the gang. He could have approached some of the higher ups within the organization to see if there was another role available to him but, as described in Chapter 8, CVNH was running a more limited operation during occupation and could not provide work for everyone.

Severino, like many of the older gang members, used this opportunity to leave the gang, forced to find a way to make money and provide for his family – a wife and two children – through other means. Unlike the many gang members that joined the NGO program I described in Chapter 9 or that turned to the informal sector, Severino sought formal employment. He had a carteira assinada, a government issued document necessary for formal employment, but with only a middle-school education, he was qualified for a limited number of jobs. Nonetheless, after a couple of months of searching, he was hired as a traffic attendant, which consisted of him arriving in the early morning hours and standing at one of several intersections directing traffic for ten hours a day. Severino was grateful to have the job but did not like the boring and tedious work. Moreover, it did not pay well, only R$724 ($250) per month, the minimum wage at the time, roughly a third of what he had previously made while in the gang.

Toward the end of my fieldwork, I seldom saw Severino as he was working most days and spent a lot less time at his corner. I never even had the chance to say goodbye before I returned to the US in 2015. In the intervening years, I often wondered, how he was doing. So, when I returned to Maré in July 2018 and saw him standing at his old corner one afternoon, I was very happy to see him. We greeted one another in typical Brazilian fashion, with a hug and lots of smiling. I told him I had returned to do some follow-up research and to see how things were going for some of the people I had interviewed, including him. We arranged to meet the following afternoon at one of the local NGOs which allowed me to use their offices or classrooms to conduct interviews.

The next day, surrounded by whiteboards and computer monitors, I repeated the consent script to Severino for the last time.[1] He was different than I remembered him. His thinking was much clearer. He had been a habitual marijuana smoker for virtually his entire adult life (not uncommon among gang members) and sometimes during our conversations at the corner I could tell that he was high. His eyes would be red and swollen. He would be less talkative, more withdrawn. I avoided asking him for interviews or touching on more serious subjects when he was like this as I knew he was likely dealing with serious stresses in his life and did not want to add to those in any way. This day, Severino was more lucid than in some of our previous interviews, perhaps the result of not smoking as much or the reduced need to self-medicate after leaving the gang.

We talked for a couple of hours. Severino did most of the talking as I scribbled furiously in my notebook. Our interviews had a way of meandering to various topics, depending on what he wanted to talk about and the various questions I had for him. We started by addressing how things had changed in the community since the end of the military occupation, then he began recalling his time in prison, which he had always seemed reticent to talk about in previous interviews. He described how he was arrested in 2006 near his corner.

---

[1] Even if I conducted multiple interviews with the same person, I always repeated the consent script to make sure they remembered their rights and how I would use the information, protect their confidentiality, and ensure their anonymity.

"All of a sudden, a police operation happened. No one expected it. There were a couple of firecrackers set off, but it was too late. They caught me running away and took me to the Battalion where I was put in a small cell with eight other guys. We were all from the Zona Norte. Two of them were TCP," he said.

"How did you know?" I asked.

"Because I heard them talking about it. I told them that I was a thief. We were in that cell for three days straight. I didn't sleep. How could I? If you sleep, it's the same thing as death. If they found out I was CV, they would kill me. The police also abused us and there were some fights between the guys in the cell. After three days they sent me to Frei Caneca [one of Rio's large prison complexes] where I was put in a cell with 22 other CV guys from all over – Campo Grande, Penha, and lots of other places. The room was about half the size of this classroom," he said, looking around. The classroom was about 15 feet by 15 feet, so the cell was only 100 square feet.

"How did you sleep?" I asked.

"On the floor. There were no hammocks, just paper mats so we slept one on top of the other. Some rested standing up. I was there for six months. The other part of the 18 months I was in another room right next door. The same size only with more guys in it. They only let us out onto the patio for an hour each day. We got visitors once a week. There were books but I can't read very well."

"Did anyone visit you?"

"Yes, my mother."

"Did your wife or your kids come?"

"No."

"Why not?"

"I'm not sure. The kids were little. I was only 18 years old at the time."

"How did you pass the time?"

"We talked. We talked about what it was like where each of us lived. What the drug trade was like, how they organized themselves, the wars, the police, the women… We talked about everything."

"Did it help you?"

"It helped me to understand reality of my situation."

"And what was that?"

"That there was no escape."

"When you got out, what did you do?"

"I started trafficking the first day I was back. How was I gonna eat or drink otherwise?"

We eventually talked about his life after leaving the gang. I asked if it was easy to leave. "Yeah, you can leave and come back anytime. It didn't always used to be this way. You used to have to leave through the church but now you can just tell the gerente geral that you're leaving." After eventually quitting his job as a traffic attendant, Severino had found a position as a custodian at a large building in a nearby neighborhood. He'd been there for a year or so. He liked the evening shift but was still not paid very well, only the minimum wage at the time, R$950 ($250) per month.² Moreover, he found getting paid only once every two weeks difficult. With the money he gave his ex-wife to take care of their kids and rent for his one-room apartment, it didn't leave him very much for food and other expenses. "I don't even have a fan," he lamented. Having lived in Maré in a one-room apartment without air conditioning for nearly eighteen months, I knew how a fan could save your life in the summer months.

"How are things with your ex?" I asked.

"Not good," he said and looked down at his hands for a moment. "Last Christmas she told me she couldn't take it anymore. I don't know why. When I try to talk to her about it, we just end up fighting," he said, visibly upset by the situation. I waited to see if he wanted to say anything more, not wanting to press him. We sat in silence for a while.

"What do you think about your time in the gang now that you've been out for a while?" I asked finally, changing the subject. Severino thought for a moment. "I think the gang members themselves don't even understand how important they are in the community. They help the residents a lot. They give money and solve problems all the time. And that's why the people support the gangs more than they do the police."

"What would you like people to know about the gangs in Maré?"

"We aren't bad people. Others might think they know who we are, but they don't know our hearts."

We finished around lunchtime and I asked if he had eaten yet. Severino shook his head vigorously. We exited the NGO and went over to a small diner across the street, where I ordered a few sandwiches and some sodas. After we ate, I asked him if he would like to go to the grocery store with me. I needed to pick up a few things and we could get some things for him too. He readily agreed and said he would pay me back once his paycheck came. He took out his salary receipt and showed me how much he was owed. I said that was not necessary. In the grocery store, I told him to buy whatever he wanted. A few minutes later, he came back with a basket with several large bags of rice and dried beans.

"Is that all you want?" I asked.

"Maybe some meat," he said.

"Of course. Anything you want."

He ordered several different kinds of meat from the butcher. In total, the bill came to R$150 ($40 at the time). This was the first and only time I paid for anything other than small snacks and meals for my interlocutors. I never felt like Severino (or anyone else) wanted or expected such gifts from me, despite

---

² The Brazilian Real's value has fluctuated significantly over the last ten years.

giving so generously of his time and attention. He had allowed me to conduct several hours-long interviews with him, we had had dozens of conversations, and he had always warned me of impending violence or other dynamics within the community, all of which were essential not only for my research but my personal safety as well. I could tell that despite having left the gang and no longer being subject to the many stressors of gang life, Severino was struggling financially, and his personal life was in turmoil.

He thanked me profusely for the groceries. I told him it was I that should be thanking him for everything he had done for me. "*Estamos juntos*" (We are together), he said. "*Estamos juntos*," I repeated. We embraced again and parted ways. I watched him until he turned the corner out of sight then headed in the opposite direction, toward Avenida Brasil, and world beyond Maré.

Appendices

Int. #	Date	Age	Gender	Category	Residence of interviewee	Pseudonym
1	1/28/13	30s	F	Community leader	Outside of Maré	
2	1/28/13	30s	M	Community leader	Outside of Maré	
3	2/12/13	20s	F	Community leader	Complexo da Maré: TCP	Nanda
4	2/12/13	50s	F	Community leader	Complexo da Maré: TCP	Tainá
5	3/15/13	40s	M	Former gang member	Outside of Maré	Lucas
6	3/15/13	40s	M	Former gang member	Outside of Maré	Davi
7	4/5/13	40s	M	Former gang member	Outside of Maré	Dazio
8	4/5/13	40s	M	Former gang member	Outside of Maré	Zacarias
9	4/9/13	50s	M	Former gang member	Outside of Maré	Tuco
10	4/9/13	30s	F	Scholar	Outside of Maré	
11	4/24/13	40s	M	Former gang member	Outside of Maré	Guilherme
12	6/19/13	50s	F	Community leader	Outside of Maré	
13	7/8/13	40s	M	Former gang member	Outside of Maré	Robinho

(*continued*)

TABLE A.I *(continued)*

Int. #	Date	Age	Gender	Category	Residence of interviewee	Pseudonym
14	7/16/13	40s	M	Resident	Complexo da Maré: CVNH	Fausto
15	7/17/13	30s	M	Former gang member	Complexo da Maré: CVNH	Francisco
16	7/17/13	40s	M	Former gang member	Outside of Maré	Lucas
17	7/17/13	40s	M	Resident	Complexo da Maré: CVNH	Fausto
18	7/18/13	30s	M	Former gang member	Outside of Maré	Teodoro
19	7/23/13	30s	F	Former gang member	Outside of Maré	Nina
20	7/28/13	30s	M	Resident	Outside of Maré	
21	7/31/13	50s	F	Community leader	Complexo da Maré: TCP	Fátima
22	7/31/13	50s	F	Community leader	Complexo da Maré: TCP	
23	7/31/13	50s	F	Resident	Complexo da Maré: TCP	
24	7/31/13	60s	F	Resident	Complexo da Maré: TCP	
25	7/31/13	60s	F	Resident	Complexo da Maré: TCP	
26	8/2/13	40s	M	Resident	Complexo da Maré: CVNH	Fausto
27	8/8/13	40s	M	Former gang member	Outside of Maré	Natan
28	8/11/13	30s	M	Resident	Outside of Maré	
29	8/20/13	30s	M	Former gang member	Complexo da Maré: CVNH	Francisco
30	8/22/13	40s	M	Former gang member	Outside of Maré	Natan
31	8/26/13	20s	M	Former gang member	Outside of Maré	
32	8/29/13	50s	F	Community leader	Complexo da Maré: CVNH	Eduarda
33	9/5/13	20s	F	Community leader	Outside of Maré	
34	9/5/13	20s	F	Community leader	Outside of Maré	
35	9/5/13	20s	M	Community leader	Outside of Maré	
36	9/9/13	40s	M	Former gang member	Outside of Maré	Davi
37	9/19/13	50s	F	Community leader	Complexo da Maré: CVNH	Eduarda
38	9/20/13	40s	M	Former gang member	Outside of Maré	Lucas

TABLE A.1 *(continued)*

Int. #	Date	Age	Gender	Category	Residence of interviewee	Pseudonym
39	10/2/13	40s	M	Community leader	Complexo da Maré: TCP	Carlitos
40	10/2/13	20s	M	Current gang member	Complexo da Maré: CVNH	Severino
41	10/3/13	40s	M	Community leader	Complexo da Maré: TCP	Carlitos
42	10/4/13	40s	M	Former gang member	Outside of Maré	Dazio
43	10/8/13	50s	M	Resident	Complexo da Maré: CVPU	Beto
44	10/10/13	40s	F	Community leader	Complexo da Maré: TCP	Yuliana
45	10/11/13	50s	M	Community leader	Complexo da Maré: CVNH	Eduardo
46	10/15/13	20s	M	Former gang member	Outside of Maré	
47	10/16/13	50s	M	Community leader	Complexo da Maré: CVNH	João
48	10/17/13	40s	M	Former gang member	Outside of Maré	Robinho
49	10/17/13	40s	M	Former gang member	Outside of Maré	Lucas
50	10/17/13	40s	F	Former gang member	Outside of Maré	Talia
51	10/18/13	40s	M	Former gang member	Complexo da Maré: CVPU	
52	10/28/13	40s	M	Former gang member	Complexo da Maré: CVNH	Reinaldo
53	10/31/13	40s	M	Former gang member	Outside of Maré	Lucas
54	10/31/13	40s	M	Former gang member	Outside of Maré	Robinho
55	11/1/13	40s	M	Resident	Complexo da Maré: CVPU	Eusebio
56	11/6/13	50s	M	Community leader	Complexo da Maré: TCP	Lúcio
57	11/6/13	60s	M	Community leader	Complexo da Maré: TCP	Vicente
58	11/7/13	40s	F	Former gang member	Outside of Maré	Talia
59	11/14/13	40s	M	Current gang member	Complexo da Maré: CVNH	Flávio
60	3/6/14	30s	M	Community leader	Complexo da Maré: CVPU/CVNH	Breno

(continued)

TABLE A.1 *(continued)*

Int. #	Date	Age	Gender	Category	Residence of interviewee	Pseudonym
61	3/12/14	30s	M	Former gang member	Complexo da Maré: CVNH	Angelo
62	3/18/14	40s	M	Community leader	Complexo da Maré: CVPU/CVNH	Artur
63	3/20/13	40s	M	Current gang member	Complexo da Maré: CVNH	Nelson
64	3/20/14	20s	F	Community leader	Complexo da Maré: CVPU	Andrea
65	3/20/14	50s	F	Community leader	Complexo da Maré: CVNH	Eduarda
66	3/26/14	30s	M	Community leader	Complexo da Maré: CVPU/CVNH	Breno
67	3/26/14	40s	M	Current gang member	Complexo da Maré: CVNH	Inácio
68	3/27/14	50s	F	Resident	Complexo da Maré: CVNH	
69	4/1/14	40s	F	Community leader	Complexo da Maré: CVNH	Sofia
70	4/1/14	60s	F	Community leader	Complexo da Maré: CVNH	Doroteia
71	4/3/14	30s	M	Current gang member	Complexo da Maré: CVNH	Inácio
72	4/8/14	30s	M	Community leader	Complexo da Maré: CVNH	
73	4/9/14	20s	F	Community leader	Outside of Maré	
74	4/9/14	50s	M	Community leader	Outside of Maré	
75	4/17/14	20s	M	Current gang member	Complexo da Maré: CVNH	Márcio
76	4/17/14	30s	M	Current gang member	Complexo da Maré: CVNH	Everton
77	4/17/14	20s	M	Former gang member	Complexo da Maré: CVNH	Tomás
78	4/18/14	40s	M	Former gang member	Outside of Maré	Lucas
79	4/24/14	40s	M	Current gang member	Complexo da Maré: CVNH	Inácio
80	4/24/14	30s	F	Scholar	Outside of Maré	Isabel
81	4/29/14	50s	M	Community leader	Complexo da Maré: TCP	Neto
82	5/13/14	40s	M	Community leader	Complexo da Maré: CVNH	
83	5/15/14	30s	M	Current gang member	Complexo da Maré: CVNH	Severino
84	6/11/14	30s	M	Community leader	Outside of Maré	Dudu

TABLE A.I *(continued)*

Int. #	Date	Age	Gender	Category	Residence of interviewee	Pseudonym
85	6/11/14	30s	M	Current gang member	Complexo da Maré: CVNH	Severino
86	6/13/14	40s	M	Community leader	Complexo da Maré: CVPU/CVNH	Artur
87	6/16/14	40s	M	Resident	Complexo da Maré: CVNH	Fausto
88	6/18/14	40s	M	Resident	Complexo da Maré: CVNH	Lino
89	6/24/14	20s	M	Scholar	Outside of Maré	
90	6/24/14	20s	M	Scholar	Outside of Maré	
91	6/27/14	40s	M	Community leader	Complexo da Maré: CVPU	Patrício
92	6/28/14	40s	M	Community leader	Complexo da Maré: CVPU	Patrício
93	6/30/14	20s	M	Resident	Complexo da Maré: TCP	Feliciano
94	7/1/14	20s	F	Community leader	Complexo da Maré: CVNH	Luana
95	7/1/14	30s	M	Community leader	Complexo da Maré: CVNH	
96	7/1/14	40s	F	Resident	Complexo da Maré: CVNH	Felícia
97	7/3/14	30s	M	Former gang member	Complexo da Maré: TCP	Fulton
98	7/10/14	30s	M	Former gang member	Complexo da Maré: TCP	Josué
99	7/15/14	20s	M	Former gang member	Complexo da Maré: TCP	Timo
100	7/15/14	20s	M	Former gang member	Complexo da Maré: TCP	Josué
101	7/15/14	20s	M	Former gang member	Complexo da Maré: TCP	
102	7/15/14	20s	M	Former gang member	Complexo da Maré: TCP	
103	7/15/14	20s	M	Former gang member	Complexo da Maré: TCP	Felipão
104	7/15/14	30s	M	Former gang member	Complexo da Maré: TCP	Fulton
105	7/15/14	30s	M	Former gang member	Complexo da Maré: TCP	
106	7/22/14	30s	M	Former gang member	Complexo da Maré: TCP	Josué
107	7/23/14	30s	M	Former gang member	Complexo da Maré: TCP	Josué
108	7/29/14	30s	M	Former gang member	Complexo da Maré: TCP	Luiz

(continued)

TABLE A.1 (*continued*)

Int. #	Date	Age	Gender	Category	Residence of interviewee	Pseudonym
109	7/30/14	30s	M	Former gang member	Complexo da Maré: TCP	Luiz
110	7/31/14	30s	M	Former gang member	Complexo da Maré: TCP	Luiz
111	8/7/14	30s	M	Community leader	Complexo da Maré: CVPU/CVNH	Breno
112	8/7/14	30s	M	Current gang member	Complexo da Maré: CVPU	
113	8/21/14	30s	M	Former gang member	Complexo da Maré: TCP	Daniel
114	8/28/14	20s	M	Former gang member	Complexo da Maré: TCP	
115	8/28/14	20s	M	Former gang member	Complexo da Maré: TCP	Timo
116	8/28/14	30s	M	Former gang member	Complexo da Maré: TCP	Fulton
117	8/29/14	30s	F	Resident	Complexo da Maré: TCP	
118	8/29/14	50s	F	Community leader	Complexo da Maré: TCP	Susana
119	8/29/14	50s	M	Community leader	Complexo da Maré: TCP	Lúcio
120	8/29/14	50s	M	Community leader	Complexo da Maré: TCP	Carlitos
121	8/29/14	60s	M	Community leader	Complexo da Maré: TCP	Vicente
122	9/8/14	40s	M	Former gang member	Outside of Maré	Plínio
123	9/15/14	30s	M	Community leader	Complexo da Maré: CVNH/TCP	Manoel
124	9/22/14	50s	F	Scholar	Outside of Maré	Luna
125	9/26/14	20s	F	Community leader	Complexo da Maré: TCP	Olívia
126	9/26/14	40s	M	Scholar	Outside of Maré	
127	9/26/14	40s	M	Scholar	Outside of Maré	
128	9/27/14	40s	M	Community leader	Complexo da Maré: CVPU/CVNH	Artur
129	10/2/14	20s	F	Former gang member	Complexo da Maré: CVNH	Luiza
130	10/6/14	40s	M	Community leader	Complexo da Maré: CVPU/CVNH	Artur
131	10/6/14	30s	M	Former gang member	Complexo da Maré: CVNH	Bruno
132	10/6/14	30s	F	Resident	Complexo da Maré: CVPU	
133	10/7/14	60s	M	Resident	Complexo da Maré: CVNH	

TABLE A.1 *(continued)*

Int. #	Date	Age	Gender	Category	Residence of interviewee	Pseudonym
134	10/27/14	30s	M	Former gang member	Complexo da Maré: CVNH	Bruno
135	11/3/14	40s	M	Community leader	Complexo da Maré: CVPU/CVNH	Artur
136	11/3/14	20s	M	Former gang member	Complexo da Maré: CVNH	Marcos
137	11/3/14	40s	M	Resident	Complexo da Maré: CVNH	Lino
138	11/3/14	60s	M	Resident	Complexo da Maré: CVNH	Joaquim
139	11/5/14	40s	M	Community leader	Complexo da Maré: TCP	Bras
140	11/5/14	50s	M	Community leader	Complexo da Maré: TCP	Neto
141	11/9/14	40s	M	Community leader	Complexo da Maré: CVPU	Artur
142	11/9/14	40s	M	Resident	Complexo da Maré: CVPU	Vinícius
143	11/12/14	50s	F	Resident	Complexo da Maré: CVNH	Fernanda
144	11/19/14	30s	M	Community leader	Complexo da Maré: CVNH	Gilson
145	11/19/14	70s	M	Resident	Complexo da Maré: CVPU	Gustavo
146	11/19/14	70s	F	Resident	Complexo da Maré: TCP	Silvia
147	11/19/14	70s	M	Resident	Complexo da Maré: TCP	Ademir
148	12/1/14	30s	F	Community leader	Complexo da Maré: CVNH	Elisangela
149	12/1/14	40s	M	Community leader	Complexo da Maré: TCP	Valdemir
150	12/4/14	70s	M	Resident	Complexo da Maré: TCP	Ademir
151	12/8/14	30s	M	Resident	Complexo da Maré: TCP	Thiaguinho
152	12/10/14	20s	F	Former gang member	Complexo da Maré: CVNH	Gabriela
153	12/11/14	50s	F	Community leader	Complexo da Maré: CVNH	Veronica
154	12/15/14	20s	F	Former gang member	Complexo da Maré: CVPU/CVNH	Lidiane
155	12/16/14	30s	M	Community leader	Complexo da Maré: CVPU/CVNH	Breno
156	12/17/14	20s	F	Former gang member	Complexo da Maré: CVNH	Luiza
157	12/17/14	20s	M	Former gang member	Complexo da Maré: CVNH	Marcos

(continued)

TABLE A.I *(continued)*

Int. #	Date	Age	Gender	Category	Residence of interviewee	Pseudonym
158	12/17/14	20s	M	Former gang member	Complexo da Maré: CVNH	
159	12/17/14	20s	M	Former gang member	Complexo da Maré: CVNH	
160	12/17/14	20s	M	Former gang member	Complexo da Maré: CVNH	
161	12/17/14	20s	M	Resident	Complexo da Maré: CVPU	Sergio
162	12/17/14	20s	M	Resident	Complexo da Maré: TCP	Naldo
163	12/23/14	30s	M	Community leader	Complexo da Maré: CVPU	Evaristo
164	1/7/15	30s	M	Resident	Complexo da Maré: TCP	Osvaldo
165	1/9/15	40s	M	Community leader	Complexo da Maré: TCP	Valdemir
166	1/9/15	20s	M	Resident	Complexo da Maré: TCP	Thiago
167	1/9/15	60s	F	Resident	Complexo da Maré: TCP	Rosalyn
168	1/12/15	40s	M	Police	Outside of Maré	Delegado I
169	1/12/15	40s	M	Police	Outside of Maré	Delegado II
170	1/13/15	20s	M	Resident	Complexo da Maré: TCP	Mateo
171	1/14/15	50s	F	Community leader	Complexo da Maré: CVNH	Eduarda
172	7/24/15	30s	F	Community leader	Complexo da Maré: TCP	Julia
173	8/3/15	60s	F	Resident	Complexo da Maré: CVPU	Angela
174	8/15/15	20s	M	Former gang member	Complexo da Maré: CVNH	Márcio
175	8/17/15	50s	M	Community leader	Complexo da Maré: CVNH	Julio
176	8/22/15	40s	M	Community leader	Outside of Maré	Vitor
177	8/25/15	50s	M	Community leader	Outside of Maré	
178	8/25/15	50s	M	Scholar	Outside of Maré	
179	1/2/17	30s	M	Resident	Complexo da Maré: CVNH	Wagner
180	1/9/17	40s	M	Community leader	Complexo da Maré: CVPU/CVNH	Artur
181	1/10/17	30s	M	Community leader	Complexo da Maré: CVPU/CVNH	José
182	1/11/17	40s	M	Community leader	Complexo da Maré: CVPU/CVNH	Artur
183	1/13/17	60s	M	Resident	Complexo da Maré: CVPU	Beto
184	1/13/17	40s	M	Scholar	Outside of Maré	Rui

TABLE A.1 (*continued*)

Int. #	Date	Age	Gender	Category	Residence of interviewee	Pseudonym
185	1/14/17	20s	F	Community leader	Complexo da Maré: CVNH	Fabiene
186	1/16/17	20s	M	Resident	Complexo da Maré: CVPU	Bernardo
187	1/17/17	20s	M	Resident	Complexo da Maré: CVPU	Ramón
188	1/17/17	30s	F	Scholar	Outside of Maré	
189	1/18/17	50s	F	Community leader	Complexo da Maré: CVPU	Octavia
190	1/18/17	20s	M	Resident	Complexo da Maré: CVPU	Dagobert
191	4/4/17	30s	M	Community leader	Complexo da Maré: CVPU/CVNH	Breno
192	7/3/18	60s	M	Community leader	Complexo da Maré: CVPU	Danilson
193	7/4/18	30s	M	Former gang member	Complexo da Maré: CVNH	Severino
194	7/10/18	30s	F	Resident	Complexo da Maré: CVNH	Josie
195	7/14/18	30s	M	Resident	Complexo da Maré: CVNH	Wagner
196	7/24/18	20s	F	Community leader	Complexo da Maré: CVNH	Fabiene
197	7/24/18	20s	M	Resident	Complexo da Maré: CVPU	Bernardo
198	7/24/18	20s	M	Resident	Complexo da Maré: CVPU	Sergio
199	7/24/18	20s	M	Resident	Complexo da Maré: TCP	Naldo
200	7/24/18	30s	M	Resident	Complexo da Maré: CVPU/CVNH	Breno
201	7/24/18	30s	F	Resident	Complexo da Maré: TCP	Neusa
202	7/29/18	30s	F	Resident	Complexo da Maré: CVNH	
203	7/30/18	40s	M	Resident	Complexo da Maré: CVNH	Fausto
204	7/30/18	40s	M	Community leader	Outside of Maré	
205	7/31/18	30s	F	Community leader	Complexo da Maré: CVPU/ CVNH	Andrea
206	7/31/18	40s	M	Community leader	Complexo da Maré: CVPU	Ronaldo

* If interviewees lived or worked in more than one gang territory, each is listed as residence.
** 18–20 year olds have been included in the twenties category. No minors were interviewed.

Appendices

TABLE A.2 *Summary of interviews*

Category	Breakdown	Total	Percent*
Gender**	Male (inc. trans men)	154	75%
	Female (inc. trans women)	52	25%
Residence of interviewee***	CVNH	78	35%
	CVPU	39	17%
	TCP	55	25%
	Outside of Maré	51	23%
Age	20s	45	22%
	30s	56	27%
	40s	62	30%
	50s	28	14%
	60s	11	5%
	70s	4	2%
Interview type	Current/Former gang member	73	35%
	Community leader	73	35%
	Resident	48	23%
	Other	12	6%

* Percentages rounded.
** Gender identities were not asked about directly.
*** Interviewees with multiple residences have been counted separately.

TABLE A.3 *List of public and private meetings attended*

Meeting #	Date	Meeting participants	# of Attendees
1	8/5/13	NGOs, AMs	20
2	8/24/13	NGOs, AMs	25
3	9/5/13	NGOs, AMs, PSIs	50
4	9/26/13	NGOs, AMs	20
5	10/21/13	NGOs	20
6	10/29/13	NGOs, PSIs	30
7	11/5/13	NGOs, AMs, PSIs	25
8	2/21/14	NGOs	75
9	3/25/14	NGOs	15
10	3/27/14	NGOs, AMs, PSIs, Public	50
11	3/29/14	NGOs	15
12	4/1/14	NGOs	35
13	4/3/14	NGOs, AMs, PSIs, Public	200
14	4/6/14	NGOs	10
15	4/6/14	NGOs, PSIs	10
16	4/29/14	NGOs	10
17	4/29/14	NGOs, PSIs	30

TABLE A.3 *(continued)*

Meeting #	Date	Meeting participants	# of Attendees
18	5/6/14	NGOs, AMs, PSIs, Public	50
19	5/6/14	NGOs, PSIs	20
20	5/8/14	NGOs, PSIs	10
21	5/13/14	NGOs, PSIs	20
22	6/16/14	NGOs, AMs, Public	50
23	6/24/14	NGOs, AMs	25
24	7/3/14	NGOs, AMs, Public	50
25	7/15/14	NGOs	12
26	7/16/14	NGOs	10
27	8/7/14	NGOs, AMs, PSIs	50
28	8/29/14	NGOs, AMs	30
29	9/1/14	NGOs	20
30	9/5/14	NGOs, AMs, PSIs	50
31	9/15/14	NGOs	30
32	9/17/14	NGOs	30
33	9/30/14	NGOs	20
34	10/13/14	NGOs	20
35	10/24/14	NGOs, AMs	40
36	10/27/14	NGOs	20
37	11/5/14	NGOs, AMs, PSIs, Public	40
38	11/20/14	NGOs	25
39	12/1/14	NGOs	20
40	12/5/14	NGOs, AMs, PSIs, Public	50
41	12/8/14	NGOs	20

* Meetings were held at schools, NGOs, public buildings, and public security installations in Maré. They involved members of the following groups:
NGOs = Non-governmental Organizations
AMs = *Associações de Moradores* (Residents' Associations)
PSIs = Public Security Institutions, including both the military and police
Public = Residents of Maré
** The exact names of the organizations have been removed for security considerations.

PRIMARY SOURCES CITED

O Globo

6/17/1954. "O Exército ainda não mandou fazer despejos."
7/24/1967. "Garrucha e Faca Contra Táxis."
6/12/1969. "Disparo mata o bom rapaz na fuzilaria com homem mau."
5/26/1973. "Comerciante comprou arma de bandido e não pagou. Morreu."
6/26/1976. "Policiais acham o caso da menina morta 'de difícil solução'."
1/15/1979. "Fogem da delegacia 16 assaltantes e só um é recapturado."

4/10/1979. "Sem Título."

7/18/1980. "Pele confessa, rindo, assassinato da menina."

7/19/1980. "Será pedida preventive dos matadors da menina."

4/4/1981. "Cinco mortos em cerco a assaltantes na Ilha."

5/21/1981. "Presa quadrilha de nove assaltantes, todos jovens."

10/20/1981. "Vinte e outo presos fogem e sete são recapturados."

12/7/1981. "Bando armado com escopetas tocaia dois PMs em Ramos."

2/8/1982. "PM prende 5 suspeitos de roubo em Manguinhos."

4/1/1982. "Padaria."

10/20/1982. "Conjunto Esperança tem novas invasões e arrombamentos."

12/21/1982. "Carro Roubado aparece sem o equipamento radiotivo."

7/26/1983. "Sete morreram em 'guerra' na Nova Holanda."

9/10/1983. "Polícia controla os saques. Em Ramos, bandidos lideram ataque."

12/16/1983. "Sem palafitas, esvazia-se poder dos 'Irmãos Metralha'."

12/28/1983. "'Irmão Metralha' nega ter matado Delegado Guimarães."

1/9/1984. "Homem morto com pancada na cabeça."

3/26/1984. "Nas drogas, o desajuste."

12/28/1984. "Rivalidades esquentam o clima no Parque União."

4/4/1985. "No Presídio Ary Franco o domínio de três falanges."

4/13/1985. "Desipe confirma: ataques a bancos tiveram participação de ex-detentos."

11/26/1985. "Dez homens roubam Cr$30 milhões de banco em Ramos."

12/6/1985. "Lista revela nomes de outros possíveis envolvidos."

2/20/1986. "PM cerca favela e mata 4 traficantes em tiroteio."

4/10/1986. "Guarda enfrenta 5 ladrões a bala e Evita assalto a banco na Penha."

6/11/1986. "Quatro homens levam Cz$130 mil de banco."

11/16/1986. "Silêncio e medo no dia-a-dia da Nova Holanda."

3/25/1988. "Soldados são acusados por furto de armas."

4/10/1988. "Sem Drogas, traficantes roubam bancos."

6/5/1988. "Os 'donos' dos morros do Rio."

8/13/1989. "Os contrastes da Favela do Parque União."

11/23/1989. "Desipe apura a participação de guardas em fuga de sete presos."

12/9/1989. "Perseguição, tiroteio e mortes em Bonsucesso."

9/1/1990. "Perseguição e morte no assalto em Bonsucesso."

9/22/1990. de Bonis, Rodolfo, and Letícia Helena. "Bandidos seqüestram motorista de escola para saber endereço de alunos."

1/19/1991. "Favela vira campo de batalha após prisão de traficante e seqüestrador."

10/29/1991. "Três facções disputam o comando."

7/21/1991. "Parque União, a 'Zona Sul' da Maré."

4/21/1992. "Traficantes invadem e matam na Maré."

5/1/1992. Lopes, Jorge Luiz. "'Comando Vermelho' ocupa Complexo da Maré."

7/2/1992a. "Em oito anos, pelo menos dez amantes assassinadas."
7/2/1992b. "Polícia Federal mata chefe do tráfico na favela Nova Holanda."
7/18/1992. Duarte, Solange. "'Comando Vermelho' promove guerras para manter poder."
9/28/1992. "Confundidos com policiais, 4 garçons são baleados."
12/10/1992. "Traficante é morto em operação na Maré."
4/2/1993. "Comércio em favela fecha por ordem de traficante."
4/15/1993. "Os detentos no presidio de segurança máxima Bangu I."
9/28/1993. "Traficantes distribuem doces na favela."
10/30/1993. "Traficante morre e PMs são baleados."
11/14/1993. "Tiroteio na Maré causa morte de um homem."
3/18/1994. "Dois ônibus são depredados em confront entre gangues no Centro."
11/11/1994. "Italianos têm intteresses na cidade."
3/14/1995. "Guerra do tráfico mata 8 na Vila do João."
3/30/1995. "Militares caçarão bandidos até no interior."
5/1/1995. "Operações passam a utilizar táticas militares nas ruas."
5/7/1995. Leite, Marcelo. "Bangu I abre as celas para as flechas de Cupido."
6/9/1995. "Bandidos recebem PMs a tiros na Ilha do Governador."
10/22/1995. "PMs baleados com fuzil AR 15."
12/15/1995. "Quadrilhas rivais estão em Guerra."
12/16/1995a. "Policiais ocupam favelas da Maré."
12/16/1995b. "Policiais ocupam favelas onde torcedores foram metralhados."
12/17/1995. "Ocupação da Maré começa com dia calmo."
12/19/1995. "Polícia prende traficantes que atiraram em torcedores."
12/26/1995. "Invasão de favela cantada em rap."
1/15/1996. Werneck, Antônio. "Querra do tráfico mata seis e policiais militares são encurralados na Vila do João."
2/23/1996. Arruda, Edgar. "PM caça os traficantes da Maré."
2/24/1996. Leite, Marcelo. "Comandante prevê nova guerra entre quadrilhas na Maré."
3/20/1996. "Odir, chefe do tráfico nas favelas da Maré, é preso pela Polícia em São João de Meriti."
3/26/1996. "Traficante do segundo escalão é preso em Itaboraí."
5/4/1996. Werneck, Antônio. "Onda de seqüestros assusta Luz, que chama 'banda podre'."
10/2/1996. Seabra, Cátia, Selma Schmidt, and Victor Javoski. "Canteiros de obras viram vala comun."
8/16/1997. "Área invadida só será desocupada se Justiça mandar."
12/4/1997. "Complexo da Maré tem novos moradores."
3/12/1999. "Escolas no meio do fogo cruzado."
6/30/1999. "Traficantes usavam creche de favela na Maré como depósito."
9/22/1999. "Casa em Santa Teresa é invadida por assaltantes."
2/5/2000. Amora, Dimmi, and Jorge Martins. "Guerra na Favela Nova Holanda mata seis."

2/12/2000a. Goulart, Gustavo, and Renato Garcia. "Fugitivos teriam invadido a Nova Holanda."

2/12/2000b. Matheus, Letícia, and Vannildo Mendes. "Conheça as novas versões da fuga e da invasão."

3/25/2000. "Três mulheres são assassinadas com tiros na cabeça em Bonsucesso."

5/26/2000a. Bottari, Elenilce, and Letícia Matheus. "Onze horas como reféns do tráfico."

5/26/2000b. Antunes, Laura. "Ficamos os três aguardando a morte chegar."

10/2/2000. "Motoristas apavorados fogem pela contramão."

12/29/2000. "Secretário de Segurança admite indenizar família de bandido morto."

7/4/2001. "Políca acusa o tráfico de organizer protesto."

8/31/2001. Torres, Ana Carolina, Gustavo Goulart, and Taís Mendes. "PMs ocupam Maré para garantir batalhão."

9/1/2001. de Cássia, Cristiane. "Empresa estuda solo de terreno em favela onde ficará quartel da PM."

5/9/2002. "Um tráfico milionário."

5/21/2002. Goulart, Gustavo, and Berta, Ruben. "Violência fecha parte da Linha Amarela."

7/26/2002. "Via Expressa Fechada."

9/12/2002. "Guerra do tráfico já dura mais de 20 anos."

9/20/2002. "Linho, traficante de Maré, é o próximo alvo."

9/22/2002. "Linho, o empresário do narcotráfico."

10/18/2002. "Violência fecha parcialmente a Linha Amarela."

12/18/2002. Pessoa, Flávio. "Protesto fecha Linha Vermelha cinco vezes."

3/6/2003. "Tiroteio deixa um morto e oito feridos na Maré."

3/8/2003. "Tráfico fecha Linha Vermelha por 20 minutos."

4/22/2003. "Microônibus da PM é emboscado por 'bonde'."

5/3/2003. Matheus, Letícia. "Operação com 250 policiais vasculha a Maré."

5/7/2003. "Terror de novo na Avenida Brasil."

5/18/2003. "Famílias são separadas pelo tráfico na Maré."

6/22/2003. Bottari, Elenilce. "Guerra à corrupção na PM."

7/1/2003. "A tomada da Maré."

7/9/2003. "Comerciante é morto a tiro no Complexo da Maré."

7/26/2003. "Delegado é morto durante cerco a traficantes."

10/5/2003. "Tiroteio fecha linhas Amarela e Vermelha."

10/12/2003. "Um batalhão da PM no meio do fogo cruzado."

12/9/2003. "Ameaça fecha vila olímpica."

12/13/2003. "Polícia prende traficante e pára-quedista."

12/17/2003. "Traficantes acusados de torturer e matar menina de 13 anos em favela."

1/22/2004. "O perigo nas vias expressas."

1/23/2004. "Um dia com 14 baixas."

4/4/2004. "Angolanos estariam treinanado traficantes do Rio."

8/16/2004. "Seis mortos em operaçõ da PM na Maré."

11/4/2004. "Guerra na Maré mata 5 e deixa 9 feridos."

11/29/2004. "Tiroteio fecha a Linha Vermelha por uma hora."

1/31/2005. "Famílias em fuge invadem fábrica desativada."

2/11/2005. "Cesar: traficantes da Maré estariam indicando pessoas para seis postos."

11/5/2005. "Preso chefe do tráfico em 11 favelas da Maré."

11/9/2005. "Tráfico da Maré planejava ataques no asfalto."

10/10/2007. "Presos 12 bandidos que invadiram favela."

1/14/2008. "Faltou inteligência."

12/20/2008. "Tiroteio em favela da Maré mata quarto e fere 7."

6/1/2009. "Guerra do tráfico na Maré faz 8 mortos e 8 feridos."

6/2/2009. "Medo deixa 7.232 alunos sem aulas."

6/12/2009. "Sete morren em confronta na Maré."

6/13/2009. "PM reforça policiamento na Maré."

9/17/2009. "Bando invade favela e mantém família refém."

9/27/2012. Carvalho, Janaína. "Polícia investiga ação do tráfico em execução de DJ em favela no Rio." http://g1.globo.com/rio-de-janeiro/noticia/2012/09/policia-investiga-acao-do-trafico-em-execucao-de-dj-em-favela-no-rio .html.

10/18/2012. "Em menos de 4h, o previsível retorno ao 'curral do crack'."

11/12/2012. "Cracolândia itinerante toma a Avenida Brasil."

4/27/2013. Barreto, Diego. "Polícia apura tortura contra jogador."

3/12/2013. "Polícia do Rio prende suspeito de assassinar DJ Chorão." https:// g1.globo.com/rio-de-janeiro/noticia/2013/03/policia-do-rio-prende-suspeito-de-assassinar-do-dj-chorao.html.

4/4/2014. Ramalho, Sérgio. "Beltrame Anuncia Ouvidoria Para UPPs."

4/6/2014. Costa, Ana Claudia. "Comandante Da Força de Pacificação Reconhece Que Ainda Há Bandidos Na Maré." https://oglobo.globo .com/rio/comandante-da-forca-de-pacificacao-reconhece-que-ainda-ha-bandidos-na-mare.

4/12/2014. "Homem Morre Em Confronto Com o Exército Na Maré, Rio." http://g1.globo.com/rio-de-janeiro/noticia/2014/04/homem-morre-em-confronto-com-o-exercito-na-mare-rio.html.

4/16/2014. Brito, Guilherme. "Idosa Baleada Em Farmácia Na Maré é Enterrada No Rio." http://g1.globo.com/rio-de-janeiro/noticia/2014/04/ idosa-morta-apos-disparos-na-mare-e-velada-no-rio.html.

4/21/2014. "Exército Intensifica Segurança e Troca Tiros Com Criminosos Na Maré, Rio." http://g1.globo.com/rio-de-janeiro/noticia/2014/04/ exercito-intensifica-seguranca-e-troca-tiros-com-criminosos-na-mare-rio .html.

5/26/2014. Werneck, Antônio. "Presença de Militares Na Maré Custa R$ 1,7 Milhão Por Dia." https://oglobo.globo.com/rio/ presenca-de-militares-na-mare-custa-17-milhao-por-dia-12601748.

5/27/2014. "Vídeo Da PF Mostra Menor P Sendo Preso Em Apartamento No Rio." http://g1.globo.com/rio-de-janeiro/noticia/2014/03/video-da-pf-mostra-menor-p-sendo-preso-em-apartamento-no-rio.html.

6/9/2014. Lo-Bianco, Alessandro. "Força de Pacificação Da Maré é Atacada Por Moradores e Traficantes Durante Festa Na Região." http://oglobo .globo.com/rio/forca-de-pacificacao-da-mare-atacada-por-moradores-traficantes-durante-festa-na-regiao-12770366.

7/29/2014. Coelho, Henrique. "Ministro Aprova Forças Armadas Na Maré, Rio, e Ocupação é Prorrogada." http://g1.globo.com/rio-de-janeiro/ noticia/2014/07/ministro-aprova-forcas-armadas-na-mare-rio-e-ocupacao-e-prorrogada.html.

8/28/2014. "Na Maré, TRE apreende remédios e panfletos da empresa de Garotinho." https://oglobo.globo.com/politica/na-mare-tre-apreende-remedios-panfletos-da-empresa-de-garotinho-13755701.

10/1/2014. Costa, Ana Claudia. "Guerra Do Tráfico Na Maré Fecha Avenida Brasil e Leva Pânico a Motoristas e Pedestres." http://oglobo.globo .com/rio/guerra-do-trafico-na-mare-fecha-avenida-brasil-leva-panico-motoristas-pedestres-14102267.

11/3/2014. Costa, Celia, and Gustavo Goulart. "Tiroteio No Complexo Da Maré Deixa Mais de 4 Mil Alunos Sem Aula." https://oglobo.globo.com/ rio/tiroteio-no-complexo-da-mare-deixa-mais-de-4-mil-alunos-sem-aula-14446818.

11/28/2014. "Baleado Na Cabeça, Cabo Se Torna o Primeiro Militar Morto Na Maré." https://oglobo.globo.com/rio/baleado-na-cabeca-cabo-se-torna-primeiro-militar-morto-na-mare-14694567.

4/14/2015. Junior, Paulo Roberto, and Magalhães, Luiz Ernesto. "Complexo Da Maré Começa a Ganhar 18 Escolas Em Tempo Integral Para Dez Mil Estudantes." https://oglobo.globo.com/rio/complexo-da-mare-comeca-ganhar-18-escolas-em-tempo-integral-para-dez-mil-estudantes-15865158.

5/25/2015. "Em 1 Ano, 23 Homens Do Exército Se Feriram Na Maré; Vídeo Mostra 'Guerra'." http://g1.globo.com/rio-de-janeiro/noticia/2015/05/ em-1-ano-23-homens-do-exercito-se-feriram-na-mare-video-mostra-guerra.html.

6/29/2015. "Tropas Federais Deixam Complexo Da Maré Após 83 Mil Ações Em 15 Meses." http://g1.globo.com/rio-de-janeiro/noticia/2015/06/tropas-federais-deixam-complexo-da-mare-apos-83-mil-acoes-em-15-meses .html.

8/15/2015. Barreira, Gabriel. "PM Do RJ Poderá Usar 'touca Ninja' Em Atos Violentos e Ações Com Refém." https://g1.globo.com/rio-de-janeiro/ noticia/2015/08/policia-do-rj-podera-usar-touca-ninja-em-protestos-e-operacoes-especiais.html.

6/8/2017. Bottari, Elenilce. "Apreensões de Crack Despencam No RJ, 14 Anos Após Chegada Da Droga Ao Estado." https://oglobo.globo.com/ rio/apreensoes-de-crack-despencam-no-rj-14-anos-apos-chegada-da-droga-ao-estado-21450753.

5/6/2021. Haidar, Diego et al. "Operação No Jacarezinho Deixa 25 Mortos, Provoca Intenso Tiroteio e Tem Fuga de Bandidos." https://g1.globo .com/rj/rio-de-janeiro/noticia/2021/05/06/tiroteio-deixa-feridos-n o-jacarezinho.ghtml.

10/25/2023. Soares, Rafael. "A Guerra das milícias no Rio de Janeiro." https:// oglobo.globo.com/podcast/noticia/2023/10/25/a-guerra-das-milicias-no-rio-de-janeiro.ghtml.

Other Primary Sources

Bom Dia Brasil. 6/23/2015. "Força de Pacificação Teve Avanços Na Maré, Mas Ainda Enfrenta Dificuldades." http://g1.globo.com/bom-dia-brasil/ noticia/2015/06/forca-de-pacificacao-teve-avancos-na-mare-mas-ainda-enfrenta-dificuldades.html.

Comissão Parlamentar de Inquérito. 8/14/2008. "Relatório Final Da Comissão Parlamentar de Inquérito Destinada a Investigar a Ação de Milícias No Âmbito Do Estado Do Rio de Janeiro." www.marcelofreixo.com.br/ cpi-das-milicias.

CrimeNews. 3/19/2015. "História do Traficante Linho ou Chuck – Líder e Fundador do ADA." https://crimesnewsrj.blogspot.com/2015/03/historia-do-traficante-linho-ou-chuck.html.

Departamento Penitenciário Nacional. 2022. *Quantidade de Incidências por Tip Penal.* Retrieved from https://app.powerbi.com/ view?r=eyJrIjoiMTMwZGI4NTMtMTJjNSooZjM3LThjOGGQtZ jlkZmRlZTEyMTcxIiwidCI6ImViMDkwNDIwLTQoNGMtND NmNyo5MWYyLTRiOGRhNmJmZThlMSJ9.

Driss Ghali: La Vie Est Politique. 8/11/2017. Ghali, Driss. "Entrevista Com o General Roberto Escoto." www.drissghali.com/2017/08/11/ entrevista-com-general-roberto-escoto/.

Estadão. 9/21/2014. Constancio, Thaise. "Quadrilhas Trocam Tiros Em Disputa Por Controle Do Complexo Da Maré." https://brasil.estadao .com.br/noticias/rio-de-janeiro,quadrilhas-trocam-tiros-em-disputa-por-controle-do-complexo-da-mare,1563833.

6/26/2015. Bacelar, Carina. "Ocupação Das Forças Armadas Na Maré Acaba Após Usar 85% Do Efetivo Militar Do Haiti." https:// brasil.estadao.com.br/noticias/rio-de-janeiro,ocupacao-das-forcas-armadas-na-mare-termina-apos-usar-85-do-efetivo-militar-do-haiti,1713771.

Extra. 11/9/2013. Soares, Rafael. "Cinco Meses Após Operação Do Bope Na Maré, Simulação Pode Apontar Quem Matou Garçom Dentro de Bar."

https://extra.globo.com/casos-de-policia/cinco-meses-apos-operacao-do-bope-na-mare-simulacao-pode-apontar-quem-matou-garcom-dentro-de-bar-10733270.html.

11/20/2013. "Comandante Da UPP Da Rocinha Diz Que Tráfico Fatura R$ 10 Milhões Por Mês Na Favela." http://extra.globo.com/casos-de-policia/comandante-da-upp-da-rocinha-diz-que-trafico-fatura-10-milhoes-por-mes-na-favela-10733178.html.

7/8/2014. "Complexo Da Maré Tem Tiroteio e Confronto Com Militares Na Noite Desta Terça-Feira." http://extra.globo.com/casos-de-policia/complexo-da-mare-tem-tiroteio-confronto-com-militares-na-noite-desta-terca-feira-13188844.html#ixzz36ydhigQL.

9/23/2014. Heringer, Carolina. "Polícia Investiga Tentative de Invasão Por Faction Rival Na Maré." http://extra.globo.com/casos-de-policia/policia-investiga-tentativa-de-invasao-por-faccao-rival-na-mare-14016583.html.

Folha de São Paulo. 8/15/1997. Torres, Sergio. "Líder do tráfico é idolatrado." www1.folha.uol.com.br/fsp/1997/8/15/cotidiano/16.html

11/29/2004. Pequeno, João, and Talita Figueiredo. "Guerra Sem Trincheira: Traficantes Atiram Granadas Em Baile Funk." www1.folha.uol.com.br/fsp/cotidian/ff2911200424.htm.

11/5/2014. Brito, Diana. "Moradores Do Rio Denunciam Supostos Abusos de Militares Na Maré." www1.folha.uol.com.br/cotidiano/2014/11/15 43902-moradores-do-rio-denunciam-supostos-abusos-de-militares-na-mare.shtml.

Jornal do Brasil. 10/21/1980. "Comandos."

5/15/1983a. "Na cadeia, grupos brigam por poder e dinheiro."

5/15/1983b. "Terceira galleria contesta o Comando."

Lei N⁰ 11.343. 8/23/2006. Sistema Nacional de Políticas Públicas sobre Drogas. www.planalto.gov.br/ccivil_03/_ato2004-2006/2006/lei/l11343 .htm.

Lei N⁰ 13.840. 6/5/2019. Sistema Nacional de Políticas Públicas sobre Drogas. www.planalto.gov.br/ccivil_03/_ato2019-2022/2019/lei/L13840.htm.

Ministério da Defesa. 1/31/2014. *Garantia de Lei e Ordem.* Pub. L. No. MD33- M–10. www.gov.br/defesa/pt-br/arquivos/2014/meso2/md33-m-10-garantia-da-lei-e-da-ordem-2a-ed-2014-31-jan.pdf.

Montedo.com. 11/7/2014. Valdevino, Diego, and Thiago Antunes. "'Nós Perdemos a Paz e a Tranquilidade Desde Que o Exército Entrou Na Maré', Diz Líder Comunitário. Bom, Mesmo, Era No Tempo Dos Traficantes, Digo Eu." www.montedo.com.br/2014/11/07/nos-perdemos-paz-e-tranquilidade-desde/.

O Dia. 9/17/2009. "Guerra do tráfico toma dois bairros da zona norte do Rio." www.terra.com.br/noticias/brasil/policia/guerra-do-trafico-toma-dois-bairros-da-zona-norte-do-rio,57de6ce675e4b310VgnCLD200000bbcc eboaRCRD.html.

6/30/2014. Araujo, Adriano. "UPP Na Maré é Adiada de Novo." http://odia
.ig.com.br/noticia/rio-de-janeiro/2014-06-29/upp-na-mare-e-adiada-de-
novo.html.

9/16/2014. Antunes, Thiago. "Líder comunitário foi executado com sete
tiros na Maré." https://odia.ig.com.br/noticia/rio-de-janeiro/2014-09-15/
lider-comunitario-foi-executado-com-sete-tiros-na-mare.html.

11/5/2014. Antunes, Thiago. "Moradores Do Complexo Da Maré
Relatam Supostas Torturas de Militares." http://odia.ig.com.br/
noticia/rio-de-janeiro/2014-11-05/moradores-do-complexo-da-mare-
relatam-supostas-torturas-de-militares.html.

2/22/2015. Cadu, Bruno. "Ocupantes de van São Baleados Na Maré."
https://odia.ig.com.br/noticia/rio-de-janeiro/2015-02-21/ocupantes-de-
kombi-sao-baleados-na-mare.html.

7/7/2015. Martins, Felipe. "Ex-sargento do Bope treinou bando da
Maré sobre como usar armas." https://odia.ig.com.br/noticia/rio-
de-janeiro/2015-07-07/ex-sargento-do-bope-treinou-bando-da-mar
e-sobre-como-usar-armas.html.

Piauí. 4/19/2008. Tardáguila, Cristina. "Dentro Do Caveirão." https://piaui
.folha.uol.com.br/materia/dentro-do-caveirao/.

Pública. 10/31/2018. Viana, Natalia. "Exército é Acusado de Matar
Inocentes Em Operações de Segurança Pública." https://apublica
.org/2018/10/exercito-e-acusado-de-matar-inocentes-em-operacoes-de-
seguranca-publica/.

Rio On Watch. 7/16/2017. Jones, Claire. "História do 'Projeto Rio' na Maré
Parte 1: O Canto da Sereia." https://rioonwatch.org.br/?p=26789.

9/5/2017. Jones, Claire. "História do 'Projeto Rio' na Maré Parte 2: Aliados
Juntem-se à Luta." https://rioonwatch.org.br/?p=26952.

9/20/2017. Jones, Claire. "História do 'Projeto Rio' na Maré Parte 3:
Desagregação do Governo." https://rioonwatch.org.br/?p=28188.

The Guardian. 4/12/2010. Phillips, Tom. "Rio de Janeiro Police Occupy
Slums as City Fights Back against Drug Gangs." www.theguardian.com/
world/2010/apr/12/rio-de-janeiro-police-occupy-slums.

União da Maré. 5/1980. "Um Presidente Solitário."

UOL. 1/26/2002. de Souza, Mário Vieira. "Reengenharia Do Crime." https://
web.archive.org/web/20090131172242/http://mail-archive.com/policia-
br@grupos.com.br/msg05780.html.

3/30/2014. de Andrade, Hanrrikson, and Henrique Coelho. "Forças Policiais
Do Rio Ocupam Favelas Do Complexo Da Maré." https://noticias
.uol.com.br/cotidiano/ultimas-noticias/2014/03/30/forcas-policiais-do-
rio-comecam-a-ocupar-favelas-do-complexo-da-mare.htm.

4/4/2014. Platinow, Vladimir. "Operação Na Maré Resultou Em 16 Mortes
Em 15 Dias; 162 Foram Presos." https://noticias.uol.com.br/cotidiano/
ultimas-noticias/2014/04/04/operacao-na-mare-resultou-na-prisao-de-
162-pessoas-e-apreensao-de-101-armas.htm.

1/7/2019. Mello, Igor, and Lola Ferreira. "A mão invisível da milícia." https://noticias.uol.com.br/reportagens-especiais/com-milicia-em-expansao-confrontos-policiais-no-rio-miram-trafico-e-somam-so-3-em-areas-de-milicianos/.

Veja. 7/6/2015. Leitão, Leslie. "Policial Do Bope Comprou Até Uniforme de Guerra Para o Tráfico." https://veja.abril.com.br/brasil/policial-do-bope-comprou-ate-uniforme-de-guerra-para-o-trafico/.

12/15/2015. Leitão, Leslie. "Policiais Do Bope São Presos Por Envolvimento Com o Tráfico No Rio." https://veja.abril.com.br/politica/policiais-do-bope-sao-presos-por-envolvimento-com-o-trafico-no-rio/.

References

Abello-Colak, Alexandra, and Valeria Guarneros-Meza. 2014. "The Role of Criminal Actors in Local Governance." *Urban Studies* 51(15): 3268–89.

Acebes, César Muñoz. 2016. *"Good Cops Are Afraid": The Toll of Unchecked Police Violence in Rio de Janeiro*. New York: Human Rights Watch. www.hrw.org/report/2016/07/07/good-cops-are-afraid/toll-unchecked-police-violence-rio-de-janeiro.

Acemoglu, Daron, James A. Robinson, and Rafael J. Santos. 2013. "The Monopoly of Violence: Evidence from Colombia." *Journal of the European Economic Association* 11(Suppl. 1): 5–44.

Albarracín, Juan. 2018. "Criminalized Electoral Politics in Brazilian Urban Peripheries." *Crime, Law and Social Change* 69(4): 553–75.

Albarracín, Juan, and Nicholas Barnes. 2020. "Criminal Violence in Latin America." *Latin America Research Review* 55(2): 397–406.

Alonso, Angela, and Ann Mische. 2017. "Changing Repertoires and Partisan Ambivalence in the New Brazilian Protests." *Bulletin of Latin American Research* 36(2): 144–59.

Alves, Jaime Amparo. 2018. *The Anti-Black City: Police Terror and Black Urban Life in Brazil*. Minneapolis, MN: University of Minnesota Press.

Alvito, Marcos. 2001. *As Cores de Acari: Uma Favela Carioca*. Rio de Janeiro: Fundação Getúlio Vargas.

Amorim, Carlos. 1993. *Comando Vermelho: A História Secreta Do Crime Organizado*. Rio de Janeiro: Record.

2000. *CV-PCC: A Irmandade Do Crime*. Rio de Janeiro: Record.

2010. *Assalto Ao Poder: O Crime Organizado*. Rio de Janeiro: Record.

Andreoni, Manuela, and Ernesto Londoño. 2020. "'License to Kill': Inside Rio's Record Year of Police Killings." *The New York Times*. www.nytimes.com/2020/05/18/world/americas/brazil-rio-police-violence.html (August 21).

Arias, Enrique Desmond. 2006a. *Drugs & Democracy in Rio de Janeiro: Trafficking, Social Networks, and Public Security*. Chapel Hill, NC: University of North Carolina Press.

2006b. "The Dynamics of Criminal Governance: Networks and Social Order in Rio de Janeiro." *Journal of Latin American Studies* 38(2): 293–325.

2013. "The Impacts of Differential Armed Dominance of Politics in Rio de Janeiro, Brazil." *Studies in Comparative International Development* 48(3): 263–84.

2017. *Criminal Enterprises and Governance in Latin America and the Caribbean.* New York: Cambridge University Press.

2019. "Social Responses to Criminal Governance in Rio de Janeiro, Belo Horizonte, Kingston, and Medellín." *Latin American Research Review* 54(1): 165–80.

Arias, Enrique Desmond, and Nicholas Barnes. 2017. "Crime and Plural Orders in Rio de Janeiro, Brazil." *Current Sociology* 65(3): 448–65.

Arias, Enrique Desmond, and Daniel M. Goldstein, eds. 2010. *Violent Democracies in Latin America.* Durham: Duke University Press.

Arias, Enrique Desmond, and Corinne Davis Rodrigues. 2006. "The Myth of Personal Security: Criminal Gangs, Dispute Resolution, and Identity in Rio de Janeiro's Favelas." *Latin American Politics and Society* 48(4): 53–81.

Arjona, Ana. 2015. "Civilian Resistance to Rebel Governance." In *Rebel Governance in Civil War*, eds. Nelson Kasfir Arjona, and Zachariah C. Mampilly. New York: Cambridge University Press, 180–202.

2016. *Rebelocracy: Social Order in the Colombian Civil War.* Cambridge: Cambridge University Press.

2017. "Civilian Cooperation and Non-Cooperation with Non-State Armed Groups: The Centrality of Obedience and Resistance." *Small Wars & Insurgencies* 28(July): 755–78.

Arjona, Ana, Nelson Kasfir, and Zachariah C. Mampilly, eds. 2015. *Rebel Governance in Civil War.* New York: Cambridge University Press.

Arjona, Ana, Zachariah C. Mampilly, and Wendy Pearlman. 2019. "Research in Violent or Post-Conflict Political Settings." Final Report of QTD Working Group IV.2 (December).

Asbury, Herbert. 2008. *The Gangs of New York: An Informal History of the Underworld.* New York: Vintage.

Aspholm, Roberto R. 2020. *Views from the Streets: The Transformation of Gangs and Violence on Chicago's South Side.* New York: Columbia University Press.

Auyero, Javier. 2001. *Poor People's Politics: Peronist Survival Networks and the Legacy of Evita.* Durham, NC: Duke University Press.

2007. *Routine Politics and Violence in Argentina: The Gray Zone of State Power.* New York: Cambridge University Press.

Auyero, Javier, and María Fernanda Berti. 2015. *In Harm's Way: The Dynamics of Urban Violence.* Princeton, NJ: Princeton University Press.

Auyero, Javier, Philippe Bourgois, and Nancy Scheper-Hughes, eds. 2015. *Violence at the Urban Margins.* Oxford: Oxford University Press.

Baird, Adam. 2018. "Dancing with Danger: Ethnographic Safety, Male Bravado and Gang Research in Colombia." *Qualitative Research* 18(3): 342–60.

Bakke, Kristin M., Kathleen Gallagher Cunningham, and Lee J. M. Seymour. 2012. "A Plague of Initials: Fragmentation, Cohesion, and Infighting in Civil Wars." *Perspectives on Politics* 10(02): 265–83.

Balcells, Laia. 2017. *Rivalry and Revenge: The Politics of Violence during Civil War.* Cambridge: Cambridge University Press.

Barcellos, Caco. 2003. *Abusado: O Dono Do Morro Dona Marta.* Rio de Janeiro: Record.

Barkey, Karen. 1994. *Bandits and Bureaucrats: The Ottoman Route to State Centralization*. Ithaca, NY: Cornell University Press.

Barnes, Nicholas. 2013. "The Rio Protests: Who, What, Why, and Will They Matter?" *The Monkey Cage*. https://themonkeycage.org/2013/06/the-rio-protests-who-what-why-and-will-they-matter/ (November 7, 2021).

2016. "Mobilization in the Wake of Rio's Olympics." *Mobilizing Ideas*. https://mobilizingideas.wordpress.com/2016/08/29/mobilization-in-the-wake-of-rios-olympics/ (May 15, 2021).

2017. "Criminal Politics: An Integrated Approach to the Study of Organized Crime, Politics, and Violence." *Perspectives on Politics* 15(4): 967–87.

2022a. "The Global Comparative Study of Gangs and Other Non-State Armed Groups." In *The Oxford Encyclopedia of International Criminology*, eds. Edna Erez and Peter R. Ibarra. Oxford University Press, 447–65.

2022b. "The Logic of Criminal Territorial Control: Military Intervention in Rio de Janeiro." *Comparative Political Studies* 55(5): 789–831.

2023. "The Enduring Influence of The Logic of Violence in Civil War." *Civil Wars* 25(2): 569–76.

Barnes, Nicholas, and Juan Albarracín. 2020. "Criminal Governance in the Time of COVID-19." *Urban Violence Research Network*. https://urbanviolence.org/criminal-governance-in-the-time-of-covid-19/ (July 10, 2020).

Barnes, Nicholas, Desirée Poets, and Max Stephenson Jr., eds. 2021. *Maré from the Inside: Art, Culture, and Politics in Rio de Janeiro, Brazil*. Blacksburg, VA: VT Publishing.

Barnes, Nicholas, and Stephanie Savell. 2018. "Giving the Military Control in Rio Threatens Brazilian Democracy." *US News and World Report*. www.usnews.com/opinion/world-report/articles/2018-02-23/giving-the-military-control-in-rio-threatens-brazilian-democracy (May 15, 2021).

Bateson, Regina. 2013. "Order and Violence in Postwar Guatemala." PhD Dissertation, Yale University.

2021. "The Politics of Vigilantism." *Comparative Political Studies* 54(6): 923–55.

Benmergui, Leandro, and Rafael Soares Gonçalves. 2019. "Urbanismo Miliciano in Rio de Janeiro." *NACLA Report on the Americas* 51(4): 379–85.

Berg, Louis-Alexandre, and Marlon Carranza. 2018. "Organized Criminal Violence and Territorial Control: Evidence from Northern Honduras." *Journal of Peace Research* 55(5): 566–81.

Berti, Benedetta. 2023. "From Cooperation to Competition: Localization, Militarization and Rebel Co-Governance Arrangements in Syria." *Studies in Conflict & Terrorism* 46(2): 209–27.

Bianchi, Paula. 2021. "Polícia do Rio está há 153 dias desobedecendo o STF." *Intercept Brasil*. www.intercept.com.br/2021/03/02/policia-pm-rio-desobedecendo-stf/ (June 13, 2023).

Biderman, Ciro, João M. P. de Mello, Renato S. de Lima, and Alexandre Schneider. 2019. "Pax Monopolista and Crime: The Case of the Emergence of the Primeiro Comando Da Capital in São Paulo." *Journal of Quantitative Criminology* 35: 573–605.

Bill, MV, and Celso Athayde. 2006. *Falcão: Meninos Do Tráfico*. Rio de Janeiro: Objetiva.

Biondi, Karina. 2009. "Junto e Misturado: Imanência e Transcendência No PCC." Master's Thesis, Federal University of São Carlos.

2014. "Etnografia No Movimento: Território, Hierarquia e Lei No PCC." PhD Dissertation. Federal University of São Carlos.

Blattman, Christopher, Gustavo Duncan, Benjamin Lessing, and Santiago Tobón. 2021. "Gang Rule: Understanding and Countering Criminal Governance." *NBER Working Paper* (28458).

2023. "Civilian Alternatives to Policing: Evidence from Medellín's Community Problem-Solving Intervention Operación Convivencia." *NBER Working Paper* (29692).

Bleich, Erik, and Robert Pekkanen. 2015. "Data Access, Research Transparency, and Interviews: The Interview Methods Appendix." *Qualitative & Multi-Method Research* 13(1): 8–13.

Blitzer, Jonathan. 2022. "The Rise of Nayib Bukele, El Salvador's Authoritarian President." *The New Yorker.* www.newyorker.com/magazine/2022/09/12/the-rise-of-nayib-bukele-el-salvadors-authoritarian-president (September 5).

Blume, Laura R. 2021. "Narco Robin Hoods: Community Support for Illicit Economies and Violence in Rural Central America." *World Development* 143(July): 105464.

Blume, Laura R., Laura Aileen Sauls, and Christopher A. C. J. Knight. 2022. "Tracing Territorial-Illicit Relations: Pathways of Influence and Prospects for Governance." *Political Geography* 97: 102690.

Bobea, Lilian. 2013. "How Caribbean Organized Crime Is Replacing the State." *Insight Crime.* www.insightcrime.org/news-analysis/the-benefits-of-organized-crime-in-the-caribbean (August 31).

Borges, Doriam. 2016. *Diagnóstico Dos Homicídios Em Municípios Do Rio de Janeiro e Do Espírito Santo.* Rio de Janeiro: Programa das Nações Unidas para o Desenvolvimento.

Bourdieu, Pierre. 1992. *The Logic of Practice.* Cambridge: Polity Press.

Bourgois, Philippe. 2002. *In Search of Respect: Selling Crack in El Barrio.* New York: Cambridge University Press.

Brenneman, Robert. 2011. *Homies and Hermanos: God and Gangs in Central America.* Oxford: Oxford University Press.

Brotherton, David C. 2015. *Youth Street Gangs: A Critical Appraisal.* London: Routledge.

Brotherton, David C., and Luis Barrios. 2004. *The Almighty Latin King and Queen Nation: Street Politics and the Transformation of a New York City Gang.* New York: Columbia University Press.

Brotherton, David C., and Rafael Gude. 2021. "Social Control and the Gang: Lessons from the Legalization of Street Gangs in Ecuador." *Critical Criminology* 29(4): 931–55.

Bunker, Robert. 2015. "Gangs & Drug Trafficking in Central America Conference." *Small Wars Journal.* https://smallwarsjournal.com/blog/gangs-drug-trafficking-in-central-america-conference.

Burgos, Marcelo Baumann. 2006. "Dos Parques Proletários Ao Favela-Bairro: As Políticas Públicas Nas Favelas Do Rio de Janeiro." In *Um Século de Favela*, eds. Alba Zaluar and Marcos Alvito. Rio de Janeiro: Editora FGV, 25–60.

Caldeira, Teresa P. R. 2001. *City of Walls: Crime, Segregation, and Citizenship in São Paulo.* Berkeley, CA: University of California Press.

2002. "The Paradox of Police Violence in Democratic Brazil." *Ethnography* 3(3): 235–63.

Calderón, Gabriela, Beatriz Magaloni, Gustavo Robles, and Alberto Diaz-Cayeros. 2015. "The Beheading of Criminal Organizations and the Dynamics of Violence in Mexico." *Journal of Conflict Resolution* 59(8): 1455–85.

Cano, Ignacio. 2008. "Seis Por Meia Dúzia?: Um Estudo Exploratório Do Fenômeno Das Chamadas 'Milícias' No Rio de Janeiro." In *Segurança, Tráfico e Milícias No Rio de Janeiro*. Rio de Janeiro: Justiça Global, 48–83.

2012. "Os Donos Do Morro": Uma Avaliação Exploratória Do Impacto Das Unidades de Polícia Pacificadora (UPPs) No Rio de Janeiro*. Rio de Janeiro: Fórum Brasileiro de Segurança Pública e Laboratório de Análise da Violência.

Cano, Ignacio, and Thais Duarte. 2012. *No Sapatinho: A Evolução Das Milícias No Rio de Janeiro (2008–2011)*. Rio de Janeiro: Laboratório de Análise da Violência (LAV-UERJ) & Fundação Heinrich Böll.

Carey, Sabine C., and Neil J. Mitchell. 2017. "Progovernment Militias." *Annual Review of Political Science* 20: 127–47.

Carvalho, Leandro, and Rodrigo R Soares. 2016. "Living on the Edge: Youth Entry, Career and Exit in Drug-Selling Gangs." *Journal of Economic Behavior & Organization* 121: 77–98.

Cavalcanti, Mariana. 2007. "Of Shacks, Houses, and Fortresses: An Ethnography of Favela Consolidation in Rio de Janeiro." PhD Dissertation, The University of Chicago.

CCSPJ (Consejo Ciudadano para la Seguridad Pública y la Justicia). 2021. *Ranking 2021 de Las 50 Ciudades Más Violentas Del Mundo*. https://geoenlace.net/seguridadjusticiaypaz/webpage/archivos.php (April 2, 2023).

Centeno, Miguel Angel. 2002. *Blood and Debt: War and the Nation-State in Latin America*. University Park, PA: The Pennsylvania State University.

Chalhoub, Sidney. 1996. *Cidade Febril: Cortiços e Epidemias Na Corte Imperial*. Rio de Janeiro: Companhia das Letras.

Chazkel, Amy. 2011. *Laws of Chance: Brazil's Clandestine Lottery and the Making of Urban Public Life*. Durham, NC: Duke University Press.

Christia, Fotini. 2012. *Alliance Formation in Civil Wars*. Cambridge: Cambridge University Press.

Cloward, Richard A., and Lloyd E. Ohlin. 1960. *Delinquency and Opportunity: A Theory of Delinquent Gangs*. New York: Free Press.

Collier, David, and James E. Mahon. 1993. "Conceptual 'Stretching' Revisited: Adapting Categories in Comparative Analysis." *American Political Science Review* 87(4): 845–55.

Contreras, Randol. 2013. *The Stickup Kids: Race, Drugs, Violence, and the American Dream*. Berkeley, CA: University of California Press.

Córdova, Abby. 2022. "Living in Gang-Controlled Neighborhoods: Impacts on Electoral and Nonelectoral Participation in El Salvador." *Latin American Research Review* 54(1): 201–21.

Correa-Cabrera, Guadalupe. 2017. *Los Zetas Inc.: Criminal Corporations, Energy, and Civil War in Mexico*. Austin, TX: University of Texas Press.

Costallat, Benjamin. 1995. *Mistérios Do Rio*. Rio de Janeiro: Biblioteca Carioca.

Cruz, José Miguel. 2010. "Central American Maras: From Youth Street Gangs to Transnational Protection Rackets." *Global Crime* 11(4): 379–98.

Cruz, José Miguel, and Angélica Durán-Martínez. 2016. "Hiding Violence to Deal with the State: Criminal Pacts in El Salvador and Medellin." *Journal of Peace Research* 53(2): 197–210.

Cruz, José Miguel, and Jonathan D. Rosen. 2024. "Leaving the Pervasive Barrio: Gang Disengagement under Criminal Governance." *Social Problems* 71(1): 254–70.

Cunningham, Kathleen Gallagher. 2018. *Understanding Fragmentation in Conflict and Its Impact on Prospects for Peace.* Centre for Humanitarian Dialogue.

Cunningham, Kathleen Gallagher, and Cyanne E. Loyle. 2021. "Introduction to the Special Feature on Dynamic Processes of Rebel Governance." *Journal of Conflict Resolution* 65(1): 3–14.

Curry, G. David. 2011. "Gangs, Crime and Terrorism." In *Criminologists on Terrorism and Homeland Security*, eds. Brian Forst, Jack R. Greene, and James P. Lynch. Cambridge University Press, 97–112.

Daly, Sarah Zukerman. 2016. *Organized Violence after Civil War: The Geography of Recruitment in Latin America.* New York: Cambridge University Press.

  2022. "How Do Violent Politicians Govern? The Case of Paramilitary-Tied Mayors in Colombia." *British Journal of Political Science* 52(4): 1852–75.

Daly, Sarah Zukerman, and Elena Barham. 2024. "A Bargaining Theory of Criminal War." *International Studies Quarterly.* In press.

Dancing with the Devil. 2009. Jon Blair Film Company.

Davis, Diane E. 2010. "Irregular Armed Forces, Shifting Patterns of Commitment, and Fragmented Sovereignty in the Developing World." *Theory and Society* 39(3–4): 397–413.

Davis, Diane E., and Anthony W. Pereira, eds. 2003. *Irregular Armed Forces and Their Role in Politics and State Formation.* Cambridge: Cambridge University Press.

Davis, Mike. 2006. *Planet of Slums.* London: Verso.

Decker, Scott H., and David C. Pyrooz. 2015a. "Street Gangs, Terrorists, Drug Smugglers, and Organized Crime: What's the Difference?" In *The Handbook of Gangs*, eds. Scott H. Decker and David C. Pyrooz. Hoboken, NJ: John Wiley & Sons, Inc., 294–308.

  eds. 2015b. *The Handbook of Gangs.* John Wiley & Sons, Inc.

Delgado, Fernando Ribeiro. 2009. *Lethal Force: Police Violence and Public Security in Rio de Janeiro and São Paulo.* New York: Human Rights Watch. www .hrw.org/report/2009/12/08/lethal-force/police-violence-and-public-security- rio-de-janeiro-and-sao-paulo.

Dell, Melissa. 2015. "Trafficking Networks and the Mexican Drug War." *American Economic Review* 105(6): 1738–79.

Denyer Willis, Graham. 2014. "The Gun Library." *Boston Review.* www .bostonreview.net/world/graham-denyer-willis-pcc-gun-library-sao-paulo-prisons- crime#.UoakDrSFtn4.facebook (April 10).

  2015. *The Killing Consensus: Police, Organized Crime, and the Regulation of Life and Death in Urban Brazil.* Berkeley, CA: University of California Press.

Denyer Willis, Graham, and Pedro Mendes Loureiro. 2023. "The Prison Consensus: Incarceration, Prison Financing, and the Politics of Agreement in Neoliberal Brazil." *Unpublished manuscript.*

Denyer Willis, Laurie. 2018. "'It Smells like a Thousand Angels Marching': The Salvific Sensorium in Rio de Janeiro's Western Subúrbios." *Cultural Anthropology* 33(2): 325–49.

2023. *Go with God: Political Exhaustion and Evangelical Possibility in Suburban Brazil.* Berkeley, CA: University of California Press.

Dias, Camila Caldeira Nunes. 2013. *PCC: Hegemonia Nas Prisões e Monopólio Da Violência.* São Paulo: Saraiva.

Dickie, John. 2007. *Cosa Nostra: The Definitive History of the Sicilian Mafia.* London: Hodder Paperbacks.

Dowdney, Luke. 2003. *Children of the Drug Trade.* Rio de Janeiro: 7 Letras.

Doyle, Caroline. 2016. "Explaining Patterns of Urban Violence in Medellin, Colombia." *Laws* 5(3): 1–17.

Dubet, François. 1987. *La Galere: Jeunes En Survie.* Paris: Fayard.

Durán-Martínez, Angélica. 2018. *The Politics of Drug Violence: Criminals, Cops and Politicians in Colombia and Mexico.* Oxford: Oxford University Press.

Escobar, Gipsy A. 2012. "Using Social Disorganization Theory to Understand the Spatial Distribution of Homicides in Bogota, Colombia." *Revista Invi* 27(74): 21–85.

Fahlberg, Anjuli N. 2018. "Rethinking Favela Governance: Nonviolent Politics in Rio de Janeiro's Gang Territories." *Politics and Society* 46(4): 485–512.

Felbab-Brown, Vanda. 2010. "Conceptualizing Crime as Competition in State-Making and Designing an Effective Response." *Security and Defense Studies Review* 10(Spring-Summer): 155–58.

Feltran, Gabriel de Santis. 2010a. "Crime e Castigo Na Cidade: Os Repertórios Da Justiça e a Questão Do Homicídio Nas Periferias de São Paulo." *Caderno CRH* 23(58): 59–73.

2010b. "The Management of Violence on the São Paulo Periphery: The Repertoire of Normative Apparatus in the PCC Era." *Vibrant:* 109–34.

2018. *Irmãos: Uma História Do PCC.* São Paulo: Companhia das Letras.

2022. "Variações nas taxas de homicídios no Brasil: Uma explicação centrada nos conflitos faccionais." *Dilemas: Revista de Estudos de Conflito e Controle Social* 15(Especial 4): 311–48.

Fischer, Brodwyn. 2008. *A Poverty of Rights: Citizenship and Inequality in Twentieth-Century Rio de Janeiro.* Palo Alto, CA: Stanford University Press.

Fjelde, Hanne, and Desirée Nilsson. 2012. "Rebels against Rebels: Explaining Violence between Rebel Groups." *Journal of Conflict Resolution* 56(4): 604–28.

Flores-Macías, Gustavo A. 2018. "The Consequences of Militarizing Anti-Drug Efforts for State Capacity in Latin America: Evidence from Mexico." *Journal of Comparative Politics* 51(1): 1–20.

Flores-Macías, Gustavo A., and Jessica Zarkin. 2021. "The Militarization of Law Enforcement: Evidence from Latin America." *Perspectives on Politics* 19(2): 519–38.

Franco, Marielle. 2014. "UPP – A Redução da Favela a Três Letras: Uma Análise da Política de Segurança Pública do Estado do Rio de Janeiro." Master's Thesis, Federal Fluminense University.

Fujii, Lee Ann. 2009. *Killing Neighbors: Webs of Violence in Rwanda.* Ithaca, NY: Cornell University Press.

2012. "Research Ethics 101: Dilemmas and Responsibilities." *PS: Political Science & Politics* 45(4): 717–23.

2016. "Politics of the 'Field'." *Perspectives on Politics* 14(4): 1147–52.

2021. *Show Time: The Logic and Power of Violent Display.* Ithaca, NY: Cornell University Press.

Gade, Emily Kalah. 2020. "Supplementary Materials: Social Isolation and Repertoires of Resistance." *American Political Science Review* 114(2): 309–25.

Gambetta, Diego. 1993. *The Sicilian Mafia: The Business of Private Protection.* Cambridge, MA: Harvard University Press.

Garotinho, Anthony, and Luiz Eduardo Soares. 1998. *Violência e Criminalidade No Estado Do Rio de Janeiro: Diagnóstico e Propostas Para Uma Política Democrática de Segurança Pública.* Rio de Janeiro: Hama.

Gay, Robert. 1990. "Neighborhood Associations and Political Change in Rio de Janeiro." *Latin American Research Review* 25(1): 102–18.

  1994. *Popular Organization and Democracy in Rio De Janeiro: A Tale of Two Favelas.* Philadelphia, PA: Temple University Press.

  1999. "The Broker and the Thief: A Parable (Reflections on Popular Politics in Brazil)." *Luso-Brazilian Review* 36(1): 49–70.

  2005. *Lucia: Testimonies of a Brazilian Drug Dealer's Woman.* Philadelphia, PA: Temple University Press.

  2015. *Bruno: Conversations with a Brazilian Drug Dealer.* Durham, NC: Duke University Press.

Gerring, John. 2012. "Mere Description." *British Journal of Political Science* 42(4): 721–46.

Gilsing, Sterre. 2020. "The Power of Silence: Sonic Experiences of Police Operations and Occupations in Rio de Janeiro's Favelas." *Conflict and Society* 6(1): 128–44.

Glenny, Mischa. 2016. *Nemesis: One Man and the Battle for Rio.* New York: Knopf Doubleday.

Goldstein, Daniel M. 2004. *The Spectacular City: Violence and Performance in Urban Bolivia.* Durham, NC: Duke University Press.

Goldstein, Donna. 2003. *Laughter Out of Place.* Berkeley, CA: University of California Press.

Gomes, Simone. 2020. "A Cultura Como Alternativa: Uma Aproximação a Partir de Sociabilidades Militantes Na Zona Oeste Do Rio de Janeiro." *Dilemas: Revista de Estudos de Conflito e Controle Social* 13(1): 57–76.

Gooderson, Philip. 2010. *The Gangs of Birmingham.* Preston, UK: Milo Books.

Grillo, Carolina Cristoph. 2013. "Coisas Da Vida No Crime: Tráfico e Roubo Em Favelas Cariocas." PhD Dissertation, Federal University of Rio de Janeiro.

Guevara, Che, Isidor Feinstein Stone, and Joseph P. Morray. 2012. *Guerrilla Warfare.* Hawthorne, CA: BN Publishing.

Hagedorn, John M. 1988. *People and Folks: Gangs, Crime, and the Underclass in a Rustbelt City.* Chicago, IL: Lake View Press.

  2005. "Institutionalised Gangs and Violence in Chicago." In *Neither Peace Nor War*, ed. Luke Dowdney. COAV, 316–34.

  2008. *A World of Gangs: Armed Young Men and Gangsta Culture.* Minneapolis, MN: University of Minnesota Press.

Hagedorn, John M., and Brigid Rauch. 2007. "Housing, Gangs, and Homicide: What We Can Learn from Chicago." *Urban Affairs Review* 42(4): 435–56.

Hallward, Maia, Juan Masullo, and Cécile Mouly. 2017. "Civil Resistance in Armed Conflict: Leveraging Nonviolent Action to Navigate War, Oppose Violence and Confront Oppression." *Journal of Peacebuilding and Development* 12(3): 1–9.

Hanson, Rebecca, and Patricia Richards. 2019. *Harassed: Gender, Bodies, and Ethnographic Research*. Berkeley, CA: University of California Press.

Harig, Christoph. 2015a. "Peacekeeping in Haiti: A Laboratory for Pacification in Rio de Janeiro?" *Strife*. https://isnblog.ethz.ch/humanitarian-issues/peacekeeping-in-haiti-a-laboratory-for-pacification-in-rio-de-janeiro (August 1, 2020).

2015b. "Synergy Effects between MINUSTAH and Public Security in Brazil." *Brasiliana-Journal for Brazilian Studies* 3(2): 142–68.

Hazen, Jennifer M., and Dennis Rodgers. 2014. *Global Gangs: Street Violence across the World*. Minneapolis, MN: University of Minnesota Press.

Hazlehurst, Kayleen M., and Cameron Hazlehurst. 1998. *Gangs and Youth Subcultures: International Explorations*. New Brunswick, NJ: Transaction Publishers.

Heinle, Kimberly, Cory Molzah, and David Shirk. 2015. *Drug Violence in Mexico: Data and Analysis Through 2014*. San Diego, CA: Justice in Mexico Project.

Herbst, Jeffrey Ira. 2015. *States and Power in Africa: Comparative Lessons in Authority and Control*. Princeton, NJ: Princeton University Press.

Hidalgo, F. Daniel, and Benjamin Lessing. 2014. "Endogenous State Weakness in Violent Democracies: Paramilitaries at the Polls." *NBER Summer Institute* 24 (July): 24–25.

Hirata, Daniel Veloso, Adauto Lúcio Cardoso, et al. 2021. *A Expansão Das Milícias Do Rio de Janeiro: Uso Da Força Estatal, Mercado Imobiliário e Grupos Armados*. Rio de Janeiro: GENI/UFF.

Hirata, Daniel Veloso, and Maria Isabel Couto. 2022. *Mapa Dos Grupos Armados Do Rio de Janeiro*. Rio de Janeiro: Fogo Cruzado.

Hirata, Daniel Veloso, Shyrlei Rosendo Dos Santos, et al. 2021. "Impactos de Ações Judiciais na Preservação de Vidas Negras nas Favelas: ACP da Maré e ADPF das Favelas." *Boletim de Análise Político-Institucional* (26): 21–28.

Hirata, Daniel Veloso, and Carolina Christoph Grillo. 2019a. *Operações Policiais no Rio de Janeiro*. Heinrich Böll Stiftung.

2019b. "Movement and Death: Illicit Drug Markets in the Cities of São Paulo and Rio De Janeiro." *Journal of Illicit Economies and Development* 1(2): 122–33.

Hirata, Daniel Veloso, Carolina Christoph Grillo, Renato Coelho Dirk, and Diego Azevedo Lyra. 2021. *Operações Policiais e Violência Letal No Rio de Janeiro: Os Impactos Da ADPF 635 Na Defesa Da Vida*. Rio de Janeiro: GENI.

2023. *Chacinas Policiais No Rio de Janeiro: Estatização Das Mortes, Mega Chacinas Policiais e Impunidade*. Rio de Janeiro: GENI.

Hobsbawm, Eric J. 1959. *Primitive Rebels: Studies in Archaic Forms of Social Movement in the 19th and 20th Centuries*. New York City: W. W. Norton.

2000. *Bandits*. New York: The New Press.

Hoelscher, Kristian, and Per M. Norheim-Martinsen. 2014. "Urban Violence and the Militarisation of Security: Brazilian 'Peacekeeping' in Rio de Janeiro and Port-Au-Prince." *Small Wars & Insurgencies* 25(5): 957–75.

Holland, Bradley E., and Viridiana Rios. 2017. "Informally Governing Information: How Criminal Rivalry Leads to Violence against the Press in Mexico." *Journal of Conflict Resolution* 61(5): 1095–119.

Holmes, Carolyn E. 2021. "Standing Out and Blending In: Contact-Based Research, Ethics, and Positionality." *PS – Political Science and Politics* (July): 443–47.

Holston, James. 2009. *Insurgent Citizenship: Disjunctions of Democracy and Modernity in Brazil.* Princeton, NJ: Princeton University Press.

Horan, James D. 1997. *Desperate Men: The James Gang and the Wild Bunch.* Lincoln, NE: University of Nebraska Press.

Horowitz, Ruth. 1983. *Honor and the American Dream: Culture and Identity in a Chicano Community.* New Brunswick, NJ: Rutgers University Press.

Huang, Reyko. 2017. *The Wartime Origins of Democratization: Civil War, Rebel Governance, and Political Regimes.* New York: Cambridge University Press.

Huggins, Martha Knisely. 1991. *Vigilantism and the State in Modern Latin America: Essays on Extralegal Violence.* New York: Praeger.

Idler, Annette. 2012. "Exploring Agreements of Convenience Made among Violent Non-State Actors." *Perspectives on Terrorism* 6(4–5): 63–84.

Idler, Annette, María Belén Garrido, and Cécile Mouly. 2015. "Peace Territories in Colombia: Comparing Civil Resistance in Two War-Torn Communities." *Journal of Peacebuilding and Development* 10(3): 1–15.

Igarapé Institute. 2023. "Homicide Monitor." https://homicide.igarape.org.br/?l=es (June 17, 2023).

Imbusch, Peter, Michel Misse, and Fernando Carrión. 2011. "Violence Research in Latin America and the Caribbean: A Literature Review." *International Journal of Conflict and Violence* 5(1): 87–154.

Informação Demográfica e Socioeconômica. 2022. *Desigualdades Sociais Por Cor Ou Raça No Brasil.* Instituto Brasileiro de Geografia e Estatística.

Institute for Crime & Justice Policy Research. 2023. "World Prison Brief." www.prisonstudies.org/country/brazil (June 12, 2023).

Instituto Pereira Passos. 2018. "Limite Favelas e Urbanização." www.data.rio/datasets/limites-de-favelas-e-urbanização (June 12, 2023).

2023. "Data Rio." www.data.rio/ (June 12, 2023).

ISP-RJ. 2023a. *Dados.* Rio de Janeiro: Instituto de Segurança Pública. www.ispvisualizacao.rj.gov.br.

2023b. *Segurança Em Números 2022.* Rio de Janeiro: Instituto de Segurança Pública. http://arquivo.proderj.rj.gov.br/isp_imagens/Uploads/SN2022_rev.html#crimes_vida (June 7, 2023).

Jackman, David. 2019. "The Decline of Gangsters and Politicization of Violence in Urban Bangladesh." *Development and Change* 50(5): 1214–38.

Jacobs, Alan M. et al. 2021. "The Qualitative Transparency Deliberations: Insights and Implications." *Perspectives on Politics* 19(1): 171–208.

Jaffe, Rivke. 2013. "The Hybrid State: Crime and Citizenship in Urban Jamaica." *American Ethnologist* 40(4): 734–48.

2015. "From Maroons to Dons: Sovereignty, Violence and Law in Jamaica." *Critique of Anthropology* 35(1): 47–63.

Jensen, Steffen. 2008. *Gangs, Politics & Dignity in Cape Town.* Oxford: James Currey.

Jentzsch, Corinna. 2022. *Violent Resistance: Militia Formation and Civil War in Mozambique.* Cambridge: Cambridge University Press.

Johnson, David T., and Jon Fernquest. 2018. "Governing through Killing: The War on Drugs in the Philippines." *Asian Journal of Law and Society* 5(2): 359–90.

Kalyvas, Stathis N. 2001. "'New' and 'Old' Civil Wars: A Valid Distinction." *World Politics* 49(October): 99–118.

2006. *The Logic of Violence in Civil War.* Cambridge: Cambridge University Press.

2015a. "How Civil Wars Help Explain Organized Crime–and How They Do Not." *Journal of Conflict Resolution* 59(8): 1517–40.

2015b. "Rebel Governance during the Greek Civil War, 1942–1949." In *Rebel Governance in Civil War*, eds. Ana Arjona, Nelson Kasfir, and Zachariah C. Mampilly. New York: Cambridge University Press, 119–37.

Kant de Lima, Roberto. 1986. "Legal Theory and Juridical Practice: Paradoxes of Police Work in Rio de Janeiro City." PhD Dissertation, Harvard University.

Kaplan, Oliver. 2013. "Protecting Civilians in Civil War: The Institution of the ATCC in Colombia." *Journal of Peace Research* 50(3): 351–67.

2017. *Resisting War: How Communities Protect Themselves*. Cambridge: Cambridge University Press.

Kasfir, Nelson. 2005. "Guerrillas and Civilian Participation: The National Resistance Army in Uganda, 1981–86." *The Journal of Modern African Studies* 43(2): 271–96.

2015. "Rebel Governance – Constructing a Field of Inquiry: Definitions, Scope, Patterns, Order, Causes." In *Rebel Governance in Civil War*, eds. Ana Arjona, Nelson Kasfir, and Zachariah C. Mampilly. New York: University of Cambridge, 21–46.

Katz, Jack. 1988. *Seductions of Crime: Moral and Sensual Attractions in Doing Evil*. New York: Basic Books.

Katz, Jack, and Curtis Jackson-Jacobs. 2004. "The Criminologists' Gang." In *The Blackwell Companion to Criminology*, ed. Colin Sumner. Hoboken, NJ: Wiley-Blackwell, 91–124.

Kenny, Paul D., and Ronald Holmes. 2020. "A New Penal Populism? Rodrigo Duterte, Public Opinion, and the War on Drugs in the Philippines." *Journal of East Asian Studies* 20(2): 187–205.

Khan, Iqbal Alam. 2000. "Struggle for Survival: Networks and Relationships in a Bangladesh Slum." PhD Dissertation, University of Bath.

Killebrew, Robert. 2011. "Criminal Insurgency in the Americas and Beyond." *Prism* 2(3): 33–52.

King, Gary, Robert O. Keohane, and Sidney Verba. 1994. *Designing Social Inquiry: Scientific Inference in Qualitative Research*. Princeton, NJ: Princeton University Press.

Klein, Malcolm W. 1995. *The American Street Gang: Its Nature, Prevalence, and Control*. Oxford: Oxford University Press.

Klein, Malcolm W., and Cheryl L. Maxson. 1996. *Gang Structures, Crime Patterns, and Police Responses*. Washington, DC: National Criminal Justice Reference Service.

2006. *Street Gang Patterns and Policies*. Oxford: Oxford University Press.

Koenders, Sara. 2020. "'Pedagogy of Conversion' in the Urban Margins: Pacification, Education, and the Struggle for Control in a Rio de Janeiro Favela." *Journal on Education in Emergencies* 6(1): 118–47.

Koivu, Kendra L. 2016. "In the Shadow of the State: Mafias and Illicit Markets." *Comparative Political Studies* 49(2): 155–83.

Koonings, Kees, and Dirk Kruijt. 2004. *Armed Actors: Organised Violence and State Failure in Latin America*. London: Zed Books.

Kostelnik, James, and David Skarbek. 2013. "The Governance Institutions of a Drug Trafficking Organization." *Public Choice* 156(1–2): 95–103.

Krause, Jana. 2018. *Resilient Communities: Non-Violence and Civilian Agency in Communal War*. Cambridge: Cambridge University Press.

Krystalli, Roxani C. 2021. "Narrating Victimhood: Dilemmas and (in)Dignities." *International Feminist Journal of Politics* 23(1): 125–46.

Kynoch, Gary. 1999. "From the Ninevites to the Hard Livings Gang: Township Gangsters and Urban Violence in Twentieth-Century South Africa." *African Studies* 58(1): 55–85.

2005. *We Are Fighting the World: A History of the Marashea Gangs in South Africa, 1947–1999*. Athens, OH: Ohio University Press.

Lamb, Robert D. 2010. "Microdynamics of Illegitimacy and Complex Urban Violence in Medellín, Colombia." PhD Dissertation, University of Maryland.

Lambrechts, Derica. 2012. "The Impact of Organised Crime on State Social Control: Organised Criminal Groups and Local Governance on the Cape Flats, Cape Town, South Africa." *Journal of Southern African Studies* 38(4): 787–807.

LeBas, Adrienne. 2013. "Violence and Urban Order in Nairobi, Kenya and Lagos, Nigeria." *Studies in Comparative International Development* 48(3): 240–62.

Leeds, Elizabeth. 1996. "Cocaine and Parallel Polities in the Brazilian Urban Periphery: Constraints on Local-Level Democratization." *Latin American Research Review* 31(3): 47–83.

Lessing, Benjamin. 2008. "As Facções Cariocas Em Perspectiva Comparativa." *Novos Estudos – CEBRAP* (80): 43–62.

2015. "The Logic of Violence in Criminal War." *Journal of Conflict Resolution* 59(8): 1486–516.

2017. *Making Peace in Drug Wars: Crackdowns and Cartels in Latin America*. Cambridge: Cambridge University Press.

2020. "Conceptualizing Criminal Governance." *Perspectives on Politics* 19(3): 854–73.

Lessing, Benjamin, and Graham Denyer Willis. 2019. "Legitimacy in Criminal Governance: Managing a Drug Empire from behind Bars." *American Political Science Review* 113(2): 584–606.

Levi, Margaret. 1989. *Of Rule and Revenue*. Berkeley, CA: University of California Press.

Levitt, Steven D., and Sudhir Venkatesh. 2000. "An Economic Analysis of a Drug-Selling Gang's Finances." *The Quarterly Journal of Economics* (August): 755–89.

Ley, Sandra, Shannan Mattiace, and Guillermo Trejo. 2019. "Indigenous Resistance to Criminal Governance: Why Regional Ethnic Autonomy Institutions Protect Communities from Narco Rule in Mexico." *Latin American Research Review* 54(1): 181–200.

de Lima, Renato Sergio et al. 2018. *Anuário Brasileiro de Segurança Pública: 2014–2017*. São Paulo: Fórum Brasileiro de Segurança Pública.

Lima, William da Silva. 1991. *Quatrocentos Contra Um: Uma História Do Comando Vermelho*. Rio de Janeiro: Instituto de Estudos da Religião.

Loveman, Mara. 2014. *National Colors: Racial Classification and the State in Latin America*. Oxford: Oxford University Press.

Loyle, Cyanne E., et al. 2022. "Revolt and Rule: Learning about Governance from Rebel Groups." *International Studies Review* 24(4): viac043.

Magaloni, Beatriz et al. 2020. "Living in Fear: The Dynamics of Extortion in Mexico's Drug War." *Comparative Political Studies* 53(7): 1124–74.

Magaloni, Beatriz, Edgar Franco-Vivanco, and Vanessa Melo. 2020. "Killing in the Slums: Social Order, Criminal Governance, and Police Violence in Rio de Janeiro." *American Political Science Review* 114(2): 552–72.

Malejacq, Romain, and Dipali Mukhopadhyay. 2016. "The 'Tribal Politics' of Field Research: A Reflection on Power and Partiality in 21st-Century Warzones." *Perspectives on Politics* 14(04): 1011–28.

Mampilly, Zachariah C. 2011. *Rebel Rulers: Insurgent Governance and Civilian Life during War*. Ithaca, NY: Cornell University Press.

Mampilly, Zachariah C., and Megan A. Stewart. 2021. "A Typology of Rebel Political Institutional Arrangements." *Journal of Conflict Resolution* 65(1): 15–45.

Manso, Bruno Paes. 2020. *A República das Milícias: Dos Esquadrões da Morte à Era Bolsonaro*. Rio de Janeiro: Todavia.

Manwaring, Max G. 2005. *Street Gangs: The New Urban Insurgency*. Carlisle, PA: Strategic Studies Institute, US Army War College.

Marx, Anthony W. 1996. "Race-Making and the Nation-State." *World Politics* 48(2): 180–208.

Masullo, Juan. 2021a. "Civilian Contention in Civil War: How Ideational Factors Shape Community Responses to Armed Groups." *Comparative Political Studies* 54(10): 1849–84.

2021b. "Refusing to Cooperate with Armed Groups Civilian Agency and Civilian Noncooperation in Armed Conflicts." *International Studies Review* 23(3): 887–913.

Mattos, Carla dos Santos. 2016. "Uma Etnografia Da Expansão Do Mundo Do Crime No Rio de Janeiro." *Revista Brasileira de Ciencias Sociais* 31(91): 1–15.

McCann, Bryan. 2014. *Hard Times in the Marvelous City: From Dictatorship to Democracy in the Favelas of Rio de Janeiro*. Durham, NC: Duke University Press.

Melde, Chris, Terrance J. Taylor, and Finn Aage Esbensen. 2009. "'I Got Your Back': An Examination of the Protective Function of Gang Membership in Adolescence." *Criminology* 47(2): 565–94.

Méndez, María José. 2018. "The Violence Work of Transnational Gangs in Central America." *Third World Quarterly* 40(2): 373–88.

Menezes, Palloma Valle. 2014. "Os Rumores Da 'Pacificação': A Chegada Da UPP e as Mudanças Nos Problemas Públicos No Santa Marta e Na Cidade de Deus." *Dilemas-Revista de Estudos de Conflito e Controle Social* 7(4): 665–84.

Merriam-Webster. 2023. "Gang." Merriam-Webster Dictionary. www.merriam-webster.com/dictionary/gang.

Metelits, Claire. 2009. *Inside Insurgency: Violence, Civilians, and Revolutionary Group Behavior*. New York: NYU Press.

Misse, Michel. 1999. "Malandros, Marginais e Vagabundos & a Acumulação Social Da Violência No Rio de Janeiro." PhD Dissertation, Instituto Universitário de Pesquisas do Rio de Janeiro.

Misse, Michel, Carolina Christoph Grillo, César Pinheiro Teixeira, and Natasha Elbas Neri. 2011. *Quando a Polícia Mata: Homicídios Por "Autos De Resistência" No Rio de Janeiro (2001–2011)*. Rio de Janeiro: Núcleo de Estudos da Cidadania, Conflito e Violência Urbana.

Mobekk, Eirin, and Anne M. Street. 2006. *Disarmament, Demobilisation and Reintegration: What Role Should the EU Play in Haiti?* London: ActionAid.

Moncada, Eduardo. 2017. "Varieties of Vigilantism: Conceptual Discord, Meaning and Strategies." *Global Crime* 18(4): 403–23.

2019a. "Resisting Protection: Rackets, Resistance, and State Building." *Comparative Politics* 51(3): 321–39.

2019b. "The Politics of Criminal Victimization: Pursuing and Resisting Power."
Perspectives on Politics 18(3): 706–21.

2022. *Resisting Extortion: Victims, Criminals, and States in Latin America.*
Cambridge: Cambridge University Press.

Moore, Joan W. 1978. *Homeboys: Gangs, Drugs, and Prison in the Barrios of Los
Angeles.* Philadelphia, PA: Temple University Press.

Morenoff, Jeffrey D., Robert J. Sampson, and Stephen W. Raudenbush. 2001.
"Neighborhood Inequality, Collective Efficacy, and the Spatial Dynamics of Urban
Violence." *Criminology* 39(3): 517–60.

Muggah, Robert, ed. 2014. *Stabilization Operations, Security and Development: States
of Fragility.* New York: Routledge.

Müller, Markus-Michael, and Andrea Steinke. 2020. "The Geopolitics of Brazilian
Peacekeeping and the United Nations' Turn towards Stabilisation in Haiti."
Peacebuilding 8(1): 54–77.

Neocleous, Mark. 2011. "'A Brighter and Nicer New Life': Security as Pacification."
Social & Legal Studies 20(2): 191–208.

Nobles, Melissa. 2000. *Shades of Citizenship: Race and the Census in Modern Politics.*
Palo Alto, CA: Stanford University Press.

Noite das Estrelas. 2021. Entidade Maré.

Nordstrom, Carolyn. 1997. *A Different Kind of War Story.* Philadelphia, PA: University
of Pennsylvania Press.

Notícias de Uma Guerra Particular. 1999. Coleção VideoFilmes.

Núñez, Javier, Ximena Tocornal, and Pablo Henríquez. 2012. "Determinantes
Individuales y Del Entorno Residencial En La Percepción de Seguridad En Barrios
Del Gran Santiago, Chile." *Revista Invi* 74(27): 87–120.

O'Donnell, Guillermo. 1993. "On the State, Democratization and Some Conceptual
Problems." *World Development* 21(8): 1355–69.

O'Hare, Greg, and Michael Barke. 2002. "The Favelas of Rio de Janeiro: A Temporal
and Spatial Analysis." *GeoJournal* 56: 225–40.

Olivier, Djems. 2021. "The Political Anatomy of Haiti's Armed Gangs: In Port-Au-
Prince, Botched NGO and Military Inventions Have Fragmented Urban Space,
Triggering an Explosive Proliferation of Violent Armed Groups." *NACLA Report
on the Americas* 53(1): 83–87.

Olson, Mancur. 1993. "Dictatorship, Democracy, and Development." *American
Political Science Review* 87(3): 567–76.

Ortiz, Jennifer M. 2018. "Gangs and Environment: A Comparative Analysis of Prison
and Street Gangs." *American Journal of Qualitative Research* 2(1): 97–117.

ed. 2023a. *Critical and Intersectional Gang Studies.* New York: Routledge.

2023b. "'Gang Ain't in My Dictionary': Utilizing Insider Perspectives to Develop a
Critical Gang Definition." In *Critical and Intersectional Gang Studies,* ed. Jennifer
M. Ortiz. New York: Routledge, 6–22.

Osorio, Javier. 2015. "The Contagion of Drug Violence: Spatiotemporal Dynamics of
the Mexican War on Drugs." *Journal of Conflict Resolution* 59(8): 1403–32.

Pachirat, Timothy. 2017. *Among Wolves: Ethnography and the Immersive Study of
Power.* New York: Routledge.

Parkinson, Sarah E. 2013. "Organizing Rebellion: Rethinking High-Risk Mobilization
and Social Networks in War." *American Political Science Review* 107(03):
418–32.

2023. *Beyond the Lines: Social Networks and Palestinian Organizations in Wartime Lebanon*. Ithaca, NY: Cornell University Press.

Penglase, Benjamin. 2008. "The Bastard Child of the Dictatorship: The Comando Vermelho and the Birth of 'Narco-Culture' in Rio de Janeiro." *Luso-Brazilian Review* 45(1): 118–45.

2014. *Living with Insecurity in a Brazilian Favela: Urban Violence and Daily Life*. New Brunswick, NJ: University of Rutgers Press.

Perlman, Janice E. 1976. *The Myth of Marginality: Urban Poverty and Politics in Rio de Janeiro*. Berkeley, CA: University of California Press.

2010. *Favela: Four Decades of Living on the Edge in Rio de Janeiro*. Oxford: Oxford University Press.

Perpétuo, Maria Eduarda Barroso. 2021. "Turf Wars in Rio de Janeiro." Master's Thesis, Federal University of Rio de Janeiro.

Petersen, Roger D. 2001. *Resistance and Rebellion: Lessons from Eastern Europe*. Cambridge: Cambridge University Press.

Phillips, Brian J. 2017. "Inequality and the Emergence of Vigilante Organizations: The Case of Mexican Autodefensas." *Comparative Political Studies* 50(10): 1358–89.

Pimenta, Marília Carolina B. Souza, Marcial Alécio Garcia Suarez, and Marcos Alan Ferreira. 2021. "Hybrid Governance as a Dynamic Hub for Violent Non-State Actors: Examining the Case of Rio de Janeiro." *Revista Brasileira de Política Internacional* 64(2): 1–21.

Pinnock, Don. 1984. *The Brotherhoods: Street Gangs and State Control in Cape Town*. Cape Town, SA: David Philip.

2016. *Gang Town*. Cape Town, SA: Tafelberg.

Pischedda, Costantino. 2020. *Conflict Among Rebels: Why Insurgent Groups Fight Each Other*. New York: Columbia University Press.

Rasmussen, Jacob. 2014. "'We Are the True Blood of the Mau Mau': The Mungiki Movement in Kenya." In *Global Gangs: Street Violence across the World*, eds. Jennifer M. Hazen and Dennis Rodgers. Minneapolis, MN: University of Minnesota Press, 213–35.

Redes da Maré. 2019a. *Censo Populacional da Maré*. Rio de Janeiro: Redes da Maré.

2019b. Direito à Segurança Pública Na Maré Edição Especial. www.redesdamare .org.br/media/downloads/arquivos/BoletimSegPublica_EdicaoEspeci.pdf (June 7, 2023).

2021. Direito à Segurança Pública Na Maré No. 6. www.redesdamare.org.br/media/ downloads/arquivos/06E2021_segpub.pdf (June 7, 2023).

2023a. "Ação Civil Pública da Maré." www.redesdamare.org.br/br/info/49/acao-civil-publica-da-mare (June 7, 2023).

2023b. Direito à Segurança Pública Na Maré No. 7. www.redesdamare.org.br/ media/downloads/arquivos/RdM_Boletim_direito_SegPubli23.pdf (June 7, 2023).

Reuter, Peter. 1983. *Disorganized Crime: The Economics of the Visible Hand*. Cambridge, MA: MIT Press.

Revkin, Mara Redlich. 2020. "What Explains Taxation by Resource-Rich Rebels? Evidence from the Islamic State in Syria." *Journal of Politics* 82(2): 757–64.

2021. "Competitive Governance and Displacement Decisions Under Rebel Rule: Evidence from the Islamic State in Iraq." *Journal of Conflict Resolution* 65(1): 46–80.

Ribeiro da Silva, Cláudia Rose. 2006. "Maré: A Invenção de Um Bairro." PhD Dissertation, Fundação Getúlio Vargas.

Rios, Viridiana. 2013. "Why Did Mexico Become so Violent? A Self-Reinforcing Violent Equilibrium Caused by Competition and Enforcement." *Trends in Organized Crime* 16(2): 138–55.

Robb Larkins, Erika. 2015. *The Spectacular Favela: Violence in Modern Brazil*. Berkeley, CA: University of California Press.

Rodgers, Dennis. 1999. "Youth Gangs and Violence in Latin America and the Caribbean: A Literature Survey." *The World Bank Sustainable Development Working Paper* (4): 1–39.

2006a. "Living in the Shadow of Death: Gangs, Violence and Social Order in Urban Nicaragua, 1996–2002." *Journal of Latin American Studies* 38(02): 267–92.

2006b. "The State as a Gang: Conceptualizing the Governmentality of Violence in Contemporary Nicaragua." *Critique of Anthropology* 26(3): 315–30.

2009. "Slum Wars of the 21st Century: The New Geography of Conflict in Central America." *Development and Change* 40(5): 949–76.

2017. "Bróderes in Arms: Gangs and the Socialization of Violence in Nicaragua." *Journal of Peace Research* 54(5): 648–60.

Rodgers, Dennis, and Adam Baird. 2015. "Understanding Gangs in Contemporary Latin America." In *The Handbook of Gangs*, eds. Scott H. Decker and David C. Pyrooz. Hoboken, NJ: John Wiley & Sons, Inc., 478–502.

Rodgers, Dennis, and Robert Muggah. 2009. "Gangs as Non-State Armed Groups: The Central American Case." *Contemporary Security Policy* 30(2): 301–17.

Rosenau, James N. 1992. "Governance, Order, and Change in World Politics." In *Governance without Government: Order and Change in World Politics*, ed. James N. Rosenau. Cambridge: Cambridge University Press, 1–29.

Rosner, Nicole E. 2018. "Detouring Urban Futures: Experience, Expectation and de-Democratization in Two Rio de Janeiro Peripheries." Paper presented at the *American Anthropological Association Annual Meeting*, San Jose, CA.

Rubin, Michael A. 2020. "Rebel Territorial Control and Civilian Collective Action in Civil War: Evidence from the Communist Insurgency in the Philippines." *Journal of Conflict Resolution* 64(2–3): 459–89.

Sampson, Robert J. 2012. *Great American City: Chicago and the Enduring Neighborhood Effect*. Chicago, IL: The University of Chicago Press.

Sampson, Robert J, and W. Byron Groves. 1989. "Community Structure and Crime: Testing Social-Disorganization Theory." *American Journal of Sociology* 94(4): 774–802.

Sampson, Robert J., Stephen W. Raudenbusch, and Felton Earls. 1997. "Neighborhoods and Violence Crime: A Multilevel Study of Collective Efficacy." *Science* 277: 918–24.

Samset, Ingrid. 2014. *"For the Guarantee of Law and Order": The Armed Forces and Public Security in Brazil*. Bergen, NO: Chr. Michelsen Institute.

Sánchez-Jankowski, M. 1991. *Islands in the Street: Gangs and American Urban Society*. Berkeley, CA: University of California Press.

2003. "Gangs and Social Change." *Theoretical Criminology* 7(2): 191–216.

Santo, Andréia Martins de Oliveira, Dalcio Marinho Gonçalves, and Eliana Sousa Silva. 2013. "Contextualizando a Maré." In *Vivências Educativas Na Maré: Desafios e Possibilidades*, eds. Andréia Martins de Oliveira Santo and Eliana Sousa Silva. Rio de Janeiro: Redes da Maré, 19–34.

Santos, Carlos Ferreira dos. 1983. *O Morro Do Timbau.* Rio de Janeiro: Federal Fluminense University.

Sartori, Giovanni. 1970. "Concept Misformation in Comparative Politics." *American Political Science Review* 64(4): 1033–53.

1991. "Comparing and Miscomparing." *Journal of Theoretical Politics* 3(3): 243–57.

Savell, Stephanie. 2014. "The Brazilian Military, Public Security, and Rio de Janeiro's Pacification." *Anthropoliteia.* https://anthropoliteia.net/2014/07/07/the-brazilian-military-public-security-and-rio-de-janeiros-pacification/ (May 18, 2019).

2015. "'I'm Not a Leader': Cynicism and Good Citizenship in a Brazilian Favela." *PoLAR: Political and Legal Anthropology Review* 38(2): 300–17.

2016. "Performing Humanitarian Militarism: Public Security and the Military in Brazil." *Focaal* 75: 59–72.

Saviano, Roberto. 2008. *Gomorrah: A Personal Journey into the Violent International Empire of Naples' Organized Crime System.* London: Picador.

Schelling, Thomas C. 1971. "What Is the Business of Organized Crime?" *The American Scholar* 40(4): 643–52.

Schuberth, Moritz. 2015. "A Transformation from Political to Criminal Violence? Politics, Organised Crime and the Shifting Functions of Haiti's Urban Armed Groups." *Conflict, Security & Development* 15(2): 169–96.

Secretaria da Segurança Pública do Estado de São Paulo. 2023. "Dados Estatísticos." *Portal do Governo.* www.ssp.sp.gov.br/estatistica/pesquisa.aspx (June 16, 2023).

Sen, Atreyee. 2014. "'For Your Safety': Child Vigilante Squads and Neo-Gangsterism in Urban India." In *Global Gangs: Street Violence Across the World*, eds. Jennifer M. Hazen and Dennis Rodgers. Minneapolis, MN: University of Minnesota Press, 193–212.

Shaw, Clifford, and Henry D. McKay. 1942. *Juvenile Delinquency and Urban Areas.* Chicago, IL: The University of Chicago Press.

Siddiqui, Niloufer A. 2022. *Under the Gun: Political Parties and Violence in Pakistan.* Cambridge: Cambridge University Press.

Silva, Eliana Sousa. 2012. *Testemunhos da Maré.* Rio de Janeiro: Aeroplano Editora.

2017. *A Ocupação da Maré Pelo Exército Brasileiro.* Rio de Janeiro: Redes da Maré.

Silva, Jailson de Souza e, ed. 2006. *Caminhada de Crianças, Adolescentes e Jovens Na Rede Do Tráfico de Drogas No Varejo Do Rio de Janeiro, 2004–2006.* Rio de Janeiro: Observatório de Favelas.

Silva, Jailson de Souza e, Fernando Lannes Fernandes, and Raquel Willadino Braga. 2008. "Grupos Criminosos Armados Com Domínio de Território Reflexões Sobre a Territorialidade Do Crime Na Região Metropolitana Do Rio de Janeiro." In *Segurança, Tráfico e Milícias No Rio de Janeiro.* Rio de Janeiro: Justiça Global, 16–24.

Siman, Maíra, and Victória Santos. 2018. "Interrogating the Security–Development Nexus in Brazil's Domestic and Foreign Pacification Engagements." *Conflict, Security & Development* 8802: 1–23.

Simmons, Erica S., and Nicholas Rush Smith. 2019. "The Case for Comparative Ethnography." *Comparative Politics* 51(3): 341–59.

Simpson, Audra. 2007. "On Ethnographic Refusal: Indigeneity, 'Voice' and Colonial Citizenship." *Junctures* 9: 67–80.

Siqueira, Italo Barbosa Lima, Francisco Elionardo De Melo Nascimento, and Suiany Silva De Moraes. 2022. "Dinâmicas inter-regionais de mercados e governança criminal em perspectiva comparada entre Fortaleza e Manaus." *Dilemas: Revista de Estudos de Conflito e Controle Social* 15(Especial 4): 441–68.

Skaperdas, Stergios. 2001. "The Political Economy of Organized Crime: Providing Protection When the State Does Not." *Economics of Governance* 2(3): 173–202.

Skaperdas, Stergios, and Constantinos Syropolous. 1995. "Gangs as Primitive States." In *The Economics of Organised Crime*, eds. Gianluca Fiorentini and Sam Peltzman. Cambridge: Cambridge University Press, 61–82.

Skarbek, David. 2011. "Governance and Prison Gangs." *American Political Science Review* 105(04): 702–16.

   2012. "Prison Gangs, Norms, and Organizations." *Journal of Economic Behavior & Organization* 82(1): 96–109.

   2014. *The Social Order of the Underworld: How Prison Gangs Govern the American Penal System*. Oxford: Oxford University Press.

Smith, Nicholas Rush. 2019. *Contradictions of Democracy: Vigilantism and Rights in Post-Apartheid South Africa*. Oxford: Oxford University Press.

Sneed, Paul. 2007. "Bandidos de Cristo: Representations of the Power of Criminal Factions in Rio's Proibidão Funk." *Latin American Music Review* 28(2): 220–41.

   2008. "Favela Utopias: The 'Bailes Funk' in Rio's Crisis of Social Exclusion and Violence." *Latin American Research Review* 43(2): 57–79.

Soares, Luiz Eduardo. 2000. *Meu Casaco de General: 500 Dias No Front Da Segurança Pública Do Rio de Janerio*. Rio de Janeiro: Companhia das Letras.

Soares, Luiz Eduardo, MV Bill, and Celso Athayde. 2005. *Cabeça de Porco*. Rio de Janeiro: Objetiva.

Sobel, Russell S., and Brian J. Osoba. 2009. "Youth Gangs as Pseudo-Governments: Implications for Violent Crime." *Southern Economic Journal* 75(4): 996–1018.

de Souza, Maria Julieta Nunes. 2007. "Apontamentos sobre a Maré: uma compreensão." *Revista Brasileira de Estudos Urbanos e Regionais* 9(1): 53–68.

Souza, Renata. 2020. *Cria Da Favela: Resistência à Militarização Da Vida*. Rio de Janeiro: Boitempo Editorial.

de Souza, Stefanie Israel. 2019. "Pacification of Rio's Favelas and the 'Pacification of the Pacification Police': The Role of Coordinating Brokerage in Police Reform." *Sociological Forum* 34(2): 458–82.

Staniland, Paul. 2012. "States, Insurgents, and Wartime Political Orders." *Perspectives on Politics* 10(02): 243–64.

Starn, Orin. 1999. *Nightwatch: The Politics of Protest in the Andes*. Durham, NC: Duke University Press.

Steele, Abbey. 2017. *Democracy and Displacement in Colombia's Civil War*. Ithaca, NY: Cornell University Press.

Stewart, Megan A. 2017. "Civil War as State Building: Strategic Governance in Civil War." *International Organization* 72(1): 205–26.

   2021. *Governing for Revolution: Social Transformation in Civil War*. Cambridge: Cambridge University Press.

Straus, Scott. 2012. "Wars Do End! Changing Patterns of Political Violence in Sub-Saharan Africa." *African Affairs* 111(443): 179–201.

Sullivan, John P. 2010. "Criminal Insurgency in the Americas." *Small Wars Journal*. https://smallwarsjournal.com/blog/journal/docs-temp/364-sullivan.pdf.

Suska, Marta-Laura. 2015. "Recommendations for Two Violence-Reducing Policing Programs in Brazil: The Pacification Police Unit in Rio de Janeiro and the Pact for Life in Recife." *BPC Policy Brief* 5(7): 1–9.

Suttles, Gerald. 1968. *The Social Order of the Slum: Territoriality and Ethnicity in the Inner City*. Chicago, IL: The University of Chicago Press.

Tajima, Yuhki. 2018. "Political Development and the Fragmentation of Protection Markets: Politically Affiliated Gangs in Indonesia." *Journal of Conflict Resolution* 62(5): 1100–126.

Tapscott, Rebecca. 2021a. *Arbitrary States: Social Control and Modern Authoritarianism in Museveni's Uganda*. Oxford: Oxford University Press.

2021b. "Vigilantes and the State: Understanding Violence through a Security Assemblages Approach." *Perspectives on Politics* 21(1): 209–24.

Telles, Edward. 2004. *Race in Another America: The Significance of Skin Color in Brazil*. Princeton, NJ: Princeton University Press.

2014. *Pigmentocracies: Ethnicity, Race, and Color in Latin America*. Chapel Hill, NC: University of North Carolina Press.

Theidon, Kimberly. 2014. "'How Was Your Trip?' Self-Care for Researchers and Writers Working on Violence." *Social Science Research Council DSD Working Papers on Research Security*. http://webarchive.ssrc.org/working-papers/DSD_ResearchSecurity_02_Theidon.pdf.

Thrasher, Frederic. 1927. *The Gang: A Study of 1,313 Gangs in Chicago*. Peotone, IL: New Chicago School Press.

Tilly, Charles. 1985. "War Making and State Making as Organized Crime." In *Bringing the State Back In*, eds. Peter Evans, Dietrich Rueschemeyer, and Theda Skocpol. Cambridge: Cambridge University Press, 169–91.

1992. *Coercion, Capital, and European States, A.D. 990–1992*. Cambridge, MA: Blackwell.

Trejo, Guillermo, and Sandra Ley. 2018. "Why Did Drug Cartels Go to War in Mexico? Subnational Democratization, the Breakdown of Criminal Protection, and the Onset of Large-Scale Violence." *Comparative Political Studies* 51(7): 900–37.

2020. *Votes, Drugs, and Violence: The Political Logic of Criminal Wars in Mexico*. Cambridge: Cambridge University Press.

2021. "High-Profile Criminal Violence: Why Drug Cartels Murder Government Officials and Party Candidates in Mexico." *British Journal of Political Science* 51(1): 203–29.

Trudeau, Jessie. 2022. "Limiting Aggressive Policing Can Reduce Police and Civilian Violence." *World Development* 160: 105961.

Tuck, Eve, and K. Wayne Yang. 2014. "Unbecoming Claims: Pedagogies of Refusal in Qualitative Research." *Qualitative Inquiry* 20(6): 811–18.

"Turf Wars." *The Economist*. 2012. www.economist.com/united-states/2012/02/04/turf-wars (July 18, 2019).

UN-Habitat. 2016. *Urbanization and Development: Emerging Futures*. United Nations Human Settlements Programme.

United Nations. 2023. "Global Issues: Youth." *UN.org*. www.un.org/en/global-issues/youth (September 4, 2023).

United Nations Department of Economic and Social Affairs Population Division. 2019. *World Urbanization Prospects 2018: Highlights*. New York: United Nations.

Uribe, Andres, Benjamin Lessing, Noah Schouela, and Elayne Stecher. 2024. "Criminal Governance in Latin America: An Initial Assessment of Its Prevalence and Correlates." *Social Science Research Network*. https://papers.ssrn.com/sol3/papers.cfm?abstract_id=4302432.

Utas, Mats. 2014. "'Playing the Game': Gang-Militia Logics in War-Torn Sierra Leone." In *Global Gangs: Street Violence Across the World*, eds. Jennifer M. Hazen and Dennis Rodgers. Minneapolis, MN: University of Minnesota Press, 171–91.

Valladares, Licia. 2008. *A Invenção Da Favela – Do Mito de Origem a Favela.Com.* Rio de Janeiro: Fundação Getúlio Vargas.

Van Der Borgh, Chris, and Wim Savenije. 2015. "De-Securitising and Re-Securitising Gang Policies: The Funes Government and Gangs in El Salvador." *Journal of Latin American Studies* 47(1): 149–76.

Varella, Drauzio, Ivaldo Bertazzo, and Paola Berenstein Jacques. 2002. *Maré: Vida Na Favela*. Rio de Janeiro: Casa da Palavra.

Varese, Federico. 2010. "What Is Organized Crime?" In *Organized Crime*, ed. Federico Varese. Abingdon, UK: Routledge, 1–35.

2017. *Mafia Life: Love, Death and Money at the Heart of Organised Crime*. London: Profile Books.

Vargas, Robert. 2016. *Wounded City: Violent Turf Wars in a Chicago Barrio*. Oxford: Oxford University Press.

Varsori, Andrea. 2021. "'The Elite Troops of Trafficking'. An Assessment of the Phenomenon of Military-Trained Gang Members in Rio de Janeiro." *Small Wars and Insurgencies* 32(1): 80–102.

Vaz, Lilian Fessler. 1985. "Contribuição Ao Estudo Da Produção e Transformação Do Espaço Da Habitação Popular: As Habitações Coletivos No Rio Antigo." PhD Dissertation, Federal University of Rio de Janeiro.

1994. *História Dos Bairros da Maré: Espaço, Tempo e Vida Cotidiana No Complexo da Maré*. Rio de Janeiro: Federal University of Rio de Janeiro.

Venkatesh, Sudhir. 1997. "The Social Organization of Street Gang Activity in an Urban Ghetto." *American Journal of Sociology* 103(1): 82–111.

2000. *American Project: The Rise and Fall of a Modern Ghetto*. Cambridge, MA: Harvard University Press.

2008. *Gang Leader for a Day: A Rogue Sociologist Takes to the Streets*. New York: Penguin Press.

Ventura, Zuenir. 1994. *Cidade Partida*. Rio de Janeiro: Companhia das Letras.

Vianna, Hermano. 1988. *O Mundo Funk Carioca*. Rio de Janeiro: Jorge Zahar Editor.

1997. *Galeras cariocas: territórios de conflitos e encontros culturais*. Rio de Janeiro: Federal University of Rio de Janeiro.

Vieira, Antônio Carlos Pinto. 1998. *Histórico da Maré*. Rio de Janeiro: CEASM.

Vigil, James Diego. 1988. *Barrio Gangs: Street Life and Identity in Southern California*. Austin, TX: University of Texas Press.

2002. *A Rainbow of Gangs: Street Cultures in the Mega-City*. Austin, TX: University of Texas Press.

2007. *The Projects: Gang and Non-Gang Families in East Los Angeles*. Austin, TX: University of Texas Press.

Villarreal, Andrés, and Bráulio F. A. Silva. 2006. "Social Cohesion, Criminal Victimization and Perceived Risk of Crime in Brazilian Neighborhoods". *Social Forces* 84(3): 1725–53.

Wacquant, Loïc. 2008. *Urban Outcasts: A Comparative Sociology of Advanced Marginality*. Cambridge: Polity Press.

Weber, Max. 1965. *Politics as a Vocation*. Philadelphia, PA: Fortress Press.

Wedeen, Lisa. 2010. "Reflections on Ethnographic Work in Political Science." *Annual Review of Political Science* 13: 255–72.

2015. *Ambiguities of Domination: Politics, Rhetoric, and Symbols in Contemporary Syria*. Chicago, IL: The University of Chicago Press.

Weinstein, Jeremy M. 2007. *Inside Rebellion: The Politics of Insurgent Violence*. Cambridge: Cambridge University Press.

Weinstein, Liza. 2008. "Mumbai's Development Mafias: Globalization, Organized Crime and Land Development". *International Journal of Urban and Regional Research* 32(1): 22–39.

2013. "Demolition and Dispossession: Toward an Understanding of State Violence in Millennial Mumbai." *Studies in Comparative International Development* 48(3): 285–307.

Whyte, William Foote. 1993. *Street Corner Society: The Social Structure of an Italian Slum*. Chicago, IL: The University of Chicago Press.

Wickham-Crowley, Timothy P. 1987. "The Rise (and Sometimes Fall) of Guerilla Governments in Latin America." *Sociological Forum* 2(3): 473–99.

Wilkinson, Steven. 2004. *Votes and Violence: Electoral Competition and Ethnic Riots in India*. Cambridge: Cambridge University Press.

Willadino, Rachel, Rodrigo Costa Nascimento, and Jailson de Souza e Silva. 2018. *Novas Configurações Das Redes Criminosas Após a Implantação Das UPPs*. Rio de Janeiro: Observatório de Favelas.

Wolf, Sonja. 2017. *Mano Dura: The Politics of Gang Control in El Salvador*. Austin, TX: University of Texas Press.

Wolff, Michael Jerome. 2015. "Building Criminal Authority: A Comparative Analysis of Drug Gangs in Rio de Janeiro and Recife." *Latin American Politics and Society* 57(2): 21–40.

2018. "Violence and Criminal Order: The Case of Ciudad Juarez." *Urban Geography* 39(10): 1465–83.

Wood, Elisabeth Jean. 2003. *Insurgent Collective Action and Civil War in El Salvador*. Cambridge: Cambridge University Press.

2009. "Ethnographic Research in the Shadow of Civil War." In *Political Ethnography: What Immersion Contributes to the Study of Power*, ed. Edward Schatz. Chicago, IL: The University of Chicago Press, 119–41.

Yashar, Deborah J. 2018. *Homicidal Ecologies: Illicit Economies and Complicit States in Latin America*. New York: Cambridge University Press.

Zaluar, Alba. 1985. *A Máquina e a Revolta*. São Paulo: Brasiliense.

1994. *Condomínio Do Diabo*. Rio de Janeiro: Editora Revan/UFRJ.

2000. "Perverse Integration: Drug Trafficking and Youth in the Favelas of Rio de Janeiro". *Journal of International Affairs* 53(2): 653–71.

Zaluar, Alba, and Isabel Siquiera Conceição. 2007. "Favelas Sob o Controle Das Milícias No Rio de Janeiro." *São Paulo em Perspectiva* 21(2): 89–101.

Zedong, Mao. 2000. *On Guerrilla Warfare*. Champagne, IL: University of Illinois Press.

Zizumbo Colunga, Daniel. 2015. "Taking the Law into Our Hands: Trust, Social Capital, and Vigilante Justice." PhD Dissertation, Vanderbilt University.

Index

Note: Page numbers in "n" followed by footnotes.

Stephen B. Kaplan, *Globalization and Austerity Politics in Latin America*

Edward L. Gibson, *Boundary Control: Subnational Authoritarianism in Federal Democracies*

Andreas Wimmer, *Waves of War: Nationalism, State Formation, and Ethnic Exclusion in the Modern World*

Leonardo R. Arriola, *Multi-Ethnic Coalitions in Africa: Business Financing of Opposition Election Campaigns*

Milan W. Svolik, *The Politics of Authoritarian Rule*

Guillermo Trejo, *Popular Movements in Autocracies: Religion, Repression, and Indigenous Collective Action in Mexico*

Cathie Jo Martin and Duane Swank, *The Political Construction of Business Interests: Coordination, Growth, and Equality*

Pablo Beramendi, *The Political Geography of Inequality: Regions and Redistribution*

Roger D. Petersen, *Western Intervention in the Balkans: The Strategic Use of Emotion in Conflict*

Jane R. Gingrich, *Making Markets in the Welfare State: The Politics of Varying Market Reforms*

Sidney Tarrow, *Power in Movement: Social Movements and Contentious Politics, Revised and Updated Third Edition*

Pepper D. Culpepper, *Quiet Politics and Business Power: Corporate Control in Europe and Japan*

Eric C. C. Chang, Mark Andreas Kayser, Drew A. Linzer, and Ronald Rogowski, *Electoral Systems and the Balance of Consumer-Producer Power*

Karen E. Ferree, *Framing the Race in South Africa: The Political Origins of Racial Census Elections*

Layna Mosley, *Labor Rights and Multinational Production*

Pauline Jones Luong and Erika Weinthal, *Oil is Not a Curse: Ownership Structure and Institutions in Soviet Successor States*

Dan Slater, *Ordering Power: Contentious Politics and Authoritarian Leviathans in Southeast Asia*

Sven Steinmo, *The Evolution of Modern States: Sweden, Japan, and the United States*

Stephen E. Hanson, *Post-Imperial Democracies: Ideology and Party Formation in Third Republic France, Weimar Germany, and Post-Soviet Russia*

Timothy Frye, *Building States and Markets After Communism: The Perils of Polarized Democracy*

Lauren M. MacLean, *Informal Institutions and Citizenship in Rural Africa: Risk and Reciprocity in Ghana and Côte d'Ivoire*

Ben W. Ansell, *From the Ballot to the Blackboard: The Redistributive Political Economy of Education*

Herbert Kitschelt, Kirk A. Hawkins, Juan Pablo Luna, Guillermo Rosas, and Elizabeth J. Zechmeister, *Latin American Party Systems*

James Mahoney, *Colonialism and Postcolonial Development: Spanish America in Comparative Perspective*

Monika Nalepa, *Skeletons in the Closet: Transitional Justice in Post-Communist Europe*

Orit Kedar, *Voting for Policy, Not Parties: How Voters Compensate for Power Sharing*

Maria Victoria Murillo, *Political Competition, Partisanship, and Policy Making in Latin American Public Utilities*

Henry Farrell, *The Political Economy of Trust: Institutions, Interests, and Inter-Firm Cooperation in Italy and Germany*

Andy Baker, *The Market and the Masses in Latin America: Policy Reform and Consumption in Liberalizing Economies*

Wolfgang C. Müller and Kaare Strøm, *Policy, Office, or Votes?*
Herbert Kitschelt, Zdenka Mansfeldova, Radek Markowski, and Gabor Toka, *Post-Communist Party Systems*
Herbert Kitschelt, Peter Lange, Gary Marks, and John D. Stephens, eds., *Continuity and Change in Contemporary Capitalism*
Carles Boix, *Political Parties, Growth, and Equality: Conservative and Social Democratic Economic Strategies in the World Economy*
Sidney Tarrow, *Power in Movement: Social Movements and Contentious Politics, Revised and Updated Fourth Edition*
Geoffrey Garrett, *Partisan Politics in the Global Economy*
Anthony W. Marx, *Making Race, Making Nations: A Comparison of South Africa, the United States, and Brazil*
Michael Bratton and Nicolas van de Walle, *Democratic Experiments in Africa: Regime Transitions in Comparative Perspective*
J. Rogers Hollingsworth and Robert Boyer, eds., *Contemporary Capitalism:The Embeddedness of Institutions*
Miriam Golden, *Heroic Defeats: The Politics of Job Loss*
Robert O. Keohane and Helen B. Milner, eds., *Internationalization and Domestic Politics*
Frances Hagopian, *Traditional Politics and Regime Change in Brazil*
David Knoke, Franz Urban Pappi, Jeffrey Broadbent, and Yutaka Tsujinaka, eds., *Comparing Policy Networks*
Doug McAdam, John McCarthy, and Mayer Zald, eds., *Comparative Perspectives on Social Movements*
Donatella della Porta, *Social Movements, Political Violence, and the State*
Roberto Franzosi, *The Puzzle of Strikes: Class and State Strategies in Postwar Italy*
Ashutosh Varshney, *Democracy, Development, and the Countryside*
Marino Regini, *Uncertain Boundaries: The Social and Political Construction of European Economies*
Paul Pierson, *Dismantling the Welfare State? Reagan, Thatcher, and the Politics of Retrenchment*
Theda Skocpol, *Social Revolutions in the Modern World*
Joel S. Migdal, Atul Kohli, and Vivienne Shue, eds., *State Power and Social Forces: Domination and Transformation in the Third World*
Herbert Kitschelt, *The Transformation of European Social Democracy*
Thomas Janoski and Alexander M. Hicks, eds., *The Comparative Political Economy of the Welfare State*
Catherine Boone, *Merchant Capital and the Roots of State Power in Senegal, 1930–1985*
Sven Steinmo, Kathleen Thelen, and Frank Longstreth, eds., *Structuring Politics: Historical Institutionalism in Comparative Analysis*
David D. Laitin, *Language Repertoires and State Construction in Africa*

For EU product safety concerns, contact us at Calle de José Abascal, 56–1°, 28003 Madrid, Spain or eugpsr@cambridge.org.

www.ingramcontent.com/pod-product-compliance
Ingram Content Group UK Ltd.
Pitfield, Milton Keynes, MK11 3LW, UK
UKHW040621240426
470322UK00011B/248